Peyote and the Yankton Sioux

The Civilization of the American Indian Series

To my wife, Cassandra, for her love and support through my many trips to South Dakota and the lonely hours of writing; and to my parents, Mike Maroukis and Mary Tsavlis (now deceased), for their encouragement in my early years and for giving me the confidence to pursue my dreams.

Peyote and the Yankton Sioux

THE LIFE AND TIMES OF SAM NECKLACE

THOMAS CONSTANTINE MAROUKIS

Foreword by Leonard R. Bruguier (Tashunka Hinzi)

UNIVERSITY OF OKLAHOMA PRESS : NORMAN

This book is published with the generous assistance of The McCasland Foundation, Duncan, Oklahoma.

The author's proceeds from the sale of this book will be donated to the Institute of American Indian Studies, University of South Dakota.

Maroukis, Thomas Constantine, 1938–
    Peyote and the Yankton Sioux : the life and times of Sam Necklace / Thomas Constantine Maroukis ; foreword by Leonard R. Bruguier.
        p. cm.—(Civilization of the American Indian series ; v. 249)
    Includes bibliographical references and index.
    ISBN 0–8061–3616–2 (alk. paper)
        1. Necklace, Sam, 1881–1949. 2. Yankton Indians—Biography. 3. Priests—South Dakota—Yankton Indian Reservation—Biography. 4. Yankton Indians—Religion. 5. Yankton Indians—Rites and ceremonies. 6. Native American Church of North America—History. 7. Peyotism—South Dakota—Yankton Indian Reservation. 8. Yankton Indian Reservation (S.D.)—Religious life and customs. 9. Yankton Indian Reservation (S.D.)—Social life and customs. I. Title. II. Series.

E99.Y25N43 2004
299.7'852'0092—dc22
[B]

2004041200

Peyote and the Yankton Sioux: The Life and Times of Sam Necklace is Volume 249 in The Civilization of the American Indian Series.

The paper in this book meets the guidelines for permanence and durability of the Committee on Production Guidelines for Book Longevity of the Council on Library Resources, Inc. ∞

Contents

Illustrations

FIGURES

PHOTOGRAPHS

Following page 182:

Peyote meeting for Adam Sitting Crow, Jr.'s fifth birthday
Yankton Native American Church
Tipi belonging to Asa and Loretta Primeaux
Mazanapi–Iron Necklace headstone
Sam Necklace headstone
Asa Primeaux, Sr.
Parnell Necklace, 2000
Parnell Necklace and seven great-grandchildren of Sam and
    Mary Necklace, 1997
Peyote drum
Peyote motif pillow
Jennie Necklace Franklin and granddaughters, ca. 1976
Yankton Sioux Peyote Singers, 1977
Young generation of Yankton Peyotists, 2003

MAP

Foreword

Sioux Native American Church members embrace an indigenous spirituality that originated in the Western Hemisphere over four thousand years ago. It came to us from the Huichol Indians who live in Mexico's northern mountain ranges. The diffusion started northward in the long ago, reaching us through visits of our people to our Indian relatives of the southern nations. Many of the rituals surrounding the sacred use of Peyote have been modified in its travels to fit into our worldview, yet the basic tenets remain the same as they were through the millennia. The medicine itself still carries a message of eternal hope to its communicants.

The story that follows contains a universal message to those who seek goodness and mercy within their lifetimes. Reverend Samuel Necklace was a man who sought the soothing balm necessary to make life good for him and for his family. Through the many trials and tribulations of an Indian man living in tumultuous times, we learn of individual human beings and their quest to find eternal salvation by the use of the sacred herb Peyote. Reverend Necklace's life encompassed many challenges, both internal and external. Growing up on the Yankton Sioux Reservation, which had suffered near-total economic depression since its inception in 1858, he sought the means to enhance the lives of his family and his relatives. Employment on the reservation was seasonal, with few available full-time jobs. Therefore, he found it necessary in the mid-1940s to move into a neighboring town to work. Being an Indian living off-reservation presented other hurdles that called on all the resources available to an enterprising person. Perhaps the biggest problems were racism and discrimination. Obtaining affordable housing with the basic amenities was particularly difficult. Once this was overcome, finding an employer who hired people for their skills and determination proved equally difficult, if not impossible.

The spiritual side of Reverend Necklace's life also caused problems. Often Christian denominations looked down on the Native American Church and its members in a very disparaging and demeaning manner. In some places on the reservation Church members were ostracized and faced unbridled criticism for following their belief system. The problems emanating from disparate groups caused the Peyote Church members to become much more closely associated with each other, and perhaps this accounts for their non-proselytizing. They were content to lead sober, spiritual lives, caring for all members of the Church and other relatives who were in need.

Reverend Necklace carried one more burden with dignity and grace: he was a leader of the Church and its congregations scattered throughout the five-state area. When called by another Native American Church, he was bound to travel to minister to the people. Hardships included transportation, food, and of course preparing for the services he would perform. All these difficulties produced a sense of trauma that we label post-traumatic stress disorder today. For the Native American, the commonly accepted rights of life and liberty and the pursuit of happiness were not applicable. Yet Reverend Necklace overcame these hurdles and left a lasting legacy to his family and relatives that is worth the retelling. This legacy continues through five generations of a Peyote family. It is a rich and complicated story from the perspective of those who live it. This history also reflects the voices of our Peyote community and the Necklace family.

Reverend Necklace's life story exemplifies the four Dakota, Lakota, and Nakota cardinal virtues of courage, fortitude, bravery, and wisdom. This book gives the reader a basic understanding of the Peyote religion and an Indian man who used the tenets of the Church in his everyday life. Reverend Necklace lived the life of a good Peyote man and trained many of his relatives to succeed him when he was gone. This is a story that deserves telling, for its strong message of faith is worthy of emulation.

Indian people have always traveled and been accepted into other people's homes, where they are treated with great hospitality. In this fashion they learned about the Peyote ways and carried its teachings home to use in their own manner. Today other people come into our communities; and with the hospitality that is seemingly typical of Indians everywhere, they are invited into our homes and given the best we can offer them. Some of the visitors join us in all our social, spiritual, and other activities and become adopted members. This book was written by such a man, who came to visit us and was accepted into our family over the last fifteen years. Over the course of these years he has participated in our traditional spiritual ceremonies and has attended many of our Peyote services. That he would write about our relatives speaks well of his feelings for us and for the way we live. In this book readers will find not only our spiritual side but also our humanity and how we try to make a living and get along in this world and try to make it better for coming generations.

Ho, hečhitu yedo. Tahunška Tanka, he miyedo.

Leonard R. Bruguier (Tashunka Hinzi), Director
Institute of American Indian Studies
University of South Dakota

Preface

The Yankton Sioux were among the earliest groups in the northern Plains to adopt the Peyote religion. Sam Necklace was one of the men who helped establish it on a firm basis and shape it into the institution it is today. He not only played an important leadership role on the local level but also was well known to other Peyote communities in North and South Dakota. Necklace began practicing Peyotism in the early twentieth century, and he played a key role in the incorporation of the local Yankton Peyote community into the Native American Church of Charles Mix County, South Dakota. He later became chief priest, a position he held for the remainder of his life. Sam Necklace is the focus of this study, as a person who helped establish a large extended family network that has continued his spiritual traditions into the present. I have called this a biography, but it could just as easily be called a family history or, more specifically, a social history of a Native American family. This study covers seven generations of one Native American family. The last five generations, starting with Sam and Mary Necklace, have been active members of the Native American Church. Such a study of five generations of one family is a first in the history of the Peyote religion. The history of this family, with their spiritual and cultural heritage and their interaction with local, state, and national historical trends, provides insights into the everyday lives of Native Americans during an era of great change.

The genesis of this study of the Necklace family involved a fortuitous series of events. Life has a way of opening unintended paths for us to follow. Whether it is serendipitous or meant to be part of some greater scheme of events is unclear to me. I did not intend to undertake such a study, yet I find myself involved in Native American life and culture both personally and academically. It began in 1987 when I met Asa Primeaux, a Yankton Sioux spiritual leader and the grandson of Sam and Mary Necklace. His cousin Selma Sully Walker, director of the Native American Indian Center of Central Ohio, invited him to Columbus in order to provide spiritual support and direction for the center's activities. For the next ten years he traveled back and forth between South Dakota and Ohio, becoming a spiritual mentor to the American Indian community in central Ohio. I met Asa after I received a telephone call asking me if I would like to have a "medicine man" speak at Capital University. It was Asa. After getting to know him and other members of the local Indian community, I was invited to join them for a Sweat Lodge ceremony. I did not consider saying no.

In 1988 Asa invited me to his home on the Yankton Reservation in South Dakota. Things have never been the same. I have been back every summer since then and spent most of my 1991–92 sabbatical on the reservation and at the Institute for American Indian Studies at the University of South Dakota, where I had an appointment as a visiting scholar. I knew Asa for a year or more before we had an in-depth talk about his grandfather. All I knew was that he had been chief priest of the local Native American Church. Asa told me about his own childhood. His parents, Jennie and Harry Primeaux, divorced when he was an infant; and his grandparents raised him to become a devout member of the Native American Church. Asa always spoke about his grandpa and grandma with great reverence. One day in 1991 he took me to the old church where the Peyote services were held and the adjoining cemetery where his grandparents and many members of the Peyote community are buried. As I was standing at the gravesite, the dates on Sam Necklace's tombstone seemed to glare out at me. It suddenly struck me that they were almost exactly the same dates as the birth and death dates of my grandfather, for whom I was named. Both died in 1949; both were born in the 1880s (1881 and 1886). The date 1949 has always been indelibly etched in my mind's eye. I have vivid memories of my grandfather's funeral (I was twelve) and always have felt a bit unnerved by seeing a tombstone with the name "Tom Maroukis" on it. Looking at Sam Necklace's tombstone brought back a rush of memories. As time passed, I could not help thinking of other parallels and ironies about our grandfathers.

My grandfather was reared on the Greek island of Samos when it was under Turkish rule. Samos did not gain independence from Turkey until 1913. Like many Greeks, I was brought up with a rather negative view of Turkish rule. Now here was Asa's grandfather, born and reared on a reservation as a ward of the state. I thought it ironic that our grandfathers had grown up in a colonial environment, as subjects living under authoritarian conditions with virtually no political rights and economic deprivation. I also pondered their responses. My grandfather fled Samos and entered the United States in 1908; Asa's grandfather fled the assimilationist agenda of the U.S. government and maintained his cultural identity and spiritual values through the Peyote faith. Sam Necklace was educated in a boarding school, learned to read and write English, but chose not to live in two worlds. Instead he chose to live within the spiritual milieu of the Peyote religion and the social and cultural environment of Yankton traditional values. As some of his contemporaries with boarding-school educations began "talking back to civilization," a term used by historian Frederick Hoxie to describe those American Indians whose collective voices protested federal policies, Sam Necklace "talked back," not with spoken or written words but by living a spiritual and cultural life rooted in the Native American Church and traditional Yankton cultural values. Sam and his wife, Mary, passed this heritage on to their descendants or, as it is commonly described today, passed their heritage on to the Seventh Generation.

Many American Indians, including the Yanktons, use the term "Seventh Generation" as a metaphor for practicing, protecting, and transmitting their culture to future generations. It implies a conscious effort to preserve cultural and spiritual values for one's descendants. Sam and Mary Necklace accepted this responsibility as they transmitted the cultural values of their generation to their descendants. For example, Mary attended boarding school and became fluent in English; however, she only spoke Dakota to her grandchildren. These values are alive and well today in the Necklace/Primeaux family as the fifth generation in the Peyote religion. During my third summer in South Dakota Asa and I discussed the possibility of writing about his grandfather.

Once I had decided to pursue a biography of Sam Necklace, I met with Dr. Herbert Hoover, a historian at the University of South Dakota and a recognized scholar on Yankton history. He pointed out that the historical record on Sam Necklace was not extensive; but with the use of existing records, oral history, and ethnographic research, I could put together a life and times biography of Necklace and his era. I also met with Dr. Leonard Bruguier, a historian and director of the Institute of American Indian Studies at the University of South Dakota, who provided ideas and directions. Dr. Bruguier is a

Yankton Sioux and a member of the Native American Church. Through Asa and his family, and Dr. Hoover and Dr. Bruguier, I had access to many people on the reservation who could assist in this project.

As I pondered the difficulty of initiating a study in a new area, it became evident that the methodology for such a project was not new to me. My academic training, research, and teaching were in the field of African history, specializing in the precolonial era. The methodologies of African historiography could be applied to American Indian history. In the 1960s I was trained at Boston University's African Studies Center to use oral tradition in writing African history and did so in my doctoral dissertation. My dissertation advisor, Daniel McCall, was a strong advocate of the use of oral tradition. Jan Vansina's writing on oral tradition was required reading. McCall, who was both professor of history and professor of anthropology, was an early advocate of integrating the two disciplines for the study of African history and one of the first to use the term "ethnohistory" in African historiography. As I prepared for this project, I read back issues of *Ethnohistory* and was pleasantly surprised to find a special issue on ethnohistory and Africa, with an introduction calling for more communication between historians of Africa and American scholars practicing in the ethnohistorical tradition.[1]

In addition to oral sources, I relied on archival sources as well. I reviewed the Yankton material in the National Archives in Washington, D.C., and the regional branch in Kansas City. The Richardson Archives at the University of South Dakota also contained helpful material. Most important for writing the history of the Necklace family was the annual census of the Yanktons. Other sources included probate records, death certificates, Yankton Enrollment Books, and, most significantly, Sam Necklace's notebook on church activities.

I also have made extensive use of two types of oral sources. I used the oral history collection at the University of South Dakota, which contains interviews with many Yanktons. I also conducted interviews with people who knew Sam Necklace and/or the history of the Yankton Peyote community. In many cases I was able to corroborate written and oral sources.

A third source is ethnographic: more than fifteen years of fieldwork on the Yankton Reservation with the Necklace/Primeaux family. Aside from being involved in the ebb and flow of everyday life with several families, I attended and participated in many spiritual ceremonies. I went to as many Peyote meetings as possible; I also was involved with Sun Dances, Vision

Quests, and Sweat Lodge ceremonies. It was after several years of active participation in Peyote meetings and traditional Yankton spiritual activities that I began to recognize the many parallels between the two. While there certainly are differences, I was struck by the similarities. I did not begin this study with the idea of comparing Peyotism with traditional Yankton spirituality. Eventually I developed the view that many of the Yanktons accepted Peyotism because they saw it as traditional Indian religion, not just in ceremony and ritual but also in Peyotism's underlying theology.

The use of oral sources has been crucial to this study. Most of the sources can be characterized as oral history, which is the recollection of the past by individuals who have directly experienced the events. I also have used and collected oral tradition. These are the narratives that have been passed down by word of mouth from generation to generation. They are a very significant aspect of Yankton culture, where the narratives about the ancestors are held in high esteem. Today's cultural and spiritual practices and beliefs are rooted in the past; thus references to the past validate the present.

The Yanktons place a high value on oral tradition. It is not only the record of their history but the spiritual and cultural charter for the present; it also teaches values and beliefs. In everyday language people often mention grandparents, great-grandparents, and ancestors. This is a source of identity and place for the individual or group. Asa Primeaux prefaces comments with "I heard from my grandpa [Sam Necklace] who raised me, and he talked about his grandpa that did this, and his great-grandpa down there, he did that . . ."[2] Another example is a 1936 quote from a Yankton elder, Simon Antelope, recorded by Ella Deloria: "I have heard my grandfather say that his grandfather told him of the days when . . ."[3] Another example occurred when I was interviewing Yankton elder Joe Packard, who knew Sam Necklace. Packard kept referring to the preservation of knowledge for "your children, grandchildren, and great-grandchildren."[4] When I spoke with younger members of the Necklace/Primeaux family about the Peyote religion, they almost always began with something like: "My father told me that his father or grandfather told him." Or they would say they learned about a specific skill, like playing a Peyote drum, from their father, grandfather, or uncles. The use of the ethnohistorical approach in employing oral sources means that this study focuses on the Necklace/Primeaux family's representation of their own history through the use of their traditions as well as the oral history of family members. Oral history and oral tradition are living parts of contemporary Yankton culture. I have attempted to incorporate this into the life and times of Sam Necklace. (Pending permissions the majority of the taped interviews will be deposited in the Oral History Center at the Institute of American Indian Studies, University of South Dakota.)

This study is based on a methodology of ethnohistory informed by the developments in social history of the late 1960s, particularly the qualitative social history that deals with the everyday lives of ordinary people or history from the bottom up. In considering an approach to family history I was influenced by Richard Werbner's *Tears of the Dead: The Social Biography of an African Family*.[5] The phrase "social biography of a family" is relevant to this study, as is Werbner's method of recording life histories and integrating them into the wider historical framework. The history of the Necklace family is microhistory; but the life of Sam and Mary Necklace, and their extended family, is contextualized by placing it within the wider framework of local, regional, and national history. I also have included the story of Mary Necklace. I discuss her boarding-school experience, her marriage and relationship with Sam, her children and grandchildren, her later years as a widow, and the significance of her memory to her descendants. It is a life story that lends insight into the everyday lives of Native American women—in this case, a woman who was a member of the Native American Church for more than half a century.

Although there is considerable work published on the history of the Peyote religion, the literature rarely includes family history and certainly not five generations of one family. Most of it is either broad-based narrative or analytical studies, such as Omer Stewart's *Peyote Religion*, Weston LaBarre's *The Peyote Cult*, Ake Hultkrantz's *The Attraction of Peyote*, J. S. Slotkin's *The Peyote Religion*, or tribal-based studies such as David F. Aberle's *The Peyote Religion among the Navaho*. The same is true with local history, such as the history of Peyotism in a particular community. This study includes a comprehensive history of the Yankton Peyote community—or, as they called themselves after incorporating in 1922, the Native American Church of Charles Mix County—from the introduction of Peyotism early in the twentieth century to developments at the end of the century. It is a hundred-year history of struggle and perseverance, as the Peyote community had to face opposition, suppression, and hostility from many quarters.

It would have been impossible to write a meaningful history of the Necklace family without integrating them into the local, regional, and national history of the Peyote religion. Nationwide efforts to eradicate Peyotism had local repercussions. The Peyote religion began in the 1870s in the southern Plains and spread throughout the West. Wherever it was accepted by American Indians, it faced stiff opposition from federal, state, and local officials as well as from missionary and reform groups. In spite of the opposition, the Peyote religion thrived. In 1918 it adopted the formal name "Native American Church," and it currently has a membership of approximately 250,000. The religion aroused so much hostility for two reasons: first and foremost, because it challenged the assimilationist agenda of federal policymakers and Christian missionaries; and second, because the central theological element is the use of Peyote, a small cactus with mild hallucinogenic properties that is ingested as a holy sacrament during religious services (like bread and wine in Christian communions). The history of the Necklace/Primeaux family and the local Native American Church community is woven into this larger historical fabric. While situating the history of the Necklace/Primeaux family and the Yankton Native American Church in the wider historical milieu, I have focused on human agency, demonstrating how the members of the Peyote community developed an identity and established a place within the reservation system to exercise spiritual and cultural autonomy.

This study would not have been possible without the support and cooperation of Sam Necklace's descendants, particularly his grandson Asa and his wife, Loretta, and their sons and daughters. They welcomed me into their home and treated me as part of the family. The same is true with the other relatives, especially the Necklace grandchildren, and Parnell Necklace in particular. They all supported this project, shared their memories of the family's history, and taught me about the Native American Church and Yankton traditional religion. I learned from observation and participation. I am thankful to all the family members for allowing me to share the family's spiritual heritage. What I have recorded in taped interviews and in preparing field notes only scratches the surface of what I have learned. In fifteen years there have been hundreds of hours of conversation, interaction, and participation in family activities that are part of my experience but are not recorded. For example, Asa, who is my primary source of information, stayed at my home in Columbus for three months. Almost every morning we would sit at my kitchen table, with plenty of black coffee, and discuss everything from family to politics to religion. None of this was recorded. This was two people talking, sharing, not a scholar/informant relationship. During my sabbatical

I borrowed a small trailer, parked it next to Asa and Loretta's home, and lived there for part of an academic year. Asa and I spent almost every morning talking. In the afternoons we traveled throughout the reservation for me to meet various people. We went to the cemeteries on the reservation; we visited the small towns, traveling along the Missouri River and through the rolling hills, as Asa explained the significance of each area. Among other places, he took me to a deserted home in a remote area on the eastern side of the reservation where, he said, his grandfather secretly attended Sweat Lodge ceremonies when the government was trying to suppress them. It was at this point, while I was staying on the reservation, that I began to record some of the conversations.

As mentioned above, Asa Primeaux is the primary source of information. As he was raised by his grandparents, his memories of them are extensive, particularly of his grandfather. Asa accompanied him virtually everywhere as he carried out his responsibilities as a chief priest. Asa eventually became a roadman (one who conducts Peyote services) and is well known to Peyote communities throughout the West. The Primeaux family (including Asa, his father, Harry, his brother Francis, and the sons of Asa and Francis) are well-known Peyote singers. Almost all of them have been recorded commercially. In 1999 the Native American Church of South Dakota dedicated its Seventy-seventh Annual Convention to Asa in recognition of his lifelong service to the church.

In addition to Asa's life in the Native American Church, he is involved in Yankton traditional religion. In the late 1960s and early 1970s Asa became involved in the emerging renaissance of American Indian spirituality. By the early 1980s he had become a respected spiritual leader who conducted Sweat Lodge ceremonies, Vision Quests, and Sun Dances as well as healing and naming ceremonies. He was the spiritual leader of a large extended family and made his spiritual services available to anyone in need. He also shared his knowledge and experience as a speaker. From the early 1970s (as a spokesperson for the local Yankton chapter of the American Indian Movement) to the mid-1990s (when his health deteriorated), he spoke throughout the country. For example, whenever Asa was in Columbus, he spoke to a variety of classes at Capital University. He spent considerable time with our students. In recognition of his contributions to the Capital students and faculty in 1990, he was awarded an honorary Doctorate of Humanities degree.[6] In many ways Asa represents the spiritual legacy of his grandfather. When he teaches people about the ways of the Native American Church, he credits his learning to his grandfather. He believes that it is his responsibility to transmit his grandfather's spiritual legacy to future generations of his family.

Most of the chapter titles include dates that define watershed events in Sam Necklace's life. He was born in 1881, married in 1906, participated in the incorporation of the Yankton Peyote Church in 1922, was ordained chief priest in 1929, and died in 1949. The dates provide a structure to the narrative. The text begins with a brief analysis of the early history of the Lakota, Dakota, and Nakota (Sioux) nation or people of the Seven Council Fires (Očeti Šakówin) in chapter 1. Chapter 2 reviews early Yankton history to their removal to a reservation in 1859.

Chapter 3 examines life on the Yankton Reservation, with a description of the everyday lives of the Yankton people as seen through the experiences of the Necklace family. Sam Necklace matured, attended boarding school, and married, amidst a rapidly changing environment. This provides the opportunity to assess the impact of federal policies on American Indian lifestyles. It is also the era (chapter 4) of the emergence and expansion of the Peyote religion and its introduction onto the Yankton Reservation. Sam Necklace and his family became members of the Peyote church.

Chapter 5 analyzes the opposition to Peyotism and the various strategies of the Peyote community to quell the impact of the opposition. This chapter also contains an in-depth analysis of why some of the Yankton people accepted the Peyote religion and presents the central thesis of the study concerning the diffusion of Peyotism among the Yanktons. Chapter 6 reviews the impact of the Depression, the New Deal, and World War II on the Yanktons in general and the Necklace family in particular. These are Sam Necklace's years of church leadership, when he struggled to protect the rights of the Peyote community. This led him to become involved in reservation politics, as the members of the Peyote community, who were full-bloods, believed their rights and status among the Yanktons were being threatened by a younger generation of so-called mixed-bloods. During the 1930s Sam Necklace became a spokesperson of the full-blood faction in Yankton politics.

Chapter 7 analyzes the last half-century of federal policy and the American Indian struggle for self-determination. This includes the growth and development of the Native American Church, the continuing battles for religious freedom, and an in-depth analysis of the local Yankton Peyote community. It also covers the last years of Mary Necklace's life and Mary and Sam's descendants as they continue the family's commitment to both the Native American Church and Yankton traditional spirituality.

The use of certain terminology in this study needs explanation. For those not familiar with the history of the Native American Church the terms that are used for religious services may be confusing. Many Peyotists use the term "meeting," as in "Peyote meeting"; others say "prayer service." Sometimes one encounters the terms "Peyote ceremony" or "Peyote religious service." All of these phrases refer to the same thing: a spiritual service that begins at dusk and ends the next morning, usually ten to twelve hours in duration. When a member of the Native American Church says, "I'm going to a meeting" or "Let's sponsor a meeting," this refers to the dusk to dawn religious service.

The term "tradition" or "traditional" is problematic in the field of ethnohistory, whether in African studies or American Indian studies. The simplistic traditional/modern dichotomy was discarded several decades ago, yet scholars need terms to describe the cultural life of the past and contrast it with subsequent change. The use of the terms "traditional life" and "traditional religion" by Western scholars when describing non-Western people has been criticized because it implies an unchanging past. When "traditional" is used, for example, with the Sioux, how far back does it go? Does it mean before the introduction of the horse? In order to clarify the use of the term "traditional," as in "Yankton traditional religion" or "traditional culture," I use it in a very precise manner to refer to the spiritual, cultural, and social values and structures that existed on the eve of the reservation era.[7]

The terms "full-blood" and "mixed-blood" are also problematic, as any reference to a connection between blood and culture is viewed as discredited racist diatribe. These terms, however, have historic significance and are commonly used. They are also relevant today, because the federal government and almost all tribal governments have a "blood quantum" requirement for membership and access to federal services and programs. As historic terms they have a double usage: as derogatory terms or as descriptive terms referring to a group's reference point in politics or culture. Earlier in the twentieth century "full-blood" and "mixed-blood" were used in a derogatory manner when each group used them referring to the other. A full-blood was backward, superstitious, pagan; a mixed-blood was a sellout, sacrificing American Indian values for immediate gain in the Anglo-American world. When "full-blood" was used as a reference point, as the Yankton full-bloods used the term to define themselves, it meant being part of a value system whose beliefs and practices were rooted in the ancestors and the spiritual world. In the 1930s politics on many reservations, particularly in South Dakota, was divided by a full-blood/mixed-blood dichotomy. This is relevant to this study, because Sam Necklace was a leader of the Yankton full-blood faction in the 1930s as it struggled to maintain power vis-à-vis a growing mixed-blood population.

Another concern as a point of consistency is the capitalization of "Peyote," "Peyotism," "Peyotist," "Peyote religion," and "Peyote church." The tendency in recent scholarship is to capitalize "Peyote," "Peyotism," and "Peyotists" but not to capitalize "Peyote community," "Peyote prayers," "Peyote music," or "Peyote drum." I have chosen to expand recent usage and capitalize virtually all use of the word "Peyote," because it refers to the holy sacrament of the Native American Church. This capitalization is also out of respect to the church membership, as Peyote is considered a gift of God and central to their theology. The members also capitalize the word "Peyote" in all its usages (see the convention program in appendix II). Here it is lowercase only in botanical references to the peyote cactus.

What follows is the story of a family, a religion, and a people. It is the accumulation of material from many sources, particularly the Necklace/Primeaux family and the Yankton Native American Church community. I consider myself very fortunate that they would share their remembrances of the past with me. This is a history of people who struggled to maintain spiritual and cultural autonomy when political and economic autonomy was not possible. It is an illustration of how a marginalized people maintained some degree of control over their lives under stressful circumstances during an era of intense change. This examination of family history and local history will add to the understanding of the everyday lives of American Indian men and women. The credit belongs to the people in this study; it is their story. Any errors in judgment or fact are my responsibility.

Acknowledgments

A project such as this, which included visits to archives and libraries as well as interviews and interactions with a large number of people, requires many thanks to many individuals. I want to thank the staff at the National Archives in Washington, D.C., and Kansas City for their valuable help in making materials readily available. I also thank Karen Zimmerman, former director of the Richardson Archive at the University of South Dakota (USD), who made my hours there both pleasant and fruitful. Margaret Quintal, assistant director of the Institute of American Indian Studies at USD, who aided me in a hundred ways, deserves a very special thank you for her support. I owe a huge debt of gratitude to Leonard Bruguier, director of the institute, colleague, and *koda* [friend], who supported this work from its inception to completion. And thanks to Professor Herb Hoover of USD for help in the early planning of this study. I would like to thank Judy Warnement, director of Harvard University Botany Libraries, for help in accessing material on Peyote. I also would like to mention Jo Ann Reece, an acquisitions editor at the University of Oklahoma Press. Her help, support, and advice have been invaluable. I could not have worked with a more pleasant person.

At my home base I want to thank colleagues Harry Jebsen and Andy Carlson for reading the manuscript and making suggestions. I want to thank Earnesta Davie, our departmental secretary, for her hard work in helping to prepare the various versions of the manuscript. I also want to thank my former student assistant Jerry McMannamy, who helped with the intricacies of endnotes and in formatting the complicated genealogies. I would like to thank Lindsay Jones, a comparative religion scholar at Ohio State University, for his advice. Longtime friend Don Wallis, an author and teacher from Yellow Springs, Ohio, helped make my paragraphs and sentences a little more coherent.

I received considerable support and friendship from many people at the Native American Indian Center of Central Ohio, especially the executive director, Carol Welsh, and associate director, Mark Welsh. Their friendship has been steadfast. I also must mention Carol's mother, Selma Walker, the founder of the Indian Center. Selma was raised on the Yankton Reservation and was a lifelong member of the Native American Church. We spent many hours discussing reservation life. During the last years of Selma's life I spent pleasant afternoons in her home, where she shared her experiences with me. Her help was invaluable.

My deepest appreciation of all goes to the Necklace and Primeaux families and all the descendants of Sam and Mary Necklace. They always welcomed me and made me feel like part of the family, particularly Asa and Loretta. Without Asa's initial ideas this study would not have started. Loretta opened her home to me and welcomed me with a smile, a hug, and her special fry-bread. All nine children—Edith, Sonny, Jolene, Junior, Gerald, Mike, Sylvia, Tina, and Jennifer—taught me much about Yankton spirituality, especially as they were consciously maintaining the traditions of their family. And special thanks to Gerald and Mike, who taught me a great deal about the Native American Church, the Sun Dance, Vision Quests, and the Sweat Lodge. I would like to offer a very special prayer for Mike, who tragically passed away in 1997. This special thanks also goes to Parnell Necklace and his family for their hospitality and friendship. Finally, thanks to Germaine Sitting Crow for her help. I will never forget my first night in Vermillion, when she made me a huge Indian taco.

Pidamayedo to all.

Notes on Orthography

There is no standard orthography for the Dakota language. The following pronunciations generally follow Stephen Riggs, *A Dakota-English Dictionary*.

á	vowel sound as in "y<u>a</u>hoo"
č	<u>ch</u> sound as in "<u>ch</u>ase" or "<u>ch</u>in"
é	long vowel sound like the French acute accent as in *gravit<u>é</u>*
ĥ	<u>ch</u> guttural sound as in German *ach*
í	long vowel double <u>ee</u> sound as in "w<u>ee</u>"
ó	long vowel sound as in "<u>o</u>we" or "<u>oh</u>"
š	<u>sh</u> sound as in "<u>sh</u>ip" or "<u>sh</u>op"
ž	<u>s</u> sound as in "plea<u>s</u>ure" or "fu<u>s</u>ion"

Peyote and the Yankton Sioux

CHAPTER ONE

The Sioux

NATION OF THE SEVEN COUNCIL FIRES

Sacred Pipe carved by Parnell Necklace, grandson of
Sam Necklace. Drawn by Dr. Cassandra Tellier, director,
Schumacher Gallery, Capital University.

On a warm September afternoon in 1949, Sam Necklace and his family were traveling home to the Yankton Sioux Reservation. In the car with Sam were his wife, Mary; his son Dan, who was driving, and his wife; and Sam's eighteen-year-old grandson, Asa. They had just come from Devil's Lake (renamed Spirit Lake) Reservation near Tokio, North Dakota, where Sam had conducted a Peyote meeting for a relative with epilepsy. He never refused a request to conduct a Peyote meeting, whether it was for a funeral, a marriage, or an illness or to celebrate a birthday or graduation. He believed it was his calling and his responsibility. As a priest in the Native American Church, he had been conducting such Peyote meetings for more than three decades. Sam Necklace, now sixty-eight years old, had been an active member of the Native American Church since his late twenties. While in Tokio, Sam and his family stayed with his niece Violet Blue Shield and her husband, Lincoln. The Peyote service was held all night Saturday and into Sunday morning. They decided to stay on another day or two in order to rest and visit with relatives they did not see very often. They left on Tuesday morning for a 400-mile trip back to the Yankton Reservation that would take twelve to fourteen hours on two-lane highways. Violet had prepared food for their long journey home, because in 1949 there were few roadside restaurants that served Native Americans. They headed straight south on state route 281, going through Jamestown and Aberdeen and on to the reservation.

In September the countryside was still green, with barely a hint of fall in the air. The corn was high, and the acres and acres of sunflower fields were bright with many shades of yellow and green. The flowers, full of seeds, were tilting toward the ground, ready to be harvested. It was a pleasant trip. They drove mile after mile through the unchanging scenery. Grandpa Sam, as everyone called him, was sitting in the back with his wife and grandson. He said he was tired and wanted to sleep. He had a favorite star quilt that had been given to him as a gift many years before; as he started to doze off, he pulled the quilt up over his lap and fell into a heavy sleep. Sam never woke up; he died peacefully while sleeping. There was nothing they could do except continue on home. His grandson remembered, "He wasn't sick or anything, he just died all of a sudden."[1]

Sam actually had been sick. His death certificate lists tuberculosis as the cause of death. Pulmonary tuberculosis ravaged American Indian communities. Early in the twentieth century TB (called consumption) was the leading cause of death in the United States. It is a highly contagious disease that literally consumes its victims. The bacteria are present in the material sprayed into the air from the lungs when an infected person coughs or sneezes. The high incidence of TB among American Indians was due to their low resistance as well as living in crowded indoor quarters in areas of economic deprivation. Overcrowding facilitated the spread of this very communicable disease. There were similar epidemics among African Americans living in crowded urban areas. The tubercle bacilli may be in the system years before overt symptoms appear. By the time the symptoms are noticed, the disease is well advanced. The first symptoms are fatigue and weight loss, followed by coughing and eventually spitting up blood. Inadequate medical care allowed the disease to advance to the point where a cure was almost impossible. This accounts for the high mortality rate.

Sam Necklace lived a full life that revolved around family, religion, and community. His life reflected reservation conditions. Daily existence was difficult; constant adjustment, if not accommodation, was required. Economic conditions were unstable, and Necklace experienced turmoil in both his personal and public life. His family and his spiritual life, however, brought him solace. Born in 1881, he grew up in an era when traditional culture was still predominant. From his parents and his parents' parents, he learned the old ways. His roots were in the Yankton past. These ties to the past helped prepare him for the era of incredible change that his life spanned. The Yankton people had known change such as the introduction of the horse and the use of iron in the form of kettles, axes, knives, and firearms; but now the change was more rapid. A rapidly evolving, unpredictable world was becoming the norm. In Necklace's lifetime the unpredictability of change made adjustment virtually impossible. His later years must have seemed so different from his early years, a span of just a half-century. Yet some things remained the same. For example, there was the transmission of knowledge. As he had learned from his elders, he passed on to his children and his children's children. Some of what he taught was different from what he learned, but the method of transmitting culture, values, and knowledge had not changed. From his grandparents to his great-grandchildren he was the link in the middle of seven generations. This was not unusual. It was the Yankton way—as it was the way of many Native American people—of using the past as a model for the present in order to prepare for the future. This allowed for a certain degree of continuity at the core, in spite of a rapidly changing exterior.

Sam Necklace was born on the Yankton Sioux Reservation in South Dakota. His parents were Yankton Sioux or more correctly Ihanktonwan Dakotas. "Yankton" is the anglicization of the Dakota name: Ihanktonwan. They are one of the seven major divisions of the great Sioux nation, one of the Seven Council Fires (Očeti Šakówin). Today the Sioux are located primarily on reservations in North and South Dakota, Minnesota, Nebraska, and Montana and in south-central Canada. Many, however, live in urban centers throughout the Plains states. The Yanktons live in south-central South Dakota in Charles Mix County. The location of the earliest homeland of the Sioux is uncertain. The French first came in contact with people they called the Sioux in the 1660s in present-day Minnesota. It is unclear how long the Sioux had been in Minnesota. Other questions remain, such as the location of an earlier homeland, their coalescence into a group that eventually referred to itself as the Seven Council Fires, the length of time they have spoken a common language, and the subsequent emergence of three dialects.

There is some indirect evidence as well as speculation for an eastern origin of the Sioux. The evidence comes from linguistics and oral tradition. Lakota, Dakota, and Nakota are considered three dialects of a single language that is part of the larger Siouan language family (called Siouan-Catawba by earlier scholars). Siouan is a linguistic grouping of a large family of Native American languages that extends from the Gulf region to the Carolinas, Virginia, the upper Midwest, and the Plains. Recent scholarship lists the following Siouan subgroups:

Subgroup	Language
1. Missouri River	Crow, Hidatsa
2. Mandan	Mandan
3. Mississippi Valley	Sioux, Assiniboine, Stoney
4. Chiwere-Winnebago	Chiwere, Winnebago
5. Dhegiha	Omaha-Ponca, Kansa-Osage, Quapaw
6. Ohio Valley Virginian Siouan	Tutelo, Saponi, Moniton, Occaneechi
7. Mississippi Siouan	Biloxi, Oto

Charles E. Voegelin established the basic grouping of Siouan languages in 1941; but more recent scholarship has placed Mandan in a separate subgroup, and the more distantly related Catawba is no longer included as a Siouan subgroup. There has been considerable debate about the age and the homeland of proto-Siouan. Douglas Parks and Robert Rankin suggest a 2,000- to 3,000-year time depth for proto-Siouan and speculate about a possible eastern origin. Several linguists, especially John P. Swanton, have speculated about an Ohio Valley origin, followed by two subsequent movements: one northwesterly and one eastern and southern, thus accounting for the wide dispersal of Siouan subgroups. This speculation is not supported by convincing linguistic evidence, however, so the question of a Siouan homeland is still unsettled.[2]

Among the Yanktons there are widespread oral traditions concerning an eastern origin.[3] In a 1912 speech DeWitt Hare, a Yankton elder, said: "I shall here give a brief sketch of their originality as is handed down by our tribal historians from generation to generation from time immemorial up to the present. They had migrated from afar. Centuries before the time of Columbus they lived near, or upon the Atlantic Seaboard in what is now North Carolina."[4] He went on to describe their migration through the Ohio Valley and westward. In 1943 John Swanton, while collecting material on Sioux origins, wrote that, "according to the traditions of the western Siouan tribes, they, or at least some of them, formerly lived in the east, the Ohio River being in some cases specifically mentioned."[5] Another example is Paul Picotte (eighty-nine years old), a Yankton highly respected for his knowledge of the Yankton traditions, who told an interviewer that "our Dakota Indians came from the eastern seaboard and finally they got to the Mississippi River." Yankton scholar Ella C. Deloria held the same view.[6] Other Yanktons have similar beliefs. The grandson of Sam Necklace, Asa Primeaux, reiterated on many occasions that his grandfather told him stories about Sioux origins in the Ohio Valley and their eventual migration west. More linguistic studies are needed; and the oral traditions need to be collected, analyzed, and compared in a more systematic manner before any conclusions can be drawn concerning Sioux origins. There is also no archaeological evidence at this time to support a theory of an eastern origin for the Sioux.

The first mention of the Sioux in a European source is 1640. Jean Nicollet, who was visiting the Winnebagos in present-day Wisconsin, referred to them as the "Nadisieu." The first contact was in 1660, when French explorer Pierre-Esprit Radisson called them "the Nation of the Beef" in reference to their buffalo hunting. The first extended encounter occurred in 1680, when Louis Hennepin, a Catholic priest, and two companions were taken captive by the Sioux. Hennepin became ill and was taken into a Sweat Lodge. This is the first European recording of one of the Sioux's Seven Sacred Rites. During that century the Sioux were located in a region between Mille Lacs (present-day Minnesota) in the east and the Missouri River in the west. Their homeland encompassed a woodlands environment in the East, among the lakes and rivers, and a Prairie/Plains environment in the West.

At this initial contact the French recognized the distinctions among the various divisions of the Sioux. The French referred to them as eastern Sioux and western Sioux. Two brothers, Guillaume and Joseph-Nicholas Delisle, published a series of maps showing this distinction. Their information was based on the accounts of various French explorers. One map published in the early eighteenth century was titled *L'Amérique Septentrionale* (North America). It places the *Pays des Nadouessis* (Country of the Sioux) on both sides of the upper Mississippi River and then further distinguishes between the *Sioux de l'Ouest* and the *Sioux de l'Est* on opposite sides of the river. Map 21 (1719), titled *Carte du Canada ou de la Nouvelle France*, labels the headwaters of the Mississippi as *Sioux ou Madouessi ou Issatti* (Santee). Below this is *Sioux de l'Ouest* and *Sioux de l'Est*. This map also labels an area below the Sioux of the West as the *Nation des Tintons* (Tetons). A map published in 1752, *Carte de Nouvelle Découverts,* also by Joseph-Nicholas Delisle, shows the eastern and western Sioux divided by the Mississippi River. The map locates the western Sioux just east of a mountain range. In addition to recognizing an eastern and western division of the Sioux, Hennepin mentions their further division into four eastern Sioux groups and three western Sioux, indicating that at the time of this contact the Sioux were already divided into seven groups. There is, however, no evidence in European sources that they called themselves the Očeti Šakówin or Seven Council Fires at this time.

Recent scholars, such as Raymond DeMallie, divide the Sioux into three groups (Teton, Yankton-Yanktonai, and Santee), not using the traditional division of Lakota, Dakota, and Nakota of earlier scholars. The eastern Sioux, known collectively as the Santees or Isantis, are the Sissetonwans (Sissetons), Wahpekutewans (Wahpekutes), Wahpetonwans (Wahpetons), and Mdewankantonwans (Mdewakantons). The western Sioux are the Titonwans (Tetons). The middle Sioux are the Ihanktonwannas (Yanktonais) and the Ihanktonwans (Yanktons).[7] The general tendency of Sioux groups was to move in a westerly direction. By the late eighteenth century the Tetons were located west of the Missouri River, the Yanktons and Yanktonais were in present-day eastern North and South Dakota and northwest Iowa, and the Santees were in what is now Minnesota and northwest Iowa.[8] After the expansion of the Sioux from the Upper Mississippi Valley, their late eighteenth century structure was as follows.

Structure[9]

DESIGNATION	SEVEN COUNCIL FIRES
Yankton (Middle Sioux)	1. Yankton (People of the End Village)
	2. Yanktonai (Little People at the End Village)
Santee (Eastern Sioux)	3. Mdewakanton (Spirit Lake People)
	4. Wahpeton (Dwellers among the Leaves)
	5. Sisseton (People of the Boggy Ground)
	6. Wahpekute (Shooters among the Leaves)
Teton (Western Sioux)	7. Teton (Dwellers of the Prairie)
Teton Bands	a. Oglala (They Scatter Their Own)
	b. Sičangu or Brule (Burnt Thighs)
	c. Hunkpapa (Campers at the End of the Circle)
	d. Minneconjou (Planters beside the Water)
	e. Sihasapa (Blackfoot)
	f. Oohenonpa (Two Kettles)
	g. Itazipčo or Sans Arcs (Those without Bows)

In the late seventeenth and eighteenth centuries the economic life of the Sioux people was based on hunting, fishing, and gathering, with limited agri-

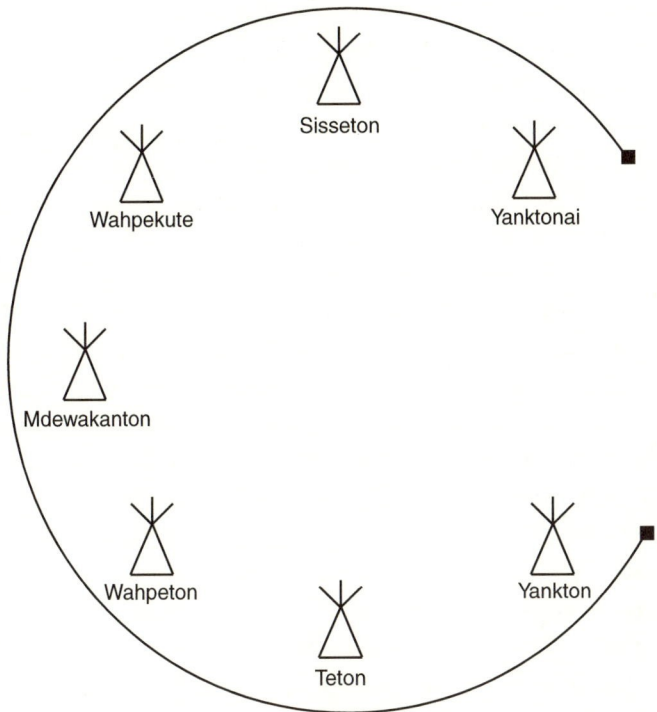

Figure 1. Camping Circle of the Seven Council Fires

culture among the eastern groups. In the woodlands region, living on both sides of the Mississippi River, the Sioux resided in small-scattered villages with five to six families per village. In some areas there were larger villages. Families lived in round lodges or tipis covered with animal skins. They practiced limited agriculture, growing mostly tobacco and some corn. The bulk of their diet was buffalo (*Bison americanus*) and wild rice. In the summer the villages organized communal hunts for buffalo, taking entire families to the west, where herds of buffalo were located. After a successful hunt there was plenty of food for the summer. The remainder, cut into narrow strips and dried in the sun, was a major source of food for the winter. Buffalo hides were used for blankets and tipi covering. When the people returned home in the fall, harvesting of wild rice began. The rice was dried and stored for the winter. With numerous lakes, rivers, and streams in this region, fishing also provided a significant source of food. Canoes, rafts, and small covered boats facilitated fishing and gathering wild rice. The canoes were essential for harvesting the rice, because the elongated shape of the canoe made it easy to glide into the wild rice marshes. The rice shoots were pulled over the canoe, and with a little shaking or tapping the loosened grains of rice fell into it. In addition to rice and fish, fruits, berries, nuts, and roots were collected and sometimes dried and stored. The supply of buffalo meat was supplemented by hunting deer, moose, antelopes, rabbits, squirrels, ducks, and geese. Deer were especially important, as tanned skin provided clothing and moccasins.[10]

The western Sioux were hunters in the open prairies from present-day western Minnesota to the Missouri River, surviving primarily on buffalo. They did not practice horticulture or (given their location) collect wild rice. Before the introduction of the horse, buffalo were hunted on foot. It took large groups of hunters and required coordination. Buffalo herds could be difficult to find in the vastness of the Plains. When they were located, they were surrounded and approached slowly, as buffalo have a keen sense of smell. The buffalo were killed with bows and arrows or spears or on rare occasions were driven over a cliff. During the winter the hunters wore snow-shoes, while the snow slowed the mobility of the buffalo. When on the hunt they slept in tipis. The women with the hunting group set up and took down the tipis. Their equipment and supplies were carried on a travois, pulled by dogs. Made of two poles tied together at one end, with the other ends spread apart (forming a V-shaped frame), the travois could be loaded with a con-siderable amount of goods. The narrow part of the frame was attached to the dog's harness. Hunting took time and endurance, but if the hunting parties were successful they provided their communities with meat and hides.[11]

In the seventeenth and eighteenth centuries the appearance of the French explorers and traders in the Great Lakes region had a significant impact on the Sioux. The Sioux never had an isolated subsistence economy. They had been trading with their neighbors for centuries and were also linked directly and indirectly to the wide-ranging intracontinental trade. The French, how-ever, introduced new factors: an insatiable demand for furs and the introduc-tion of iron products. The French presence initiated a series of confrontations between Europeans and American Indians and sometimes between Indian groups in a struggle over dwindling resources and land.

From the early to mid-eighteenth century the Sioux began moving west, southwest, and south. This was not a large-scale mass migration. Various bands and extended families (*tiošpayes*) began moving in a series of outmi-grations that lasted several generations. Some Sioux did not move or did not move very far, choosing to remain in present-day central Minnesota. It was at this time that the Tetons crossed the Missouri River and occupied part of the vast wide-open Plains. Some theories on the causes of the migrations have emphasized warfare. Supposedly the Sioux's eastern enemy, the Ojibwas (Chippewas), developed a trade network with the French and were able to acquire firearms. The Sioux, without firearms, moved away to avoid confrontations with a more heavily armed neighbor.[12] This interpretation seems to rely on Ojibwa oral tradition, which claims that their military strength drove the Sioux from their woodland homes. More recent research has shown that other factors were involved.

At this time patterns of economic life as well as the ecology of the western Great Lakes region were undergoing significant change due to European trapping and trading. Fur-bearing game was in decline, as furs became a highly valued commodity. Dependence on European markets that were affected by international events created alternate patterns of scarcity and surplus, resulting in political and economic instability. As game was hunted more for trade than for food, resources dwindled, tension increased, and groups of Sioux began to migrate. By the 1730s the French found few Sioux in their traditional area of present-day Minnesota.[13] Professor Herbert Hoover summarizes the causes of these migrations: the Sioux migrated "to avoid a war with these neighbors [Ojibwas], and to find better gleaning and hunting lands as well as trade connections to meet the needs of their growing population." By moving west they found more trade opportunities along the Des Moines and Missouri Rivers.[14]

By the mid-eighteenth century the Sioux were spread out across the Great Plains. The Tetons (or western Sioux) continued west to the Black Hills. They did not move into unfamiliar territory; they already had hunted buffalo across the Plains. Now seeking food, trade, and a secure life, they made present-day western South Dakota their home. The eastern Sioux (the Mdewakantons, Wahpetons, Wahpekutes, and Sissetons) moved from north-central Minnesota to southeast and south-central Minnesota, many settling along the Minnesota River. These groups continued limited agriculture, still relying primarily on hunting, fishing, and gathering. They were also in a location where they could carry on considerable trade. The Yanktonais moved west and southwest into eastern North and South Dakota. They now relied more on hunting as they adjusted to a drier prairie environment. The Yanktons migrated southwest. First they moved into the area of the Red Pipestone Quarry, the location of the red pipestone (catlinite) that is used to make the Sacred Pipes (*čannupa wakan*). The Yanktons had the responsibility to keep the pipestone quarry safe and secure so that all Sioux could still have access to the pipestone. The Yanktons continued south along the Big Sioux River and south to the Missouri River in what is now southeast South Dakota, northeast Nebraska, and northwest Iowa. From there they expanded westward along the Missouri River to the Vermillion and James Rivers. Like the Yanktonais, they now relied more and more on hunting. Their location along the Missouri River also gave them greater trade opportunities.

From the late eighteenth century until the reservation era began, the seven divisions of the Sioux nation were more or less permanently located in home areas. For all seven branches, trade with each other was essential. From the far reaches of Sioux territory they gathered together periodically not only for trade but for social as well as spiritual renewal. Old ties were reestablished, and spiritual activities such as the Sun Dance were held in common. According to Sioux oral tradition, these gatherings go back several centuries. At some point (the date is not clear) they began referring to themselves as Očeti Šakówin, the Seven Council Fires. This name was certainly in use by the early nineteenth century. In the late spring the seven groups gathered in a large circle, where each group was referred to symbolically as a council fire and given a specific location in the camp circle. For example the Yanktons' name "end dwellers" or "people of the end village" derives from their relative position in the great circle. These "annual reunions" or "trade fairs" were described by a number of explorers and merchants. The gatherings were in a central location, usually along a waterway such as the James River. According to French merchant Pierre-Antoine Tabeau, the gatherings were quite large. He reported seeing 1,000 to 1,200 lodges and about 3,000 men bearing arms. He noted that the Tetons traveled east to "exchange horses, lodges of leather [tipi coverings], buffalo robes, shirts and leggings of antelope-skin" for mostly European goods such as firearms and iron kettles. They also traded for red-stone pipe bowls and bows made of walnut. Meriwether Lewis and William Clark reported that the Santees acquired horses from the Tetons. The Santees functioned as "middlemen" traders, bringing European goods to trade for goods from the Plains. By the mid-nineteenth century the frequency of the gatherings declined as the continuing dispersal of the Sioux made travel more difficult, and as other factors such as the decline of the buffalo and series of epidemics added to the problems of travel.[15]

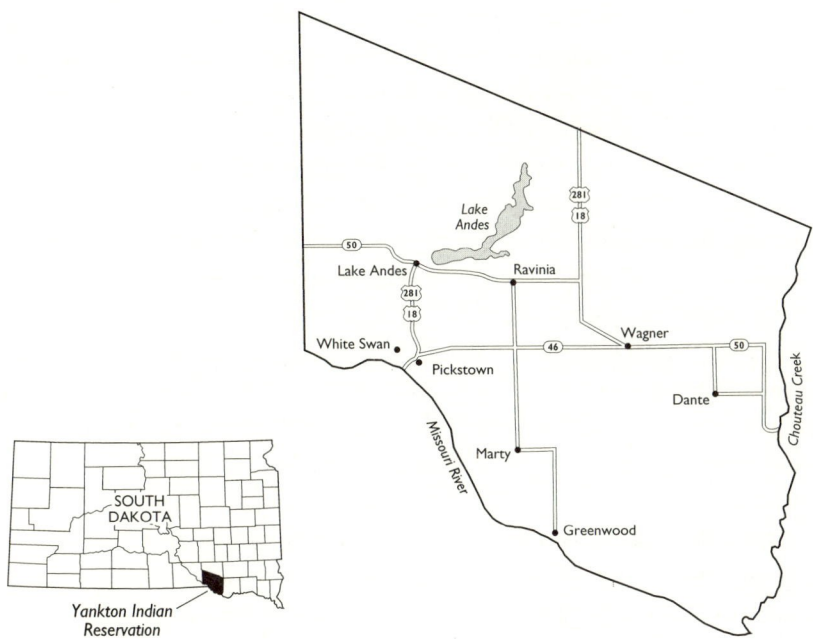

Yankton Sioux Reservation

LANGUAGE

Today many Lakota, Dakota, and Nakota speakers hold the term "Sioux" in disdain. There is not a universally accepted name for this language, made up of three mutually intelligible dialects. "Sioux" was not the name they used for themselves. The Ojibwas (Chippewas), their more powerful neighbors, applied the name to them. The Ojibwas called the Sioux *Nadowe-is-iw-ug* or *Nadouessioux;* the French corrupted it to *Naduesiu* then shortened it to "Sioux." The Sioux people believe the Ojibwa term for them means rattlesnake or adder and was intended to be pejorative as a reference to them as an enemy. Thus the term "Sioux" was born and was then applied by European traders and missionaries and eventually by American officials to wide-ranging groups who spoke Lakota, Dakota, or Nakota. All three of these terms can be translated as "friends" or "allies."[16]

In the mid-nineteenth century several anthropologists and historians began using "Dakota" as the name for all Sioux. In 1891 the name "Dakota" received "official" blessing in John Wesley Powell's *Indian Linguistic Families of America North of Mexico*. Powell, the director of the Smithsonian Institution, was influenced by the work of Stephen Return Riggs (1812–83), a missionary among the Sioux. In the 1830s Riggs and others developed a written form for Dakota. Riggs based his work on the eastern or Santee Sioux (Dakota dialect), but "Dakota" became the generic term for the three dialects. In 1852 Riggs published *Grammar and Dictionary of the Dakota Language*. It was later expanded and published posthumously (1890) by James Owen Dorsey, an ethnologist from the Smithsonian. In an introductory note for the new edition, Powell wrote that "the Dakota language now consists of three well defined dialects, the Santee, Yankton and Teton." Powell and others argued that because "Sioux" was a derogatory name it should not be used. Powell did not use the linguistic terms "Lakota," "Dakota," and "Nakota," but along with Riggs and Dorsey he established the term "Dakota" for all Sioux groups.[17]

Today some linguists still use "Dakota" as the collective term for the three dialects yet also continue to use it as the name for the eastern dialect. This is confusing. Lakota speakers would never call their language Dakota or refer to themselves as Dakota. In spite of a wider usage of "Dakota," many government officials and the popular press have continued to use the name "Sioux," making use of the name "Dakota" for all Sioux people unsatisfactory. Recent scholarship still divides the Sioux language into three dialects: the Santee-Sisseton and Yankton-Yanktonai dialect is Dakota; the Teton dialect is Lakota; and the closely related Assiniboine and Stoney groups of Montana and Canada speak the Nakota dialect. These are also the distinctions made by contemporary Sioux speakers. The basic difference is the *L, D,* and *N* sounds. There is no *D* sound in the Lakota dialect just as there is no *L* sound in the Dakota dialect. Lakota, Dakota, and Nakota use the *L, D,* and *N* sound, respectively. For example, in Lakota the word for "thank you" is *palama;* in Dakota it is *padama.* Some linguistic classification systems place Yankton-Yanktonai in the Nakota category; however, DeMallie and Parks claim that this was an error made in the early twentieth century and repeated by later scholars. They contend that there is no historical evidence that the Yanktons and Yanktonais ever spoke Nakota. Today these two groups call themselves Dakota speakers.[18] This association of the Yankton people with the Nakota dialect has confused many scholars. This is best illustrated by reference to a recent statement in the foreword to the 1992 reprint of Riggs's 1890 *A Dakota-English Dictionary* that "the N or Nakota is used by the Yankton."[19] As mentioned above, the Yanktons call themselves Dakota and speak Dakota.

The name "Sioux" causes consternation, but it is still the most well-known collective term for Lakota, Dakota, and Nakota speakers. This is changing, however. In 1993 the Sisseton-Wahpeton Sioux Tribe officially changed its name to the Sisseton-Wahpeton Dakota Nation.[20] Non-Indians are generally unfamiliar with the designations "Lakota," "Dakota," and "Nakota," yet almost all Americans know the name "Sioux." It is interesting to note that in the film *Dances with Wolves* the Lakota speakers refer to themselves as Lakota; but in the English subtitles "Lakota" is translated as Sioux. Which term one uses depends on whom one is speaking to and the context of the conversation. "Sioux" is usually used when speaking English and when speaking to non-Sioux. "Lakota," "Dakota," or "Nakota" is used when speaking in one of the three dialects. On the Pine Ridge Reservation people may refer to themselves as Oglala, Lakota, or Sioux or sometimes in combination as Oglala Lakota or Oglala Sioux or, as is becoming quite common, as the Oglala Lakota Nation. On the Yankton Reservation people may refer to themselves as Yankton, Dakota, or Sioux or sometimes in combination as Yankton Dakota or Yankton Sioux and, when speaking to each other, as Ihanktonwan Dakota. It should be noted that the term "Sioux" is slowly falling in disuse. Fewer and fewer people are using it. Several reservation governments are debating whether to delete "Sioux" from their official name. For example, one may still see the name "Rosebud Sioux Reservation," but in some places it is now referred to as Sicangu Lakota Reservation or Sičangu Lakota Oyáte (nation).

WESTWARD MIGRATION: THE HORSE AND THE BUFFALO

As the Sioux were migrating and expanding westward, they acquired the horse, which had been spreading northward since its introduction into the Americas by the Spanish. The horse entered the Plains from several directions. Horses first appeared in the eastern Rockies among the Crows, Nez Perces, and Shoshones and in the southern and central Plains among the Comanches, Plains Apaches, Kiowas, Cheyennes, and Arapahos. Specific dates are difficult to establish for most groups, but the Crows were probably using horses by 1730 and the Cheyennes by 1766. Horses were acquired through trade, by capturing wild horses, and by raids against neighboring peoples. The Sioux were certainly using horses by the 1770s, and possibly earlier. The horse had a great impact on all branches of the Sioux, changing their lives in dramatic fashion. This was an innovation that served as an "intensifier" of Sioux cultural patterns. The horse became central to their existence. It made the Sioux more effective hunters and made them the most powerful military force in the Plains. With the horse, the western or Teton Sioux now began expanding even farther, pushing the Cheyennes, Kiowas, and Crows to the west and forcing the Pawnees to the south. The Tetons named the horse *šunka wakan*, which literally translates as "sacred dog" or "holy spirit dog."[21] *Wakan* is a powerful word in Lakota (as well as in Nakota and Dakota), meaning sacred or holy, imbued with powerful spiritual or creative qualities. Its most profound uses are Wakan Tanka meaning God or Creator and *wičaša wakan*, holy man.[22] In Dakota the word for horse is *šunka tanka,* meaning large dog.

The impact of the horse varied from region to region; it nevertheless affected all branches of Sioux society, although the eastern Sioux used fewer horses. The greatest impact was in the open Plains west of the Missouri River, where the horse could best be used to assure a sufficient supply of buffalo meat. In the open terrain a good horse could outrun a buffalo. It was also much easier to find and follow a herd, and fewer hunters were needed for a successful hunt. Buffalo hunting required superb horsemanship, especially the need to control the horse by using pressure from the rider's legs while the hands held weapons. Boys literally grew up on the backs of horses; and by the time they became young men they were some of the best riders in the world. In the eastern Plains, where there were higher grasses, more hills, and fewer buffalo, the horse played a less significant role. In the semiwoodlands and woodlands of Minnesota the horse was important, but it did not lead to any drastic change in lifestyle.[23]

Regardless of how the horse was used in relationship to the terrain, it became a symbol of status and prestige everywhere. Wealth was measured in horses. They were used as a medium of exchange and were most highly valued gifts at "giveaways." They were also the object of many raids, because acquiring horses brought additional prestige to young men and their families. In the early nineteenth century many of the Sioux began using firearms, including, after mid-century, breech-loading rifles. This made them even more formidable warriors. In sum, the horse, used in hunting, warfare, trade, travel, and recreation, had a profound impact throughout the Plains.[24]

As the horse became central to the social and political structure of the Sioux, the buffalo became more crucial to their economic survival. Millions of buffalo roamed the Plains. They were a major source of food: a large male buffalo weighing 2,000 pounds could provide 900–1,000 pounds of meat.[25] It was the main part of the diet. Almost nothing was wasted, as it could be eaten immediately or preserved. Much of the meat was transformed into buffalo jerky (*papa*) by cutting it into long thin strips and hanging them to dry in the hot sun. The dried meat was also used in a mixture called pemmican (*wašna* or *wakapapi*). The meat was pounded and then mixed with melted fat or marrow and any type of berries or plums. This mixture was rolled into small balls and preserved. It was a high-energy food essential for travel.[26] The same mixture, but in a looser or powdery form (also called *wašna*), is used as a sacred food eaten at the close of many ceremonies. *Wašna* is offered as a gift to the spirits.[27]

Scholars have listed close to a hundred nonfood uses for the buffalo, including using the hides for tipi coverings, blankets, moccasins, and heavy clothing for winter as well as the gear for riding horses. In many ways the most significant nonfood use of the buffalo was for trade. Buffalo hides were the most important item, because they became a medium of exchange. This became a lucrative trade, as buffalo hides were in demand in the United States and Canada. Much of the trade was along the Missouri River, with the French and the Spanish and later with the Americans. The tanning of hides was a major activity for the Sioux. Some hides were tanned with the hair on and became buffalo robes. Others were tanned further and sold as finished leather.[28] The market for buffalo products was tremendous. In the early nineteenth century this trade increased substantially, as buffalo robes shipped down the Missouri River increased from an annual average of 2,600 between 1815 and 1830 to 40,000 to 50,000 in 1833. In 1848 Father Pierre-Jean De Smet reported an annual figure of 25,000 buffalo tongues and 110,000 robes shipped to St. Louis. In addition to the hides, buffalo meat was sold. The most valued part of the buffalo was the tongue. Pickled tongue, considered a delicacy by many Americans, brought exceptionally high prices. The Sioux also sold tallow. The fat from the buffalo was melted and allowed to cool into solid form. It was in great demand for use as cooking oil and to make candles and soap. Through this trade the Sioux acquired firearms, knives, axes, metal kettles, beads, and cloth. These new elements, especially the iron trade goods, had a significant impact on Sioux material culture.[29]

Although the buffalo provided for material comforts, its true value was its spiritual significance in everyday life. The heart of Sioux spirituality is the Sacred Pipe. After being carved from red pipestone and connected to a wooden stem, the pipe is blessed by a spiritual leader. It now serves as the main channel to Wakan Tanka (God). According to all branches of the Sioux, the Sacred Pipe was sent to earth by Wakan Tanka and given to the Sioux nation by White Buffalo Calf Woman. Although there are minor variations in the details of this narrative, the account summarized below is the generally accepted version. This account is from Arvol Looking Horse, a Minneconjou Sioux from the Cheyenne River Reservation in South Dakota. He is the official keeper of the Sacred Pipe. His ancestors have been the keepers and protectors of the pipe for nineteen generations. The pipe is kept in a medicine bundle, which is housed at Green Grass on the Cheyenne River Reservation. It is brought out periodically when there are special spiritual needs. According to Looking Horse, "the Sacred Pipe is very powerful; it is at the center, and all other pipes are like its roots or branches. The Sacred Pipe transfers its power to the other pipes. All pipes have to be blessed, made sacred." It is this Sacred Pipe that was brought to earth by White Buffalo Calf Woman.[30]

Two warriors were out hunting buffalo. . . . As they stood on top of a hill, looking into the distance, they saw something white coming. They went closer to look and found a woman walking toward them, carrying a bundle. One of the young men had good thoughts toward the woman. He realized that buffalo were scarce and the people needed some kind of help. But the other young man had bad thoughts. "This woman is pretty," he said, "so I want to have her." The first young man said, "No, Wakan Tanka must have sent this woman." But the young man who was thinking evil reached out to touch the woman. Suddenly a cloud came over them. The good young man heard rattlesnakes inside the cloud. When the cloud lifted, the young man saw that his companion was nothing but bones. . . . Then the woman said to him: "Tomorrow make preparations for me to come to bring the bundle for the Sioux people. With this you will survive on the earth." The man went back to the village and told the people what he had seen and what had happened. . . . The next day she arrived and presented them with the Sacred Calf Pipe. The woman taught them how to use the Pipe, how to pray with it, and how to do different things to take care of it. She gave the Pipe to Buffalo Standing Upright, a medicine man. . . . She explained everything about it, and then she left. She left the camp circle in a clockwise direction, then headed west. As she went she changed into four animals. The last was a white buffalo calf, which disappeared over the horizon.[31]

Looking Horse says that almost every family has a pipe. He adds that "the pipe is very sacred, for the stem represents a man, and the bowl, which is red, represents a woman. The Sacred Pipe is the center. . . . the Sioux people believe in the Sacred Pipe."[32] When used in a proper way, the Sacred Pipe is the channel or path to Wakan Tanka; and in turn, through ceremony, ritual, and prayer, the Sacred Pipe can imbue humans with spiritual power. This unity of all things is the heart of the Sioux worldview. This represents a theology where there is no separation between the natural and the supernatural world, where there is no separation between the sacred and the profane, a unity in which the two-legged, the four-legged, the winged, and the finned creatures are all related as in the Lakota, Dakota, and Nakota prayer *Mitakuye Oyasin*, which means "for all my relations." One's relations are all living things. This oneness is also expressed by Black Elk, quoting White Buffalo Calf Woman: "With this sacred pipe you will walk upon the Earth; the Earth is your Grandmother and Mother, and She is sacred. Every step that is taken upon Her should be as a prayer."[33]

Because Wakan Tanka sent White Buffalo Calf Woman to deliver the Sacred Pipe, both the pipe and the buffalo became the essential core of Sioux spirituality. In Black Elk's account the Buffalo Woman said: "From this time on, the holy pipe will stand upon this red Earth, and the two-leggeds will take the pipe and will send their voices to *Wakan-Tanka*."[34] Along with the pipe and the sacred ceremonies associated with it, the teachings of White Buffalo Calf Woman established the cosmological view of the inherent unity of all things in the universe. This essential unity included a close relationship between humans and buffalo. The buffalo would be honored and respected, and in return humans would be provided sustenance. This spiritual significance is reflected in the role that the buffalo plays in Sioux cosmology. *Tatanka kin wakanpi*, "the buffalo are sacred," is a commonly used phrase. White Buffalo Calf Woman was not only a messenger from Wakan Tanka; she also represents the buffalo nation *(pté oyáte)*. This indicates how powerful a symbol the buffalo is, because in a spiritual sense it represents all four-legged creatures.

The buffalo also plays a major role in ritual and ceremony such as the Sun Dance, which is the most significant spiritual event for the Sioux. The Sun

Dance is considered an essential method of communicating with Wakan Tanka. It is a ceremony of sacrifice and renewal that in its entirety embodies the cosmological structure of the Sioux universe. During the Sun Dance, with the fasting, dancing, purification, piercing of the skin, and four days of intense prayer under a bright, hot sun, the dancers beseech Wakan Tanka to take pity on them as humble human beings and to answer their prayers. Led by a Sun Dance chief, they dance around a sacred cottonwood tree. In order to create the most efficacious environment for the prayers to be answered, the dancers, singers, drummers, Sun Dance chief, and Sun Dance site are continually purified. All the dancers are purified in a Sweat Lodge; and while dancing they wear garlands of sage on their heads and wristlets and anklets of sage. The spiritual power of the eagle is also used to protect the dancers. All the dancers wear eagle feathers or eagle plumes attached to the sage garland on their heads. They blow on eagle-bone whistles while dancing, and the Sun Dance chief carries an eagle-feather fan. Cedar is burned on hot coals, creating smoke that serves as a protective shield. Cedar smoke is also used to cleanse and protect the Sun Dance arena, the Sacred Pipes, the cottonwood tree, the dancers, the singers, and anyone else who is gathered around the Sun Dance circle. Throughout the day everyone is "cedared-off" many times.

The buffalo is a central element in the Sun Dance. A figure of a buffalo is cut from rawhide and hung in the Sacred Tree. According to Black Elk: "He [the buffalo] represents the people and the universe and should always be treated with respect, for was he not here before the two-legged peoples, and is he not generous in that he gives us our homes and our food? The buffalo is wise in many things, and, thus, we should learn from him and should always be as a relative with him."[35] When the Sun Dance begins at sunrise of the first day, the Sun Dance chief carries a buffalo skull into the Sun Dance arena. The buffalo skull serves as an altar, as the spirits of the buffalo nation are there to support and protect all. Sometimes one or two of the dancers use buffalo skulls as part of their piercing. After the dancer is pierced twice on the back, several buffalo skulls are tied to the piercing pegs by means of leather thongs or rope. The dancer then circles the Sun Dance arena four times while dragging the skulls along the ground, eventually causing the pegs to be torn from the skin and completing the most difficult part of the dancer's personal sacrifice. With four days of fasting, dancing, prayer, and piercing, the individual dancers are offering themselves, their bodies, which are all that they have to offer as humble human beings. They are making this sacrifice of themselves so that Wakan Tanka may answer their prayers.[36]

The buffalo play a significant role in other aspects of the Sioux belief system. Because the buffalo are considered the closest to humans of all the four-legged relatives, praying to them for support and protection honors that essential relationship. There is a purification ceremony, sometimes called a Buffalo ceremony, for young girls marking their transition into womanhood at the time of their first menstruation. The young women are instructed in their responsibilities to their family and their nation and are taught "proper" behavior. The ceremony also establishes a relationship between the young women and White Buffalo Calf Woman, who, along with the buffalo people, offers spiritual protection for women.[37]

The spirits of the buffalo are called upon in many other ceremonies. During prayers one may ask the buffalo spirits for support and protection before going on a Vision Quest and then give thanks upon one's return. One may include such prayers in naming ceremonies or in the Yuwipi healing ceremony. The most frequently held ceremony takes place in a Sweat Lodge or *inipi*. The "sweat" is a combination prayer, purification, and/or healing ceremony. It may be held just for itself or in conjunction with other ceremonies in order to purify the participants. Purification takes place inside the lodge when steam is produced by pouring water over hot rocks. For example, sun dancers enter a Sweat Lodge before and after they dance each day, and individuals purify themselves before and after going out on Vision Quests. Sweat Lodge ceremonies are also part of naming ceremonies as well as the Yuwipi ceremony.[38] A buffalo skull is usually placed in front of the Sweat Lodge to serve as an altar. The path between the skull and the Sweat Lodge is a sacred path that facilitates the entrance of spirits, representing the sacred path of life that all individuals should follow. Throughout Sioux spiritual life, whether in the belief system or in ceremonies, the role of the buffalo and buffalo spirits is ever present and all pervasive, indicating how thoroughly the buffalo is integrated into the social, economic, and spiritual life of the Sioux nation.

The importance of the buffalo in the life of the Plains Indians was not lost on government officials, who were well aware that the Sioux and other Plains tribes were dependent on the buffalo herds. The military leadership in the West and officials in Washington realized that by exterminating the buffalo they would force the Plains Indians onto the reservations. This coincided with the great demand for buffalo products throughout the United States.

The process of eliminating the buffalo herds was facilitated first by the use of steamboats on the Mississippi and Missouri Rivers and then in the 1860s and 1870s by the expansion of the railroads. The improved transportation network not only brought more non-Indians into Indian land but also opened new markets for buffalo products. By the early 1870s there was massive hunting of the buffalo for both profit and sport. For example, in 1872, according to one estimate, there were 10,000 to 20,000 American hunters slaughtering buffalo, killing them at a rate of a million a year. For many hunters the motive was profit through the sale of buffalo hides and buffalo tongues. For others it was sport. Taxidermists did a booming trade, preparing stuffed buffalo heads for display in homes and businesses. As the herds diminished in numbers, more and more "sportsmen" rushed to the Plains in order to get their kill and their trophy before the herds were gone. Buffalo-killing contests were part of this "sport." Prizes were awarded to those who killed the most buffalo in a specified time. William F. (Buffalo Bill) Cody excelled in these contests.[39]

The full responsibility for the destruction of the buffalo herds, however, must rest with the United States Army. Its top generals in the West, William Tecumseh Sherman and Philip Sheridan, both advocated the deliberate destruction of the buffalo as a way to break Indian resistance. The military developed a calculated policy to destroy the buffalo. Not only did various army units participate in the slaughter, but the military leadership also helped U.S. private citizens and European dignitaries to participate in killing. For example, when Grand Duke Alexis, son of the tsar of Russia, was touring the United States in 1872, he was given a military escort led by General Sheridan. In five days of hunting in Nebraska, they slaughtered hundreds of buffalo. The United States Army provided free ammunition and use of weapons to private citizens. The army also offered protection, supplies, equipment, markets, storage, and horses and wagons to anyone who was engaged in the slaughter of the herds. Generals Sheridan and Sherman did not hide their feelings. Sheridan wrote: "If I could learn that every Buffalo in the northern herd were killed I would be glad. The destruction of this herd would do more to keep Indians quiet than anything else that could happen, *except the death of all Indians . . .*" (emphasis added). Sherman gloated about how American soldiers "in so short a time replaced the wild buffaloes by more numerous herds of tame cattle, and by substituting for the useless Indians the intelligent owners of productive farms and cattle-ranches."[40]

By the 1880s the massive slaughter had led to the virtual extinction of the buffalo in the United States. The impact of this loss is impossible to overstate. It was even a severe loss to the eastern and middle Sioux, who were less dependent on the buffalo than the western Sioux. This was not only an economic loss but a spiritual loss of tremendous magnitude. In a melancholy tone, ethnographer George Bird Grinnell, writing in 1892 on the last of the buffalo, said: "Of the millions of buffalo which even in our own time ranged the plains in freedom, none now remain. From the prairies which they used to darken, the wild herds, down to the last straggling bull, have disappeared."[41]

The extermination of the buffalo herds ended the independence of the Sioux people. The Lakotas, Dakotas, and Nakotas in the United States were now forced to live on reservations. The people of the Seven Council Fires were officially wards of the United States government.

CHAPTER TWO

The Ihanktonwan (Yankton) Nation

THE EARLY YEARS TO 1858

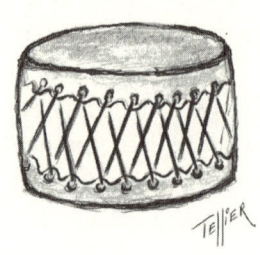

Drum used at family Sun Dances, made by Parnell Necklace and given to the author as a gift. Drawn by Dr. Cassandra Tellier.

The experiences of the Yanktons or Ihanktonwans were not essentially different from those of other Sioux groups. They were located geographically between the western Sioux or Tetons and the eastern Sioux or Santees. The Yanktons' material culture and lifestyle reflected both their Woodlands background and a Plains/Prairie way of life. They were also part of a wider movement of Sioux groups to the west. From their woodland villages in what is now central Minnesota, the Yanktons began migrating in a southwestern direction. The first European references to the Yanktons located them in the Mille Lacs region of present-day central Minnesota, west of the Mississippi River. Their economic life was based on a mixture of hunting, fishing, gathering, and limited agriculture, as described in chapter 1. Around 1700 Pierre-Charles Le Sueur, a French trader, came in contact with a Yankton group in a village or villages near Red Pipestone Quarry and thus called them the "nation of stone." It is difficult to be certain if all the Yanktons had moved when they met Le Sueur or if only a smaller group was temporarily at Pipestone mining the red stone. Some of the Yanktons, either in bands or extended families, probably had already moved to the Southwest by 1700.[1] In any case the Yanktons certainly did not all move at once. Their migration took place over several years, if not several decades.

By the mid-eighteenth century the move was more or less complete. The Yanktons, located in the region between the headwaters of the Des Moines and Big Sioux Rivers, migrated farther west along the Missouri River into what is now southeast South Dakota. Two merchants, Peter Pond in the 1770s and Jean-Baptiste Trudeau in the 1790s, visited the Yanktons in this region. Pond reported that the Yanktons had horses; Trudeau described much of the trade along the rivers. In moving into the prairie areas of the Big Sioux and the Missouri Rivers, the Yanktons along with the Tetons pushed the Omahas to the west. The Tetons were already moving west and left this region to the Yanktons. The area that the Yanktons would eventually occupy was approximately 13 million square acres.[2] This prairie environment would have a significant impact on Yankton economic life.

Most of the Yankton villages were located on the northern branches of the Des Moines River and along the banks of the Missouri near the mouth of the Big Sioux River. Villages were also located farther up the Missouri near the mouths of the Vermillion and James Rivers. The remainder of the region was used for hunting and gathering.[3] Even though the Yanktons continued some of their agricultural practices, this large area was essential to their survival because of the Prairie ecology. They had to rely more and more on hunting, as they could no longer collect and store wild rice. The western portion of the new Yankton homeland is typical Prairie. Moving to the western end of Yankton land and across the Missouri River, one enters the true Great Plains. The Prairie region is typified by high grasses with a wet subsoil, while the Plains have short grasses and a dry subsoil. The difference between the two regions is rainfall. The Prairie area may have twenty to forty inches of rain per year, whereas rainfall in the Plains is between ten and twenty inches per year. In both areas summer rain may be in the form of thunderstorms, with a heavy runoff of rainwater. Game flourished in both areas, particularly the buffalo. The Yanktons also hunted deer, elk, antelope, fox, rabbit, and muskrat as well as duck, goose, pheasant, and quail. They hunted the beaver for its fur and the porcupine for its quills, which were essential to Sioux arts and crafts.[4]

The Prairie region was not totally treeless. Groves of deciduous trees grew along the lakes, streams, and rivers. The trees were important, not only because they provided firewood. The Yanktons used willows to build Sweat Lodge frames, ash to make stems for Sacred Pipes, and cottonwoods in the Sun Dance. Pine used for tipi poles was harvested on the western edge of the Great Plains in the Black Hills.[5]

The Yankton area was also suitable for gathering a wide range of wild fruits, berries, and vegetables. The most important plant was the wild turnip (*Psoralea esculenta pursh*), called *tinpsina* in Dakota and *pomme blanche* by the French explorers. Women harvested *tinpsina* in early summer. They used a special digging stick called a *wiwopta*. The white starchy root could be eaten raw or could be boiled with buffalo meat (beef or chicken today) and other vegetables in a stew or soup. Turnips were important because they could be dried and preserved. In the winter they could be ground into flour or soaked in water and cooked in soups. The process of collecting and drying the turnips was a communal activity of women. After the turnips were harvested, the green top was cut off; but the long stringy roots below the bulb were left on. Using the stringy roots, the women braided the turnips. The result was a string of turnips from one to three feet long. The largest turnips were on the bottom and the smaller ones on the top, making the braid symmetrical. When hung to dry, braided turnips could be kept for several years. After drying for several months, the turnips turn a beautiful golden brown color. Some Yanktons have them hanging in their homes today as aesthetically pleasing decorative items.

The Yanktons also harvested wild artichokes, wild onions, red plums, raspberries and june berries, and delicious dark-red chokecherries. Chokecherries are made into a pudding called *wožapi* by crushing the berries and adding a little flour for thickening and sugar for sweetness. It may be served with any meal but is especially important as one of the Yanktons' sacred foods. The chokecherries are valued so highly that in Dakota the month of July is called *čanpaša wi*, "moon when the chokecherries are red."[6] The Yanktons also harvested a wide variety of roots, plants, leaves, and bark used for spiritual and medicinal purposes. This was supplemented by several methods of fishing in the lakes and rivers of their more westerly home, although fishing was not as central to Yankton subsistence as it had been in their earlier homeland. One method was called "crowding." A line of people waded along a shallow lakeshore, driving the fish into narrow inlets where they could be grabbed and thrown ashore. Fishing baskets made of willow branches were used in rivers and streams. The closed lower end of the basket was weighted down while the upper open end floated on the top of water, so the fish could enter the basket but not exit.[7]

The Yanktons now relied more heavily on hunting. In this new homeland they had easier access to the buffalo herds on the Plains. As noted, they had acquired horses by the 1770s and possibly earlier. This new mobility allowed a greater range for their hunting expeditions. Like other Plains Indians, the Yanktons not only used the meat of the buffalo but incorporated various buffalo parts into their material culture. They also collected antlers from large animals and carved them into tools such as scrapers and spoons. The Yanktons hunted in groups, with two major excursions each year. Usually entire families went on the hunts, carrying their tipis and other necessary items. They hunted throughout Sioux territory, sometimes going as far west as the Black Hills.[8]

When not on hunting expeditions, the Yanktons lived in villages. They hunted in their local area and collected and stored wild fruits, nuts, and vegetables. They also stored dried buffalo meat to help survive the long winter. The Yanktons maintained their villages as more or less permanent sites. By the mid-nineteenth century many of the villages along the rivers had gardens, where they grew several types of corn, squash, and beans. Along with buffalo meat, much of this was dried and stored for winter. In addition to living in tipis, many Yanktons lived in circular earth lodges similar to ones used by the Poncas, Otos, and Omahas. These villages often grew quite large. Scattered about the villages were scaffolds for drying meat, vegetables, and fruits; racks for scraping, drying, and curing deer, antelope, or buffalo hides; outdoor cooking fires; piles of firewood; and sometimes several Sweat Lodges. The villages were usually located along the rivers in order to facilitate both transportation and trade. In Yankton oral tradition this era is remembered as a happy time.[9]

In the late eighteenth century, given the location of their villages along major rivers, the Yanktons were in the forefront of contact between the Sioux and non-Indians. Merchants and explorers visited the Yanktons regularly. During this period French merchants appeared along the Missouri River. Spanish and English traders also competed for the lucrative fur trade. After the Louisiana Purchase, Americans began to enter the area, coming up the Missouri River from St. Louis. This area from the Mississippi River through the headwaters of the Des Moines River to the Missouri River and its tributaries became a region of widespread trade with subsequent cultural and material impact on the Yanktons. There was also considerable trade among American Indian groups. Some tribes such as the Arikaras, Mandans, and Hidatsas used their location along the Missouri River to become "middlemen." They bought manufactured items from non-Indians and resold them to other Native Americans. People living in the eastern regions or riverine groups who practiced horticulture traded food products for horses and buffalo skins with people in the western Plains who relied primarily on hunting. The

Europeans and Americans wanted buffalo robes and beaver skins as well as buffalo meat and corn from Native Americans. These products were traded for firearms, kettles, cloth, beads, knives, axes, and other manufactured goods. The trade was extremely competitive, and the region was rife with conflict. As the various branches of the Sioux expanded westward, they came into conflict and warfare with other American Indian groups.[10]

The French were the first Europeans to trade with the Yanktons in their new homeland. Some of the French merchants lived with the Yanktons and took Yankton wives. As the expanding trade became more important to the Yanktons, they increased the range of their hunting trips in order to acquire the buffalo, beaver, and deerskins so much in demand by French traders. This brought the Yanktons farther west, up the Missouri River near present-day Pierre, South Dakota. At the same time the Yanktons continued to hunt to the north along the Minnesota River, the upper part of the Des Moines River, and the Big Sioux River. The expanding trade and contact with non-Indians would have a significant impact on Yankton society.[11]

THE YANKTONS AND THE UNITED STATES

The Yanktons increasingly came into contact with Americans. In 1803 President Thomas Jefferson purchased a vast track of central North America from France. The boundaries of the Louisiana Purchase were vague, but it clearly included the land of the Sioux. In 1804 Jefferson commissioned Meriwether Lewis and William Clark to undertake a major expedition to explore so-called unknown territory in order to map its geography and assess its potential for trade. This was also the first official mission of the United States to the Native American people west of the Mississippi River. Lewis and Clark began their expedition in St. Louis. They traveled up the Missouri River, across the Rocky Mountains, and down the Columbia River to the Pacific Ocean. In traveling west and on the return trip, they passed through Yankton territory. Their expedition opened this region to a massive migration of Americans. They not only wrote reports on the tremendous potential for trade but identified locations for future trading sites. They proclaimed American sovereignty and demonstrated it not only through the display of the American flag but also by intruding into Native American affairs, albeit encouraging an end to intertribal warfare. Lewis and Clark were followed by traders, hunters, missionaries, ranchers, farmers, soldiers, and bureaucrats, the first steps toward reducing the sovereignty of the Yanktons and the other branches of Seven Council Fires.[12]

On 27 August 1804, as Lewis and Clark proceeded up the Missouri River, west of the mouth of the James River, several Yankton youths swam out to greet them. Lewis and Clark sent their interpreters, Pierre Dorian, Sr., and Sergeant Nathaniel Pryor, to a nearby village to ask the Yankton chiefs to meet with them. The two men were received enthusiastically. On the morning of 30 August Lewis and Clark met with a large Yankton delegation at Calumet Bluffs, located on the Missouri River about ten miles upstream from the James River. The meeting was held with full diplomatic protocol. As the delegation arrived, Lewis and Clark sent gifts of tobacco, corn, and iron kettles. The Yankton chiefs were preceded by musicians singing, drumming, and shaking rattles. After proper ceremonial introductions, everyone sat down and listened to speeches given by the Americans. Captain Lewis said he was interested in peace between the Indian nations and hoped that a delegation of chiefs from all the Sioux could be arranged. After the speeches the two explorers gave bronze presidential peace medals to five chiefs. They also gave the head chief an American flag and an artillery corps uniform and distributed tobacco to all. In return the Yanktons offered the Sacred Pipe as a symbol of peace and friendship. They sat in a circle and smoked the pipe. That evening in front of a large fire they sang, danced, and celebrated.

The next morning the head chief, whom Lewis called Weuche or Shake Hand in English and *Le Libérateur* in French, told the American delegation that the Yanktons needed trade opportunities and wanted firearms and ammunition. He offered to organize a Sioux delegation and said he would be happy to help establish intertribal peace and provide his services as an intermediary. All went well. The negotiations were hospitable and friendly and ended with the further distribution of gifts by Lewis and Clark. The Americans departed on 2 September, continuing up the Missouri River into Teton country. They left their interpreter, Pierre Dorian, Sr., and his son with the Yanktons. They hoped Dorian would continue facilitating intertribal peace and work toward fulfilling the major objective of the mission, which was to prepare the way for American merchants to follow Lewis and Clark.[13]

The members of the expedition left significant historical and ethnographic documentation of their contact with the Yanktons. They described the Yanktons as a trading people who saw their economic stability based on an expanding trade network. The Yanktons traded deer, raccoon, bear, and beaver skins. Lewis suggested to them that they should also trade buffalo skins, buffalo tallow, and dried meat. Lewis and Clark reported that the Sioux held an extensive trade fair every year, located up the Missouri River. The explorers' field notes and maps indicate that the village they visited was on the western edge of Yankton territories and that the larger body of Yanktons was still located between the Big Sioux and Des Moines Rivers. It was obvious to Lewis and Clark that the Yanktons were moving westward.[14] While in the area they documented much of Yankton daily life. For example, they described a tipi as "a conical form, covered with buffalo robes, painted with various figures and colors, with an aperture in the top for smoke to pass through. The lodges contain from ten to fifteen persons, and the interior arrangement is compact and handsome."[15] They also described a short trip up the Vermillion River, a tributary of the Missouri, to search for the large hill that the local Yanktons said was inhabited by "little people" or "little spirits." Spirit Mound, as it is called today, is located nine miles up the Vermillion River and four miles to the west along present Route 19 north of Vermillion, South Dakota.

The state of South Dakota has erected a historical marker commemorating Lewis and Clark's visit to the mound, which they described as a natural formation three hundred yards long, seventy yards wide, and seventy feet high, with a flat plain on top. Lewis called it the Hill of Little Devils. From this vantage point they saw several herds of buffalo grazing at a distance. They found nothing unusual on the hill and mocked the beliefs of the Yanktons, saying that they were happy to have escaped the vengeance of the little people. Nevertheless, many Yanktons, both past and present, believe in the existence of spirits in dwarfed human form. They are said to be about eighteen inches tall, with oversized heads. It is believed that they not only inhabit Spirit Mound but also live in some of the woods on the Yankton Reservation. These spirits, who are armed with sharp arrows, are considered evil and will kill anyone who approaches them. Local people would not go to Spirit Mound with Lewis and Clark.[16] The spirits are called *čanotina* in Dakota (*čan* is "tree" in both Dakota and Lakota). Riggs's *Dakota-English Dictionary* defines *čanotidan* as the Dakota "god of the woods."

These "little people" are described by such respected elders as Henry Hare, Sr., Joe Rockboy, and Asa Primeaux. Rockboy said that "they were the enemies of the Sioux from the time the Sioux entered this region."[17] Asa Primeaux said that the "little people" inhabit some of the woods between Chouteau Creek and Greenwood, just north of the Missouri River. While we were touring near the area, Asa explained that people avoided the woods even though they contained plenty of dead trees for firewood. He added that the "little people" are dangerous but that they are here for a reason: "This is God's land and you have to respect God's ways. If you follow God's ways you can get through the woods okay, but if not, if you are a doubter, you may see one of the little people and they will get you."[18] Lewis and Clark may have doubted the existence of the "little people," but they are part of the Yankton belief system. Their presence in Yankton tradition has been documented for almost two hundred years.

Lewis and Clark's skepticism about "little people" did not affect discussions and negotiations. They described a negotiating process that reflected Yankton cultural patterns. There was always a preliminary exchange of gifts and the smoking of a Sacred Pipe. Each chief took a turn speaking in response to the American speeches. The chiefs then retired to discuss the negotiations. They again addressed Lewis and Clark, each chief expressing his own opinion. This multitude of opinions was confusing to Lewis and Clark; but allowing each chief to express his own views reflected the Yankton manner of negotiation and dialogue. This initial contact between the United States government and the Yankton nation ended in a friendly manner, at least according to Lewis and Clark.[19]

In the years following the Lewis and Clark expedition the Yanktons were visited by an increasing number of American explorers and traders. American companies set up trading posts near Yankton territory. This was part of the United States' policy to expand trade into the Louisiana Territory; it would eventually lead to the U.S.-Yankton Treaty of 1858. The treaty phase of U.S. expansion across the Mississippi gave Americans open access to the newly acquired territory. The treaties were also aimed at regulating relations between the Indian nations, because the United States considered intertribal strife inimical to its economic interests.

Between the War of 1812 and their removal to a reservation in 1859, the Yanktons signed a number of treaties with the American government. After 1815 government diplomats were instructed to establish diplomatic relations with Indian nations west of the Mississippi River. The goals were to establish good relations after the confusing allegiances of the War of 1812, to end intertribal strife, to prepare the way for trade, and, most importantly, to establish American protection. For example, in 1815 a "Treaty of Peace and Friendship" was signed with the Yanktons. In addition to declaring peace and friendship, the treaty placed the Yanktons under the "protection" of the United States of America. Meanwhile, the American government built a series of forts to enforce "peace" and facilitate trade.[20]

Forts were built along the Mississippi, Minnesota, and Missouri Rivers. By guaranteeing protection for the extension of American trade, these military outposts became the cutting edge of U.S. expansion into the trans-Mississippi region. In order to facilitate expansion and trade, the federal government signed a series of treaties with Native American nations. Two treaties were signed in 1825. One was with various branches of the Sioux, including the Yanktons, the other with a wide range of groups. Both treaties established territorial boundaries in order to lessen the growing tension over land and trade. Establishing boundaries between Indian groups proved very difficult, because the presence of U.S. traders, such as the American Fur Company, created additional tension and competition over access to the dwindling supplies of fur.[21]

In order to coordinate expansion and protection, Congress established the Office of Indian Affairs within the War Department. In 1849 it was transferred to the Department of the Interior. A commissioner of Indian Affairs, appointed by the president, coordinated diplomatic relations with Native Americans.[22] The commissioner was charged with moving Native American groups westward. This resulted in a new round of treaties, including for the first time a visit to Washington, D.C., by a Yankton delegation. It was led by Chief War Eagle, who received a bronze peace medal from President Martin Van Buren. One of the signers was Padaniapapi (Struck by the Ree), future head chief of the Yanktons. In this treaty (1837) the Yanktons ceded virtually all their land in present-day Iowa except for a small area near Sioux City.[23]

During these decades a flood of outsiders besieged Yankton territory, including more merchants, government agents, land speculators, explorers, and missionaries. In 1839 Father Pierre-Jean De Smet, a Roman Catholic missionary, visited the Yanktons. As a result of his visit, future chief Struck by the Ree converted to Catholicism. Naturalist and painter John James Audubon passed through by way of steamboat in 1843, as did other artists such as the Swiss painter Karl Bodmer and the American painter George Catlin. Trade continued to be essential for the Yanktons. Trade companies had posts in Yankton territory. Fort Vermillion and Fort Pierre both attracted large volumes of trade. The Yanktons traded hides and furs for blankets, cloth, beads, and iron implements. Unfortunately, the growing contact with American traders brought alcohol as a trade item; thus with the benefits of trade came the debilitating effects of alcohol.

During this era of the great fur trade, the demand for fur products in America and Europe was insatiable. By the mid-1840s, however, fur-bearing animals (especially the beaver) began to disappear. This meant the Yanktons and the other tribes of the region needed to expand their hunting range. The Yanktons had to cross the lower Missouri River (into present-day Nebraska) to hunt. This created tension and conflict with the Omahas, Pawnees, and Otos. Further north the Yanktons crossed the upper Missouri more frequently in order to hunt buffalo in the Great Plains. On the eastern side of the upper Missouri in the Prairie region, the buffalo herds were declining. Reports in 1840s by government agents and missionaries such as Father De Smet commented on this decline. The economic difficulties of the late 1840s and 1850s help to explain the Yankton decision to sign the Treaty of 1858 and surrender almost their entire homeland.[24]

The general scarcity of game and food would be offset by the goods, services, or cash provided by the government as stipulated in various treaties. In 1846 the Yanktons received their last large annuity until 1859. They got $5,000 in goods, an overdue payment from the 1830 treaty. This was mentioned in a 1849 report by Alexander Ramsey of the Minnesota Superintendency. His report, titled "Background of the Dacotah or Sioux Nation," described all the branches of the Seven Council Fires. Ramsey translated "Ihank Ton Wan" as "People of the Further End" and said they numbered 3,200. He also commented on the great gathering: "the Sioux themselves tho [sic] scattered, meet annually on the Jacques [James River], those on the Missouri trading with those on the Mississippi."[25]

The Yanktons faced other problems in addition to the competition for scarce resources. Reports from this period indicate that smallpox, cholera, and measles were taking their toll on life. Alan Woolworth argues that there was a slow decline in the Yankton population from 1840 to 1858. He also believes that the government figure of 3,200 for 1849 is too high and that between 1825 and 1860 the population ranged between 2,000 and 3,000.[26] While the Yanktons were facing economic hardships, other problems emerged. American settlers, actually squatters, appeared on the eastern side of Yankton territory. There was also the problem of settlers passing through Sioux territory on their way west. "Oregon fever" spurred Americans westward. In 1845 the term "Manifest Destiny" entered the American lexicon; a rallying cry for expansion, it proclaimed America's God-given destiny to possess the continent from coast to coast. The politicians expounded upon it, the press praised it, and the public bought it. It mattered little that Native Americans and Mexicans already occupied the land. They did not count. They must not stand in the way of America's destiny. In reality, Manifest Destiny was the moral justification for expansionism; it was a racial and cultural manifesto proclaiming the inherent superiority of Anglo-American ideas, institutions, and people. It was a rationalization for greed, ambition, and exploitation that led the United States government to sign a myriad of treaties with Native American nations—treaties it later ignored.

A growing population helped fuel America's westward expansion. Between 1840 and 1860 hundreds of thousands of immigrants streamed into America, increasing the population from 17.1 million to 31.5 million. Iowa was granted statehood in 1846, Wisconsin in 1848, and Minnesota in 1858. Cities emerged west of the Mississippi. On the eastern side of Yankton territory the number of squatters increased. Along with land speculators they became pressure groups, demanding that Congress remove the Yanktons as well as other Indian people. In response the government pursued the policy of further compressing Indian land into smaller tracts with clearly defined boundaries. The tribes would be required to live within the boundaries, allowing more land for settlers and making it easier for the U.S. military to control the Indian nations.

Thus began the concentration policy or reservation system west of the Mississippi. These reservations would be located in remote areas away from the newly arriving settlers. For the Plains Indians this began the government policy of turning hunting people into sedentary farmers. In 1851 Indian agents gathered together a large number of Plains tribes at Fort Laramie, Wyoming, for treaty negotiations. Thousands of Native Americans appeared, including several branches of the Sioux, Shoshones, Gros Ventres, Cheyennes, Arapahos, Mandans, Arikaras, Assiniboines, and Crows. They agreed to cease hostilities among themselves and to allow American settlers unmolested passage through their lands. They also agreed to allow the government to build roads and forts and to draw boundaries between their lands. The government in return agreed to protect the Indians from Anglo-American deprivations and to divide among the Native American nations that signed the treaty $50,000 per year for fifty years. Congress reduced this to ten years with an optional five-year extension. The money would be paid in merchandise, domestic animals, and agricultural tools. The Yanktons were represented by Smutty Bear (Mato Sabi Ceya, 1790?–1865). He was their most experienced negotiator, having participated in almost all previous treaty talks between the United States government and the Yanktons. It is also significant to note that the Fort Laramie Treaty clearly stated that the Black Hills belonged to the "Sioux or Dahcotah [*sic*] Nation."[27]

In 1856 the Yanktons underwent a change in leadership. Padaniapapi (Struck by the Ree) became head chief. He replaced War Eagle (ca. 1785–1851), the highly respected and popular leader. Chief War Eagle was not a Yankton; he was from the Mdewakanton or Santee Dakota but moved into the Yankton area near present-day Sioux City, Iowa, during the War of 1812. Much of what is known about him comes from oral tradition that has been preserved by his family. War Eagle was adopted by the Yankton people; and when head chief Little Dish died (in the 1830s), War Eagle was chosen as the *itančhan*, the new head chief. His rise in status and influence is attributed to his trade connections and the benefits that they brought to the Yanktons. He invited merchants into Yankton territory. One of these merchants was the French-Canadian fur trader Theophile Bruguier, who settled among the Yanktons and married two of War Eagle's daughters. Before War Eagle died, he chose a bluff overlooking the Missouri River for his gravesite. In 1975 a memorial to War Eagle was erected on this same bluff. The memorial is a large granite statue of War Eagle that faces the Missouri River; very appropriately, War Eagle is holding a Sacred Pipe in outstretched arms, offering it to those who pass below.[28]

The career of Struck by the Ree, sometimes called Old Strike, is crucial to Yankton history. He headed a Yankton contingent to Washington to negotiate the Treaty of 1858; he led the Yanktons to their new home; and he was the essential person in helping the Yanktons adjust to reservation life. Under his leadership the Yanktons had to deal with the pressures of acculturation from the Bureau of Indian Affairs (BIA), Christian missionaries, and the encroaching American squatters. Struck by the Ree is a controversial figure in Yankton history, but part of the controversy involved his entrapment by the reality of an expanding America. He lived in tumultuous times. His people were being forced to adjust to the loss of sovereignty and freedom and to live under restrictions and dependence. The position of head chief did not include any autocratic or arbitrary powers. One led through example, verbal persuasion, a reputation for integrity and generosity, personal honor, and prestige. With these skills, a head chief would attempt to develop a consensus among Yankton band chiefs and elders. The Yanktons were divided into seven bands. It is not clear how old the Yankton bands are, but it seems from extant reports that they were in existence in the early nineteenth century. Generally there were four bands living along the Missouri River, who were referred to as the lower Yanktons. The other three bands lived farther north and northwest and were called the upper Yanktons.

During the 1850s and 1860s relations with the United States government and the encroaching settlers exacerbated the division between upper and lower bands. It seems that the lower bands wanted to follow a policy of cooperation and accommodation with non-Indians, whereas the upper bands supported resistance and noncooperation. The Yankton bands remained constant through the remainder of the century. According to information collected by Stephen R. Riggs in 1878, the seven bands that existed at the beginning of reservation era (1859) were:

Lower bands:	Čagu	(Lungs) [Struck by the Ree's band]
	Oyáte Sica	(Bad Nation)
	Wačeunpa	(Roasters or the Ones That Cook)
	Igmu	(Cat People)
Upper bands:	Iha Ishdaye	(Mouth Greasers)
	Wakmuha Oin	(Pumpkin Rind Earrings)
	Čankute	(Shooters at Trees)[29]

Later, probably in the 1860s, the government established an eighth band, called Wašičun Činča (white man's sons or "half-breeds"), with Philip J. Deloria as the band chief. In 1897 anthropologist James O. Dorsey listed the same eight bands. They functioned as social, economic, and political units. As such they threatened federal programs, representing a traditional structure that could resist acculturation, because each band lived as a unit in its own district. The Dawes Act, allotment, and scattered housing stripped the bands of their various functions. The bands were further weakened when the local BIA agents appointed band chiefs rather than allow leadership to emerge in the traditional way. In the Yankton census of 1887 the BIA lists the Yankton population by band for the last time, leaving out the Dakota name of the band:

Band One: Struck by the Ree's Band
Band Two: Jumping Thunder's Band
Band Three: Medicine Cow's Band
Band Four: White Swan's Band
Band Five: William Bean, Sr.'s Band
Band Six: Feather in His Ear's Band
Band Seven: Frank Jandron, Sr.'s Band
Band Eight: Philip J. Deloria's Band.[30]

In the years before the Treaty of 1858, the Yanktons faced an increasing U.S. military presence. One can understand why the Yanktons would question the wisdom of armed resistance. In 1855 General William S. Harney led an expedition of 1,200 troops against their neighbors the Sičangu Lakotas (Brules). In the ensuing battle Harney's troops killed eighty-five Sičangus and took seventy-five women and children prisoner. Harney spent the following winter at Fort Pierre on the edge of Yankton country. Even more threatening was the building of Fort Randall on the Nebraska side of the Missouri River just across from the Yanktons. As the military situation created problems for the Yanktons, so did the settlers. By the mid-1850s small settlements had turned into the towns of Sioux Falls and Sioux City. Yankton villages began having serious confrontations with settlers along the Big Sioux River. In 1856 head chief Struck by the Ree and Smutty Bear, Igmu band chief, began negotiations with General Harney at Fort Pierre. The Yankton leaders drafted a petition to President Franklin Pierce asking for funds that were due from previous treaties. They said that game was scarce and that they would use these funds for agricultural purposes.[31]

These developments form part of the background for understanding the Yankton motives in negotiating the Treaty of 1858. Not only were the Yanktons threatened by U.S. troops to their west and northwest, but they had to deal with mounting demands for land cessions on their eastern border from land speculators and settlers. The Yanktons also faced very difficult economic circumstances. In 1857 Alfred Cumming, the superintendent in St. Louis, recommended to James W. Denver, the commissioner of Indian Affairs, that a treaty be negotiated with the Yanktons for the purchase of their land and that they be moved to a reservation on the western part of their land. The Yanktons, of course, were well aware of the fact that their eastern relatives (the Sissetons, Wahpekutes, Mdewakantons, and Wahpetons) had already signed treaties and were confined to reservations.

All this was part of the larger plan now being debated by the Department of the Interior in Washington. Two commissioners of Indian Affairs whose names live on in Yankton history, Charles E. Mix and Alfred B. Greenwood, were staunch supporters of the concentration policy, the suppression of American Indian culture, and eventual assimilation. The reservation was the tool to accomplish these ends. Mix was commissioner for only eighteen months; but for eighteen years he was chief clerk, the number two position behind the commissioner. As such Mix had a significant impact on the direction of federal Indian policy. Charles Mix County, the home of the Yankton Reservation, is named after him. Greenwood served as commissioner from 4 May 1859 to 13 March 1861. The headquarters of the Yankton Agency at Greenwood was named after him. One week after the inauguration of President Abraham Lincoln, Greenwood resigned and joined the Confederacy to recruit Native Americans to fight for the South.[32]

Facing many pressures from a variety of sources, the Yankton leadership decided to negotiate with the government. Meetings were held at Fort Pierre in 1857, and soon afterward a delegation led by Struck by the Ree traveled to Washington, D.C. Band chiefs such as Smutty Bear and Mad Bull of the Oyáte Sica band were part of the entourage. Other prominent Yanktons included Jumping Thunder (1830?–1901), Little White Swan (1813–98), and Walking Elk (1825–90s?). Also in attendance and a key player in the negotiations was Charles F. Picotte (1830–96). He was the son of French fur trader Honoré Picotte and Eagle Woman, sister of Struck by the Ree. A close advisor to his uncle, the head chief, and fluent in several languages, Picotte was the key interpreter during the negotiations.

As a result of disagreements among some of the Yanktons, the negotiations took almost four months. Smutty Bear and several other members of the delegation argued against the treaty. After considerable pressure Smutty Bear agreed to sign it. The main negotiator for the United States was commissioner Charles E. Mix. The treaty was signed on 19 April 1858 and ratified by the U.S. Senate on 16 February 1859. In the treaty the Yanktons ceded more than 11 million acres of land to the United States. In return they were guaranteed 431,000 acres on the western side of their homeland along the Missouri River. This became the Yankton Reservation. The Yanktons also believed that they were guaranteed title to a small tract of land in Minnesota that contained the Red Pipestone Quarry. They surrendered all rights and claims acquired in other treaties except their annuity rights from the Fort Laramie Treaty of 1851. The Yanktons also agreed to move to "said reservation" within one year. In return for ceding this large tract of land, the government would pay the Yanktons $1,600,000 in annual installments ($32,000 per year) for the next fifty years. The government would also send an agent to reside on the reservation and agreed to build a school and a mill to grind grain and saw lumber. Charles Picotte and Zephier Rencontre, another interpreter, each received 640 acres from the government for their "valuable services." Finally, and most significantly, Article 11 states: "The Yancton acknowledge their dependence upon the Government of the United States."[33]

There were sixteen Yankton signatories to the treaty. Twelve of the signers represented the four lower Yankton bands, the main supporters of the treaty. Charles Picotte also signed the treaty. Three band chiefs (White Medicine Cow, Little White Swan, and Pretty Boy) represented the upper Yankton bands. Their names are on the treaty, but they did not personally put their mark on the document. Their mark was made by their "duly authorized delegate and representative, Chas. F. Picotte." Did these three band chiefs give this authority to Picotte because they could not attend the signing? Did they return home in protest? Did Picotte, whose self-interest was tied to the treaty, simply usurp the right to sign for them in their absence? The answer is unclear.[34]

The Treaty of 1858 created controversy among the Yanktons. Ceding such a large amount of land and the small amount of the payment were criticized. The Yanktons ceded 96 percent of their land. The remaining 4 percent was not the best land. The $1,600,000 in annuities over a fifty-year period figures out to be (if we assume a cash value of $32,000 per year) $16 per capita per year for 2,000 Yanktons. Even by nineteenth-century standards this is an insubstantial amount of money. When Chief Struck by the Ree returned home, waiting for the Senate to ratify the treaty, he faced opposition not only from the upper bands but also from Smutty Bear, who now condemned the treaty. Another leader of the opposition was future band chief Feather in His Ear (1818–1901), from one of the upper bands. He not only opposed the treaty but opposed the presence of Christian missionaries on the reservation. The lower bands were the most numerous of the Yanktons. They tended to live along the river and depended on agriculture and trade for their primary livelihood and hunting to a lesser degree. Given their location, they had long-standing contact with non-Indians and had confronted many issues of accommodation. The upper bands relied primarily on hunting and less on agriculture and trade. They also had less contact with non-Indians and were more intolerant of accommodation with Anglo-American society. The leaders of the upper bands claimed that they had not been properly represented at the negotiations. Many blamed and were angered at both Struck by the Ree and his nephew, Charles Picotte. There were threats, unrest, and a legacy of controversy.[35] According to Yankton elder Henry Hare, Sr., a descendant of Mad Bull's band: "Our people never did have a chance to vote on the Treaty that Struck by the Ree and Charles Picotte and others made with the government. A lot of us went on a hunt, for buffalo, and when we came back, here we found out they sold our land to the whites."[36]

In considering the motives of Struck by the Ree and his supporters, one must analyze the options available in the 1850s. He could have chosen resistance, armed or otherwise, against American expansionism; but this would have been doomed to failure. Struck by the Ree knew the power of the U.S. military, and he knew the military would protect American squatters. Militarily the Yanktons were in an impossible position. Their population was small, disease was common, and food was scarce. Out of 1,972 Yanktons in 1859, there were 440 adult men.[37] They could not muster an effective fighting force. The feared General Harney, stationed at Fort Randall with 1,200 troops, made armed resistance an untenable option. Another possible option was voluntary migration west. This would have been possible but very difficult. It would have required a location, funding, and consensus from the Yanktons. Voluntary migration, even if successful, would only have postponed an eventual collision with American expansion. The third option, accommodation with the United States, must have seemed like the only viable choice to Chief Struck by the Ree. Accommodation meant a guaranteed permanent homeland for the Yanktons and fifty years of annuity payments. This was much better than fruitless resistance where all could be lost. From his point of view, he had only one option.[38]

Struck by the Ree weathered the storm. Within several years opposition to him withered away, and he became a very popular and respected leader until his death in 1888. He continued to support accommodation with Anglo-American culture, including the acceptance of Christianity.[39] When he died, he was buried in the Presbyterian cemetery near Greenwood. In the 1930s a large granite monument was placed at his gravesite as a memorial. It reads in part: "He was in his days the strongest and most faithful friend of the whites." When the United States Senate ratified the treaty, the Yankton people began moving to their reservation. Struck by the Ree's legacy was the survival of the Yanktons as a nation.

CHAPTER THREE

Sam Necklace and Reservation Life

THE GROWING YEARS, 1881–1906

Water bird, symbol of the Native American Church. It represents swift flight
as it carries prayers skyward. Drawn by Dr. Cassandra Tellier.

In the summer of 1859 many of the Yanktons gathered at the mouth of the
James River awaiting the new government agent and a shipment of goods for
the move west. There was still tension between those who supported the
treaty and those who opposed it. The steamboat *Carrier* came up the Missouri River with Major Alexander Redfield, the new agent for the reservation,
and several tons of supplies. It was not a difficult trip in a physical sense. The
Yanktons packed their belongings on wagons and horses, and many were on
foot, but it was difficult in another sense. They were moving against their will;
they were entering a new era, now dependent on the federal government.
They traveled seventy to eighty miles onto the reservation and into an uncertain future. Two of the migrants were Sam Necklace's grandfather, Mazanapin
(Iron Necklace), and his grandmother, Hintunkasanwin (Weasel Woman).
They were respectively forty-two and thirty years old. They had three children,
including thirteen-year-old Peter Iron Necklace, Sam's future father. On the
reservation they lived in the village of their band chief, Jumping Thunder,
one of the signers of the Treaty of 1858.

Greenwood, located on the Missouri River, became the site for the Yankton
Agency headquarters, built on 160 acres of land. In addition to government
buildings, Greenwood would eventually have schools, a hotel, churches, and a
commercial center made up of many small businesses. The Yanktons settled
on the reservation in villages organized by band. They lived in tipis and tents

and were geographically organized into upper and lower bands. The three upper bands were located on the west and northwestern side of the reservation, and the four lower bands were located in the center and on the eastern side. It was a period of adjustment that was difficult for everyone. For example, on arrival in Greenwood, agent Redfield, who considered himself a devout Episcopalian, instituted the Christian Sabbath throughout the reservation. He prohibited a variety of activities, such as work or hunting on Sunday, and held Episcopal prayer services for the recent arrivals.[1]

The Treaty of 1858 established the reservation in present-day Charles Mix County. The Missouri River is the southern boundary; the eastern boundary went from the mouth of Chouteau Creek north to where the present county line goes northwest. The northern boundary is a straight line from Chouteau Creek to the intersection of present state routes 50 and 44. The western border descends straight south to the Missouri River. The reservation, 431,000 square acres, consists of flat plains and rolling hills, sometimes called the Missouri Hills, running east to west in the south. There is a lowland riverine area between the hills and the Missouri River. The area is generally within the rainfall line of twenty inches per year. The summer rains can be in the form of violent thunderstorms, causing heavy runoff. The weather consists of hot summers and cold winters. The high temperatures in summer are accompanied by a strong southerly wind, which creates a high rate of evaporation. A torrential thunderstorm may pass through at night, but by midafternoon it can be extremely dry again. The winters can be exceedingly difficult. Temperatures are often below zero. Generally there is a wide year-to-year variation, punctuated by periodic summer droughts, blizzards in winter, and inconsistent rainfall.

The area has scattered stands of deciduous trees along the creeks in the east and throughout the hills to the west as well as a heavy growth of trees along the Missouri River. The lowland along the river is the best area for agriculture, despite occasional floods prior to the installation of Fort Randall Dam after World War II. Parts of the reservation could support corn or wheat crops; but except for the narrow strip along the river the area was not good agricultural land. The natural grasses of the open areas allowed for the grazing of horses and cattle. There were also small buffalo herds that passed through to the watering areas along the river. By 1859, however, there were few buffalo in the immediate area. Yankton hunters crossed the Missouri River to hunt buffalo on the Plains. The river was essential to the reservation in the early years. It facilitated travel and the shipment of government supplies and provided a source of water for people, animals, and crops.[2]

During the early years of reservation life the Yanktons were dependent on distributions of government supplies as outlined in the Treaty of 1858. Some people still hunted and gathered wild foods, and some had small gardens, but this was not sufficient. Life was difficult, options were limited, the future was uncertain, and they had to cope with a powerful government that was determined to change their culture and their way of life. In 1861 Congress established the Dakota Territory, bringing more settlers, miners, land speculators, soldiers, and government personnel into the Dakotas. The Civil War and the Minnesota Sioux War added to the sense of crisis. The Yanktons also had to cope with Walter A. Burleigh, the corrupt agent who was sent to Greenwood to replace agent Redfield. The Yankton people remember Burleigh's four-year administration with much anger. Burleigh arrived in Greenwood during the early days of the Civil War. Totally unqualified for such a position, with no background working with American Indians, he had been hired by the BIA as part of the "political spoils" from the 1860 presidential campaign. He had been an organizer and campaigner for Abraham Lincoln in Pennsylvania.

According to the treaty, the Yanktons received annuities in the form of cash, services, and supplies. The agent at Greenwood was responsible for distributing the annuities to the band chiefs, who in turn distributed them to their people. The event that most rankled the Yanktons was the shipment of goods that was supposed to arrive in August 1861. The *J. G. Morrow*, a steamboat that brought the new agent and supplies up the Missouri River, ran aground. Burleigh had some of the supplies removed from the vessel and hidden away. He did not know that Yanktons from the eastern end of the reservation had heard about the accident and the subsequent unloading of the supplies. Upon arriving in Greenwood, Burleigh told the Yanktons that he was not able to deliver their supplies or money. The Yanktons, understandably furious and convinced he was lying, surrounded the agency headquarters. Somehow Burleigh got word of the confrontation to Fort Randall. In three hours a detachment of U.S. troops arrived to protect Burleigh. Later there was an investigation, but Burleigh was not charged. The Yanktons continued to accuse him of fraud, misappropriation of funds, and nepotism. For example, he charged the government $10,000 to build a school that was never built, he was reimbursed for providing students with meals when there were no students, he had members of his family on the agency payroll, and he paid his wife to teach in the nonexistent school. The four years of Burleigh's corrupt administration set the tone for mistrust. The hostility against Burleigh increased until he resigned in 1865.

After the Civil War, Burleigh and several other agents were charged with fraud. Yankton head chief Struck by the Ree testified. He had three complaints: Burleigh stole the Yankton annuity goods; drunken U.S. soldiers harassed his people, especially women; and the above-ground scaffold graves were being destroyed and body parts stolen. Unfortunately, reforms came slowly. Burleigh was not convicted; but on a salary of $2,000 a year he somehow became a wealthy and influential person in the politics of the new Dakota Territory.[3]

During the Burleigh years the Yanktons faced a major dilemma with the outbreak of the Minnesota Sioux War. The Minnesota Sioux, or Santees, had been living on small reservations and were being victimized by unscrupulous agents and the encroachment of squatters on their land. In addition, they had not received their annuities from the government as guaranteed by treaty. Hunger was rampant; anger and rebellion followed. In August 1862 the discontent exploded. Led by Chief Little Crow, they attacked settlers in an attempt to drive them from their land. A brutal war ensued. The Yanktons were in a dilemma. The Santees were their kin. Little Crow sent emissaries asking the Yanktons to join them. The Yanktons had just signed a treaty with the United States, however. In a very difficult decision, Chief Struck by the Ree chose neutrality. By September U.S. troops, with the help of local militia groups, had suppressed the Santee rebellion. Many hundreds of people died on both sides, as thousands of settlers fled from Minnesota. The American military found 303 Santees guilty of crimes and sentenced them to death. President Lincoln intervened and set aside the death sentences of 265 of the prisoners. In December 1862 the remaining 38 Santees were hanged in the largest mass execution in American history. The Yankton decision not to join the war protected them from much death and destruction. It was a war that could not be won.[4]

The years of Burleigh, the *J. G. Morrow* affair, and the Minnesota Sioux War, as well as the reliance on government annuities for subsistence, made it clear that life for the Yanktons would never be the same. They were subjected to the caprices of local agents and policies of powerful officials in Washington. These policies included an enforced peace to be followed by the implementation of acculturation programs. This was initiated within a framework of government policy that subjected Native Americans to military confrontation and reservation life. Between 1851 and 1881 the Sioux became subjects of the U.S. government. Once on reservations, they faced an onslaught of government bureaucrats, missionaries, teachers, and merchants.

By the 1870s the main BIA policies for the Yankton Reservation were in place. One key policy was to develop agriculture and animal husbandry. Subsistence came mostly from federal annuities supplemented by hunting, gathering, and gardening, although hunting was in rapid decline. According to Yankton elder Paul Picotte, the last buffalo was hunted on the reservation in 1869. He also said that the Yanktons had hunted in this area for several generations, but there was little large game left. Some large game could still be found off the reservation, but it was not enough.[5] The agent or superintendent in charge coordinated the government programs. Each year the agent prepared an Annual Report for the commissioner of Indian Affairs. From these reports one can gain some insights into the government policies and their impact. The Annual Reports, however, have their limitations as sources. They were written by low-level bureaucrats, many of whom were political appointees working inside a large government agency and who certainly wanted to be seen as successful administrators. As noted, one of their main activities was the promotion of agriculture on the family level. The goal was not only to create economic growth but also to create an independent nuclear family. As a result of inadequate resources, poor land, and unpredictable weather, agriculture would never be very successful.

In the mid-1870s, out of 431,000 acres, the Yanktons had only 1,200 to 2,000 acres planted. The government agency planted 1,000 acres. The success of the crops varied from year to year. There were periodic droughts, unpredictable hailstorms, recurrent infestations of grasshoppers, and a shortage of water away from the river. The ultimate disaster was a summer-long drought with hot southerly winds that dried the crops to a crisp. Agriculture could not create self-sufficiency; government supplies were essential. In 1874 agent John Gassman reported that reliance on the government supplies was mandatory. They usually received beef, flour, sugar, salt, coffee, tobacco, and clothing.[6]

The government also introduced the raising of livestock. The Yanktons already had horses. Now the horses along with mules could be used for agriculture. Horses continued to have considerable social and cultural value. A Yankton was proud of a fine horse, especially one that could run a good race. One could acquire prestige by giving a horse at a "giveaway." The government also introduced cattle, sheep, hogs, and chickens. Cattle and sheep seemed ideal, given the available grazing. Hog pens and chicken coops began to appear near family settlements. The agency built its own slaughterhouse. In 1873 Gassman reported that the Yanktons possessed 1,500 horses, 100 mules, 250 cattle, and 150 hogs. The agency itself had a flock of 800 sheep and hoped to use the wool to make cloth. The problem with raising livestock was the severe weather. Few people had barns or shelters, and often feed was not available throughout the winter. In the spring of 1873 a three-day snowstorm killed many cattle. In 1875 many of the sheep died of exposure during an extremely cold winter.[7]

The government developed other facilities on the reservation, including a blacksmith shop, a tin shop, a carpenter shop, and a flourmill. These facilities were run by government employees who were supposed to teach a variety of skills to the Yanktons. In 1874, however, there were only fourteen Yanktons serving as apprentices. Building new homes was a government priority. In 1873 Gassman reported that half the Yanktons lived in Anglo-style houses. Another hundred were built in 1874. The BIA was trying to establish family farming and free enterprise to replace the traditional communal nature of Yankton society. It was a difficult transition. New homes were being built, but "nearly every Indian retains his tipi for summer use, next to his home," reported Gassman. The continued use of the tipi was not just social but was essential for health. In the summers the log houses were hot and stuffy and poorly ventilated. They were conducive to the spreading of contagious diseases. The overall health of the Yanktons was not good. One hundred Yanktons died of a measles epidemic in 1873. The government also encouraged the Yanktons to change their style of clothing. Young boys and girls had to wear non-Indian clothing in school and church. The agency kept statistics on the number of Yanktons who wore "citizens dress." These appear in the Annual Reports and on the census rolls. For example, in 1873 it was reported that one-fourth of the Yanktons "wear citizens dress." Pressure was exerted to use English, although the process of spreading English progressed quite slowly.[8]

In 1869 the Reverend John P. Williamson (1837–1917), a Presbyterian, became the first resident missionary to settle on the Yankton Reservation. Some Yanktons were not happy with his arrival. Band chief Feather in His Ear led the opposition to the missionaries. He warned his people that missionaries would mean trouble for them. Chief Struck by the Ree, however, supported Williamson. In a biography of her father, Williamson's daughter

Winifred Barton, who grew up on the Yankton Reservation, describes the opposition to him and the difficulties in establishing a mission. She said her father's ministry was supported by agent Patrick Conger, who defended him on the basis of the First Amendment's guarantee of freedom of religion. She said that "the agent pointed to the waving Stars and Stripes and told them that religion was free and the missionary could do as he pleased."[9] This is a rather interesting perspective, because missionaries and government agents did not extend the concept of religious freedom to the Yanktons. Barton also described Feather in His Ear as a "strong heathen" and the Yankton people as "idolaters."

In 1871 Williamson founded the Ihanktonwan Presbyterian Church. Two years later he built a new church and established a Presbyterian cemetery on a hill overlooking Greenwood. Chief Struck by the Ree attended this church. Fluent in Dakota and one of the few missionaries who believed it was important to teach and preach in the indigenous language, Williamson published a monthly newsletter in Dakota. Its motto was "Helping the Right, Exposing the Wrong." Two years later it was published in English and Dakota. Williamson used it to promote Christianity and "civilization." He wrote that "we shall be satisfied only when the Dakota nation becomes a civilized people." Williamson and other missionaries played a significant role in bringing about change. For example, Williamson encouraged the government to abolish the Sun Dance. When it was abolished he reportedly said, "Thank God." He also organized women into small groups "to pray and to work." They made quilts and learned to prepare and serve meals in Anglo-American style. Williamson's goal was direct: replace the Yankton traditional religion with Christianity.[10]

In 1870 Father Joseph Cook, an Episcopalian, founded a mission on the reservation. He built a church, established an Episcopal cemetery, and supported the building of a series of schools. Eventually a second Episcopal church was established near Chouteau Creek, a third near White Swan, and a fourth near Bon Homme. In 1873 the Episcopal bishop William Hobart Hare (1838–1909) arrived on the Yankton Reservation to establish two boarding schools for girls near the eastern boundary of the reservation. St. Mary's School was opened on the Nebraska side of the Missouri River on the Santee Reservation; across the river in Springfield, South Dakota, he established Hope Indian School, which Mary Chinn, future wife of Sam Necklace, attended. In Greenwood, Bishop Hare opened Emmanuel House for girls and St. Paul's Boarding School for boys, which Sam Necklace attended.

Hare's goal for St. Paul's was to train Native Americans to become teachers and missionaries. He called them "living epistles," as he tried to fulfill the Episcopal mission "to civilize through Christianity, to Christianize through civilizing."[11]

As the boarding school movement emerged in the 1870s, Bishop Hare and other missionaries believed that Indian children should be separated from their parents and from the "negative" influence of their culture. Both the missionaries and the government agents at Greenwood favored boarding schools. Agent Gassman reported: "The schools are disappointing. The young Indians simply will not attend regularly." He added that the day school would "never suffice" and advocated boarding schools. By the late 1870s there were six churches (two Presbyterian, four Episcopal) with nine missionaries on the reservation. There were also seven schools, five day schools, and two boarding schools, with thirteen teachers employed to teach approximately two hundred students. These were all denominational schools. According to the Treaty of 1858, the government was required to build educational facilities for the Yanktons. As of the mid-1870s none had been built, although the BIA was channeling funds into the mission schools. The government boarding school in Greenwood did not open until 1882.[12]

By the 1870s the Catholics had made their presence felt on the reservation but had yet to establish a permanent facility. There was a small Catholic congregation with a lay leader. The Catholics did not establish a permanent facility until 1913, and it was not until 1920 that a Catholic priest took up permanent residency on the reservation. As mentioned before, the widely traveled Jesuit priest Father De Smet visited the Yanktons in 1839. He returned in 1844 and established a life-long friendship with Struck by the Ree. He and other priests were called "blackrobes"; according to Sister Mary Duratschek of the Marty Catholic mission, the Yanktons called the Presbyterians "short coats" and the Episcopalians "white gowns." In the years before Father De Smet died in 1873, he made periodic visits to the reservation. He described his 1866 visit in a letter to his superiors. He wrote that he baptized 100 Yankton children and fifteen adults, including Chief Struck by the Ree, who subsequently wore a Catholic crucifix around his neck. Father De Smet was followed by Martin Marty, a Benedictine priest from Indiana. He visited the Yanktons periodically and conducted mass for Catholics on the reservation. He became the first Catholic bishop in South Dakota. The Marty Mission and the town of Marty, South Dakota, were named after him.[13]

This rapid increase of Christian missions, missionaries, and schools in the 1870s was related to a new government policy initiated by President Ulysses S. Grant, dubbed Grant's "Peace Policy." Grant wanted more church involvement with the reservation system. He thought a broader mission presence would reduce graft and fraud by reservation agents, who, for the most part, were political appointees. Grant believed it would provide more effective administration. Part of the motivation behind this so-called reform movement was to protect American Indians from the likes of Walter Burleigh, but there were also other motives. Grant, as well as his successor, President Rutherford B. Hayes, saw the Peace Policy as a way to "civilize" American Indians. Grant wanted missionaries or former missionaries to be appointed to governmental positions on the reservations or, if this was not possible, at least to require a close working relationship between missionaries and BIA agents. The Grant administration embarked on a policy that allocated a reservation to a particular denomination, preferably one that was already active on the reservation. This led to the appointment of John Gassman, a former Episcopal priest, as the agent on the Yankton Reservation (1872–78). In order to carry out this new initiative Congress authorized the president to establish a Board of Indian Commissioners. The impetus for such a board came from a broad range of groups that supported missionary and humanitarian work in the tradition of Protestant evangelism. Historian Francis Prucha writes that the establishment of the Board of Indian Commissioners "set post-Civil War Indian policy ever more firmly in the pattern of American evangelical revivalism."[14] President Grant appointed ten wealthy Protestant businessmen to the board.

The Peace Policy and the board may have set the tone for governmental policy toward American Indian religion and culture; but as a bureaucratic structure it created confusion and controversy. In 1881 Carl Schurz, the secretary of the interior, declared an end to the Peace Policy and opened the reservations to all denominations.[15] This Peace Policy of both the Grant and Hayes administrations was one of the most pronounced entanglements between church and state in American history.

By the end of the 1870s the everyday life of the Yankton people was undergoing change. It was still modest compared to the degree of change that would occur just before and after the turn of the century, yet the paradigm of change was firmly established. Christian missions were functioning, boarding schools and day schools had been established, and the government introduced Anglo-American concepts and practices of farming and property ownership. Pressure was also being applied to the Yankton religion, culture, and language. Many Yanktons lived in log homes and wore Anglo-American–style clothing; but many Yanktons still followed traditional patterns of everyday life. They all spoke Dakota and referred to each other by their Dakota names or by kinship terms. Most people were still engaged in the Yankton traditional religion based on the centrality of the Sacred Pipe. Many were also participating in Sun Dances and Sweat Lodge ceremonies (*inipi*) and undertaking Vision Quests (*hanblečeya*). Most Yanktons were still getting married in a traditional ceremony, with husband and wife preparing a marital bundle of sacred items. Traditional medicine was being practiced, giveaways were still common, and social rights and responsibilities were carried out through the *tiošpaye* (extended family) and the band. The kinship network was still the focus of everyday life.

THE NECKLACE *TIOŠPAYE*

Sam Necklace grew up at a time when the social, cultural, and economic environment was shifting. He was part of the first generation of Yanktons who had to deal with the full implications of life in two different worlds. The world he was born into in 1881 was quite different from the world he would live in when he was married and rearing his children. Sam Necklace learned to live in both worlds. He did not really try to integrate the two worlds, but he did learn to live with the new while refusing to surrender the old. This took considerable adjustment not only for him but also for all the Sioux who were now on reservations facing the dilemmas posed by the loss of sovereignty, contending with economic dislocation, and coping with the clash of cultures. It was a time of loss, when some sought peace and comfort in a reaffirmation of the past such as the Ghost Dance movement; others sought solace by assimilating into Anglo-American culture. This was a difficult path to navigate. For some it caused dislocation, alienation, and anomie. For others there was searching, building, and growing while coping with difficult realities.

The life of Sam Necklace was not unlike the life of William Wash (1865–1926), a Northern Ute. In a brief biography of Wash, David Lewis—rejecting the simplistic traditional/progressive dichotomy of analyzing American Indian lives—discusses the growing trend of studying the lesser-known "bicultural individuals who spend their lives on the borders between ethnic groups, mastering the knowledge of two cultures without being immobilized by the process."[16] William Wash, like Sam Necklace, struggled to hold onto the culture of his forebears while coping with the changes developing around him. Both men became active members with leadership positions in the Native American Church. They led significant lives and made valuable contributions to their families and their communities. Both men may have been victimized by the reservation system, but they were not victims. They maintained the necessary agency to shape and control their social, cultural, and spiritual lives, albeit less so their economic and political lives. We study their lives as a way to focus on the larger themes of American Indian history during the early years of the reservation era.

Through a study of the life of Sam Necklace one can gain insights into the complexity of everyday reservation life and the adjustments to new social patterns and economic realities. More specifically, we can ascertain how the Native American Church affected the lives of its members. This is not so much a study of Necklace's impact on the Yanktons—there were others who had a much greater impact; it is a study of his life for what it tells us about the Yankton people as well as the historical forces that created the environment he lived in. Although Sam Necklace was an important person in the emergence and development of the Native American Church among the Yanktons, including almost forty years of membership and twenty years as chief priest, there are gaps in the historical record for certain periods of his life. There is material on Sam from the 1930s, when he was active in Yankton politics as one of the leaders of the full-blood faction, as well as documentation involving leasing and fee patents and all the personal financial information that was submitted as part of those dealings and census data and probate records. His name appears on many tribal petitions. There are references to him in various tribal council minutes, as he took part in political debates. Letters written by him and his records as a student at the Flandreau Indian School have survived. One of the most valuable extant sources is a notebook he kept for twenty years (see appendix I). He recorded many of the activities of the Native American Church of Charles Mix County, including the first draft of the Church's constitution.

If the written record of Sam Necklace's life is not as complete as one would hope, the oral record is strong. There are many people who remember him, including family and friends and members of the Native American

Church. Others recall what their parents and grandparents told them about him. This is not surprising; a vibrant oral tradition is part of the cultural heritage of the Yanktons. This was the way in which knowledge, beliefs, and values were transmitted from generation to generation. Oral tradition was the cultural, spiritual, and social charter of a people. It provided legitimacy, created social order, and offered an explanation for virtually the entire natural and supernatural world. It also provided the individual with a basic source of familial/ethnic/spiritual identity. For example, all Yanktons know and can recite the narrative of White Buffalo Calf Woman. In everyday conversation Yanktons refer to ancestors, grandparents, children, grandchildren, and future generations as a continuous cyclical flow that links the family to all living things as in the prayer *Mitakuye Oyasin* (for all my relations). Oral tradition is dynamic, as it provides meaning to life and reproduces the inner core of a culture.

In addition to interviews with people who knew Sam Necklace, the oral history collection at the University of South Dakota contains a wealth of material, including recorded interviews with many Yankton people. These interviews do not relate to Sam Necklace specifically, but they do contain considerable material on the Peyote religion as well as on Yankton history. They give us a historical context in which we can place the life of Sam Necklace and the development of the local Native American Church.

The most valuable source for this study has been Asa Primeaux, Sr., of Marty, South Dakota. The grandson of Sam and Mary Necklace, Asa is the son of their daughter Jennie. After Asa's birth in 1931, Jennie and her husband, Harry Primeaux, separated, and Asa was sent to live with his grandparents. He lived with them until his grandfather died in 1949. Since Sam Necklace was chief priest of the local Native American Church, Asa grew up in an environment totally imbued with the Peyote religion and learned about it at an early age. He traveled with his grandfather when he conducted Peyote meetings in other places. As a teenager, Asa assisted his grandfather while learning the songs, prayers, and drumming of the Peyote faith. Eventually Asa became a roadman himself and has been conducting Peyote meetings for more than thirty years. Like his grandfather, he travels and teaches the Peyote way. Also like his grandfather, Asa is a well-known Peyote singer.[17] Beginning with Sam Necklace, through three of his children, his grandchildren, their children, and their children's children, we can trace five generations of the Peyote religion among the Necklace/Primeaux *tiošpaye*. The presence of five generations of one family in the Native American Church speaks strongly for the power of the Peyote religion to provide continuity and meaning to its members. It also shows how Sam Necklace, as the spiritual mentor of this family, planted firm roots for his descendants.

The origin of the Necklace *tiošpaye* dates back to the Yankton homeland in Minnesota and is part of the family's oral history. During a naming ceremony for Danny Necklace (great-grandson of Sam Necklace) in 1982, the family made a tape-recording of the traditional version of their origins. The Dakota name that young Danny received was Hehaka Mani Hokšina, Walking Elk Boy. Asa Primeaux recited the story of the family's history as it was passed down to him in order to explain the origin of Danny's name.

> The Yankton Sioux, our name came from there. They say at one time when the Sioux was coming up the country from the east, coming west, from Ohio, and on this side of the Mississippi River they split up. A group of people went north, and a group of them went southwest and they come to a river we call the Big Sioux River. When they found that they kept going and going and pretty soon the river met up with another river that was the Missouri River. So they come to a point there, so they set up a village there. Right now there is a big city there. They call it Sioux City. That time they had a big chief there by the name of War Eagle. His people settled there. Then this group that went north; they went into a wooded area. They call it *unčiapi makoče* [grandmother's land]. Now they call it Canada. They went in there and were confronted by some foreigners. They were Frenchmen. So they attacked them. This one family got scared, so he took his wife and kids, he took off. He came south, he remembered his people. They went west, he went west a little bit and then south; he comes into this Big Sioux River. He followed that, kept coming, coming here and all of a sudden he come to a village, and here, that's where it ran into the Missouri River. There was a great big village there. The people recognize him, that he was part of the band. So they accepted him and asked him his name. He said my name is Walking Elk, Hehaka Mani, he come from the north. So he stayed at the village. They say he has a grave many miles north of Sioux City, that's where he's buried. So that's where this name came from . . . so these Necklaces they're the offsprings of Hehaka Mani. So that's the name this boy is going to receive today. So I just thought I'd say this, whenever you are going to pass on an Indian name, there is a little history, a little saying how this name come about.[18]

Figure 2

Seven Generations
Descendants of Iron Necklace (Mazanapin)

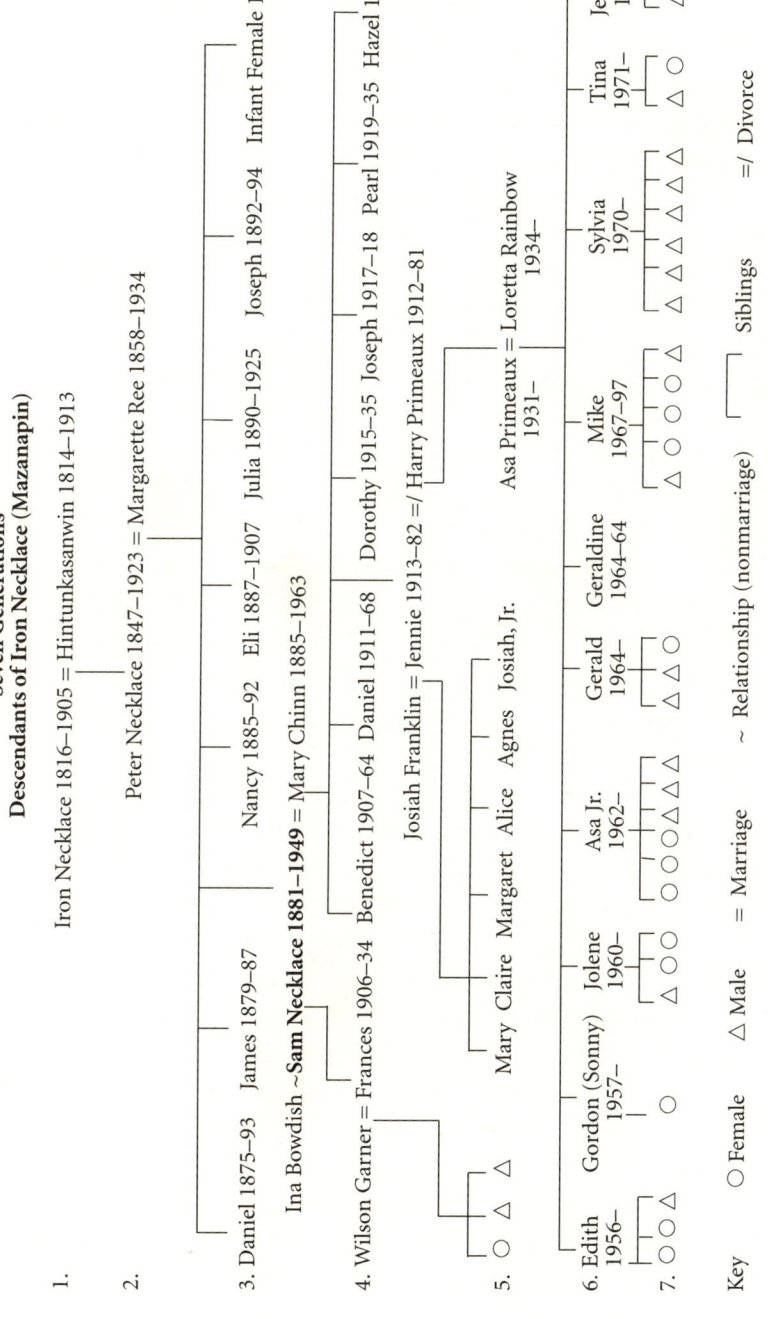

1. Iron Necklace 1816–1905 = Hintunkasanwin 1814–1913

2. Peter Necklace 1847–1923 = Margarette Ree 1858–1934

3. Daniel 1875–93   James 1879–87   Nancy 1885–92   Eli 1887–1907   Julia 1890–1925   Joseph 1892–94   Infant Female 1895–97

    Ina Bowdish ~ **Sam Necklace 1881–1949** = Mary Chinn 1885–1963

4. Wilson Garner = Frances 1906–34   Benedict 1907–64   Daniel 1911–68   Dorothy 1915–35   Joseph 1917–18   Pearl 1919–35   Hazel 1921–22

    Josiah Franklin = Jennie 1913–82 =/ Harry Primeaux 1912–81

    Asa Primeaux = Loretta Rainbow 1931–   1934–

5. Mary   Claire   Margaret   Alice   Agnes   Josiah, Jr.

6. Edith   Gordon (Sonny)   Jolene   Asa Jr.   Gerald   Geraldine   Mike   Sylvia   Tina   Jennifer
   1956–   1957–   1960–   1962–   1964–   1964–64   1967–97   1970–   1971–   1972–

7.

Key   ○ Female   △ Male   = Marriage   ~ Relationship (nonmarriage)   [Siblings   =/ Divorce

There is no family memory or historical information on the link between Hehaka Mani and the first Necklaces who enter the historical record in the Yankton census. The first, as noted, are Mazanapin and his wife, Hintunkasanwin, Sam Necklace's grandparents. Both are buried in the Presbyterian Cemetery in Greenwood. Mazanapin's tombstone reads: "Mazanapi / Iron Necklace / Born April 20, 1816 / Died August 17, 1905." The tombstone of his wife, who is buried next to him, reads: "Hintunkasanwin / 1814–1913 / Gone but not forgotten." We cannot be certain of the accuracy of the birth dates on the tombstones. They conflict with census data. On the tombstones Iron Necklace is two years younger than his wife; but on the Yankton census for the late 1880s and early 1890s he is listed as eleven years older than his wife. On the census from 1899 until his death in 1905 he is listed as three years older than his wife. Whatever their actual birth dates, they acquired considerable status as the two oldest living people on the reservation. In addition they are the first of seven generations of Necklaces and are part of the family's collective memory.

Iron Necklace was born into the Igmu (Cat) Band under Chief Smutty Bear, who was succeeded by Chief Jumping Thunder. The Necklace family has little memory of Iron Necklace, although one branch of the family uses "Iron Necklace" as its surname. Aside from the census, he is in the historical record as a signer of petitions. He was one of the Yankton adult males who signed the controversial Agreement of 1892, which sold unallotted land to the government. It is interesting to note that he did not sign the Pipestone Agreement of 1899, even though his son Peter and his grandson Sam signed it.[19] Iron Necklace was allotted 120 acres of land (Allottee No. 394) in Ree Township, located in the southeast corner of the reservation, directly below Wagner, South Dakota, near the Missouri River.

Peter Iron Necklace, son of Iron Necklace, was born in 1851. His Dakota name, Hepazasni, is emblazoned in large letters on the top of his tombstone in the Episcopal cemetery in Greenwood, with the name "Peter Necklace" below. It is remembered that he owned horses and took great pride in raising them and probably racing them, as was popular at the time. He married Margarette Ree, the daughter of John Ree, who was the band chief of Oyáte Sica (Bad Nation) band after Mad Bull II died in 1875. According to the census records, Peter and Margarette had eight children: five boys and three girls spaced over a twenty-year period. Most died at an early age. Only Sam lived into the mature years. Two of his siblings died in infancy; his brothers Eli,

Daniel, and James died at age twenty, eighteen, and ten, respectively. His sister Nancy died at age six, and Julie Ree lived until age thirty-five. There is a ninth child, Amos Henry Necklace, born in 1886, the son of Peter and another woman who is listed as deceased in the 1900 Register of Yankton Families.[20] Peter Necklace used several different names. Sometimes he used his father's name, as in "Peter Iron Necklace"; but in his later years he used the name "Peter Baker Necklace." It is unclear how Peter made a living; but like many others he leased out his allotted land to local non-Indian farmers. For example, there is a Farming and Grazing Lease for 1914 in which Peter leased 160 acres of land to a white farmer from Wagner, South Dakota. He was paid $365 a year by the lessee. The lease has the name "Peter Baker Necklace" typed in, followed by a fingerprint.[21] Peter appears in a photograph (ca. 1895) with twenty-seven other Yankton men standing in front of the Yankton Agency headquarters. Peter, with short hair, is wearing farmer-style bib overalls and a cowboy hat. There is a striking resemblance between him and his great-grandson Asa. Both are of medium height, with a muscular physique, high cheekbones, a strong-looking face, and deep, dark eyes.[22] Peter played a minor role in Yankton politics. His name appears from time to time on petitions. For example, he signed both the Agreement of 1892 and the Pipestone Agreement of 1899. He also served on the Tribal Council for a short period as well as on several enrollment and allotment committees.

Sam Necklace was the third oldest child of Peter and Margarette. They lived in Ree Township, several miles from grandpa Iron Necklace, in a village with the Oyáte Sica band, where Margarette's father, John Ree, was band chief. The Necklace family knows very little about Sam's younger years. His rearing was probably not atypical for the era. He grew up within a large nuclear family that was part of a larger Necklace extended family and the close-by Ree family. This certainly helped him grow up with a strong sense of identity. By the time of Sam's birth both the government and the missionaries were beginning to put considerable pressure on Yankton families to send their children to school. The implications of this were so severe that it created consternation for many families. Chief Struck by the Ree supported sending children to school, but many parents were opposed to it. In addition to continuing President Grant's "Peace Policy," President Hayes pursued several new initiatives. Now that forced resettlement and concentration of American Indians was virtually complete, Hayes implemented "reforms" in order to acculturate and assimilate them. The two initiatives involved land

Figure 3

Descendants of Sam and Mary Necklace

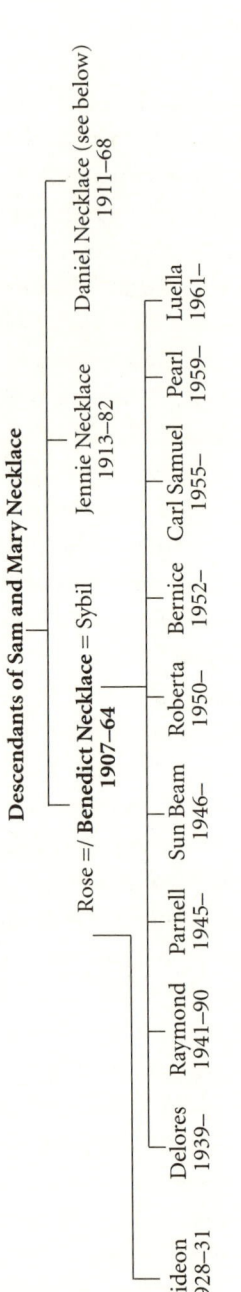

Rose =/ **Benedict Necklace** = Sybil
1907–64

Gideon	Delores	Raymond	Parnell	Sun Beam	Roberta	Bernice	Carl Samuel	Pearl	Luella
1928–31	1939–	1941–90	1945–	1946–	1950–	1952–	1955–	1959–	1961–

Jennie Necklace
1913–82

Daniel Necklace (see below)
1911–68

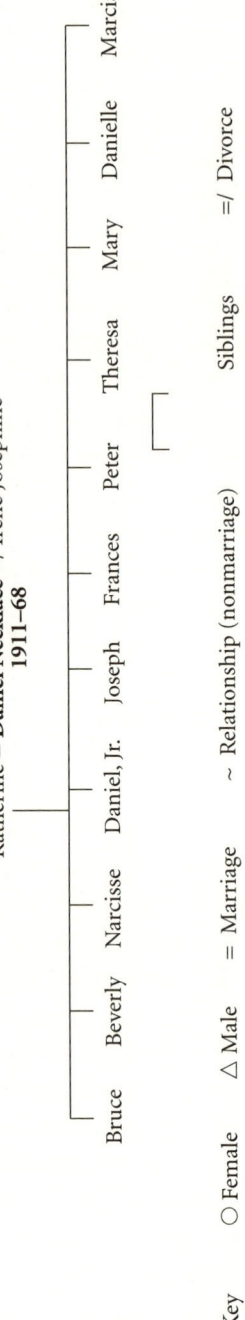

Katherine = **Daniel Necklace** =/ Irene Josephine
1911–68

Bruce Beverly Narcisse Daniel, Jr. Joseph Frances Peter Theresa Mary Danielle Marcia

Key ○ Female   △ Male   = Marriage   ~ Relationship (nonmarriage)   Siblings   =/ Divorce and education. Reservation land was to be divided into individual allotments to be held as private property; and the government began establishing day schools and boarding schools for reservation children.[23]

THE "REFORM" ERA AND THE YANKTON RESERVATION

The purpose of the "reforms" was to transform American Indian culture. Many "reformers," such as Secretary of the Interior Carl Schurz and Senator Henry L. Dawes of Massachusetts, believed that the American Indian could survive only if assimilated into Anglo-American culture. The question they posed was: how do you civilize "savages"? Their solutions were through private property, Christianity, and American-style education. Secretary Schurz said, "The enjoyment and pride of the individual ownership of property is one of the most effective civilizing agencies."[24] This would negate one of the unifying principles of Yankton life: communally owned land. The "reform" movement that led to the Dawes Allotment Act of 1887 was supported by missionaries, humanitarians, educators, and even some American Indian groups, such as the Indian Rights Association and the Women's National Indian Association. "Reform" received a considerable boost in 1881 with the publication of Helen Hunt Jackson's *A Century of Dishonor*. Jackson outlined the history of atrocities against American Indians but concluded that their salvation lay in the concept of private property. Not all support for the privatization of reservation land came from "reformers." Realtors, land speculators, farmers, and railroad, timber, and mining interests wanted access to reservation land. They lobbied for the Dawes Act, knowing that the demise of the reservation system would make millions of acres of land available for exploitation. There were 138 million acres of reservation land in the mid-1880s—and intense political pressure to take it away.[25]

The Dawes Act authorized the surveying of reservation land, the preparation of allotment population rolls, and the distribution of 160 acres of land to the head of each household and smaller amounts to other individuals. Allottees received a trust patent for twenty-five years. At the end of that time a fee patent would be given to the owner, which meant unrestricted ownership of the land. After the allotments were distributed, the so-called surplus land could be sold to the general public. By 1934 the Dawes Act had led to the loss of 86 million acres of reservation land. From the Native American perspective the Dawes Act was devastating, not only because of the sale of "surplus" land but also because many allottees lost their land through fraud and manipulation. Others sold their land when faced with oppressive poverty. The Dawes Act stimulated a broad assault on Native American culture. The impact on the Yankton people followed this pattern. There was loss of land, dislocation, and increasing poverty. In 1887 the Yanktons had 431,000 acres of land guaranteed by the Treaty of 1858; by 1934 they held less than 50,000 acres.

From the Yankton point of view the Dawes Act was a dismal failure. Much of the allotted land was marginal; and given the arid nature of parts of the reservation, agriculture would be very difficult. In addition, individuals lacked the capital or the ability to acquire credit that would be needed to work the land. The most appropriate term for this era is "dispossession," as in the title of Janet McDonnell's monograph *The Dispossession of the American Indian,* a perceptive analysis of the actual implementation of the Dawes Act. She states in her conclusion that—instead of promoting productive use of Indian land—the solution of freeing Indians from government control led to the loss of land and the pauperization of Indians.[26] The Dawes Act and the subsequent Agreement of 1892 caused considerable debate among the Yanktons; however, it was a debate that contained a mixture of consternation concerning the loss of the land and hope that the sale of reservation land could be a way out of poverty. Others saw allotments and the potential income from leasing their land in the same way. The hope was not borne out in the long run, but in the short run it seemed like an answer to some.

In the summer of 1888, during the allotment turmoil, Chief Struck by the Ree died at the age of eighty-seven. He had been head chief since 1851. Instrumental in the signing of the Treaty of 1858, Struck by the Ree led the Yanktons onto the reservation; he provided leadership in face of governmental control. He favored accommodation with the United States, believing resistance was futile. In these beliefs, as well as his Catholic baptism and regular attendance at Presbyterian Church services, Struck by the Ree represented acceptance of change. Even at the end of his life he counseled Yankton parents to send their children to school.[27] The manner in which he represented change is seen in comparing two photographs of him. In 1858, when he was in Washington, he was photographed wearing traditional Dakota clothing, including moccasins and a fur hat, with what appears to be a buffalo-hide blanket over his lap. He has long hair and is wearing an eagle feather and is carrying a ceremonial hatchet. It is a typical posed studio photo from that era, but what is most instructive is the display of the single eagle feather. There is another photograph of him (ca. 1858) in the South Dakota Historical Society in which he also has long black flowing hair and a single eagle feather attached to it. These photos are not unusual, but they are a point of departure in comparing them to a photo taken in 1885. In the later photo he has short hair, is wearing American-style clothing, and has a large Catholic crucifix around his neck. He is not wearing an eagle feather or carrying any traditional symbols of status. In many ways these photographs represent what was happening to the Yankton people.[28]

The death of Struck by the Ree marked the end of the band as an important sociopolitical-economic unit. This demise reflected BIA policy, which included the abandonment of the village system in favor of scattered housing on family allotments. It caused considerable dislocation and resentment, as the eight bands were dispersed, making communal activities very difficult.[29] The band chiefs, who at one time had a great deal of influence in a consensual form of tribal government, were becoming less and less relevant. At one time band chiefs, in council with the head chief, debated and made decisions for the Yanktons. The demise of the band is well remembered by several Yanktons who were interviewed in the 1960s. Cecil Provost (a former business manager of the Marty Mission) and Paul Picotte (born in 1880) both discuss the loss of the band with phrases such as "almost extinct," "disappeared many years ago," and "ceased having much influence."[30] Despite the subversion of the Yankton political system and the dispersal of the villages, the kinship network based on the extended family continued to function. Kinship obligations and responsibilities as well as kinship terminology remained part of everyday life. Children were still taught to function within the kinship network and to honor and respect parents and elders. There certainly was dislocation, but an inner core of Yankton culture survived the onslaught of the non-Indian world.

The implementation of the allotment system did not proceed smoothly. The government surveyors were harassed and threatened and had difficulty doing their work. Troops from nearby Fort Randall were sent to protect them. As the allotting procedure was in progress, there were accusations of fraud and mismanagement. For example, the Yankton wives and children of white men (called "squaw men") were given preferential treatment. Some were allotted 320 acres instead of the usual 160 acres. Some Yanktons were given allotments on poor, hilly land that could not be farmed. Others were given allotments that were divided into two or more parcels. This confusion, fraud, and mismanagement of allotments was common throughout the reservation system. In spite of resistance, mismanagement, and questionable decisions by the allotting agent, the land was surveyed, and allotments were distributed. It was clear to many, however, that when all allotments had been assigned there would still be unallotted reservation land. What would happen to this land was of concern to everyone.[31]

In 1892 Congress gave the Department of the Interior the authority to negotiate the sale of "surplus" reservation land. Later in the year three commissioners traveled to the Yankton Agency to negotiate for the sale of this land. Approximately 268,000 acres of Yankton land was allotted. The government wanted to negotiate the sale of the remaining 168,000 acres. The commissioners negotiated with a "committee of 24," consisting of three representatives from each of the eight bands. The commissioners also held open meetings in which dozens of people gave testimony.[32] Factions emerged to support or oppose the sale of the land. In order for the sale to be finalized, the signatures of a majority of Yankton males over age eighteen were required, followed by the ratification of the U.S. Congress. The government offered $600,000 for the 168,000 acres. The commissioners traveled throughout the reservation seeking signatures. Five of the eight band chiefs opposed the sale of land. Chief Feather in His Ear was the leader of the opposition. Band chiefs Running Bull, Jumping Thunder, and Frank Jandron supported the sale and signed the agreement. Peter Necklace also signed it.[33] The commissioners obtained 254 signatures, 24 more than the 230 necessary for a majority vote.

Congress ratified the agreement in 1894 and declared the land open for non-Indian settlement on 1 April 1895. A land rush ensued. A reporter for *Harper's Weekly* said the "squatters," or "boomers" or "sooners" as he called them, followed the principle of "possession is nine points of the law." The squatters immediately put up a wood cabin or a sod house and staked a claim to the land. They were required to pay a $14 filing fee and fifty cents an acre for a 40-, 80-, or 160-acre lot. This settlement within the reservation boundaries resulted in the present patchwork pattern of Yankton land holdings and would be a source of tension among the Yanktons, local white residents, and state and county officials for the next century. One reason why there was such a large number of people ready to buy land is that the federal government advertised the sales in a booklet, *Indian Lands for Sale*. The government also distributed posters advertising "Indian Land for Sale." For example, one poster states that 120,445 acres of Indian land had been sold in South Dakota in 1910, and 350,000 acres in twelve states would be available in 1911. The poster's sales pitch included: "Get a Home of Your Own, Easy Payments, Perfect Title, Possession within Thirty Days."[34]

Several factors must be considered when analyzing the motives of those who signed the Agreement of 1892. Many Yanktons lived in poverty, made more severe by a terrible drought that summer. The agreement (article III) promised that within sixty days $100,000 would be distributed on a per capita basis. In addition, all males over eighteen would receive a $20 gold coin. There was also a provision to pay $11,475 to fifty-one Yankton men (or their heirs) who had been employed as scouts by the U.S. Army in the Minnesota Sioux War in 1864. This helped ensure the votes of some families. The remaining $500,000 was placed with the U.S. Treasury as a trust fund to be distributed at the rate of $20,000 per year for twenty-five years. The funds were to be used "for the care and maintenance of such orphans, and aged, infirm, or other helpless persons of the Yankton tribe . . . for schools and educational purposes . . . for courts of justice and other local institutions" (article I). The Yanktons received their per capita payments in 1895.[35]

In hindsight it is clear that poverty was the major factor leading to the agreement. The question of how the signatures were acquired, however, remains. There were accusations of pressure and threats as well as charges of fraud. In November 1893 government commissioners visited the reservation to investigate these charges. Testimony was taken, but little came of these hearings. The government concluded that the signatures were obtained appropriately. In fact, in order to put any dissension to rest, the commissioners obtained an additional twenty-three signatures for the agreement. One of the new signers was Iron Necklace, Sam Necklace's grandfather, now eighty years old.[36] The government succeeded in taking more land from the Yankton people. The commissioners described this as being in their best interests. What they did not mention was the intense political pressure to provide more land for non-Indian settlers. The so-called best interests of the Yanktons were couched in humanitarian terms. Commissioners J. C. Adams and John J. Cole wrote to Congress: "We think that all proper means should be used to break up the tribal condition and tribal habits of life."[37]

YANKTON CHILDHOOD

Young Sam Necklace and his future wife, Mary Chinn, grew up in the midst of this turmoil, frustration, and displacement. They lived on the eastern side of the reservation, the area most exposed to interaction with Anglo-American culture. By the 1890s most Yankton children were in school and were generally bilingual, as were Sam and Mary. The children attended one of three types of schools: day schools, on-reservation boarding schools, and off-reservation boarding schools. The BIA concluded, however, that off-reservation boarding schools were the ideal method to "civilize" Native Americans. In 1879 army captain Richard H. Pratt opened the Carlisle Indian Industrial School in Pennsylvania. It was the first off-reservation boarding school for Indian children and served as the model for other such schools. The objective of these schools is best summed up in the famous dictum of Captain Pratt: "Kill the Indian, save the Man." "Killing" the Indian would allow the young to assimilate into American society. Reformers concluded that the best method to achieve this end was to separate the children from their family and community.

The schools were a traumatic experience for the children. Administrators and teachers changed the children's names and discarded their clothes. They were not allowed to speak their native language. "English only" was the norm, usually enforced by corporal punishment. The children had their hair cut within a day or two of arrival. The boys had almost all their hair removed and were left with military-style crew cuts. They felt humiliated. There are three photographs of Yankton boys at boarding schools in Greenwood. Two of the photographs are from the government boarding school, and the third was taken at St. Paul's in 1890. All three photos are strikingly similar. The boys are quite dressed-up, standing rigidly in rows. They do not look like they want to be in the photographs. No one is smiling; most look sad, and a few look scared. The older boys and some of the younger ones are wearing suit jackets, shirts and ties, knickers, and high shoes.[38] The photographs are clearly orchestrated to show order, discipline, and control.

An example of the boarding-school experience comes from Gertrude Simmons Bonnin, also known as Zitkala-Ša (Red Bird), a Yankton woman who became a well-known author and political activist. Born on the Yankton Reservation in 1876, she was part of the same generation as Sam Necklace. From age eight to eleven she attended White's Manual Institute, a Quaker school in Wabash, Indiana. Her experience away from home and her return from the missionary school environment sparked her creative energies. She later attended Earlham College in Indiana and the Boston Conservatory of Music. She became a writer, publishing autobiographical essays, short stories, and collections of Native American traditional narratives, including *Old*

Indian Legends. Her essays and short stories appeared in *Harper's Magazine* and *Atlantic Monthly.*[39]

Although Bonnin and Necklace belonged to the same generation and both went to boarding school, they took different life paths. Whereas Necklace spent almost his entire life on the reservation, Bonnin became a political activist, living for a time in Washington, D.C., working with the Society of American Indians and the organization she founded, the National Council of American Indians. Their paths also diverged on one other issue. While Sam Necklace was an ardent supporter and chief priest of the Native American Church, Gertrude Bonnin was a fervent opponent of the Peyote Faith (see chapter 4). As a student and a young author, Bonnin was sensitized to the negative impact that American education and Christianity had on the Yanktons. Her autobiographical writing reflects this view. She recalled her own experiences with having her hair cut:

> What caused them to stoop and look under the bed I do not know. I remember being dragged out, though I resisted by kicking and scratching wildly. In spite of myself I was carried downstairs and tied fast in a chair. . . . I cried aloud, shaking my head all the while until I felt the cold blades of the scissors against my neck, and heard them gnaw off one of my thick braids. Then I lost my spirit.[40]

Her early experiences with Christianity were no less terrifying:

> She showed me a picture of the white man's devil. I looked in horror upon the strong claws that grew out of his fur-covered fingers. His feet were like his hands. Trailing at his heels was a scaly tail tipped with a serpent's open jaws. His face was a patchwork: he had bearded cheeks, like some I had seen pale-faces wear; his nose was an eagle's bill, and his sharp-pointed ears were pricked up like those of a sly fox. Above them a pair of cow's horns curved upward. I trembled with awe, and my heart throbbed in my throat, as I looked at the king of evil spirits. Then I heard the pale face woman say that this terrible creature roamed loose in the world, and that little girls who disobeyed school regulations were to be tortured by him.[41]

The schools also subjected the children to an intense regimen of work and discipline. A martial atmosphere with drilling, marching, and total obedience became the norm. The mornings were spent in the classroom, where the typical curriculum included reading, penmanship, arithmetic, spelling, history, and geography. In the afternoon manual training and work was required. The girls were taught domestic skills; the boys were taught agriculture, animal husbandry, masonry, carpentry, and smithing. Students also did the laundry and janitorial work for the school. Disobedience brought physical and psychological punishment, including humiliation. The children's responses to school varied. Some children adjusted and did well in school; some responded with passivity or indifference and simply went through the motions of compliance as required. Others ran away. This was a serious problem at most boarding schools, as was the general pattern of active or passive resistance.[42]

Sending their children to school was not popular with many Yankton parents. Yet after the government school was opened in Greenwood in 1882, and with Chief Struck by the Ree and government agents encouraging, cajoling, and threatening parents, more and more children began attending school.[43] Yankton children attended all three types of schools and had many experiences similar to the types of trauma described above. One example is Joe Rockboy, who attended the government school in Greenwood from 1911 to 1915. He described a typical day of half-schooling, half-work, both punctuated by a series of drills and rote activities. The students were required to wear uniforms and followed a military school regimentation. He said the regulations were rigid and that the administrators, teachers, and older boys inflicted corporal punishment. He added that the older boys were used to discipline the younger boys. "They'd give 'em a paddle, or say a belt, you know like a pulley belt or a small rubber hose. You get hit with one of these belts, and you know you're hit." He noted that he was required to go to church in spite of being in a government school. There was also a problem with runaways. Rockboy said school was most difficult for the children who did not speak English very well. When they were caught "speaking Indian" they were punished. It was these children who tended to run away.[44]

In the 1890s approximately 20 percent of the children attended off-reservation boarding schools. Most of the other children attended day schools or the government boarding school in Greenwood. The Yankton people never reconciled themselves to having their children in the local boarding school. In 1906 a memorandum protesting the boarding school was sent to the commissioner of Indian Affairs by David Zephier, Sr., who lived on the reservation. A professional interpreter fluent in French, Dakota, and English, Zephier had served as an interpreter for most of the Yankton delegations that had traveled to Washington. In this case he says that he was asked to write and forward this request. "It is almost the universal desire upon our Reservation, that the Boarding-School at the Agency shall be abolished, and that in lieu of it we may have established upon the Reservation such day schools. . . . This would enable the children to live at home, which is for obvious reasons very desirable to our people. We would like to know if this can be arranged."[45] The commissioner ignored this request.

Sam and Mary Necklace both attended Episcopal boarding schools. Sam went to St. Paul's, an on-reservation boarding school located in Greenwood; later he enrolled at the Flandreau Indian School in Flandreau, South Dakota. Mary attended the Springfield Indian School (called Hope Indian School for a time). The only evidence for Sam's attendance at St. Paul's is his answer to a question about schooling on a 1920 fee patent application, where he stated that he went to St. Paul's and Flandreau. St. Paul's was a typical denominational boarding school, with rules and regulations designed to foster acculturation. There is an 1890 photograph of St. Paul's school with Father Cook, two female teachers, and thirty-four Native American children in the National Anthropological Archives. It is possible that a nine-year-old Sam is in the photo.

One of the puzzles about Sam Necklace is his use of the name "Baker." Sometimes he used it as a middle name, as in Samuel Baker Necklace, or "B." as a middle initial; but on many occasions he used it as a surname, as in Samuel Baker or Samuel Necklace Baker. No one in the family knows the origin of the name "Baker," but there is one hypothesis. At St. Paul's there was a teacher named Miss Baker. Paul Picotte, who went to St. Paul's and was probably a classmate of Sam's, mentions her in his oral history. There was also an Anna M. Baker teaching at Emmanuel school for girls, which was closed in 1878. Possibly she moved to St. Paul's, because both schools were in Greenwood. In the photograph of St. Paul's there are two female teachers. One was probably Father Cook's sister; the other may have been Miss Baker.

The reason why this is more than a pedantic note is that Native American students in boarding schools were often forced to take new names, adding to the stress of an already difficult situation. For about twenty years Sam used both "Baker" and "Necklace" as surnames. In 1899 he signed the Pipestone Agreement as Sam Baker; however, the annual census always lists "Necklace" as his surname, with "Baker" or "B." for the middle name. His records at Flandreau Indian School are under "Necklace," yet when he began to deal with agency officials over land, leases, and affidavits he used "Baker." Even Sam's father began using the name "Peter Baker Necklace." In the Family Registry of 1900 all the members of the Necklace family had "Baker" or "B." as the middle name or initial. There is an interesting affidavit from 1917 concerning forty acres of Sam's land. It began:

> Question. Your name is Samuel Baker or Samuel Baker Necklace?
>
> Answer. Yes, Samuel Baker Necklace.
>
> Question. You also sign yourself Samuel N. Baker?
>
> Answer. I never sign my name that way, Major McLaughlin told me to put it that way. I was allotted Samuel Baker Necklace.

Even Sam's wife followed suit, sometimes signing "Mary Baker Necklace" or "Mary Chinn Baker." By the 1920s Sam had stopped using "Baker" as a surname but kept it as a middle name, although many of his friends and relatives continued to call him Sam Baker. The Miss Baker of St. Paul's may or may not be the origin of the name, but it does lend some insight into the everyday life on the reservation.[46]

The Flandreau Indian School (called Riggs Institute from 1901 to 1906) was initially established as a Presbyterian mission. In 1892 it officially became a government boarding school under superintendent William V. Duggan. It was located in Flandreau, a small town in eastern South Dakota. The school's curriculum combined the classroom and physical labor with the emphasis on vocational training. The school plant contained a classroom building, a laundry, a small hospital, a dining hall, a dairy barn, and a library. The school had 480 acres of land, some of it farmed by the pupils. The students also worked in the various facilities of the school. This work was considered essential to their training as well as to the economic viability of the school. The curriculum was divided into "literary work" and "industrial work." According to a 1902 report card, the former included Mathematics, Reading, Language, Geography, Grammar, History, Physiology (Health), Writing, Drawing, Spelling, and Music. The latter included Sewing, Dressmaking, Cooking, General Housework, Farm Work, Care of Stock, Carpentry, Tailoring, Shoe Mending, and Harness Making. Students were also graded on Use of English, Deportment, and Habits of Industry.[47]

In the records of the Flandreau Indian School, Sam is listed on the enrollment forms for 1894–95 and 1900 through 1904. He may have attended during the intervening years, but the Flandreau records from 1895 to 1899 have been lost. Sam's younger half-brother, Amos Necklace, also attended Flandreau from 1901 to 1904. School records list both as full-bloods and Episcopalians. There were many other Yankton youth at Flandreau. Looking through the enrollment records is like looking through a who's who of Yankton families. The lists of surnames include Archambeau, Bruguier, Blaine, Drapeau, Blackowl, Picotte, Cook, St. Pierre, and Arrow. At the turn of the century Flandreau was similar to other government boarding schools. The regimen was structured, discipline was strict, and physical labor was required. There is no direct family memory of Sam's school days except that he did attend a boarding school and graduated. Some family members believed that Sam went to Carlisle Indian School, but there is no evidence to support this in the Carlisle records. It was Sam's niece, Auntie Pauline, who said he went to Flandreau. In addition to his name on the enrollment registers, some of his grades have survived.

There are not enough of Sam's records at Flandreau to re-create his school days, but there are a number of recorded interviews with others who attended Flandreau early in the twentieth century. They describe a military-school atmosphere with a daily routine punctuated by bells. The students were required to march to different places, such as into or out of the classrooms and the dining room. All the former students commented on the strict discipline, particularly when it came to "speaking Indian." According to Lottie Good Thunder, who attended Flandreau in 1916, the punishment for "speaking Indian" was to be placed in isolation in a locked room. The food was not appealing. A typical meal would be bread soaked in bacon-grease gravy. One student reported that at breakfast it was not unusual to see "worms floating in the oatmeal." Being hungry, they ate it anyway. The military nature of the school was not surprising. Some staff members were retired from the U.S. military.[48]

When Sam was at Flandreau, enrollment fluctuated between 350 and 400 pupils, with approximately half male, half female. The age of the students varied, even within the same grade. Sam was twenty-two years old when he finished eighth grade. School records show many students in their late teens and early twenties. Many were there to acquire the tools necessary to survive in the Anglo-American world. This meant not only vocational skills but also the communication skills that come with reading and writing in English. The daily schedule included work on the school grounds, but some of the older students worked in town or for surrounding white families. Some of the students were paid a meager wage; however, they did not receive cash. The school kept an account for each student; when students wanted spending money they were issued vouchers for small sums that they could spend at school or at certain businesses in town. Merchants would then redeem the vouchers at the school. For the year 1903–1904 Sam and Amos were listed as attending the "Evening Term," which meant that they worked in town or on a farm during the day and attended school at night. This was typical for the older students. In discussing Sam's early life, several of his descendants, including his grandson Asa, said something quite unexpected: that he was well known for having beautiful penmanship. Why his descendants made that assertion, or even why it was remembered, was puzzling until I reviewed Sam's records at Flandreau. His highest grades were always in Writing, Drawing, and Spelling. In one grading period in 1903, he received a 98, 90, and 92 in these three subjects. His poorest grades were generally in Geography and History. We can be certain that Sioux history was not part of the curriculum. He also received high grades in Deportment.

Sam's schooling provided valuable benefits to him, although it is not known if he considered his boarding-school experience positive or negative. As an older student attending class in the evening, he may have avoided some of the rigid discipline. He told his grandson Asa that he did benefit from school and always encouraged his grandson to go to school. Sam's bilingualism as well as his writing ability gave him opportunities in later life. For example, in 1922 he was chosen as secretary of the newly established Peyote Church on the Yankton Reservation. It is also significant to point out the conjunction of the family's memory of his beautiful handwriting and his actual grades in penmanship at Flandreau.[49]

Mary Chinn, Sam's future wife, attended Hope Indian School. From 1895 to 1902 it was attached to the Santee Agency as a government contract school. In 1902 it became a government boarding school for girls and was renamed Springfield Indian School. Mary was a student for four years while it was still Hope Indian School. This information about her schooling comes from an interview with her in 1960 by University of South Dakota researchers. The choice of Hope School was not just because of its nearby location but also because of its Episcopal heritage. The Chinn family, as well as the Necklaces, were Episcopalians, as were many Yanktons in the Chouteau Creek region. In 1870 band chief David Mad Bull II was baptized as an Episcopalian. Members of his band, including the Chinns and the

Necklaces, followed his lead. Holy Name Chapel was built for the new parishioners.

The Chinn family attended the new chapel, and many of them are buried in its cemetery. Mary grew up in a family of seven children. She had a very interesting birth order position as the third child between two sets of twins. She had twin brothers, George and Henry, who were four years older; twin sisters, Nancy and Lucy, who were five years younger; and a younger brother and sister, Felix and Jennie. The family was very proud having two sets of twins, for among the Lakotas, Dakotas, and Nakotas the birth of the twins is considered a blessing and a special gift from Wakan Tanka. Bishop Hare believed that schools like Hope would prove his theory that the "steady advancement" of Native Americans would occur after separation from their communities. The school, with a small enrollment of sixty to seventy students, combined academic and religious study with vocational training and daily work. Hare's schools were economically self-sufficient. Students were divided into work squads, such as the dormitory squad, outdoor squad, and table squad.[50] In spite of the school's efforts to Americanize the manners, values, and language of its students, Mary always remained a Yankton, both in her heart and in her daily life. She spoke English to outsiders, but until her death in 1963 she spoke Dakota at home. All her grandchildren attest to her Yankton ways and said she always spoke Dakota to them. The division of labor in the Necklace household was traditional, as was the value system. Mary's life is an example of the viewpoint that Native American women were essential keepers and transmitters of culture. She transmitted these values to her children and grandchildren. Mary eventually left the Episcopal Church for the Native American Church.

EVERYDAY LIFE ON THE RESERVATION

After the turn of the century the pace of the change accelerated. The Yankton political structure had been disassembled; economic life was getting worse and continuing a slide that would lead to widespread poverty by the 1920s. The land base was still shrinking, everyday life was in flux, and the future was uncertain. Language, clothing, housing, schooling, work, food, and religion were all changing. Native Americans were still reminded by government officials, educators, and missionaries that they must give up their culture for their own good. Sam Necklace was a product of this environment. He represented a new generation whose everyday life was an intense interaction of two worlds. Not all people were successful in coping with the new reality. There were the extremes of those who assimilated and, all too often, those who suffered from alcoholism. Yet there were many like Sam Necklace who took a middle path, who were able to function in both worlds, who adjusted to the harsh realities of the larger American society but were still able to maintain and pass on a strong ethnic identity. In the case of Sam Necklace it was an Ihanktonwan identity.

The acceleration of change was facilitated by a number of factors. The government played an increasingly intrusive role in everyday life. Missionaries and schools were more prolific. After 1895 American homesteaders were moving into land formerly owned by the Yanktons. Small, predominately white towns, such as Wagner, Ravinia, and Lake Andes, emerged within reservation boundaries. Roads and highways were now crisscrossing Yankton land. In 1900 the Chicago, Milwaukee and St. Paul Railroad built a track through the reservation. The railroad brought more non-Indians to the area. All these factors contributed to the patchwork pattern of Yankton land tenure. What was a single block of land according to the Treaty of 1858 was now a variegated network of landholdings, mixing tribal land, allotted land, leased land, land sold to non-Indians, and the small towns mentioned above. One could not conceive of a more complex pattern of land tenure.

It is difficult to ascertain which particular change had the greatest impact on Yankton life. Certainly the loss of land was devastating; but no one element was a dominant factor—it was the overall pattern of change. For example, language was changing. The older generation spoke Dakota as their everyday language, making interpreters necessary at public meetings. The younger generation, most of who were in school, used more and more English, which became the language of business, land transactions, and communication with the government and sometimes was a necessity for work. It was almost impossible not to allow language to change one's daily life. For instance, the customary way of recording time as "winter counts" gave way to years. The Gregorian calendar was now standard. The division of the year into "moons" now became months. *Wičatawi* or "raccoon moon" became February; *tahečapsun wi* or "moon when deer shed their horns" became December; *watsuton wi* or "moon of the ripening harvest" became August. With a new calendar and a new religion came new holidays and a changing structure of the week. The Sabbath was a day of rest, and church attendance became the norm. Many Yanktons celebrated Christmas, Easter, and Thanksgiving as well as the patriotic holidays of Memorial Day (called Decoration Day) and the Fourth of July. The BIA encouraged its agents in the field to push the Fourth of July as a major celebration on reservations.

As happened to Sam Necklace, names changed. Lakota, Dakota, and Nakota names were altered. Pressure to change one's name came from teachers, government officials, and missionaries. Native American names confused them and seemed an obstacle to assimilation. Throughout the entire Sioux nation, names and naming ceremonies were an essential ingredient of cultural identity. Children might be given a name just after their birth and another later in childhood. Sometimes it was a birth order name such as *časké* or *yamni* (first- or third-born male). Other names could be given later in life, representing physical, personal, or historic events. A name could reflect skill in hunting or warfare or a valued quality from the natural world. The use of animal names such as *četan, tatanka, mato, wanbdi, heȟaka* (hawk, buffalo, bear, eagle, elk) was common. They could be used in combination with other descriptive terms such as War Eagle, Walking Bear, Mad Bull, Iron Bear, Standing Elk, or Flying Bull. These were not surnames; everyone had one or more given names. Children did not take their father's name, and wives did not take their husband's name. The Necklace family included Mazanapin and his wife, Hintunkasanwin. That is how they are listed in the census. One typical way to change one's name was to translate the Dakota into English; thus Mazanapin becomes Iron Necklace and eventually Necklace. First names such as "Peter" or "Samuel" or surnames such as "Smith" or "Jones" could be assigned arbitrarily by school or government officials. These changes are evident as one reads through the annual census reports.

Marriages were now performed under U.S. law rather than customary law, so women took their husband's name on marriage certificates. At birth children were given their father's surname. The same types of pressure were applied to marriage ceremonies. Customary or traditional marriage ceremonies had no "legal" recognition. A couple might be accused of living in sin or given the ultimate threat that their children would not be their "legal" heirs after their death. The local government agents kept annual statistics on marriage "by tribal custom" or "by legal procedure." During the first decade of the twentieth century customary marriages virtually disappeared. The local agent reported that no "Indian custom" marriages were held on the Yankton Reservation.[51]

There were other changes. All Yanktons, not just children, were under pressure to give up traditional clothing. "Blanket Indian" emerged as a term of derision, to disparage Native Americans who still wore traditional attire. The BIA kept annual statistics on how many Native Americans "wear modern attire." Food also changed. Many traditional foods continued to be used but were supplemented with canned meats and vegetables and packaged staples such as flour and sugar. Commercial products now filled basic needs. There were also profound changes in education and religion. After the turn of the century most Yankton children were in government or missionary schools, which were powerful agents of change, as they combined academics, discipline, and work. The Episcopal and Presbyterian churches were also agents of change. To the missionaries, changing the local way of life was their holy mission. Each denomination had a church in Greenwood and smaller missions stationed throughout the reservation. In 1898 the missionaries reported that 1,140 Yanktons, out of a total 1,728, belonged to one of the denominations.[52] A year later Reverend Williamson gave a more detailed assessment: "The Yankton, who when I came here thirty years ago were all wearing long hair and the breech cloth and worshipers of idols, are now all clothed respectably in civilized costume, and a majority of them are members of one of the seven Christian churches situated among us."[53]

This type of ethnocentrism created another dilemma for many Yankton families. It concerned burials. With the arrival of Christian denominations came the denominational cemetery. During the 1860s and 1870s the aboveground scaffold graves gave way to below-ground burials. The last recorded use of a scaffold grave was in 1888.[54] The new cemeteries created a problem for families with individuals who belonged to different denominations. It actually worsened after the Catholic mission and cemetery was established. This meant that some Yanktons could not be buried alongside relatives, causing much turmoil and grief. Today there are members of the same family buried in different cemeteries, with their remains permanently separated by denominational differences. For example, Iron Necklace and his wife are in a Presbyterian cemetery, Peter Necklace and his wife are in an Episcopal cemetery, and Sam and Mary Necklace are in the Native American Church cemetery.

At the turn of the century earning a decent living on the reservation was virtually impossible. Some Yanktons were farming their allotments, but this was a difficult way to earn a meaningful livelihood. Corn was the principal crop, although oats, potatoes, cabbage, beets, tomatoes, and squash were also grown. Some people raised cattle, hogs, and chickens. Many families raised horses. In 1909 it was reported that the Yanktons owned 1,375 horses. The BIA was also active in promoting new agricultural techniques and the use of farm machinery. The government employed a "farmer" and an "assistant farmer" to carry out these tasks. They traveled from farm to farm or sometimes held general meetings with Yankton farmers. In addition to farming, some Yanktons worked for the many Anglo-American farmers in the area. Others worked for the agency government in construction or roadwork. These were not usually permanent jobs. Some men also trained and worked in government-run shops. One could train and work as a blacksmith, wheelwright, or tinsmith or in a sawmill or a harness and shoeing shop.[55] A few were employed as police officers, and some worked as missionaries or teachers. In spite of all this, there was considerable unemployment and underemployment.

In addition to the continued loss of land, many Yanktons leased allotted land to non-Indians as a way to acquire additional income. Leasing was not originally part of the allotment legislation; but in 1891 and again in 1894 Congress passed legislation to allow leasing to non-Indians. By 1901 there were 700 lease contracts in force on the Yankton Reservation, increasing to 850 in 1902. These contracts brought the lessors $16,000 per year.[56] This was not a significant amount of income on a per-capita or per-acre basis. Even when the leasing was administered with good intentions (and sometimes it was not), it seemed contradictory to the government policy of creating self-sufficient American Indian farmers. The government's encouraging of leasing meant that the Yanktons were not getting full use of their land. It was also a step toward the sale of additional land to non-Indians. For many Yanktons without capital for equipment, stock, or irrigation or without sufficient experience with farm equipment, however, farming was not a viable alternative. They would also be at a competitive disadvantage with non-Indians.[57]

The superintendent of the reservation controlled the approval of leasing contracts. This led to abuses. The lessor often had to have the right political connections or was sometimes charged a special fee to have a lease approved. One superintendent on the Yankton Reservation was approving leases that paid the lessors eight to ten cents per acre rather than the prevailing twenty-five cents. Historian Janet McDonnell has concluded: "Commissioners Sells and Burke adopted a liberal leasing policy that benefited whites more than Indians and discouraged Indian self-support. Their flawed policy was often poorly implemented by negligent or corrupt field service employees who were more concerned about the needs and desires of local whites than with protecting Indian landowners."[58]

After the turn of the century the Yankton government had been virtually abolished. In 1903 the superintendent declared that "Tribal government" was a thing of the past. The system of band chiefs and headmen had been replaced by a Board of Advisors and a Speaking Council. These groups had no real power and little voice. They were very pliable to the wishes of the superintendent. The same thing happened to Yankton culture. The Sun Dance had been outlawed, and government officials were very active in discouraging traditional dancing and giveaways. All traditional Yankton spiritual practices were officially discouraged. In fact the government officials, working in conjunction with the missionaries, were actually trying to stamp them out. Few Sacred Pipes were seen, and Sweat Lodges could only be found in remote areas of the reservation. What was left of the Yankton spiritual life was forced to go underground. In order to enforce reservation rules, a Court of Indian Offenses and an Indian police force were established during the 1880s. The three judges and the police officers were Yankton men who were appointed by the superintendent. They were required to enforce the rules and regulations of the BIA. The Yanktons did not welcome the Indian court or police force, who were resented for enforcing the "whiteman's rules."[59]

While young Sam Necklace was attending Flandreau Indian School, he spent his summers and vacation time on the reservation. With the building of railroad lines he could make part of the trip with relative ease. Sam spent considerable time with his half-brother, Amos, the son of Peter Necklace and another woman. Sam and Amos were always close. When Amos married Mary Sky in 1909, Sam witnessed and signed the marriage certificate as the best man. Amos had a son, Elmer, and three daughters, Delphine, Sun Beam, and Bernice. In spite of the high death rate, there were many aunts, uncles, cousins, and other relatives. The kinship network had not been weakened by recent changes despite the dispersal of the villages. Then, as now, the Necklace family was quite extensive. Sam's grandparents were still living. Mazanapin and Hintunkansawin, listed as eighty-six and eighty-three years old in 1900, were the oldest Yanktons on the reservation.[60] Sam was reared within this kinship network and spent the rest of his life in such an environment. It is not clear who had an influence on young Sam. His father had two older brothers, Foot Necklace and Feather Necklace or "Tasihanapin" and "Wiya-hanapin" in the Yankton census of 1892.

Peter's oldest brother, Foot, is remembered by the family as a medicine man. According to Sam's grandson Asa:

> There's another, I think that's their [Sam and siblings] uncle, that's the one I was telling you about, I just heard about it a little bit; he's blind and I don't know how long he was blind. We used to have a picture too, he used to wear a headband, he's a medicine man, he's a Necklace, he's a healer. I remember seeing him, blind, never wears nothing, his eyes are all closed shut, he never wears glasses. . . . He walks like if he was here. He'll find his way around, just like he's not blind. But that power that he had, it guides him. I was thinking about that, like at your house. I just sit back, my eyes just kind of close by themselves. I can hear these guys talking. I can see how everybody's sitting, it goes through my mind. And when I get up, to move, I just stay like that. I have to kind of blink and then I can open and I see where I'm going.[61]

Sam also told Asa that his father, Peter, took him to a Sweat Lodge at his uncle's place. This is where Sam may have had some early spiritual experiences. There is no additional information concerning Foot Necklace's life except that he and his wife, Wicahipiojanjanwin (Bright Star Woman), always went by their Dakota names in the census. This might indicate that they did not join a Christian denomination. Sam's father was also a member of the Monument Society that was founded in 1905. The society was formed to commemorate the fiftieth anniversary of the Treaty of 1858. The Monument Society had political overtones. Some of its members served on the tribal council. They represented the element of Yankton society that supported accommodation with the U.S. government; thus they honored the controversial treaty. A twenty-acre lot outside of Greenwood was surveyed and designated as a park and site for the monument. The society had an eighteen-foot obelisk monument placed on a hill overlooking the Missouri River, inscribed: "In Memory of the Yankton Chiefs, Who Made the Treaty of 1858." Eighteen names are listed, starting with Chief Struck by the Ree. Also inscribed on the monument are the names of the tribal counselors who were responsible for the monument, listed as "The Tribal Counselors Who Kept the Peace and Saw That the Agreements of the Fifty Year Treaty Were All Fulfilled." Peter Necklace's Dakota name, Iron Necklace, is one of the fourteen names. At the commemoration of the monument the members of the society had their photographs taken standing alongside it.[62]

Young Sam also became involved in local politics, although he was not involved with his father in the Monument Society. In 1902 Sam signed a petition asking the commissioner of Indian Affairs to stop "homestead filings" for Yankton land by non-Indians. The land in question involved canceled allotments. Some of the cancellations came about when fraudulent or erroneous allotments were uncovered. The petitioners claimed that such land belonged to the tribe and should not be sold to homesteaders, as the government was doing. Thomas Ryan, acting secretary of the Department of the Interior, rejected the petition and argued that the government had the right to dispose of the land as it saw fit.[63] It would be interesting to know Sam's reaction to the rejection of the petition. He had studied American history and government and was now petitioning to redress a grievance. This might have been the beginning of his discouragement with politics. Although there were times in his life when he became involved in political issues, his deepest commitment was to the spiritual life. It must be said, however, that involvement in the Peyote religion in the early twentieth century was a political act that was not inconsequential.

During Sam's school years, especially after 1900, he lived independently when back on the reservation on his own allotment (Allotment No. 139), not far from his mother and father (Allotment No. 136). According to the Yankton census of this period he was listed as living in a separate household except for 1902, when he is listed as living with his parents. The annual Yankton census lists people by household; therefore it is not difficult to trace household structures. Like many young men at this time, Sam was by necessity on his own economically. He was probably working while attending Flandreau. Full-time work on the reservation was rare, but he did earn some seasonal income by working for local white farmers near Chouteau Creek. He was also able to take advantage of his education. He could write Dakota and English and of course was bilingual. He was not employed as an official interpreter, but he did interpreting for individuals and groups. He wrote letters for people, read and explained documents, and invariably was asked to serve as secretary for various groups and committees.

These were difficult years for Sam not only because of the general uncertainty of the future but due to his own problems as a maturing young adult. His family claims that he was somewhat of a "hell-raiser," especially when it came to alcohol. Sam described some of this to his grandson Asa. He was on his own in Flandreau and was more or less on his own on the reservation. He ran with other young men who were going through similar difficulties. Sam also had trouble with his parents. Somewhere around 1903 or 1904 he became romantically involved with a white woman who lived near the eastern side of the reservation. The situation became more complicated when the white woman became pregnant about the same time that Sam began seeing Mary, his future wife. Sam ended up with a daughter, Frances, and he and Mary ran off and got married. In spite of this difficult beginning for their marriage, Mary and Sam had a long and fruitful life together. They were symbolic of a new generation that was emerging. Mazanapin, the family elder, passed away in 1905 at the age of ninety-one. He represented the generation that grew up before the move to the reservation in 1859. Chief Feather in His Ear and White Medicine Cow had died in 1901; and although people like Chief Blue Cloud (d. 1918) and Grandma White Tallow (d. 1943, age 100) lived on, the future now belonged to the people of Sam and Mary's generation. Meanwhile the Peyote religion had already been established in the southern Plains among the Kiowas, Comanches, Apaches, Caddos, Cheyennes, and Arapahos and was now spending northward into the central and northern Plains. Eventually it would penetrate many other American Indian groups, including the Yanktons.

CHAPTER FOUR

The Peyote Religion

YEARS OF STRUGGLE, 1906–22

Peyote gourd rattle. Drawn by Asa Primeaux, Jr.,
great-grandson of Sam Necklace.

Sam and Mary married during the early years of the expansion of Peyotism. They set up their household on an allotment located on the eastern side of the reservation about one mile north of the Missouri River halfway between Greenwood and Chouteau Creek. Sam's daughter Frances remained with them and became part of a growing family. Ben was born in 1907, Daniel in 1911, and Jennie in 1913. Like many younger couples, they lived in an "issued-house." The BIA issued these houses to some of the allottees. They were prefabricated and simple to erect, containing only two rooms and a wood/coal-burning stove. Poor construction made them virtually unlivable in the frigid winters.[1] Sometime in the late 1910s or early 1920s Sam and Mary built a one-story wooden frame house on a foundation of field stone and cement, with a huge red brick chimney on the west side. The entrance faced south, and the door opened onto two cement steps. Near the house was a small chokecherry orchard and a garden that Mary tended. They had an outhouse and small barn for Sam's horses. No one knows why Sam and Mary always painted it pink. Even today the family calls it "the pink house." Except for several years living in the city of Yankton, South Dakota, Mary and Sam lived in the pink house until Sam died in 1949. Mary occupied the house intermittently until she died in 1963. After her death the house was torn down; and the lumber was used by Auntie Pauline to build a barn and a chicken coop. Parts of the foundation, the cement steps, and the red brick chimney lying on the ground are the only remains today.

Sam loved horses. He used them not only for work and transportation but also for recreation. He had a horse-drawn wagon that he used to haul supplies and to carry water from the Missouri River to the pink house. The horse, with saddle or wagon, was the basic means of transportation on the reservation. Regular trips to Greenwood were necessary in order to pick up supplies as well as to visit Trader's Store with its large wood-burning stove and listen to the reservation gossip or join the endless debates on local politics. This particular store sold everything from staples to luxury items. Ella C. Deloria describes the store as having an aroma of "harness leather, cheese, spices, tobacco, wood smoke, and a thousand others."[2] Other businesses in Greenwood included a barbershop, livery stable, hotel, restaurant, sawmill, wagon shop, and blacksmith shop as well as the agency headquarters, post office, police station, warehouses, churches, schools, water storage tank, and a large flagpole that always flew the American flag. Greenwood was a thriving little community with frequent visitors. Steamboats going up and down the Missouri River stopped there regularly. There was a landing dock near the hotel and also a ferry service across the river to Nebraska. (The ferry was discontinued about 1925.) Almost everyone on the reservation spent time in Greenwood, especially the young men like Sam, who rode their horses to town in order to hangout with their buddies in and around the local stores.

Aside from their usefulness for transportation and hauling, the horses were used extensively for recreation. Horse racing had always been a joy for American Indian people living on the Plains. Many young men, including Sam Necklace, spent considerable time training and caring for their horses. Sam loved to race horses.[3] In fact gambling on the races was not unusual. Much of the racing took place along the river just east of Greenwood, the site of the later agricultural fairs. Horses were important in another way. They were essential in helping to maintain the social and kinship network or tiošpaye. Prior to the 1890s the tiošpaye occupied a village, but now housing was scattered. The horse was needed to visit family and friends, to attend special occasions such as birthdays, namings, and funerals, or to attend spiritual activities. Later, when the Native American Church was established, horses were essential for people to travel to Peyote services.

Sam regularly visited his half-brother, Amos, who lived about three miles east of the pink house in a somewhat remote area. He had a Sweat Lodge behind his house that could not be seen from the road. Reservation officials frowned on Sweat Lodges. Sam went there to take in "sweats." Years later he would take his grandson Asa to them. Asa said:

> I must have been nine or ten years old, my grandpa took me out east; that's where one of his brothers lived . . . he's the one that had them horses, he's the one that runs the Sweat Lodge. And that's where my grandpa used to go to the Sweat Lodge, he used to start up the fire, keep it going, but he never had one on his land. That's real funny how that happened, my grandpa never had a sweat lodge at his house, but he goes to his brother's all the time.[4]

Amos's deserted house is still standing, silhouetted against rolling hills. It is an empty frame of fieldstone with a wood-shingled roof. Nearby is a small windmill and a large watering trough for horses. Even as chief priest in the Native American Church, Sam continued to participate in Sweat Lodge ceremonies. He saw no contradictions in this and would have argued that the sacred origins of both derived from Wakan Tanka.

Mary and Sam ran their household according to the traditional Sioux division of labor. Mary did the gardening, raised chickens, canned fruits and vegetables, and collected wild fruits and vegetables such as turnips, chokecherries, and onions. The turnips were braided and hung in the kitchen to dry along with ears of corn and slices of squash and pumpkin. The kitchen always smelled of cooking. Virtually every day a large pot of soup or stew would be on the stove. Mary had the responsibility for the children, although by age eight or nine the boys began to spend more time with their father. A large part of everyday life was collecting firewood. It was used for cooking and was used in the winter for heat, along with coal. Obtaining supplies of coal required a trip to Greenwood with the horse and buggy. Having a sufficient supply of coal and wood required endless work, especially with winter temperatures near zero. Sam did the heavy gardening, such as the plowing. He cared for the horses and maintained the house in good repair. He also kept the family supplied with fish from the Missouri River, as well as providing the family with fresh water. Sam's grandson Asa remembers taking many trips to the river with the horse and buggy in order to fill large wooden barrels with water. Upon occasion Sam earned a few dollars working as a day laborer for Anglo-American farmers in the area.

Sam was also involved in Yankton politics, although not to any significant extent until the 1930s. It was typical for boarding-school returnees to become involved, but Sam was also following his father's footsteps. His father, who originally went by the name "Peter Iron Necklace" or sometimes just "Iron Necklace," did not play a significant role in Yankton politics; but he did serve for a time on the Yankton Tribal Council. Sam's first involvement was to serve as secretary for various committees of the tribal council. The public issues that most affected the Yanktons a decade or more into the twentieth century concerned allotments and enrollments. There were questions, debates, and petitions about fraudulent allotments; who deserved an allotment but did not receive one; who was left off the tribal enrollment list and who deserved to be added. In 1908 Samuel Baker Necklace is listed as secretary of an enrollment committee. His father was also a member of the committee. This committee appointed by the tribal council was investigating individual requests for enrollment. Testimony was given, minutes were kept, a vote was taken, and the results were sent to the commission of Indian Affairs. In this case the committee rejected the claimant's request, although the BIA held final authority in such matters.[5] Another example of such activity is a petition that the Yanktons sent to the BIA, asking that deserving but unallocated children be allocated cash in lieu of land. Both Sam and his father signed this petition. The BIA rejected it.[6] Some cases seemed to drag on for years. Decisions were appealed, requiring more debate, more correspondence, and more rejections.

Early in the century Yankton politics was divisive, and factionalism was rife. There were competing groups, conflicting interests, and endless debates over who represented the Yanktons. For example, in January 1910 two delegations left for Washington in order to meet with BIA officials concerning allotments, sale of land, enrollments, and the Pipestone Quarry. Both claimed to be the official delegation. The head of the Yankton Agency wired the commissioner that the "Yankton Indians in Washington went as individuals and have no authority from the tribe."[7] Nevertheless Commissioner Robert Valentine accepted them as an official delegation. The Tribal Council then changed the delegation by dropping five members and adding five more. The commissioner recognized them as the official delegation, only to receive the following from agent E. W. Estep: "[T]he delegation authorized by you has been wrecked on the Rocks of Discord." He then explained that there were two factions: one determined to go to Washington, the other not.[8] The issue still was not settled. The commissioner received a petition from fourteen Yanktons (including Sam's father, Peter) that protested the "so-called delegation" and opposed its expenses being paid out of tribal funds.[9]

This confusion and divisiveness as well as the indecisiveness was not surprising. In the attempts to impose social policies on the reservation, the BIA only wanted certain types of Yanktons elected to the Tribal Council or, as it was called by 1912, the Committee of Twelve. Superintendent Adelebert Leech received a directive to avoid having the tribal council take any action when "non-progressive Indians" were serving. The directive added that the Indians should be advised that the office of the BIA wanted them to overcome their factional differences and elect a body of "progressive councilmen who will represent the entire tribe and will lead their people in making progress along the lines of civilization."[10] Superintendent Leech attempted to manipulate the Yanktons by exploiting the factionalism in order to advance BIA policy. Leech tried to assemble the Yanktons for a vote. Many refused to attend, but the election proceeded anyway. There were only fifty voters present, who elected a "committee of twelve." Leech then complained that they were some of the old and "non-progressive" types.[11] In actuality the Yanktons were not allowed any significant degree of self-government—nor was any intended.

These machinations of the BIA were successful because of a deeper division within Yankton society. There were conflicts between the "full-bloods" and the "half-breeds." This division was already a generation old and getting worse. In an interview in the 1960s, elder Paul Picotte recalled that "in the early days, way back in '99, they the full-bloods kind of block together and they don't want to associate with the mixed-bloods."[12] These commonly used terms, "full-blood" and "half-breed," were sometimes descriptive but more often they were pejorative. The so-called half-breeds were obviously the result of a growing number of mixed marriages. They were also younger, with boarding-school or day-school education, mostly Christian, spoke English, and to a certain degree bought into much of the BIA's social and cultural agenda. They were increasing in numbers and were gaining more and more influence in tribal politics. The full-bloods tended to be older, more traditional, still spoke Dakota among themselves, and were labeled "non-progressives" by the BIA. Their numbers and influence had been in decline for decades. Sam Necklace did not clearly fit into either category. He was a "full-blood," with a traditional upbringing and a boarding-school education. Sam did not follow some other boarding-school students into Christianity and Anglo-American cultural norms. He turned to the Peyote religion for his spiritual sustenance and to the Peyote community for social needs.

The real source of divisiveness and factionalism among the Yanktons was their powerlessness. They were a colonized people, some of whom who had internalized the values of the conqueror. They had no real power, few options, and no recourse against BIA policy. They could petition, demonstrate, and complain, but no one would listen. In the second decade of the twentieth century they were faced with increasing poverty and a continued loss of land. They were in a dominant/subordinate relationship with the United States government, so they battled each other.

Through the 1910s and early 1920s the Yankton loss of land had reached alarming proportions. This was occurring on most reservations throughout the West. For the Yanktons the loss of land came primarily through the sale of allotted land. They had already lost all unallotted land in the Agreement of 1892. After the turn of the century government policy began to change in regard to its trust responsibility toward Native American land. In May 1902 Congress authorized the BIA to allow Native Americans to sell allotted land that had been inherited. Now the door was open for the widespread loss of Indian land.[13] The Burke Act followed in 1906. Charles Burke, a congressman from South Dakota and future commissioner of Indian Affairs, proposed that Native American allottees who were considered "competent" should be given title to their land. So-called competent American Indians would be granted a fee patent (or patent in fee), which gave them outright ownership of the land. This ended federal responsibility for that land. The superintendents in charge of the reservations were given the power to determine the "competency" of individual Indians.[14]

Part of the problem was that Franklin K. Lane, secretary of the interior, was under intense pressure from non-Indians who wanted access to more and more land. In a very short time many of the Native Americans who received fee patents lost their land. Money from the sale of the land did not last long, and eventually many of the Yanktons were not only landless but also penniless. The more or less indiscriminate issuance of fee patents by the superintendents had disastrous effects.[15] In the year following the passage of the Burke Act, fifty-seven parcels of Yankton land were approved for fee patents. In addition the superintendent approved the sale of 157 tracts of land totaling 13,200 acres. In 1908, 104 fee patents were issued for 9,558 acres.[16] The land was disappearing quickly. In 1909 the superintendent reported that "practically two-thirds of the land originally allotted to the Yankton Sioux has passed from their hands into that of white settlers." The

Yanktons had only 86,907 acres left out of the original total allotment of 268,263 acres. By 1911, 197 fee patents had been issued.[17] The entire process took a terrible toll. In 1913 Superintendent Leech reported that only 135 Yanktons were farming for themselves. A year later he reported that 75 percent of the Yanktons who had received fee patents had sold their land.[18]

Most of the members of the Necklace family did not sell their land but leased it to white farmers in the area. Sometime before 1913 Sam Necklace filled out an application for a fee patent. The superintendent declared him "competent" and granted it to him. Rather than sell his land, Sam decided to lease some of it. The income from leased land varied by location and suitability for farming or grazing. Most leases provided cash payments, but Sam had at least one agreement in which he leased 40 acres for two years for one-third of the crop. His father, Peter, leased 160 acres for one year for $365. His uncle Foot Necklace leased 40 acres of grazing land for only $20. Sam's deceased grandfather's land, 120 acres, was leased for $285 per year. Sam's friend Charlie Jones leased 80 acres for $160.[19] This was not a significant amount of money. With such low prices for leasing, some Yanktons concluded it was best to sell their land.

The wholesale issuance of fee patents and the rapid disposition of that land led to much concern in Washington, especially among government officials and reformers who had supported the assumptions of the Dawes Act that American Indian land would develop into America-style family farms. This clearly was not happening. The indiscriminate issuance of fee patents and the subsequent loss of land led to the establishment of Competency Commissions. The commissions were the brainchild of Franklin Lane, secretary of the interior, and Cato Sells, commissioner of Indian Affairs. The supposed purpose of the Competency Commissions was to stop the indiscriminate issuance of fee patents. In 1915–16 three commissions were established. Their charge was to investigate individual American Indians in order to determine if they were "competent" enough to handle their own affairs. The commissions traveled from reservation to reservation, assessing the "competence" of individuals and recommending or denying the issuance of a fee patent.[20] This policy became counterproductive. The stated goal was self-support and independence for American Indians. The reality was increasing dispossession of reservation land, dependency, and poverty. In actuality Secretary Lane and Commissioner Sells increased the issuance of fee patents. As historian Francis Prucha states, they "pursued the termination principle with a vengeance."

What was to be a systematic evaluation of "competence" through the Competency Commissions became a further tool to alienate reservation land.[21]

During January and February 1916 a Competency Commission visited the Yankton Reservation. It met with 439 Yanktons and secured 180 applications for fee patents.[22] The commission not only recommended the issuance of fee patents but also delivered the documents to the recipients. The Yanktons soon learned that they would be "honored" by a visit from the secretary of the interior. Secretary Lane used this opportunity to create a public relations event by traveling from reservation to reservation, issuing the documents and conferring citizenship himself with elaborate pomp and ceremony and considerable theatrics. He chose Greenwood, the Yankton Agency headquarters, for the first such public ceremony. It began at 9:00 a.m. on 13 May 1916. Approximately 2,000 people, including a motion picture company and newspaper reporters, attended the event. The ceremony took place in front of agency headquarters, where a tipi had been erected adjacent to the speaker's platform.[23]

The ceremony itself represented the culmination of the assimilation policy pursued by the United States government. Secretary Lane declared that he was personally sent by President Woodrow Wilson "to speak a solemn and serious word to you, a word that means more to you than any other you have ever heard," concerning the "privilege of becoming free American citizens."[24] With this introduction Lane began a public ritual that was symbolic of the ultimate purpose of the assimilation policy: the total elimination of Native American culture. In this context it is important to quote the entire ceremony as written by Lane:

> The Secretary stands before one of the candidates and says: —-
> "Joseph T. Cook, what was your Indian name?"
> "Tunkansapa," answers the Indian.
> "Tunkansapa, I hand you a bow and arrow. Take this bow and shoot the arrow."
> The Indian does so.
> "Tunkansapa, you have shot your last arrow. That means you are no longer to live the life of an Indian. You are from this day forward to live the life of the white man. But you may keep that arrow. It will be to you a symbol of your noble race and of the pride you may feel that you come from the first of all Americans."

Addressing Tunkansapa by his white name.

"Joseph T. Cook, take in your hands this plough." Cook does so. "This act means that you have chosen to live the life of the white man. The white man lives by work. From the earth we must all get our living, and the earth will not yield unless man pours upon it the sweat of his brow.

"Joseph T. Cook, I give you a purse. It will always say to you that the money you gain must be wisely kept. The wise man saves his money, so that when the sun does not smile and the grass does not grow he will not starve."

The Secretary now takes up the American flag. He and the Indian hold it together.

"I give into your hands the flag of your country. This is the only flag you ever will have. It is the flag of free men, the flag of a hundred million free men and women, of whom you are now one. That flag has a request to make of you, Joseph T. Cook, that you repeat these words."

Cook then repeats the following after the Secretary.

"Forasmuch as the President has said that I am worthy to be a citizen of the United States, I now promise this flag that I will give my hands, my head, and my heart to the doing of all that will make me a true American citizen."

The Secretary then takes a badge upon which is the American eagle, with the national colors, and, pinning it upon the Indian's breast, speaks as follows: ——

"And now, beneath this flag, I place upon your breast the emblem of citizenship. Wear this badge always, and may the eagle that is on it never see you do aught of which the flag will not be proud."[25]

This ceremony was repeated for each one of approximately 150 Yankton men and women. At its conclusion the audience supposedly shouted its greeting to the new citizens, hailing them by their "white name."[26] In this public setting, Secretary Lane used ritual and symbolism with a sober ceremony and a very officious demeanor; however, in his private correspondence he reveals a cynicism and contempt for Native Americans. Several days after the ceremony he wrote, "I am back from a trip to South Dakota, where I, by ritual, a copy of which is inclosed [sic] for your perusal, made citizens out of a bunch of Indians who never can become hyphenates."[27] This was an insult, meaning that they would always be "Indians" and could not become Americans.

In spite of the interest and attention paid to the Yanktons, the policy was a dismal failure. By the time Lane arrived in Greenwood, most of the Yanktons who were to receive fee patents had already made plans to sell their land. One report said that the reservation had been invaded by "land buyers, automobile agents and fakers of all kinds [who] were busy almost day and night."[28] So-called land sharks either bullied or tricked people into selling or mortgaging their land. For many of the Yanktons their longstanding poverty and their dearth of material possessions made them susceptible to such con artists and bootleggers, who were in every town on the reservation.[29] The land was a resource; but after years of deprivation the sale of the land provided temporary relief from poverty. In 1919, out of 1,927 Yanktons living on the reservation, 772 had received allotments of land, and 562 of those who had received fee patents had already sold their land. There were only 210 Yanktons left with their own land. After 1920 the government abolished the Competency Commissions and slowed the process of issuing fee patents. For the Yanktons, however, it was too late. Most of the land had already been lost. During the 1920s the Yanktons suffered their own depression, experiencing poverty and dependency as a result of joblessness, poor housing, and poor health.[30]

EMERGENCE OF THE PEYOTE RELIGION

Amidst the turmoil caused by the loss of land, the rapid change in everyday life, as well as the continuing political divisiveness and powerlessness of the Yankton people, the Peyote religion became established on the reservation. The first recorded government acknowledgment of its presence came from Walter Runke (who mistakenly refers to Peyote as mescal), superintendent of the Yankton Agency. In 1911 he sent the following to William "Pussyfoot" Johnson, chief special officer for the suppression of liquor traffic on reservations.

> A number of Indians of this reservation have recently taken it upon themselves to introduce the use of . . . [Peyote] among the people of this agency. In the past, the Indians here have been practically free from the use of this drug. . . . I am putting forth all possible effort to prevent the use thereof by the Indians under the jurisdiction of this Agency. It will be much easier at this time to prevent the introduction and general use of . . . [Peyote] on this reservation than it will be later to stamp out its use. I have taken drastic measures with the ringleaders of our new so-called Mescal [Peyote] Society and have them now lodged in the Agency jails.[31]

In Runke's Annual Report for 1911 he gave more details:

During the year one sporadic attempt was made by a number of Indians of this tribe to introduce the use of the Mescal bean and peyotes among the tribe, without success. It was found necessary to take some drastic action in breaking up these attempts and meetings called by the members of the cult. By use of the agency police the three Indians at the head of the new organization were lodged in the agency jail and assigned to a two-week task of labor with free board and lodging. This resulted in making membership in the "bean eaters" association very unpopular and no further trouble has since been experienced in suppressing the use of mescal or peyotes.[32]

Runke's optimism about suppressing the Peyote religion was premature.

This report indicates that Peyote had recently been introduced onto the reservation or at least that it had recently come to the attention of Runke. The exact date for the introduction of Peyote is difficult to determine but was probably between 1904 and 1910. There are several versions of how Peyote was introduced to the reservation, but all versions agree that it was Charlie Jones, a Yankton full-blood, who introduced it. Jones, born in 1865, had been a member of the reservation police. He was sworn in at the rank of private on 7 April 1900. By November he had been fired for "incompetency."[33] In 1912, the year after the Runke report, Jones gave Adelebert Leech, the new superintendent, information on the Peyote religion as a result of pressure from Leech. The new superintendent learned that Charlie Jones and others were holding Peyote meetings at the home of Charles Medicinehorn. Leech reported that "they were locked up again, until such time as they are willing to come into this office here and sign a statement to the effect that they will quit the use of Peyote and its attendant practices." Leech also confiscated the Peyote, a drum made from an iron kettle, some feathers, and a rod with symbols on it.[34]

Jones signed the statement. He also gave Leech additional information, saying that four years earlier, in 1908, Albert Hensley, a Winnebago, had introduced him to Peyote. Jones claimed that he had spent two years with the Winnebagos in Nebraska, where he attended a Peyote meeting every Saturday night. After he returned home, other Yanktons joined him in Peyote meetings. He listed the following participants: his wife and daughter, Charles Medicinehorn, Albert Blaine, Frank Felix, Louie St. Pierre and family, Louis Shunk, Kezocin, James Blaine, Towadankinyan, Robert Medicinehorn, and Adam Grimes, a non-Indian lawyer from Wagner, South Dakota. Jones added: "They met on Saturday night at Charlie Medicinehorns [*sic*] place, sing Indian songs, and prayed to the Great Spirit. They have a drum and several rattles, a bunch of feathers, and some other paraphernalia. . . . They eat the peyote and beat the drum and shake the rattles, and keep this up all night and sometimes the next day."[35] It is obvious from his statement that by this time the issue was not the Peyote buttons but the full Peyote religious ceremony. All the essential elements of the Peyote religion were in place. Also, all the names given by Jones (except for Adam Grimes) are listed on the Yankton census for this period.

Leech's incarceration of the Peyote people was a bit precipitous. In March 1912 he was told by the BIA: "The mere fact of holding such meetings or the use of peyote or mescal cannot be considered an offense . . . and if Jones is at present imprisoned he shall be released at once."[36] The fact that the Peyote was not illegal did not deter reservation officials from attempting to suppress it. In the 1913 Annual Report, Leech admits that Peyote usage has been revived and says he will continue a policy of harassment and confiscation: "the use of mescal or peyote has revived to some extent but after bringing the parties into the agency and confiscating the supply of peyote, I believe the practice has been stamped out."[37] This pattern of suppression continued throughout the decade.

In 1914 S. A. M. Young, the superintendent of Indian schools on the Yankton Reservation, wrote to the BIA that the use of "mescal or Peyote" was increasing on the reservation. He encouraged the BIA to find a legal means to punish these men, because not punishing them would have a bad effect on reservation discipline and make the Peyote people more brazen. Again, the reply was that the Yanktons could not be locked up but that "legislation is under consideration dealing with peyote."[38] Threats and arbitrary arrests did not restrain the Peyote community on the Yankton Reservation, so Superintendent Leech lobbied Washington to give him the power to eliminate Peyote by labeling it a narcotic, the same as morphine or opium. Another strategy was to have medical authorities attack Peyote usage. Dr. David A. Richardson, the BIA physician on the Yankton Reservation, reported many horrors associated with Peyote. He wrote that it "undermines health" and had caused "several sudden deaths," including children. He denied that Peyote cured alcoholism by saying that "every peyote fiend uses alcohol" and added that Peyote meetings were nothing but orgies.[39] Ironically, drug companies such as Parke, Davis and Company sold Peyote until the 1920s because of its alleged therapeutic uses.

The Necklace family has a slightly different version of events. They agree that it was Charlie Jones who first introduced Peyote to the Yanktons. Sam's grandson Asa says that his grandpa told him that Jones was having marital difficulties and went to live in Oklahoma for several years. It was in Oklahoma that he began to participate in Peyote meetings, not on the Winnebago Reservation. Asa said that his grandpa went to Oklahoma to visit his friend Charlie. Then in approximately 1904 Jones returned with Peyote. He was now a roadman and a teacher. There is no dispute about this. Everyone describes Charlie Jones as the teacher. He even described himself that way in a written report to reservation officials: "I am the teacher."[40] Almost all of what is known about Sam Necklace's early involvement comes from his grandson Asa. As mentioned earlier, Asa was reared by his grandparents. In Native American cultures there is a special relationship between grandparents and grandchildren, and this was certainly the case with Grandpa Sam and his grandson. Asa not only grew up as an active participant in the Native American Church but also heard about the history of the Peyote religion. It is in this context that Asa learned about his grandpa's early years. Asa said that his grandpa told him that it was Jones who taught him everything he knew about the Peyote religion and that it was Jones who taught him how to drum, how to tie the drum, and how to sing Peyote songs.[41]

This version of events is supported by Pauline Necklace Kezena (1916–96) or Auntie Pauline, as everyone called her, the last surviving member of the Necklace family from the generation that followed her uncle Sam. She was the daughter of Sam's younger sister Julia Ree and lived her entire life on the Yankton Reservation. In an interview held independently of the interview with Sam's grandson Asa, Auntie Pauline confirmed that Charlie Jones was having marital problems. She added that his wife ran off with one of Charlie's nephews. Feeling embarrassed and ashamed, he left for Oklahoma. It was there that he first came in contact with Peyote. Pauline also confirmed Sam's trip to Oklahoma to visit Jones and that her uncle Sam was first introduced to Peyote in Oklahoma. She added that Jones did return to the Yankton Reservation and taught the people about Peyote and that eventually her uncle Sam followed in his footsteps and began running meetings himself. The meetings were held in secret, with all the windows well covered. They feared arrest for using "drugs." Pauline said that her uncle Sam was not one of the people arrested. One of her most vivid memories was receiving a package in the mail. Even though it was addressed to her uncle, she opened it and hollered, "Look what I got." She thought it was a box of walnuts, but it was a box of dried Peyote buttons delivered by the U.S. Postal Service.[42]

A third family source is Eunice Rainbow Dog Soldier (1912–94). She was related to the Necklace family and Asa through marriage. She had been an active member of the Native American Church since the late 1920s and regularly attended Peyote meetings when Sam was the roadman. Auntie Eunice said that Charlie Jones was one of her uncles and that he did go to Oklahoma and brought back Peyote.[43] Clarence Rockboy offered a different version of these events. Clarence is a Yankton and has been a member of the Native American Church for more than fifty years. He is the son of Joe Rockboy (1903–82) a well-known roadman and singer. Clarence mentioned both versions, saying that Jones did go to Oklahoma to live among the Pawnees but that Peyote came to the Yanktons by way of the Winnebagos. Rockboy said that Jones also spent time on the Winnebago Reservation and was introduced to Peyote by Albert Hensley and John Rave.[44] (Since the mid-1990s the Winnebagos of Wisconsin have been referring to themselves by their traditional name, "Ho-Chunk.") Joe Shields, Sr., a long time Yankton roadman, also supported Rockboy's claim that Peyote came to the Yanktons by way of the Winnebagos. In 1976 seven Yankton Peyotists, including Sam's grandson Asa, recorded Peyote songs for the Indian House label. Joe Shields was interviewed at the recording session, and his verbatim comments are included with the record and the cassette. Shields said that Charlie Jones was the first person to bring Peyote to the Yanktons and that he brought it directly from the Winnebagos: "You might say that he [Charlie Jones] was the founder of this peyote, as far as the Yankton people were concerned. At that time, the agents or officials outlawed this peyote, but he was determined, because it was good, to show his people, and to teach his people about this religion. Pretty soon a few of his relatives got started using this medicine [Peyote]."[45]

Louie Stricker (1898–1974), a lifelong member of the Yankton Native American Church, gave a similar version of early events. In a 1972 interview he credited Jones and the Winnebagos for the introduction of Peyotism. Stricker, a longtime friend of Jones, said Jones introduced Peyote in 1910. He confirmed Jones's personal problems on the reservation and his subsequent stay in Nebraska. Stricker added that Jones met some Peyote people and began to attend their religious services. He accepted Peyotism and returned home to teach the Yanktons the Cross Fire way. Stricker did not mention Oklahoma.[46]

There is additional testimony by Jones. In 1916 Superintendent Leech interviewed him as part of a report on Peyote usage. A verbatim transcript of the interview, in a question and answer format, is part of the report. Jones does confirm that he was introduced to Peyote on the Winnebago Reservation in Nebraska. He does not mention Oklahoma but does confirm that marital problems caused him to leave the reservation and that he did have a problem with alcohol. In a very typical Peyote conversion testimony, Jones says that he went to a Peyote meeting and, after ingesting Peyote, "I prayed to God for what I did to repent my sins." He added that he stopped drinking after he began taking Peyote. On questions concerning his leadership and his first involvement with Peyote, he answered:

Q. You are the leader of peyote on this Reservation?
A. I guess so, I am the man that ate peyote first.
Q. When did you first use peyote, Charles?
A. About 12 years ago, when I first began to use it.

After leaving the Winnebagos he returned home and began teaching the Peyote way. In response to a question about how many Yanktons were Peyotists, he said "about 100" and added that important participants included Joshua Pretty Bull, Henry Blaine, Charles Iron Hawk, and Johnson Goodhouse.[47]

In spite of the Necklace version of an Oklahoma origin for Yankton Peyotism, we cannot ignore Jones's own 1916 testimony of the Winnebago origin and his crediting Albert Hensley with his introduction to Peyote. Based on all the existing evidence, Jones was certainly the link between the Winnebago Peyotism and the Yanktons. Jones may have been in Oklahoma with the Pawnees at a later date and was probably then visited by Sam Necklace. The confusion in the memory of the Necklace family is that Sam did visit Oklahoma in 1916. It was probably at this later date that Jones brought back Peyote from Oklahoma, but this was after it had been introduced from the Winnebagos. In attempting to ascertain an accurate date for the introduction of Peyote, the Yankton census is of little help. It does not corroborate or refute any of the above assertions, including Jones's absence from the reservation. From 1890 to 1922 (1908 and 1912 are missing) he is listed in the census as part of a household with his wife, Adelia, and their children. There is no direct evidence that he was or was not with his wife or that he left the reservation for an extended period. Thus we may never know the exact date.

We do know, however, that the government acknowledged its presence in 1911, and one oral source claims 1904.[48] Charlie Jones gave several dates. In his 1912 statement he said it was 1908; however, in his 1916 statement he said he first tried Peyote "about 12 years ago." Thus the date is very likely somewhere between 1904 and 1910.

This also fits with the known use of Peyote among the Winnebagos at this time. In 1905 the superintendent on the Winnebago Reservation warned the commissioner of Indian Affairs of its widespread use.[49] This also began a continual flow of Peyote people between the two reservations that continued through the twentieth century. Today it is not uncommon for the Yankton and Winnebago Peyotists to attend each others' meetings. In 1993, when the well-known Winnebago Peyotist Reuben Snake passed away, several Yank-tons traveled to Nebraska to attend a memorial Peyote meeting. Also, before he died in 1993, John D. Decora (Johnny Dee), a Winnebago roadman and president of Winnebago Native American Church, regularly attended Yankton Peyote meetings. Present-day Yanktons attest to this pattern. Quentin "Sonny" Bruguier, an active member of the Yankton Native American Church since 1959 and also a roadman, confirmed this close relationship.[50]

The Winnebagos of Nebraska were one of the first groups in the central Plains to adopt the Peyote religion.[51] They may have learned about Peyote as early as 1889. Soon after that, according to Omer Stewart, they "developed an active ceremonial organization."[52] The man credited with the introduction of Peyote to the Winnebagos is John Rave (ca. 1855–1917). He claimed that he first ate Peyote in 1889. In 1912 he said it has been twenty-three years since he first ate Peyote, when he was in Oklahoma with "peyote eaters."[53] He returned home convinced of its value for his people. He felt he had experienced something very holy that had turned his life around and changed him from being a heavy drinker living an irresolute life to a spiritual person with a positive direction. He began a lifetime of proselytizing, first among his own people then among people in surrounding states.[54] Paul Radin, the well-known ethnologist who did considerable fieldwork among the Winnebagos from 1908 to 1913, described Rave:

A very remarkable man, the leader and directing power of the Peyote religion. He became a convert to it in Oklahoma and introduced his version of the cult among the Winnebago. . . . he molded the cult he had borrowed into something quite new. He possessed the proselytizing zeal to an unusual degree. Through his activity the Winnebago form of the peyote cult has been spread among the Fox, Menominee, Ojibwa, and Dakota.[55]

Albert Hensley, also a Winnebago, played a similar role. Like Rave, Hensley was a person full of energy and drive. He attended the Carlisle School for Indians and became the Winnebago spokesman for Peyote. Hensley defended Peyotism against the increasing attacks from government officials and missionaries. His approach to legitimizing Peyotism was to make it part of Christianity. In 1908 he sent a letter, along with samples of Peyote, to the commissioner of Indian Affairs. He wrote: "Our favorite term is medicine [Peyote], and to us it is a portion of the body of Christ, even as the communion bread is believed to be a portion of Christ's body by other Christian denominations." In their attempts to legitimize the use of Peyote, both Rave and Hensley became informants to Paul Radin. They supplied some of the most significant accounts of the Peyote church in its early days. Scholars today credit both men with helping establish the Peyote church on a firm foundation. In 1921 Hensley helped the Peyotists in Nebraska to incorporate as the Peyote Church of Christ. The charter states: "We recognize all people who worship God and follow Christ as members of the one true church. . . . We believe in the sacrament and sacramental bread and wine, but in so much as the use of the same is forbidden to Indians, we of the people who cannot obtain or use the same have adopted the use of bread as Peyote and water as wine."[56] In 1922 they changed the name to the Native American Church of Winnebago, Nebraska.[57]

In establishing the Peyote religion among the Winnebagos, Rave and Hensley developed it as the Cross Fire ceremony. Rave, who first introduced it, apparently coined the term "Cross Fire." Hensley then added some significant innovations. What became known as the John Rave Cross Fire, however, was partially an adaptation of Jonathan Koshiway's (Sac and Fox) First Born Church of Christ and John Wilson's Big Moon ceremony. Rave, who spent several years in Oklahoma, said that he had visited the Otos and credited them with teaching him about Peyote. He also probably attended Peyote meetings with the Big Moon ceremony. Rave returned to Nebraska and modified what he had learned in Oklahoma. He eliminated the use of tobacco in the ritual and added more Christian elements to the Peyote service. The use of Christian elements and interpretations to explain Peyote symbolism did not originate with Rave. Christian elements were present when he attended Koshiway's First Born Church of Christ,[58] but Rave and Hensley are credited with a deepening of Christian influence on the ritual of the Cross Fire way, particularly the inclusion of Christian references in Peyote songs. They are also responsible for disseminating another innovation: the use of the Bible in Peyote services. Rave attended Oto services where the Bible was used, probably lying open on the altar. As Rave and Hensley were proselytizers, however, the Peyote way they taught included considerably more use of the Bible, such as midnight sermons based on biblical passages or using biblical references to sanction the eating of Peyote. One such example is from Exodus 12:8: "and they shall eat the flesh in the night, roast with fire, and unleavened bread; and with bitter herbs they shall eat it." In addition certain aspects of the Peyote religion were given Christian interpretations.[59] Hensley gave the following interpretation of the Peyote religion by drawing parallels with early Christianity:

> It is true religion. The peyote is fulfilling the work of God and the Son of God. When the Son of God came to the earth he was poor, yet people spoke of him; he was abused. It is the same now with the peyote. The plant itself is not much of a growth, yet the people are talking about it a good deal; they are abusing it, they are trying to stop its use. When the Son of God came to earth the preachers of that time were called Pharisees and Scribes. They doubted what the Son of God said and claimed that he was an ordinary man. So it is today with the Christian Church; they are the Pharisees and Scribes, they are the doubters. They say that this is merely a plant, that it is the work of the devil. They are trying to stop its use and they are calling it an intoxicant, but this is a lie.[60]

Hensley also told his followers that the Bible was intelligible only to those who partook of Peyote. This allowed for the continued primacy of Peyote as well as significant use of the Bible. Both Hensley and Rave had considerable influence on the development of the Peyote religion in general and the Cross Fire ceremony in particular. Their proselytizing among the Winnebagos was not without opposition. In the early years many traditionalists opposed the introduction of the Peyote religion.[61]

A more serious threat to the Winnebagos and the emerging Peyote religion was the Bureau of Indian Affairs, which began an active campaign to abolish Peyotism. This was particularly threatening to the Winnebagos, because BIA investigator "Pussyfoot" Johnson regarded them as major prose-lytizers. In 1908 he wrote: "The Winnebagoes have sent out missionaries to other Indian tribes, teaching this doctrine, administering the rites and arranging for the supply of peyote." Johnson was appointed by President Theodore Roosevelt in 1906 to enforce the prohibition of alcohol on Indian reservations. Johnson, who was an activist in the national prohibition movement, took to his new job with a vengeance. With approximately 100 deputies, he became the BIA's chief enforcer. The legislation outlawing intoxicants on reservations did not mention Peyote, but Johnson took it upon himself to interpret the law to include it. As reports came into his office on the use of Peyote, he began to gather information. He sent a list of eighteen questions to fifteen reservation superintendents, twelve in Oklahoma and one each in New Mexico, Nebraska, and Wyoming. No list was sent to South Dakota. Johnson wanted to know how widespread the use of Peyote was and what its effects on physiological and psychological functions were. The questions assumed that Peyote is a habit-forming narcotic with a deadly effect—for example, asking "How soon does habitual use prove fatal?" and "Just how does it cause death?"

Johnson combined a campaign of spreading negative information about the Peyote religion with efforts at eradication by attempting to stop the sale of Peyote from its sources in Texas and Mexico. One strategy he used was to buy and destroy Peyote. For example he reported in 1908 that he bought and destroyed 176,400 Peyote buttons. He did the same thing in 1909. In Laredo, Texas, he went to wholesale companies and warned them against shipping Peyote and convinced Pacific Express and Wells Fargo to refuse to ship it. "Pussyfoot" Johnson was developing an infamous reputation in the Peyote community. His campaign against Peyote was on shaky legal grounds, because Peyote had not been criminalized (except in Oklahoma by the territorial legislature); therefore authority to enforce a Peyote prohibition was unclear. Johnson, however, had no misgivings about his activities. He wrote: "I believe that we have got things in such shape now that we will be able to snuff out this peyote nuisance." It was not to be. Peyotism continued to grow, as the law enforcement community did not follow Johnson's interpretation of the ban on intoxicants to include Peyote. In 1911 Johnson left government service and joined the Anti-Saloon League of America.[62]

In spite of the efforts of the BIA and Johnson's belief that destroying the supply of Peyote would weaken Winnebago Peyotism, it continued to grow.

Johnson had claimed that the Winnebagos were renouncing Peyotism, when in reality it was expanding. In 1912 Jesse Clay, a Winnebago Peyotist, introduced the Half Moon ceremony. In an interview with Paul Radin, Clay said he attended an Arapaho Half Moon ceremony in Oklahoma. A year later a man Clay called Arapaho Bull (Jock Bull Bear) visited him in Nebraska and led a Peyote meeting in the Arapaho manner.[63] This became the Jesse Clay Half Moon ceremony of the Winnebagos. Many then claimed that the Half Moon way was more traditional than the Cross Fire, particularly with the ceremonial use of tobacco during prayer. The term "half moon" refers to the crescent-shaped altar. The ceremony differs from the Cross Fire primarily in the degree of Christian influence. Some Half Moon services do not contain any Christian elements; but some do to a limited extent, such as Christian references in Peyote songs or the use of Christian references to explain Peyote symbolism. For example, in Clay's account to Radin he says that "the reason for drinking water at midnight is because Christ was born at midnight and because of the good tidings that he brought to the earth, for water is one of the best things in life and Christ is the savior of mankind." The Bible is not used in the Half Moon; and instead of a midnight sermon, there are four special Peyote songs. Nevertheless, some Christian elements are found in certain Half Moon ceremonies. For the Winnebagos, as for other Native Americans who follow the Peyote faith, the introduction of Peyote with a lesser or greater degree of Christianity does not represent a break with the religions of the past but is considered an expansion of and integration with the spiritual beliefs of their ancestors.[64]

The Jesse Clay Half Moon ceremony became popular with many Winnebagos. Clay became the first president of the Native American Church of Winnebago, Nebraska, and like his counterparts Rave and Hensley was an active proselytizer. By 1918 the Wisconsin and Nebraska Winnebagos practiced both the Cross Fire and Half Moon ceremonies. Most people attended either one. The particular ceremony that was held usually depended upon which roadman was invited to lead the service. Both groups opened their doors to non-Winnebagos, and both traveled to spread the Peyote way. According to LaBarre, by 1914 half of the Winnebagos were Peyotists.[65] This large membership with its strong proselytizing ethic made the Winnebagos very influential in the spread of the Peyote religion. Local opposition to Peyote eventually dissipated; and after World War II a wide cross section of Winnebagos were Peyotists, including some important political leaders. By

1960 one scholar estimated that the majority of the Winnebagos were members of the Native American Church.[66] Most of what Rave and Hensley taught is still practiced among the Cross Fire Winnebagos.[67] Finally, it should be noted that—despite the scholarly interest in the patterns of diffusion of the Peyote religion and the degree of Christian influence on various Peyote ceremonies—the Winnebagos and all other Native Americans who are members of the Native American Church believe that Peyote is a "medicine" and is a direct gift from God. A Winnebago man told Radin:

> The Winnebago were decreasing in number, so the Creator gave them a medicine [Peyote] which would enable them to get accustomed to the white man's food; that, also, they might know the Creator and that he is the true bread and food. This they found out by using this medicine. They are going into it deeper and deeper all the time, they who had been lost, and this has all been accomplished by the medicine.[68]

THE DIFFUSION OF PEYOTISM

Before the use of Peyote reached the Plains in the nineteenth and twentieth centuries, American Indian people had used it for several millennia. Named *Lophophora williamsii* in 1894 by American botanist John Coulter, peyote is a rather small flowering spineless cactus, light bluish-green, and grows either as a solitary stem or upon occasion as a dense cluster of up to twenty or more stems, each with a top to be harvested. Each stem is one to two inches in diameter and grows just two or three inches above the ground. Peyote has a tuberous root similar to a turnip and is harvested by cutting off the tops of the plant, which are usually referred to as "buttons." In several months the peyote root then produces new growth with a button on top. Peyote grows in lime soils in deserts or in scrub regions underneath dense bush. Its natural habitat is in southern Texas and northern and central Mexico. In Texas it grows along a thirty- to forty-mile strip from Presidio through the Big Bend region, almost to Brownsville.[69] In order to prepare Peyote for use, the top of the plant is sliced off and dried in the sun (it can be eaten fresh). Once dried into buttons, it can be stored indefinitely. Being small and lightweight, it is easily transportable. Dried buttons measure a half inch to one and a half inches in diameter. They are chewed and swallowed. The dried buttons can also be ground into a greenish-gray granular powder. Water is added to the powder, which is mixed into a pasty consistency and swallowed. The buttons or powder can also be boiled and made into a "tea," which is sipped.

The word "peyote" comes from the Nahuatl (Aztec) word *peyotl*. The use of Peyote in ritual has roots in antiquity. Peyote buttons recovered from a rock shelter in the Lower Pecos River region (south-central Texas) have been radiocarbon-dated as 7,000 years old. In the same region, rock art that is 4,100 to 3,200 years old depicts the ritual use of Peyote. According to archaeologist Carolyn Boyd, a formal analysis shows that "4000-year-old Pecos River Style rock-art panels contain pictographic representation of Peyote ritual." She claims that the depiction of the Peyote ritual has many analogies to contemporary Huichol Peyotism. Other, more recent sites have been dated 810–1070 c.e. The Aztecs and other people as far north as the Rio Grande were using Peyote for religio-medicinal purposes when the Spanish arrived.[70] Peyote has mild hallucinogenic properties, containing about thirty alkaloids, including anhalamine, mescaline, anhalonidine, peyotine, and lophophorine. There is no evidence of developing a drug tolerance for Peyote, and there are no withdrawal symptoms. It is not habit forming and, when used in the context of a religious service, is not harmful.[71] The U.S. government did not list it as an illegal drug until 1965, when amending the Food, Drug and Cosmetic Act. There was, however, a federal exemption from prosecution for its use by a "bona fide religious organization."[72] The 1965 legislation was a response to the growing drug use of the emerging youth counterculture rather than its use by American Indians. In 1967 Texas outlawed all uses of Peyote; but after considerable protest the legislature added an exemption for members of the Native American Church.

Part of the misunderstanding concerning the danger of Peyote was its confusion with the mescal bean. In the late nineteenth century Peyote was referred to as mescal buttons or mescal beans, and its users were described as belonging to a mescal "cult." Even Smithsonian anthropologist James Mooney originally called the Peyote services a "mescal rite." The origin of the confusion is unclear. "Mescal bean plant" is the common name of *Sophora secundiflora*, an evergreen bush. The plant produces pods with red beans that are highly hallucinogenic and potentially dangerous. To refer to Peyote as mescal is a misnomer. There is also an alcoholic beverage called mescal that is made from the plant *Agave angustifolia*. Possibly this is the source of the confusion, since the agave belongs to the cactus family. In Mexico this confusion over terminology does not exist. The three different plants are known distinctly as peyote, *agave*, and *frijolillo* for the mescal bean plant. In his later writings Mooney corrected himself and said Peyote is erroneously known as mescal. Nevertheless, the confusion continued for several more decades until the terminology was fully clarified by ethnobotanist Richard Schultes.[73]

When the Spaniards arrived in Mexico in 1519, they found the indigenous population using a wide variety of psychotropic plants for medicinal and spiritual purposes. They encountered widespread use of Peyote in the northern half of Mexico.[74] The earliest extant reference to Peyote is from Bernardino de Sahagún, a Spanish missionary, around 1560. He described its effects: "those who eat or drink it see visions either frightful or laughable."[75] By the end of the sixteenth century Spanish writers took a more negative view. For example, Juan de Cárdenas, writing in 1591, described the use of Peyote as witchcraft and the work of the devil. As the missionary activity increased, the indigenous religions came under assault. Through the efforts of the Catholic Church, Peyote was declared the work of the devil and outlawed. The Inquisition enforced the restriction.[76] Part of the missionaries' concern was that indigenous converts to Christianity continued to use Peyote. Thus began a campaign to discredit the use of the so-called diabolic root. In the effort to stamp out Peyote, the church equated its usage with cannibalism and murder. In spite of this persecution, the Spanish government and the Catholic Church were not able to eradicate the use of Peyote, as it was an essential part of Mexico's Native cultures. On the individual level Peyote was used for healing. When used externally it was applied to wounds, snakebites, and burns. It was carried as an amulet for spiritual protection and ingested as a protective medicine. On the communal level it was used in religious ceremonies that included all-night singing and dancing with the participants arranged in circles. It was also used for visions and prophesying in a communal setting.[77]

This widespread use of Peyote was a challenge for the missionaries. Spanish commentary on Peyote was usually couched in theological language, although the real issue was the power of the Spanish government and the Catholic Church to impose their religion, culture, and language on the indigenous population. They made Peyote illegal for almost three hundred years, but its local use continued. In many areas Peyote, as well as other elements of indigenous culture, was integrated into Catholicism. Peyote usage continued to spread in spite of Spanish attempts to control it.[78] The survival of the medicinal-religious use of Peyote in Mexico made it possible for it to spread to the United States, where it was used primarily as a sacrament during ceremonies of the newly emerging Peyote religious complex. In a sense it is inaccurate to ask when Peyote spread into the United States. When this area was annexed by the United States in 1848, Peyote usage was already centuries old. The question is how it spread north into Oklahoma, where the contemporary Peyote religion had its roots. The Mescalero Apaches, Lipan Apaches, Carrizos, Tonkawas, Karankawas, and Caddos who lived in the Rio Grande area had all used Peyote in the eighteenth and nineteenth centuries and developed a spiritual and ceremonial usage that was the basis for the Peyotism that arose in the United States.[79]

In the 1890s Smithsonian anthropologist James Mooney produced the first written description of a Peyote ceremony. He was in the West studying the Ghost Dance movement when he heard about the growing Peyote religion. In 1891 he began attending Peyote services on the Kiowa-Comanche Reservation in Oklahoma. The services he attended were very elaborate and already well defined, meaning that they had already been in existence for some time.[80] In terms of theology, ritual, and structure the Peyote ceremony has changed very little in the past century. Mooney wrote that "it is regarded as the vegetable incarnation of a deity and the ceremonial eating of the plant has become the great religious rite of all the tribes of the southern plains." A hundred years later Reuben Snake, one of the nation's leading Peyotists, wrote: "If Jesus was God incarnate in human form, our holy Peyote is God incarnate in plant form."[81]

The Kiowa ceremony described by Mooney is the one that spread northward throughout the western United States. Stewart has written a composite description of the ceremonies described by Mooney; however, quoting Mooney directly gives the full sense of a Kiowa Peyote meeting in the 1890s:

> The ceremony occupies from twelve to fourteen hours, beginning about 9 or 10 o'clock and lasting sometimes until nearly noon the next day. Saturday night is now the time usually selected, in deference to the white man's idea of Sunday as a sacred day and a day of rest. The worshipers sit in a circle around the inside of the sacred tipi, with a fire blazing in the center. The exercises open with a prayer by the leader, who then hands each man four mescals [Peyote buttons], which he takes and eats in quick succession. . . . After this first round the leader takes the rattle, while his assistant takes the drum, and together they sing the first song four times; with full voices, at the same time

beating the drum and shaking the rattle with all the strength of their arms. The drum and rattle are then handed to the next couple, and so the song goes on round and round the circle—with only a break for the baptismal ceremony at midnight, and another for the daylight ceremony—until perhaps 9 o'clock the next morning. Then the instruments are passed out of the tipi, the sacred foods are eaten, and the ceremony is at an end. At midnight a vessel of water is passed around, and each takes a drink and sprinkles a few drops upon his head. Up to this hour no one has moved from his position, sitting cross-legged upon the ground and with no support for his back, but now any one is at liberty to go out and walk about for a while and return again. Few, however, do this, as it is considered a sign of weakness. The sacred food at the close of the ceremony consists of parched corn in sweetened water; rice or other boiled grain; boiled fruit, usually now prunes or dried apples; and dried meat pounded up with sugar. Every person takes a little of each first taking a drink of water to clear his mouth.

After midnight the leader passes the mescal around again. . . . On this second round I have frequently seen a man call for ten and eat them one after the other as rapidly as he could chew. They continue to eat at intervals until the close. There is much spitting, and probably but little of the juice is swallowed. Every one smokes handmade cigarettes, the smoke being regarded as a sacred incense. At intervals some fervent devotee will break out into an earnest prayer, stretching his hands out towards the fire and the sacred mescal the while. For the rest of the time, when not singing the song and handling the drum or rattle with all his strength, he sits quietly with his blanket drawn about him and his eyes fixed upon the sacred mescal in the center, or perhaps with his eyes shut and apparently dozing. He must be instantly ready, however, when his turn comes at the song, or to make a prayer at the request of someone present, so that it is apparent the senses are always on the alert and under control of the will. There is no preliminary preparation, such as by fasting or the sweat-bath, and supper is eaten as usual before going in. The dinner, which is given an hour or two after the ceremony, is always as elaborate a feast as the host can provide. The rest of the day is spent in gossiping, smoking, and singing the new songs, until it is time to return home.[82]

This ceremony was based on a compilation of ceremonies from the Mexican Peyote complex with Kiowa innovations. Of the six groups mentioned above, Stewart concludes that it was the Carrizos who developed much of the Peyote ceremony. Weston LaBarre reached the same conclusion in 1938, as did BIA agent "Pussyfoot" Johnson in a 1908 report. Johnson wrote that about thirty years ago the Carrizo Indians were large users of Peyote. The Carrizos, located along the Rio Grande, were the inheritors of the long tradition of Peyote usage in Mexico. They transmitted it to the Kiowa-Apaches and Comanches in the 1870s.[83] The specific Peyote ceremony described by Mooney in the 1890s seems to have developed after the establishment of reservations in Oklahoma. The Kiowas, Kiowa-Apaches, and Comanches shared a common reservation after 1867. Now a wide variety of people were living in close proximity to each other. Some of these groups certainly had been in contact with tribes along the Rio Grande before their removal to Oklahoma in 1867. Also, the Kiowas and Comanches were active in raiding and trading in Texas and Mexico and may have already had knowledge of Peyote.[84]

In Oklahoma the Lipan Apaches taught other groups about the Peyote religion. They had learned it from the Carrizos. Two Lipan Apaches, Chiwat and Pinero, are credited with being the primary teachers of Peyotism in Oklahoma. Chiwat was a well-known proselytizer. Beginning in the 1880s, the Peyote religion spread rapidly, partially as a result of easier travel and the ability to ship Peyote through an expanding postal system. In 1886 J. Lee Hall, the government agent at the Kiowa, Comanche, and Wichita Agency (several agencies were consolidated in 1878), made the first written reference to the presence of Peyote on a reservation. He claimed it was the Lipan Apaches, who themselves had been involved with Peyotism for twenty or thirty years, who introduced it to this agency. Hall recommended to the BIA that Peyote be declared contraband.[85] The BIA accepted his recommendation. For the next half-century it would do everything in its power to suppress the Peyote religion.

The Peyote ceremony that was in place among the Kiowas and Comanches had some similarities with the Mexican Peyote complex, but essentially it was different. The most obvious parallel is that Peyote was considered a sacred medicine. Other similarities include the use of tobacco, the gourd rattle, the sacredness of the number four and the four directions, and the all-night ceremonies. The major differences were the absence of dancing, the absence of bloodletting rituals, the lack of a sacred pilgrimage to collect Peyote, and no accepted nonspiritual uses of Peyote. In the United States Peyote ingestion was confined to a strict ceremonial setting and then used only in the form of a sacrament. In addition, the increasing influence of Christianity on Peyotism added some modifications. Thus in the United States there is a clearly defined Peyote religion, whereas in Mexico one can only refer to Peyote-using culture complexes. Omer Stewart has also concluded that, despite the parallels, Peyotism in the United States is not the direct diffusion of an entire system, only the diffusion of certain elements that were integrated into Native American belief systems and then transformed into the Peyote religion. In other words, Peyote usage had its roots in Mexico, but the Peyote religion as practiced in the United States is not a Mexican import.[86]

Another consideration is the relationship between Peyotism and the Ghost Dance movement, which began in 1889 and spread throughout the Plains and west to California. It started with Wovoka, a Northern Paiute from Nevada. At a time when the reservations resembled outdoor prisons, the Ghost Dance promised the restoration of Native American cultures. Wovoka preached peace and said that the changes would come from supernatural intervention. He promised the disappearance of the American settlers, the resurrection of the ancestors, and the return of the buffalo. As the Ghost Dance spread, the American government considered it a threat and declared it illegal. This resulted in the murder of Sitting Bull and the tragic massacre at Wounded Knee on the Pine Ridge Reservation in December 1890. The troops of the U.S. Seventh Cavalry massacred several hundred men, women, and children.[87]

The Ghost Dance was not related directly to the Peyote religion, although in several ways it facilitated the spread of Peyote. Peyotism predates the Ghost Dance. Many Native Americans in Oklahoma and Texas were already Peyotists. In fact some well-known Ghost Dance leaders such as John Wilson and Frank White (Pawnee) were active Peyotists before joining the Ghost Dance movement. The Peyote religion did expand in the wake of the collapse of the Ghost Dance movement (the Ghost Dance itself never totally disappeared); but this was not the result of a theological linkage or simply filling a vacuum created by the rapid decline of the Ghost Dance. It was related to the widespread movement of people and the many intertribal contacts that occurred with the Ghost Dance. Not all Ghost Dance supporters became Peyotists. There were active Peyote groups that the Ghost Dance did not penetrate, such as the Comanches, Lipan Apaches, and Mescalero Apaches. The Peyote religion had only limited appeal in some Ghost Dance areas. Some groups did not join the Ghost Dance movement but were very involved with the Peyote religion, such as the Winnebagos, Omahas, and Menominees.

The Ghost Dance certainly heightened the sense of spirituality and hope, which may have benefited the Peyote religion, but the real significance of the Ghost Dance was its intertribal nature. The Peyote religion would follow this pattern. Many similar contacts were made in the government boarding schools. For example, many of the Peyotists had attended to the Carlisle Indian School. Stewart has compiled a list of 109 Carlisle students who became Peyotists. Many contacts and friendships were made by hundreds of Native Americans who joined Wild West shows and rodeos. The expanding linkage of roads and railroads made travel easier and made it possible to develop a growing network of Peyote people. All of this facilitated the growth of the Peyote religion throughout the western states.[88]

By the mid-1880s the Peyote ceremony was widespread throughout the Kiowa-Comanche Reservation. It was from here that the Peyote religion spread to other reservations in Oklahoma. Two of the most famous roadmen from the early years of Peyotism, Quanah Parker (1845–1911), a Comanche leader, and John Wilson (1840–1901), mentioned earlier, came from the Wichita, Caddo, Delaware Reservation. Both men are legendary in the Peyote community. Parker was not the first Comanche Peyotist, but he was the most important. He is mostly responsible for the spread of the Peyote religion among the Comanches and was a proselytizer of the Half Moon way. He became well known as a defender of Peyotism against attacks by Christian missionaries and both state and federal officials. Parker was an influential figure in Oklahoma politics. In 1905 he traveled to Washington and met with President Roosevelt at his inauguration. Later he testified before various committees of the Oklahoma legislature. Peyote had been banned in Oklahoma in 1899; but Parker, testifying before the state legislature, defended it on the grounds of religious freedom. His arguments won the day. The ban on Peyote was rescinded in 1908.[89]

John Wilson, like Parker, was also held in high esteem by the Peyote community. He was of Caddo, Delaware, and French ancestry but considered himself Caddo. Wilson used Peyote as early as 1880. He claimed that he experienced a revelation during a vision, which led him to develop a Peyote ceremony that included Christian elements. This became the Big Moon ceremony (also called the Wilson Moon). The name refers to the size of the U-shaped altar that was eight to ten feet long and considerably larger than the Half Moon altar. Wilson said that while on a spirit journey he learned about the life of Jesus and saw the empty grave. Peyote, the teacher, showed him the true path that Jesus had taken following the Resurrection. The ridge along the top of the Big Moon altar was designed to show this path. A cross, symbolic of the crucifixion, was inscribed on the ground inside the altar. This Big Moon style of worship spread northward but was modified and then replaced by the Cross Fire way. Today the Osages are the only followers of the Big Moon way.[90]

Some scholars claim that the Kiowas were the first to develop the modern Peyote ceremony, but Stewart sees the Peyote religion emerging more or less simultaneously among the Comanches, Kiowas, and Kiowa-Apaches. Their ceremonies are virtually identical. According to Kiowa tradition, their earliest Peyote leader was Chief White Bear or Satanta (1830–78). The descendants of White Bear credit him with developing some of the basic elements in the Peyote ritual. In 1950 anthropologist James Howard traveled with and interviewed Levi White Bear (1887–1952), the grandson of Chief White Bear. Levi was a roadman and lifelong Peyotist. The Peyote ceremonies observed by Howard and described by Levi are virtually the same as the Kiowa Peyote ceremony described by Mooney in 1891. It is this ceremony, the Half Moon, that subsequently spread throughout the United States and Canada. Levi White Bear claimed that he had attended Peyote meetings with almost every tribe in the southern Plains. This certainly attests to the intertribal nature of the Peyote religion.[91] What is significant in comparing Mooney's account of the Kiowa Peyote ceremony with contemporary accounts is the continuity in both time and space.

In addition to leaving written accounts, Mooney took many photographs. In the *Handbook of American Indians* there is an 1894 photo of two Kiowa Peyotists. Except for their clothing, the photo could be from the 1990s. The same water drum, tilted the way it is played, the eagle feather fan, the gourd rattle and staff held by the singers, and their semi-squatting, kneeling position while drumming and singing have not changed in the past century.[92] Even with these additions and the subsequent variations among the Cross Fire, Big Moon, and Half Moon styles of worship, the Peyote ceremony is very similar throughout the United States and Canada. Comparisons by Stewart and other scholars show the common framework.[93]

One major difference in the rituals is the use of tobacco. The Cross Fire eliminated the use of tobacco in its ceremony while the Half Moon congregants used tobacco as an essential and traditional element in their ceremony. Early in the service each individual rolls his or her own cigarette, using dried cornhusks as wrappers. In the Big Moon ceremony smoking tobacco in cigarette form accompanies prayer. The roadman rolls a cigarette, smokes and prays at the beginning of a service, and then passes the cigarette around for all to use in prayer. Individuals may ask for tobacco if they feel they have a special need. In spite of these differences among the three variants, Peyote is always the essential element. It is the sacrament, a gift from God that has the power to teach right from wrong, good from evil. It has the power to heal. With prayer, devotion, and commitment it can cure illnesses. It is a cure for alcoholism. Peyote can lead to the right path, the right road, the right way. It establishes friendship, good works, and community among the congregation of believers. These are some of the essential beliefs that bring unity to all members of the Peyote community, whatever variant is used. It was from the Kiowa-Comanche Reservation that Peyotism spread. First it expanded throughout Oklahoma (with the exception of the so-called Five Civilized Tribes: Cherokees, Choctaws, Seminoles, Creeks, and Chickasaws) and then north and west. The Big Moon and/or Cross Fire ritual spread from the Caddos to the Delawares, Osages, Senecas, Wichitas, Winnebagos, Kickapoos, and Potowatomis. The proportion of people from each group who reportedly joined the Peyote faith varied from 20 percent to 50 percent and on occasion much higher, such as the Omahas, where it was almost 90 percent.[94]

Many of the early adherents were young men who went to boarding school, had exposure to Christianity, and spoke English. With English as a *lingua franca,* they were able to use it as an "enabling factor" in the spread of Peyotism. When people joined a Peyote community, they usually did so as an entire family. Sam Necklace and his family fit this profile. Many Native Americans may have seen Peyotism as a physical and spiritual curative in an uncertain and hostile environment. Stewart's statement that the spread of Peyote may in part be due to the fact that the all-night ceremony is followed by a large breakfast is an oversimplification.[95]

Peyotists had considerable contact with each other. This helps explain the pan-Indian nature of the Peyote faith. For example, Jim Blue Bird (Oglala) went to Carlisle and performed in Wild West shows, as did Sam Lone Bear (Oglala). William Black Bear (Sioux) and Sam Blowsnake (Winnebago) also performed in Wild West shows. Albert Hensley went to Carlisle, and Jonathan Koshiway attended Haskell Institute. The Southern Cheyenne Peyotists Cohoe, Roman Nose, and Little Chief attended Carlisle or Hampton Institute or both. Cleaver Warden (Southern Arapaho), Henry Murdock (Kickapoo),

Jock Bull Bear (Cheyenne/Arapaho), and Thaddeus Redwater (Northern Cheyenne) all attended Carlisle. Paul Boynton (Cheyenne/Arapaho), who was an interpreter for James Mooney, also attended Carlisle. Yankton Peyotists such as Sam Necklace and Joe Rockboy attended boarding schools. These contacts obviously facilitated the spread of the Peyote religion and continued throughout the twentieth century. Today it would be virtually impossible to find a roadman who has not conducted Peyote meetings on many reservations. The same is true for Native American Church members, who freely attend meetings wherever they happen to be. As a result of this historical experience, the contemporary members of the Native American Church perceive themselves as a nationwide Peyote community. These contacts, the ease of travel, and the spiritual needs of many people all account for the rapid dissemination of the Peyote religion. Peyote congregations emerged in all states west of the Mississippi River. By 1918, a watershed year in the history of Peyotism, the religion had also spread to the Winnebago, Omaha, Osage, Potawatomi, Sac and Fox, northern Ponca, northern and southern Cheyenne, Oto, Pawnee, northern and southern Arapaho, Goshute, Mescalero, Lipan, and Jicarilla Apache, Taos, and Lakota and Dakota peoples.[96]

THE YANKTON PEYOTE COMMUNITY AND RESERVATION LIFE

As Peyotism expanded on the Yankton Reservation, it also had a presence on other Sioux reservations. Its diffusion among the Sioux was uneven. Some groups were unaffected; others, such as the Yanktons, the Oglalas (Pine Ridge Reservation), and the Sičangus (Rosebud Reservation), developed significant Peyote communities. Although the Sioux Peyotists were a minority and sometimes a small minority, they were still very influential in the spread of Peyotism. Many Sioux became roadmen and traveled widely, helping the further spread of the Peyote faith.

The earliest known Peyote ceremony held on a Sioux reservation was at Pine Ridge in 1904. Winnebago roadmen Albert Hensley and John Rave were the teachers. Jim Blue Bird, one of the founders of the Native American Church of South Dakota and later its director, wrote to Omer Stewart in 1949: "I became a member of the peyote religion in July 1902, at Calumet, Oklahoma. Pine Ridge Sioux in South Dakota commence to use peyote in 1904." Others from Pine Ridge also credit the Winnebagos. As the teachers, Rave and Hensley introduced the Cross Fire way. The Half Moon came in a decade or two later, when Winnebago and Omaha Half Moon roadmen visited Pine Ridge. From 1904 to the present, Peyote people from the Winnebago and Pine Ridge Reservations have traveled back and forth, attending each other's meetings. By 1919 about 5 percent of the Oglalas were Peyotists. The Yanktons were the second Sioux group to establish a Peyote congregation. As described earlier, it was established between 1904 and 1910. Subsequently it spread to the Rosebud and Santee Reservations. Again it was the Winnebagos, led by Hensley and Rave, who were instrumental in its expansion. Leonard Crow Dog claims that Peyote came to Rosebud "around 1903," introduced by the Winnebagos. Jim Blue Bird was traveling to most Sioux reservations, including the Rosebud, teaching the Cross Fire way. Peyote also spread north to Fort Totten Reservation in North Dakota. Blue Bird told Stewart that he was active on the Yankton Reservation. He specifically said that it was Sam Necklace, Johnson Goodhouse, Charles Jones, and Charles Iron Hawk that established the Peyote religion among the Yanktons and it was Goodhouse who traveled to Fort Totten in order to establish a Peyote group. Later Sam Necklace traveled to Fort Totten in order to run Peyote meetings for family and friends, something he did for the rest of his life. Blue Bird also told Stewart that these same four Yankton Peyotists regularly attended meetings on the Pine Ridge Reservation and added that they very definitely followed the Cross Fire way.[97]

The Yankton Peyote congregation continued to grow in spite of opposition by the BIA and occasional jailing by local officials. Throughout the 1910s the reports from the reservation to Washington indicated this growth. These reports were not just descriptive; they were alarmist and totally condemned both Peyote and its users. For example, the reports describe Peyote as an "unmitigated evil" and its users as "the most shiftless and non-progressive members of the tribe." Another report from the Yankton Agency in 1916 stated: "No intoxicating liquor is manufactured by these Indians but they brew a tea from peyote that is used by some. They also chew the dried peyote button. The use of this drug is on the increase since they know its use is not prohibited by law and they are very open about it."[98] Just about every year the Yankton superintendent reported that Peyote usage was on the increase and then complained that he did not have the power to do anything about it. Interestingly, however, it was reported in 1914 that Peyote may "be an antidote for the liquor habit."[99]

It is difficult to determine how many Yanktons were Peyotists. In 1916 Charlie Jones said it was about one hundred. In 1922 the BIA published a report titled *Peyote*. It was an unabashed attack on the Peyote religion but nevertheless contained important data collected from all reservations, including total population, the "number affected by peyote" (including children), and the percentage of Peyotists in the population. The Yankton Agency, with a total population of 3,117, had 623 or approximately 20 percent "affected" by Peyote. These statistics include three reservations. In 1918 the BIA consolidated the Yanktons, the Poncas, and the Santees in Nebraska under the jurisdiction of the Yankton Agency. The data on Peyote was sent to the BIA on 1 May 1919, which meant that the superintendent used the official census from 30 June 1918. Of the 3,466 people under this agency, 1,921 were Yanktons, 352 were Poncas, and 1,193 were Santees. The Yanktons made up more than two-thirds of the total population, Peyotism was not very widespread among the Santees, and there were few Poncas in the total, so it can be assumed the large majority of 623 Peyotists were Yanktons. Therefore the 20 percent figure is reasonable. If this assessment is high, it would certainly not be below 15 percent of the total Yankton population. One must also consider that the 15 or 20 percent includes the children of the Peyote families. The percentage of Yanktons "affected" by Peyote is the highest for all Sioux groups. The Pine Ridge Reservation was listed at 5 percent, Fort Totten at 1 percent, Rosebud at 0.007 percent, and the other reservations in South Dakota at zero. The Yanktons' neighbors, the Winnebagos, are listed at 38 percent. These 1922 statistics show a considerable increase in the number of Yankton Peyotists. BIA officials reported approximately 100 in 1916 and approximately 300 in 1922. Most Peyote communities were growing. The same officials estimated 5,000 to 6,000 Peyotists nationwide in 1916 and 13,345 in 1922. This may not seem like a large number out of 320,000 Native Americans; however, Peyotism was practiced only west of the Mississippi River and had yet to expand to any degree into the Southwest or to the west coast. It is also difficult to assess the accuracy of the statistics. Reservation officials had a tendency to exaggerate the difficult conditions that they were working under, and it was in the interest of the Peyote communities to avoid bringing attention to themselves.[100]

In 1919 the BIA began the systematic collection of data on Peyote. After Congress failed to prohibit Peyote, the BIA initiated policies aimed at discrediting Peyotism with state legislators. They sent a questionnaire to all agency personnel as well as to missionaries on the reservations. The questions sought information on the extent and depth of Peyote usage but also asked about the "moral, mental and physical effect of peyote" and whether the Indians who used Peyote were less "civilized" than those who did not. Superintendent Leech collected the responses and forwarded them to Washington. Leech set the tone in his cover letter. He wrote that the "Indians of this reservation who are addicted to the use of Peyote are an indolent, dirty, bloated class, and if anything could be said in favor of its use it would be that it would probably result in the extermination of those who use it." The responses in general reflect the attitude of the superintendent. For example, Peyote people were described as shiftless, weak, lacking moral fiber, and less "civilized" than those who did not use Peyote. In response to the question of the sincerity of those who claimed to use Peyote as a sacrament, they said religion was used as a cloak to cover using Peyote as a narcotic. Another question asked if they had the opportunity actually to observe the effects of Peyote. They all said no. Nonetheless, there is important information in the answers. Most said Peyote had been introduced between seven and ten years ago. Several said that approximately 20 percent of the Yanktons were "Peyote users." Although unintentionally, the responses to the questionnaire show a fully functioning Peyote community. Entire families attended all-night Peyote services usually held on Saturdays. Not yet having a church facility, they alternated the services at the homes of individual members, who provided hospitality and a large noon meal the next day. This was a major social occasion for the Peyote community. They were also able to obtain a regular supply of Peyote shipped from Texas by rail.[101]

During the 1910s and early 1920s life was very difficult for the Yanktons. The process of change continued unabated, at least on the surface. According to 1920 BIA statistics, 60 percent of the Yanktons attended one of nine Episcopal, Presbyterian, or Catholic churches. These types of statistics were kept for all reservations. The purpose was to show quantitative progress in "civilizing" Native Americans. They kept track of things such as language and clothing, including a category called "number of Indians who wear modern attire." For the Yanktons it was 100 percent. There was another category on speaking, reading, and writing English. It was estimated that 1,100 Yanktons spoke English and 700 could read and write English (out of 1,945).[102]

The most vexing problem was the continued alcohol abuse. Alcohol was readily available in the many towns around the reservation. In spite of attempts at control by agency officials, they could do little. Those Yanktons who were now U.S. citizens, the large majority, could not be restricted. There was a brief lull in the supply of alcohol after South Dakota became a dry state in 1917, but within a year an illegal trade emerged, with the widespread manufacture and sale of alcohol. Soon the supplies were as plentiful as ever. Even after 1919, with the Eighteenth Amendment prohibiting alcohol, it still was widely available throughout the region. In a social and economic environment of hopelessness, alcohol abuse was not surprising. It is also not surprising that Peyotism, with its belief that Peyote was a cure for alcoholism, would continue to grow.

World War I had an impact on the Yankton people. Issues of patriotism and loyalty that were part of the home-front activities throughout the nation were also present on the reservation. Fifteen Yankton men enlisted in the army or navy. There was a Home Guard, numbering one hundred. Some Yanktons contributed to the Red Cross or bought War Savings Stamps and Liberty Bonds, although few could afford them.[103] Following the war the Yanktons had to cope with the great influenza epidemic. This was part of a worldwide epidemic that spread from 1917 to 1919. Millions of people died. In the United States more than 500,000 perished. This influenza epidemic caused loss of life on the reservation. Sam and Mary Necklace lost two children. Their infant daughter Dorothy Baker died on 22 April 1917, followed by two-year-old Joseph on 1 October 1918. Mary had been pregnant with Joseph when Dorothy died. Charlie Jones lost his 15-year-old son and then his 48-year-old wife, Adelia, in 1919. In addition to influenza, the general health of many Yanktons was not good. Both tuberculosis and trachoma (viral eye disease) were rife. In 1920, 165 cases of tuberculosis were reported.[104] All three diseases were contagious. The influenza epidemic created panic and subsequently some quarantining. Red tags were placed on gates or doors to warn of danger inside. One young man, Joe Packard, recalled helping his father dig graves. He said there was "no time to have prayers for the dead people. They just put them in, buried them right away."[105]

The progress of so-called civilization may have seemed very advanced from the perspective of agency officials, who looked at things such as church attendance, clothing, language, nontraditional marriage ceremonies, household accoutrements, cooking style, and schooling; but, underneath, Yankton or Dakota values were surviving. Sometimes they survived within the framework of the Native American Church and sometimes within the kinship network or tiošpaye. The relationship of the grandchildren to the grandparents remained special, and the sense of linkage from past generations to present and future generations was not extinguished. There were still many elders who served as role models and helped keep traditions alive. Blue Cloud (Mahpiyato), also known as William Bean, the last traditional Yankton headman, lived until 1918. Grandma White Tallow (1843?–1943) was one of the most influential people on the reservation. She was a storyteller and a historian, a practicing midwife, well known for her beadwork, and also provided food and care for the most needy. She continued to wear traditional clothing when few others did.[106] In a society that respected and valued the elderly, she was most highly respected. Grandma White Tallow and other elders provided a linkage between the past and present. Other cultural traditions survived, such as the type of mourning that followed the death of a family member. The mourning period was still four days, and ceremonies still included the traditional sacred foods and purification with sage. Also, the missionaries and agency officials could not suppress the giveaways, in spite of all their efforts. They continued in spite of discouragement and harassment and are still an essential part of Yankton life today.

Two other activities played a key role in keeping Yankton traditions and values alive: dancehalls and the government-sponsored agricultural fairs. BIA officials believed that dismantling Native American culture was in the best interests of Native Americans. Dancing was one such area. Dancing was essential to the spiritual and communal well-being of all Native Americans. In lieu of traditional opportunities to dance, dancehalls emerged on the Yankton Reservation after the turn of the century. The government allowed the dancehalls to stay open, believing that they could be supervised and traditional types of activities could be limited.[107] In actuality it became difficult to control what went on in the dancehalls. For example, Dakota songs and dances were performed. One could hear the traditional heart-beat sound of the drum coming from the dancehalls. Some people wore Yankton regalia. The dancehalls were also a place to gather and socialize. They provided an opportunity for giveaways. Once the BIA realized that the dancehalls were counter to its policies, it placed restrictions on them. In a 1911 report, Yankton superintendent Walter Runke was very clear about his intentions:

> There still are a number of the old time Indians who take considerable interest in the old Indian dances. There are six dance halls located on allotted lands in the reservation. Dances are held in four of them at stated intervals. With these regular established places for holding dances it has been possible

to a certain extent to place some measure of control over them. One very pernicious custom in connection with these dances towards the abolishment of which every effort has been lent is that of the giving away of valuable property on such occasions.[108]

The following year the superintendent ordered the six dancehalls to hold their dances on the first and third Saturday of each month. This was to cut down the number of dances that one could attend. He also issued an order that prohibited anyone under the age of thirty-five from attending the dances. He did not outlaw the dancehalls but tried to control them and hoped that by prohibiting the younger people from attending they would eventually die out.

As part of this continuing "civilizing process," the BIA decided to sponsor agricultural fairs. The first fair was held on the Crow Reservation in Montana in 1904. By 1917 there were agricultural fairs on fifty-eight reservations. The fairs were modeled after state and county fairs. While the government implemented its overall policies of encouraging nuclear families rather than extended families and individual land ownership rather than communal ownership, it saw the fairs as another way to encourage Anglo-American values and lifestyles. The fairs offered cash prizes that could be won in competition. The prizes were enticements intended to develop "better" farmers and "better" housewives. Everyone would supposedly work hard to win a prize. The best exhibits were awarded cash prizes and ribbons. For example, produce prizes were given for the biggest pumpkin, the nicest wheat, best yellow corn, and best peck of apples. Livestock prizes were given for the best stallion, best workteam, best wagon and harness, best chickens, best bull, and best milk cow. For domestic skills, there was a prize for the "healthiest and cleanest baby," "nicest display of home-made butter," and "best display of meal and table, cooked and set for four." There were also prizes for some Native American arts and crafts, such as best Indian pipe, best quill moccasins, best Indian costume, and best "Indian fried bread."[109]

In 1912 Superintendent Leech began to plan for a Yankton fair. He called a meeting of tribal members, who, much to his surprise, voted down the idea of having a fair. Leech went ahead anyway and met with "some of the progressive ones" and planned and held a small exhibit of agricultural products. He made it clear that there would be "no old time dances nor exhibition of Indian barbarity." The next year the first annual Yankton fair was held on the reservation. It was administered by a group of Yankton men under the close supervision of Superintendent Leech. They formed the Yankton Indian Fair Association, with Homer Redlightning as president. Each year they planned the fair and printed a program listing the events, competitions, and prizes. The fair, lasting four days, was held in September on a forty-acre site just east of Greenwood along the Missouri River.[110] Virtually everyone on the reservation attended as well as several thousand nonreservation people. The outer edge of the fair was ringed with tents and tipis, as people came for the full four days. In addition to cash prizes for produce, livestock, arts and crafts, and homemaking skills, the fair included a parade and many competitive events, such as horse racing, footraces for boys and girls, and even a "Fat Men's Race" as well as a tug of war and a series of baseball games between Yanktons from the different towns within the reservation. The cash prizes ranged from $1.50 to $5.00, although the winning baseball team could collect as much as $50.00. Horse racing was the fair's most popular attraction. Cash prizes were awarded, but betting was strictly prohibited. Nevertheless, betting provided the real excitement and was quite common among the people gathered to watch the racing.[111]

The Necklace family attended the fairs. Sam was appointed to the finance committee for the second annual fair in 1914, and the following year he became secretary of the Fair Association. One year his father, Peter, won first prize for "Best Indian Pipe" and his mother, Margarette, won first prize for "Best Muskmelon." The real excitement for Sam, however, was the opportunity to display his team of horses. Joe Packard was a regular at the fairs and knew Sam Necklace. Joe remembers the fairs from the 1920s. When I was interviewing him about Sam Necklace, he began to talk about the fairs. Joe became very animated in describing how much he enjoyed them. He said that one year Sam won a blue ribbon and a cash prize for his horses. Joe also said there were many dancers, singers, and drummers. The old folks especially enjoyed the dancing and wearing their dance regalia. He added: "I know my grandfather, he liked to dance, dress up, dance. All the old folks, they dance you know." He remembers seeing the grass dance and rabbit dance. You could also buy dried meat and fry bread as well as quilts and jewelry. Almost all the activity was competitive, including footraces and competitive dancing. Finally, and in spite of BIA policy, there were the giveaways. According to Packard: "You give away star quilts, quilts, sometimes maybe a horse, you have a good horse, why, you want to give him away, you give him away. Or you raise anything like squash, or pumpkins, you give 'em away. . . . I know my dad, he raise a lot of squash and cucumbers and pumpkins and lots of stuff, so he takes it down to the fair and he just give 'em away."[112]

Over the years the popularity of the Yankton fair grew. For many Yanktons, the fairs turned out to be both a communal and festive event. During the mid-1920s Superintendent Robert E. L. Daniel reported: "We are expecting 7,000 or more Indians and other people at the Yankton Indian Fair. . . . Last year it was estimated we had 10,000 to 12,000 people here."[113] It was the popularity of the fairs that brought about their demise. The BIA's purpose in using the fairs to assimilate Native Americans was not successful. In fact, it seemed as if the opposite happened. Giveaways were continuing, both young and old were dancing and singing, and the *tiošpaye*s or extended families were using the fairs as a gathering place. Thus during the mid-1920s the BIA instituted a reversal of policy and discontinued the tribal fairs. Instead it tried to encourage Native Americans to exhibit their produce and livestock at state and county fairs.[114] The Yankton fair dwindled but did not end entirely until the onset of the Depression. The fair itself lasted only four days. It was a respite but not a solution to the continuing loss of land and poverty. Herbert Hoover has written convincingly that government policy created a depression for the Yanktons in the 1920s before it hit the rest of the nation.[115] In hindsight, it seems that the fairs had a historical impact that was unnoticed. The young people, especially the teenagers who attended the fairs, became the parents and grandparents of the 1960s and 1970s. It is very plausible to see this generation as laying the groundwork for the cultural renaissance in the late 1960s. One can look back to the agricultural fairs as helping to keep Yankton culture alive during very difficult times.

THE NECKLACE FAMILY

It is uncertain when Sam and Mary began to participate in Peyote meetings or when they began to center their social and spiritual life within the Peyote community. Family oral history places their involvement in the first decade of the twentieth century or a few years later. This is very probable, because Charlie Jones had returned to the reservation and had introduced Peyote. Also, the presence of Peyote on the reservation was reported regularly starting in 1911. Documenting the time-frame for Sam's conversion is difficult. We know that in 1922, when the Yankton Peyotists incorporated, Sam was elected an officer. This could imply a long involvement. In 1912, however, when Charlie Jones listed the names of people involved with Peyote, Sam's name was not among them. Was this because he was not involved, or was it just a partial list, or was Sam's name left off to avoid getting a friend in trouble? In any case, there is an outside source to corroborate Sam's early involvement. As mentioned above, Jim Blue Bird, the Oglala roadman, told anthropologist Omer Stewart that Sam Necklace was one of the earliest members of the Peyote church among the Yanktons.[116]

The most convincing evidence for Sam's early involvement, around 1910 or a little later, is the family's oral history concerning his conversion. Family stories from several sources have a common theme: as a young man Sam was kind of wild, but after his conversion to Peyotism he became a responsible adult. The experience of a sinner finding salvation through the use of Peyote is typical of many conversion narratives. The literature, both oral and written, is replete with such testimonials. For example, as described above, anthropologist Paul Radin collected such stories from the Winnebago Peyotists at the turn of the century.[117] In the oral history collection at the University of South Dakota there are several dozen recorded conversion stories. They are similar to the conversion experience that Charlie Jones described in 1916. Even today when one attends a Peyote meeting it is quite common to hear how Peyote turned someone's life around, particularly if alcohol abuse was involved. One also hears frequent testimonials about how Peyote cured an illness and turned an unhealthy person into a healthy person. Conversion testimonials and healing testimonials have been part of the Peyote religion since its inception.

The family memories of Sam, from troubled youth to responsible adult, imply that he made this change when he was a young man. He may have been having trouble with his parents. His attendance at Flandreau Indian School was irregular. He finally completed his schooling in June 1904 and returned to the reservation. Sam is not always listed as being part of the Necklace household on the Yankton census. Between 1900 and his marriage in 1906 he was either away at school or living independently on the reservation. This is relatively easy to track, because the annual census lists the Yanktons by households. Even if he was away at school, he would be listed with the family unless living independently. Living on one's own as a single person was not the norm, especially since Sam was needed at home, where economic circumstances were always difficult. Possibly he moved onto his own allotment. He seems to have moved back home in 1902, only to move out again in 1903.

In addition to the family memories of a youth with too much interest in horses, racing, gambling, and carrying a pistol on occasion, Sam began a relationship with a young white woman who lived on the eastern side of Charles Mix County. It is possible that it was this relationship that caused turmoil with his family. Sam and the woman set up a household together. She became pregnant and on 28 January 1906 gave birth to a daughter named Frances. By the time of the birth Sam's relationship with the mother had ended. According to Sam's niece, Auntie Pauline, her family put tremendous pressure on her to end the relationship as well as to give up the child. At this time Anglo-American racial attitudes, especially in South Dakota, were extremely negative toward Native Americans. A female child who was half-white, half-Indian would have had a very difficult time in white society and most certainly would have been an embarrassment to the family of the mother. The 1906 Yankton census lists Sam and his daughter Frances living together as a separate household.

The story of Sam's involvement with the white woman and their daughter Frances was first told to me by Auntie Pauline and later confirmed by Sam's grandson Asa. Auntie Pauline was an energetic and outspoken woman. When discussing her Uncle Sam, she said rather sarcastically, "Did Asa tell you the story about his grandpa and the white woman?" I said no, glancing at Asa. Auntie Pauline proceeded to tell the story. After we left, Asa said the story was true and that he wanted to show me something. We drove east along the Missouri River; as we approached the end of the reservation, he said to look over at a hill: "that's where my grandpa and that white woman lived." Aside from these two oral sources there is the annual Yankton census, which lists Frances as part of the Necklace household until the mid-1920s. One other source also confirms this account. In 1928 the BIA ordered its agents to begin indicating the "degree of blood" for each person under their jurisdiction. Each name was followed by an "fb" for full-blood or an "mb" for mixed-blood. On the 1928 census all the Necklaces are listed as full-blood, but Frances (now married) is listed as mixed-blood, indicating that her mother was not a Native American.[118]

This human drama became more complex as Sam began a relationship with Mary Chinn. It probably started as Sam's relationship with the white woman deteriorated. Sometime during this period, probably in late 1905,

Sam and Mary decided to marry. On 12 February 1906, just two weeks after Sam's daughter Frances was born, they were married in Tyndall Courthouse (Tyndall, South Dakota) by a justice of the peace. Upon examining their marriage license, I made an interesting discovery. On the marriage license application and the marriage license itself the names are "Sam Necklace" and "Mary Shield." This is puzzling, especially since Sam's tombstone says that he married Mary Chinn on 12 February 1906, and the license says that he married Mary Shield on the same day. A thorough year-by-year search of the census rolls did not turn up a Mary Shield. There was a Shield family in the census, but there was no Mary. The only conjecture that fits the facts is that Sam and Mary eloped and that Mary was afraid to put her real name on the license. It must have caused considerable consternation for Mary's family that the man she loved was having a child by another woman, especially a non-Indian woman, and they probably did not want her to have anything to do with Sam. Also, why did Sam and Mary go to the town of Tyndall to get married? It is almost forty miles away. This was not an easy trip on horseback or buggy when they could have been married right on the reservation. The application for the marriage license is signed "Mary Shields," but the marriage license is signed "Mary Shield." If this really was her last name, would she sign it differently? A waiting period was not required. The application and the license were signed the same day. The witnesses, J. Barber and G. Kirschman, were not Yanktons but probably courthouse employees.

The exact reason why the license says "Mary Shield" may never be known for certain. When I discussed this with many members of the Necklace family, none of them know anything about it. No one had ever heard of a Mary Shield, and everyone said that Mary Chinn and Sam were only married to each other. This includes their grandson Asa, their niece Auntie Pauline, and their daughter-in-law Katherine Necklace (wife of Dan Necklace, Sam and Mary's son), who was quite close to Mary in her later years.

We do know from the census records that Sam and infant Frances were part of one household in 1906; and in 1907 Sam, Mary, Frances, and Benedict (born on 29 April 1907 to Sam and Mary, fourteen months after their marriage) were living as a family in one household. The 30 June 1907 census reads:

Census #1301	Samuel B. Necklace	M	26
Census #1302	Mary C. Necklace	F wife	21
Census #1303	Frances Necklace	F dau.	2
Census #1304	Benedict Necklace	M son	3 mos.

A key point in the census is that Sam's wife is listed as Mary C. Necklace. The "C." is for "Chinn," her maiden name. There was never a Mary S. Necklace. Another possible way to explain an elopement is through a close analysis of the census (struck each 30 June). The census has Mary living with her parents in 1906 even though she was married in February 1906; but the 1907 census has her living with Sam. It may be that after the elopement Mary returned to her parents' home and then later told her parents of her marriage to Sam when she became pregnant. Sam did marry Mary Chinn in 1906, and they remained together until his death in 1949. Sam's probate records at the BIA office in Wagner, South Dakota, acquired for me by a family member, verify this account. The probate records state that Sam "was married, but once in his lifetime to Mary Chinn, YS-571-791" (allotment number) and that Frances Necklace, YSU-2602, was the daughter of the decedent and Ina Bowdish, born in 1906.[119]

The Chinn family's hostility toward Sam did not diminish in the years following the marriage. The Chinns had a low opinion of him as a result of recent events and concern for their daughter. In 1907 Mary, under the name "Mary Chinn Baker," applied for a patent in fee for 40 acres of her 120-acre allotment. Mary wrote to the superintendent: "I wish to make some improvements on my eighty acres if I sell the forty acres." While the application was pending, Mary's father, Eli Chinn, went to the superintendent and protested against the issuance of the patent in fee to his daughter. He said that Sam was a "drinking man" and would leave his daughter as soon as he had "squandered" the proceeds from the sale of the forty acres. R. J. Taylor, the local superintendent, also had a low opinion of Sam. He referred to him in his report as "a drunken dissolute husband" and recommended to the Indian Bureau that the patent in fee be denied. The acting commissioner of Indian Affairs wrote to Mary and said that because her husband was "dissipated" and "your competency to look after your own affairs is not clearly shown" her application was denied. The following year Mary again applied for a patent in fee and again received a negative recommendation from Superintendent Taylor and a denial from the BIA.[120]

Sam now had the responsibility of a family of four, but it seems unlikely that he was settled enough to provide a solid anchor for his family. Many people commented on the negative aspects of his lifestyle, and the family memory of him reinforces the negative commentary in the documents. We have to credit Mary with creating a stable household. For example, she accepted Sam's daughter Frances as part of the family. Frances grew up with all the Necklace children and remained part of the household until she married. She eventually had three children, who are all still living. Dakota culture does not distinguish between full siblings and half-siblings. All are regarded as brothers and sisters. Sam and Mary's second son, Dan, and his wife, Katherine, named one of their children Frances.[121]

Sometime during the period from 1910 to 1915 Sam's life changed when he became involved with the growing Yankton Peyote community. In his early thirties, he was settling down, trying to support his family and to change his reputation. In 1912 he was working as a laborer at the government boarding school in Greenwood. He earned $400 a year as one of two Yankton employees at the school. What is significant about this is that the administrators at the school were the same agency officials who earlier had written such derogatory comments about him. Being self-supporting was, of course, very difficult. In 1916 both Sam and Mary applied for a patent in fee, along with 184 other Yanktons. Both were viewed as "competent." The report described Mary as English speaking, quite bright, and "fully competent" to take case of her own affairs. The patent report on Sam stated that he "leases his allotment upon which there are no buildings, but 60 acres of which is under alteration by lessee. He has 3 horses, spring wagon, set of harness and speaks English quite well. Fully competent to transmit his own business." The questionnaire also asked if the individual was "addicted to the use of intoxicants." The answer on Sam's forms was that "he has been, but has not drank for some time."[122]

Approval would seem to be a routine procedure with positive commentary, but for reasons that are unclear Sam did not receive a patent in fee. In September 1916 he went to a Mr. Caster in Lake Andes, South Dakota, and asked for help in attaining a patent. Caster said he would help if Sam agreed to sell him forty of the eighty acres in the application. They agreed on a price of $1,100 and signed and notarized a contract. The agency officials learned of the contract and called Sam in for interrogation. What he did was illegal, since the land was technically under federal trust protection and was not yet Sam's to do as he pleased. After he gave testimony three times on sworn affidavits, the contract was declared invalid. During the testimony Sam was asked many questions. The answers give us additional insights into Sam and Mary's life. For example, when he was asked if his name was Samuel Baker or Samuel Baker Necklace, he said "Samuel Baker Necklace" but that he signed his name "Samuel N. Baker" because he was "told to do so" by Major McLaughlin, a government inspector. He said he had not yet received a patent in fee and wanted one now so that he could sell some of the land and use the money to provide a better home for his family. Sam said that he used to farm with Joe Bruguier but was now a laborer for either whites or Indians. When he was asked about the use of intoxicants, he said that he had not touched any in the last two years. In May 1920 Sam again applied for a patent in fee. This time it went smoothly. The land in this case was not his original allotment but forty acres that he had inherited. It was valued at $1,800. The report on Sam's application also gave additional information. It stated without comment that he "used peyote," that he was self-supporting by farming and leasing some of his land, and that he owned four horses. Mary still held her 120-acre allotment, valued at $6,000. Sam said that he wanted to sell the forty acres to build an addition to his house and purchase farm machinery.[123]

In addition to family history concerning Sam's conversion, other sources confirm his involvement, including Jim Blue Bird's reference to Sam Necklace as one of the first Peyotists. Joe Packard also credits Sam with helping spread Peyotism. Packard was not a Peyotist but a lifelong Episcopalian who knew Sam in his younger years. Packard said that Sam "sold that idea [Peyote religion] to our Dakota people. . . . He taught them how to sing and so on. So by God, I'll tell you a lot of our Dakota people here on the Yankton Reservation they caught the ideas by golly, they sang it too and they do it too." The interview with Auntie Pauline reinforces this. She said that Charlie Jones taught the people about Peyote and that her uncle Sam followed "in these footsteps and began running Peyote meetings."[124]

The most detailed account of Sam's conversion comes from his grandson Asa. In a series of taped interviews Asa gave the details of his conversations with his grandfather concerning his conversion. On many occasions Sam told his grandson that "the Peyote is the one that calmed me down." Sam said that an uncle of his had prayed for him and had taken him in a Sweat Lodge, but it was not working "until the Peyote at the turn of the century came in, . . . that's when it got into my mind." Sam did have a hectic lifestyle. In addition to horse racing and gambling, he told his grandson that he used to drink. He also said that he and his friend Joe Bruguier had pistols and would go to powwows and other similar gatherings on their horses. They would ride around shooting their pistols in the air, scaring everyone. Many of these stories about Sam's youth were told to Asa in the form of advice to a teenaged grandson. One particularly interesting account by Asa uses a wild horse as a metaphor:

> You can't be a roughneck all your life . . . I know God's ways can calm anybody down. He said that himself. Like a wild horse, they're pretty hard to calm down, you know, you have to train them. Understand that it can be a good horse, a real good horse, but he's going to fight. He's going to challenge not to be that way, but pretty soon you're going to calm him down where he'll learn to be a real good horse. . . . That's how the horse will get, you know, so no matter how wild a person you are, if you really put your mind sincerely towards God, he said, he'll calm [you] down. . . . He said that's the way I was.[125]

Sam's conversion to Peyotism definitely occurred after he was married. He told his grandson that after going to boarding school and learning what he wanted to learn he knew something was missing and wanted a family. He added: "I slowed down, married, began to have kids, but was still kind of wild." What seems to have had an impact on Sam at this time was the increase in the abuse of alcohol among the Yanktons. As part of the conversion process Sam claimed he went from heavy drinking to total abstinence and then to proselytizing to others about abstinence. Asa adds: "After my grandfather ate that, after he calmed down, he started working on the people because the drinking was coming in, he took them kind of guys, he said you can't be that way, here use some of this Peyote."[126]

Sometime after Sam became involved with the Peyote congregation he began to run meetings himself. This was in conjunction with a series of visions that Sam had after he started to attend meetings that led him further along the Peyote way. His grandson said: "My grandpa, the music came to him, he started singing the songs. He learned that, he saw another vision. You have to have a drum, to have a gourd [rattle], to have a staff and a fire, so he learned that." Sam believed that this vision meant he should be a roadman. Again according to his grandson, "God picked my grandpa, he went into a trance during a meeting; after midnight Charlie Jones just kept singing and drumming until he came around, fanned him off [with an eagle feather fan], cedared him off, asked him what happened. They took him somewhere, spirits, the spirits took him, they came after him and took him, that's when they showed him the fireplace that we got here now."[127]

It was Charlie Jones who taught Sam the basics, such as the songs, the drumming, and how to tie a drum and use the gourd rattle, but Sam could only use the knowledge in conjunction with his visions. The visions told him that he should proceed along the Peyote Road. Becoming a roadman was not easy. After learning the basics of the ceremony, one may be asked to serve as an assistant to a roadman or as the chief drummer to the roadman or as cedarman or cedar chief, in charge of burning the cedar. One might serve as fireman or fire chief and be in charge of the all-night fire. This included the responsibilities for making the spiritual markings or designs in the ashes. It might take years before one could acquire the necessary knowledge to be invited to run a meeting as a roadman. More was required than just knowledge, however: one must possess a moral and spiritual quality to be accepted as a roadman. One must be leading a morally responsible life and have spiritual insights that may come through visions or dreams. The visions that Sam Necklace told his grandson correspond exactly with Yankton or Dakota spiritual traditions. The acceptance of visions within the Yankton Peyote community would be no different from the visions that one could receive while fasting or sun dancing. The commonality of the vision experience, whether through the Peyote community or through traditional religious experience, confirms the view that Peyotism took root among some of the Yanktons because much of it paralleled traditional Yankton religious practices. This is confirmed even more when one examines Sam's visions as described by his grandson: "It [the fireplace] belongs to the people, the Ihanktonwan, our people here. The peyote blessed my grandfather. It gave him a vision about the way the fireplace goes. There are some markings in there that you got to make, you can't just poke the fire and make whatever markings you want. You got to make those that go with the Ihanktonwan way."[128]

All the members of the Necklace/Primeaux family who are active in the Native American Church know these markings and the visions behind them. Even the fourth and fifth generations of this family know about Grandpa Sam, as everyone calls him, and his visions. The markings that are made in the ashes are part of Sam's vision concerning his calling as a roadman. His great-grandsons Asa Primeaux, Jr., and Gerald Primeaux continue to tell the story of Sam's visions. The family members claim that in the vision Grandpa Sam was transported by spirits to the Ponca Reservation in Oklahoma and carried into a Peyote meeting in a tipi. He noticed that they were making seven markings in the ashes and asked what they meant. They told him that the seven markings represent the seven Ponca bands and when you put these markings in the ashes your prayers will be answered. After experiencing this vision Sam began using these seven markings, claiming that they represented the Seven Council Fires of the Sioux. The fireman makes these seven markings in the ashes in Sam's fireplace four times during the meeting. These sacred markings create an efficacious environment so that your prayers will be heard and answered. Asa, Sam's grandson, said that when you use these markings "someone will experience something in the mind." The tradition of using these markings has now been passed on through four generations of this family. As far as they know, they are the only ones to use these specific markings. Two great-grandsons, Asa, Jr., and Gerald, are now roadmen and run meetings. They continue to use the symbolic markings of their great-grandfather.[129]

The fact that Sam Necklace used his own fireplace markings was not unusual. Adding individual minor variations was not atypical. Many roadmen were "given" a special way in a vision that they passed on to their descendants. As early as 1925 anthropologist Ruth Shonle recognized that minor features of Peyote meetings, such as drawing symbolic lines or designs in the ashes, could vary from roadman to roadman. A present-day Lakota roadman, Vincent Catches, also says that "to each leader or roadman, a way is given. It may be handed down through each generation from a father or maybe a grandfather."[130]

As the Peyote community grew in the late 1910s and early 1920s, Sam became a roadman. He assumed leadership responsibilities as his spirituality and willingness to serve others became recognized. He was also known as great singer, a quality highly valued among Peyotists. His path from wayward youth to respected member of the Peyote faith prepared him for a leadership role. Mary and the children were active in the church's activities with Sam. The three surviving children, Jennie, Dan, and Ben, all remained lifelong members of the Native American Church. Participation as a family was typical, as it was for families who practiced traditional religions or who belonged to Christian denominations. But in the case of the Yankton Peyotists, they were becoming an extended family, a *tiošpaye*. This helped establish spiritual and family unity during the poverty-stricken years of the 1920s. In this environment the Peyote community functioned as the traditional band and *tiošpaye* had functioned before there was allotment and scattered housing.

THE DEFENSE OF PEYOTE

As Peyotism expanded throughout the West, the opposition grew. It came from both the executive and legislative branches of the federal government as well as from state governments and from many Christian denominations. Opposition also came from a significant number of Native Americans who supported assimilation and saw the Peyote religion as retarding progress toward "civilization." Many of these groups formed an alliance in order to eradicate Peyotism. This occurred not only on the Yankton Reservation but also throughout the West, wherever Peyotism emerged. The response to this repression took several forms. The first was to go underground by holding Peyote meetings in secret and then publicly downplaying the expansion or significance of Peyotism. This was not a practical or effective approach. Another option was to focus on the Christian elements in the Cross Fire ceremony; or, if Christian elements were absent, to add several to the service. It was hoped that having some Christian elements in the service, such as the use of the Bible, would mute the opposition. Peyotists also developed theological interpretations to parallel Christian theology. For example, Peyotists began to compare Peyote as a sacrament that was ingested as the body of God to the Christian belief in bread and wine as the flesh and blood of Jesus Christ or said that the fire in the center of a Peyote service represented God in the Old Testament saying: "Let there be light." Blowing the eagle bone whistle to the four directions was symbolic of announcing the birth of Jesus. The fire chief could shape the ashes into a heart or cross to symbolize Jesus, or people could claim the Peyote Road represented Jesus' road. It made no difference whether some of these were contrivances or sincerely held beliefs; they had no impact on muting the opposition to Peyote. There was another option to counter the opposition to Peyotism: seeking constitutional protection.

The first fully incorporated group with a clear articulation of Peyote as a sacrament emerged in Oklahoma in 1918. This was a watershed event in the history of the Peyote religion. It was neither the first Peyote organization nor the first to incorporate, but it was the first publicly to proclaim Peyote as a sacrament. There is some evidence that in 1914 a group called the Peyote Society was organized in Wisconsin but later changed its name to the Union

Church Society. During the same year Jonathan Koshiway incorporated a group called the First Born Church of Christ but did not mention Peyote in the articles of incorporation. Koshiway told anthropologist James Slotkin that he incorporated in order to acquire legal protection. He said that he chose a biblical passage for the name First Born Church of Christ (Hebrews 12:23). They purposely focused on the Christian elements in their ceremonies and charter in order to lessen opposition to their religion.[131]

In the summer and fall of 1918 Peyotists from all over Oklahoma gathered to discuss the continuing assault on their faith. This gathering was in response to the furious effort by the anti-Peyote forces that were trying to get Congress to outlaw Peyote. Up to this point there had been many attempts to stop Peyote usage, but they all had failed. Anti-Peyote bills had been introduced in Congress since 1916. Representative Harvey L. Gandy of South Dakota introduced the first such bill (HR 10669). Support for the Gandy bill came from the Department of Interior. Christian denominations that were active on reservations supported the bill, as did many Native American converts to Christianity. Native American organizations that were committed to an assimilationist philosophy, such as the National Indian Association, Indian Rights Association, Society of American Indians, Native American Student Conference, and Lake Mohonk Conference, also supported the bill. These groups issued a steady stream of anti-Peyote literature, some of which made its way into the media, with alarming titles such as "Peyote—An Insidious Evil," a pamphlet written by Herbert Welsh, president of the Indian Rights Association. He said that Peyote was evil and that tying Peyote to religion was pretense. In 1916 journalist Gertrude Seymour wrote an article titled "Peyote Worship: An Indian Cult and a Powerful Drug." She quoted various "authorities" on the pernicious nature of Peyote and expressed concern about the "rapid spread of peyote worship in the past decade." She called for legislation outlawing Peyote. In spite of the nationwide campaign the Gandy bill failed in 1916 and again in 1917, but in 1918 the anti-Peyote forces coordinated their activities in a final push to convince Congress to criminalize the use or possession of Peyote.[132]

Representative Carl Hayden of Arizona reintroduced the anti-Peyote bill in 1918 (HR 2614). This time congressional supporters of the bill planned extensive hearings in order to build a case against Peyote through the testimony of expert witnesses. It was in this atmosphere of prohibition and repression that the Oklahoma Peyotists began to consider incorporation as a strategy that would give them First Amendment protection. The intensity of the assault on Peyote was stimulated by the growth of the Peyote religion and the fear among BIA officials that it would thwart their ongoing "civilizing" mission. The Hayden bill was pushed as a reform that would benefit Native Americans. Even groups such as the Women's Christian Temperance Union and the Anti-Saloon League lobbied for the bill. This was the most determined attempt to pass a federal law explicitly prohibiting the use of Peyote. As the anti-Peyote forces amassed their arsenal of evidence and testimonials, the Peyote community planned to defend its rights.

A House of Representatives subcommittee of the Committee on Indian Affairs held hearings in 1918. A leading spokesman for the Hayden bill was Richard H. Pratt, former director of the Carlisle Indian School. Also supporting the legislation and the key witness for the anti-Peyote group was Gertrude Bonnin, a Yankton Sioux (see chapter 3). Bonnin was a very prominent person at the time, and it was hoped that as a Native American she would carry extra weight in testifying in favor of the prohibition of Peyote. She was a noted author, an officer of the Society of American Indians, and editor of its publication *American Indian Magazine.* The Society of American Indians, founded in 1911 in Columbus, Ohio, was an organization with an assimilationist agenda. Many of its members saw the so-called benefits of Anglo-American society and "saw themselves as the bearers of these blessings to their race." Bonnin, aware of the impact of public opinion, granted an interview with the *Washington Times* four days before the hearings began (17 February 1918, Sunday edition). She appeared in a photo wearing traditional Native American clothing. The headline read "Indian Woman in Capital to Fight Growing Use of Peyote Drug—Mrs. Gertrude Bonnin, Carlisle Graduate, Relative of Sitting Bull, Describes Effects of Mind Poison." Bonnin's claim that she was the granddaughter of Sitting Bull and a graduate of Carlisle Indian School was untrue. She never attended Carlisle; nor was she related to Sitting Bull. Continuing in the self-publicist mode, she appeared before the House subcommittee wearing the same American Indian garb and proceeded to testify to the supposed horrors of Peyote. She said that the use of Peyote led to orgies that included men, women, and children. Also testifying for the Hayden bill were Dr. Charles Eastman (Santee), Arthur C. Parker (Seneca), representatives from the YMCA and the Bureau of Catholic Missions, and scholars from Yale University and the University of Utah.[133]

Anthropologist James Mooney led the defense of the Peyote religion. Mooney worked for the Bureau of American Ethnology, a branch of the Smithsonian. He was already well known for his study of the Ghost Dance movement and had been studying and participating in Peyote meetings since 1891. Mooney had argued for almost two decades that Peyote did not cause any harmful effects and that Peyotism was a religion that deserved First Amendment protection.[134] In defending Peyotism, he tried to weaken the credibility of Gertrude Bonnin. He pointed out that her regalia was not Sioux: her dress was from a southern tribe, her belt was a Navajo man's belt, and—ironically—she was holding a Peyote feather fan. Mooney said that she had never attended a Peyote meeting or tried Peyote. He added that members of the Peyote community never drank alcohol and that Peyote served a significant healing function. Truman Michelson, an anthropologist at the Smithsonian, and William Safford, a botanist from the Department of Agriculture, supported Mooney's testimony in saying that Peyote was not habit forming. Several Native Americans testified in defense of Peyotism, including Francis La Flesche (Omaha), a non-Peyotist, as well as Peyote people from the Cheyenne, Comanche, and Osage nations. La Flesche gave very moving testimony on how Peyote reduced alcoholism among the Omahas.[135]

After the hearings ended, Mooney returned to Oklahoma fearing the worst. Seeing the possibility of an outright prohibition of Peyote, he suggested to the Oklahoma Peyotists that they incorporate under Oklahoma law. The BIA was furious with Mooney and ordered him off the Kiowa-Comanche Reservation. The BIA accused him of interfering with its administrative policies. Mooney left Oklahoma, never to return. He died of a heart attack in 1921 before completing a thirty-year project of writing the history of the Peyote religion. After Mooney left Oklahoma, the Peyote community incorporated on 18 October 1918, using the name "Native American Church." The name is quite significant in that it is Pan-Indian in character and intent and also implies indigenous roots for the Peyote faith. The charter states that "this corporation is formed to foster and promote the religious belief of the several tribes of Indians in the State of Oklahoma, in the Christian religion with the practice of the Peyote Sacrament." It is also significant that they chose the word "church" as part of their official name. They hoped that would help convince Congress that they deserved First Amendment protection. Their incorporation and charter became the model for Peyotists throughout America.[136]

Back in Washington, the House of Representatives passed the Hayden bill; however, it ran into difficulties in the Senate. The two senators from Oklahoma, under pressure from their own constituents, persuaded their colleagues not to support the prohibition of Peyote. The issue of religious freedom convinced a majority of senators not to vote for the bill. The bill failed, and a federal prohibition of Peyote was not enacted into law. The BIA did not accept this defeat. It continued to promote additional legislation and also sought other means to destroy the growing Peyote religion, such as getting the U.S. Post Office to ban shipments of Peyote through the mail. This was not rescinded until 1940.[137]

Yankton Peyotists followed the events in Washington, D.C., and Oklahoma very closely. They were very cognizant of the fact that two of their own people, Gertrude Bonnin and her husband, Raymond, were nationally recognized leaders in the anti-Peyote movement. Sam and Mary Necklace and the other Peyote people were worried about their access to Peyote as well as the future of their religion. The local BIA officials and local missionaries were still harassing them. Representatives Gandy and Hayden were still trying to get an anti-Peyote bill passed in Congress, and the BIA was now engaged in a campaign to convince individual states to outlaw Peyote. The activities of Gertrude Bonnin, who was lobbying state legislators in Colorado and Utah, were particularly disturbing. In 1921 her notoriety increased with the publication of her second book, *American Indian Stories,* a collection of autobiographical stories that had appeared twenty years earlier in *Harper's Magazine* and *Atlantic Monthly.*[138] Because of her years of living and lobbying in the nation's capital, her position as secretary of the Society of American Indians (until 1919), her husband being an employee of the BIA, and now the publication of this book, her ability to publicize her views on Peyote through the media was significant. The BIA continued to publish negative information and damaging testimonials. One such publication appeared in 1919, titled *Concerning Peyote,* compiled by Edgar B. Meritt, the assistant commissioner of the BIA. He included information on Peyote that was alarming and misleading, repeating all the arguments that "the devil's root" was evil, addicting, and debilitating.[139] The BIA published similar pamphlets in 1922, 1923, and 1925.

Meanwhile the BIA's campaign to have Peyote outlawed by state legislatures had some successes. In 1917 Colorado, Utah, and Nevada passed laws making the possession, sale, and transportation of Peyote illegal. Kansas did the same in 1920. The main concern of the Yanktons, of course, was South

Dakota. With South Dakota's congressional delegation voting for the Gandy and Hayden bills, it seemed only a matter of time before the state legislature outlawed Peyote. The legislatures of Arizona, Montana, and North Dakota were already debating the issue; and other states were planning to do so.[140] The concern was not that state authorities could interfere on reservations, for they could not; but they could use such a law to prevent the shipment of Peyote into the state and could arrest or harass people carrying Peyote from one reservation to another. Gertrude Bonnin's influence with state legislatures was very worrisome to the Yankton Peyote community. She was already credited with being a major influence on the Colorado and Utah legislature. By the time she died in 1938, fourteen states had outlawed Peyote. Omer Stewart wrote: "I am ready to give Mrs. Bonnin the major credit." In the early 1920s the Bonnins were back living on the Yankton Reservation and beginning to involve themselves in Yankton politics. One of their goals was to get both North and South Dakota to outlaw Peyote. To achieve this end they began lobbying the South Dakota legislature.[141]

An additional threat (considered in more detail in chapter 5) was the establishment of a Catholic mission on the reservation in 1920. Father Sylvester Eisenman was sent by the Benedictine Order to establish a boarding school and build a church. The Presbyterian and Episcopalian missions were already working against Peyote, but now the Catholic Church with the quite formidable Father Sylvester would put its considerable influence into the attempts to suppress the Yankton Peyotists. In this environment the precedent of the incorporation of the Native American Church in Oklahoma loomed large. Also, as described earlier, the Winnebagos of Nebraska incorporated in 1921, being the first Peyote group outside of Oklahoma to do so. Because the Winnebago and Yankton Peyote communities were so closely involved with each other, one can assume that the Yanktons were influenced by the Winnebago incorporation.

It was in this context of a continuing federal threat, a growing state threat, and an intensifying local threat, combining a secular and sectarian assault on Peyote, that the Yankton Peyotists decided to follow the Native American Churches in Oklahoma and Nebraska and incorporate. Since the establishment of the Yankton Peyote community in the first decade of the twentieth century, its members had functioned in a hostile environment, doing whatever they could to resist interference in their spiritual lives. Now, in 1922, incorporation seemed to be the answer.

CHAPTER FIVE

The Native American Church
of Charles Mix County

1922–29

Peyote water drum. Drawn by Asa Primeaux, Jr.

The 1920s were a difficult decade for the Yankton people as well as for the Necklace family. The economic base of the family was never secure. Sam still worked intermittently for local white farmers. He added to the family's food supply by fishing in the Missouri River, while Mary kept a garden outside their home. Occasionally supplies were available from the Agency Head-quarters, but in the 1920s this source of food became unreliable. They still received a small annual income from leasing part of their allotted land. Their lives were punctuated by tragedy and joy, as the family experienced the cycle of birth, marriage, and death. In 1922 Sam was forty-one and Mary was thirty-seven. The household consisted of eight people, soon to be seven after illness and death took five-month-old Hazel. The death certificate lists "bowel trouble" as the cause of death. Frances was now sixteen; Ben, fifteen; Dan, eleven; Jennie, nine; and Pearl, three. Hazel was Mary's second child to die; both were under the age of two. Mary gave birth to seven children; only four survived into adulthood. After Hazel died, Sam's father died. He had not joined his son in the Native American Church; he remained an active Episco-palian and is buried in the Episcopal cemetery in Greenwood. With poor nutrition and limited access to health care, the Yanktons had a high death rate, especially among children. The census data for the 1920s show a growth rate of less than 1 percent.

The reality of illness and death was tempered by birth and marriage. Sam's daughter Frances married a non-Yankton in 1926, but they continued to live on the reservation. Benedict married in 1927. Within a year Frances had a daughter and Ben had a son. Sam and Mary were now grandparents, a highly valued status among the Yanktons. Being a grandparent brought joy and responsibility. The younger generation began to call Sam "Grandpa Sam." This is the Dakota way of showing respect to elders regardless of the blood relationship. Even today the family members and others still refer to him affectionately as Grandpa Sam. The Necklaces, like most other Yanktons, simply wanted a family life and spiritual life without outside interference. They wanted to be part of Yankton culture as well as to share a sense of family with the Peyote community. They did not want a continuing assault on their spiritual lives.

Throughout 1922 the BIA continued attacking the Peyote religion. In the BIA's annual report for 1922, Charles H. Burke, commissioner of Indian Affairs, proposed legislation "to control the growing and harmful habit among the Indians of using peyote." He also dismissed the idea that Peyotism was a religion, claiming that the Peyote community was just using this argument to prevent the prohibition of Peyote.[1] One may wonder why the BIA would go to such incredible lengths to prohibit and eliminate Peyote. The number of American Indians who were active in the Native American Church was not significant. According to BIA figures, only 4 percent of Native Americans were active Peyotists, yet the bureau expended tremendous energy in trying to stop Peyotism. Even if the 4 percent figure is low, it is hard to understand why the BIA saw Peyotism as a threat. Its fear was that Peyotism, with its integration of American Indian culture and language, might threaten the successful completion of the acculturation programs. Captain Pratt's maxim "Kill the Indian, save the Man" was threatened by Peyotism. The long-range goal to eliminate Native American culture and turn American Indians into Anglo-Americans was being challenged. For example, there was a similar campaign underway to eliminate customary marriage ceremonies. The mindset of Commissioner Burke and other BIA officials was made clear in their 1922 annual report dealing with "Indian Custom Marriage and Divorce." The commissioner wrote: "I think it not untimely to suggest the need of legislation subjecting all Indians to the laws of civilization respecting their marital relations. . . . The vicious practice of Indian custom marriage and separation is deplorable." Burke's Social Darwinism was clear when he referred to "loose marital relations of barbaric origin" and the need for decent family life before we can have "progress toward civilization."[2] This same attitude extended to Peyote because it was retarding "progress."

Peyote communities considered this a very real threat. In 1922 Congressman Hayden introduced another bill to criminalize Peyote. A number of states began debating its prohibition. In 1923, and in every year until 1934, the Indian Appropriations Bill included $25,000 for the "suppression of traffic in intoxicating liquors and deleterious drugs, including peyote."[3] One of the most alarming concerns was the continued dissemination of anti-Peyote propaganda by the BIA. The U.S. Congress refused to criminalize Peyote, forcing the BIA to seek other means to reach its ends. As noted in chapter 4, the BIA published a pamphlet in 1922 titled *Peyote,* written by Dr. Robert E. L. Newberne, chief medical supervisor of the BIA. The government printed and distributed 3,000 copies of this pamphlet. It was reprinted in 1925 and again widely distributed to individuals, libraries, and reservations until Commissioner John Collier withdrew it from circulation in 1934.[4]

The pamphlet attacks Peyotism in every conceivable way. The harshness of its language and its Social Darwinian ideas seem out of place even for the 1920s. Every social, moral, economic, and biological argument is used. It begins with a scientific tone by describing the plant and its geographic distribution and briefly analyzing its usage in Mexican history. This is followed by the use of two methods to attack Peyote: the mockery of Peyotism as a religion and the use of negative testimonials. The pamphlet reviews the writing of missionaries who saw Peyotism as "pagan" worship. The language used to attack Peyote was based on a good versus evil paradigm. For example, Christianity versus paganism or the "power of a drug" versus the "elevating influence of the Cross." The pamphlet attacks Peyote communities that were considering incorporation, contending that incorporation was a fraud, a simple ploy to gain First Amendment protection for drug usage. In a mocking tone, the author says that having a "Peyote Christian Church is as incongruous as it would be to recognize the Opium Christian Church, or the Cocaine Society of Christians."[5]

The testimonials that follow are from missionaries and medical people who had no direct contact with Peyote communities. The testimonials are consistent in viewing Peyote as a habit-forming and intoxicating drug that has a negative effect on the mind, body, and soul, causing heart failure, hemorrhage, brain disturbance, laziness, and inertia. A Reverend Mr. Vruwink writes that it is difficult to stop Peyote usage because "they are drug fiends bound hand and foot."[6] Another typical theme is that Peyote leads to sexual promiscuity. Terminology such as "lust of the flesh," "orgies," and "scenes of unbridled libertinism" is typical. One interesting comment from a medical doctor concludes that Peyote "produced imperfect coordination of movement."[7] Anyone who has ever been to a Peyote meeting and witnessed the coordination of drumming and shaking a gourd rattle would not make such an uninformed statement. None of the testimonial writers ever stated that they had attended a Peyote meeting. The pamphlet was blatant propaganda. Its goal was to influence people who had no direct knowledge of the Peyote religion so that they would support legislation making the use of Peyote in the Native American Church illegal.

The policy of the BIA, in spite of the reluctance of the U.S. Congress to challenge the First Amendment over Peyote, continued unchanged; but its strategy changed. It began targeting state legislatures. The BIA, along with church groups and assimilationist organizations such as the Indian Rights Association, started lobbying state legislators. Several states banned Peyote in 1922 (see chapter 4). This was a great concern to members of the Yankton Peyote community, because they knew the South Dakota legislature was being lobbied by two prominent Yanktons: Gertrude and Raymond Bonnin. In addition, there was a new enemy of the Native American Church on the reservation.

In 1921 the Catholic mission on the reservation was assigned a resident priest. Father Sylvester Eisenman took the appointment and established what became known as Marty Mission. For the next three decades he worked very hard to weaken if not eliminate Peyotism from the reservation. This new threat came at a time when the South Dakota legislature was considering a total ban on Peyote. In 1922 members of the Yankton Peyote community began discussing ways to protect their religion. There was only one answer: incorporation. The Oklahoma Peyotists had incorporated in 1918, and their close friends among the Winnebagos had incorporated in 1921. All the Peyote communities in South Dakota felt threatened. After some debate, it seemed that the best plan of action was not the Oklahoma model of one corporation for the entire state but for each Peyote community to incorporate separately. The first to do so were the Peyotists from the Pine Ridge Reservation. On 5 October 1922 they filed incorporation papers under the name "Native American Church of Allen, South Dakota." Between 1922 and 1939 eleven Peyote groups incorporated in South Dakota.[8] The Yanktons were the second, filing incorporation papers on 23 October 1922 and receiving their official Articles of Incorporation from the state on 28 November, under the name "Native American Church of Charles Mix County."

The purpose of incorporation was to gain constitutional protection, but there was another concern about the wording in the document. The issue in preparing the Articles of Incorporation was whether the word "Peyote" should or should not be included. This was not a theological issue; no one doubted the primacy of Peyote. It was a practical issue that was resolved by emphasizing Christianity and downplaying Peyote as a way to mute opposition to their religion. Omer Stewart states correctly that in South Dakota the word "Peyote" is not mentioned in any of the articles of incorporation of any Peyote group. Initially this was not the case with the Yanktons. In Sam Necklace's notebook (see appendix I), there is a handwritten version of the original articles that differs from the version filed with the state. The preamble of the former begins: "We, the church organization of the peyote church of christ [sic]." Article II states: "The purpose of the corporation is to foster and promote the christian religious belief of the Sioux Indians of South Dakota, and all Indians within the United States, recognizing, adopting, continuing and using the peyote for Sacramental and religious purposes, and teaching the scriptures, morality, kindly charity, right living, to cultivate a spirit of self respect, brotherly love and union among all the American Indians. . . ."[9]

The article concludes with the words "in the year of our Lord 1922 on Oct. 7th." Obviously, the word "Peyote" was used in the first sentence of the preamble in referring to the organization as "the peyote church of christ" and emphasized in Article II. When the Articles of Incorporation were notarized on 23 October and filed with the state, there was no reference to Peyote at all. The reference to "the peyote church of christ" in the preamble was deleted, and Article II was rewritten. It states: "The purpose of the corporation is to foster and promote the Christian religious belief among the Sioux Indians of South Dakota and North Dakota, and all Indians within the United States and to teach among them the scriptures, morality, charity, right living, to cultivate the spirit of self-respect, brotherly love and union among all American Indians. . . ."[10] The major difference between Article II of the Necklace notebook and the official version filed with the state is that the phrase "using the peyote for Sacramental and religious purposes" was deleted from the latter.

We can only guess at the debate over the wording between the two documents. One view was that Peyote, as a gift of God and the central sacramental element, should be included in the wording, as the Oklahoma Peyotists did in referring to themselves as a "Christian religion with the practice of Peyote sacrament." The opposite view was that the purpose of incorporation was constitutional protection and the muting of opposition; therefore Peyote should not be mentioned. The pragmatic viewpoint won out. The Yanktons may also have been influenced by the Winnebagos, who incorporated in 1921 as the "Peyote Church of Christ" but amended their charter in 1922 and changed their name to the "Native American Church of Winnebago, Nebraska."[11]

The meeting to establish a Yankton Peyote church took place on 7 October at the home of Charles Iron Hawk. He served as acting chair of the meeting, and Sam Necklace served as secretary. Following state guidelines for incorporation, they established a board of directors, elected a slate of officers, and completed bylaws. The members elected Charles Iron Hawk, Johnson Goodhouse, and Henry Wind Shooter as directors of the corporation. They then elected Johnson Goodhouse (president), Charles Iron Hawk (vice-president), Samuel B. Necklace (secretary), and Henry Wind Shooter (treasurer) as well as a "committee of six," who, with the officers, signed the articles. The committee members were Amos Shields (chair), Joshua Pretty Bull, Not Afraid of Pawnee, George Circle Fool, William J. Eaglethunder, and Francis Little Stallion. On 23 October the articles were notarized and affidavits signed verifying the election of officers. Necklace, Goodhouse, and Iron Hawk signed the affidavits and were "duly sworn" that they were the incorporators. According to Sam Necklace's notebook, the organization of the church followed the nonprofit corporate model. The president, vice-president, and Committee of Six constituted the governing board of trustees. There were other committees, biannual elections, annual dues, and bylaws outlining procedures, rights, and responsibilities. The church also had the right to own, buy, and sell property for carrying out its religious purposes. Dues were $1.25 per year for each adult member, and no one was allowed to borrow money from the church treasury. Johnson Goodhouse was elected the first chief priest. He was to conduct all the "prayer meetings for the Native American Church," which occurred the first Saturday of each month.

Once established, the Yankton Peyote church seems to have functioned relatively smoothly in terms of its internal development. There were elections, business was conducted, and, most importantly, regular Peyote meetings were held. The Peyote prayer services were conducted in the home of the chief priest or in the home of one of the members. This was the same as it had been in the early years of the church; but now as a corporation less secrecy was needed while on the reservation. In his correspondence to Washington,

Superintendent R. E. L. Daniel, who held this position for seven years (1923–30), complained about and condemned Peyote. He still supported federal prohibition of Peyote but took no overt action against the Yankton Peyote community. This was corroborated by Eunice Rainbow Dog Soldier (1912–94). She said that she remembered going to Peyote meetings with her family throughout the late 1920s and did not recall any trouble with local authorities.[12]

Nevertheless, in 1922 there were concerns about possible persecution or at least confiscation of Peyote. As noted, this led not only to excluding the word "Peyote" from the incorporation document but also to trying to make the organization sound Christian. Article II states that the purpose of the corporation is to promote the Christian religion and to teach the scriptures. The word "church" is in the title, leaders are called "priests" who are "ordained," and members are "baptized" and receive "sacraments." The question of whether these Christian elements were a strategy to acquire protection and mute opposition or a sincere reflection of the Christian beliefs of the members within the context of the Peyote religion is difficult to answer; most likely both motives were operative. Certainly incorporation was to gain First Amendment protection, yet there is no evidence to claim that the inclusion of Christian elements was hypocritical. Anyone who attends a Cross Fire meeting today would not question the sincerity of the commitment to Peyote, the Bible, and Jesus Christ. Sam Necklace's grandson Asa, one of the few Half Moon Yanktons, claims that his grandfather was really Half Moon but was forced to follow the Cross Fire way to avoid harassment. There is no evidence to support this statement, but it is clear that throughout his lifetime Sam Necklace practiced the Cross Fire way. The language in his notebook reflects this, particularly the words he wrote for baptisms: "Christ took upon him the nature of man, he died for the whole human race, without respect of persons; equally for all."[13] It is unclear whether the language is Sam's or whether, as secretary, he was recording the words of others. The only evidence we have comes from an interview with Clarence Rockboy. When asked this question, he said that his father, Joe, told him that Sam wrote the original charter.[14]

In examining the events of 1922, there is also an important reference to this year by longtime priest Reverend Joseph M. Shields, Sr., the son of Amos Shields, one of the original members of the church's Committee of Six. In 1976 Joe Shields was interviewed in Lake Andes, South Dakota, when he and six other Yankton Peyotists (including Asa Primeaux) were recording Peyote songs for Indian House Records. The interview is printed on both the record and cassette notes. Shields said that they wanted to

> become a church, and get established as other churches, so that they'd be free, so they won't be afraid to come out in the open with their religion . . . that was back then in 1922. They got themselves together, and talked this over, and then went to the State Capital, and got themselves chartered. . . . Now the Yankton people have their own church, and they have their own church grounds and cemetery, and all the principles that other churches have—Baptism, Confirmation, Marriage, Confession, and Burial. That's how they're established. From 1922, it's been coming up that way.[15]

Another longtime Peyotist and roadman, Quentin "Sonny" Bruguier, said that the purpose of getting a charter in 1922 was to avoid harassment and that they did base the charter on both the Bible and Peyote.[16] In reviewing all the evidence, as sparse as it is, there is no reason to doubt either motive. The purpose of incorporation, its language, and its integration of Christian elements was to seek legal protection as well as to express a spirituality based on Peyote and the Bible, but with all Peyotists proclaiming the preeminence of Peyote. Also, when the Yanktons were introduced to Peyote, they were taught the Cross Fire way by Charlie Jones, who had learned about it from two of its the most famous teachers, Albert Hensley and John Rave. Another viewpoint concerning these events is that Christianity was added only as a mode of protection; but after a number of years Christianity became a well-integrated and essential element of the Yankton Peyotism. Some members of the Necklace/Primeaux family say this is what happened with Sam Necklace—that Christian elements were originally only a veneer but later became integral. There is no evidence supporting this viewpoint. It is a possible explanation but not a probable one.

Following incorporation, the Yankton Peyotists hoped to conduct their activities in a routine fashion; but lurking in the background was the fear that the state of South Dakota would outlaw Peyote. The state had no jurisdiction on the reservation, but it could interfere with the transport of Peyote into the state or arrest Peyotists who were traveling between reservations. In 1923 Arizona, Montana, North Dakota, and South Dakota banned Peyote. The leader of this effort in South Dakota was Representative Harvey L. Gandy, already known to Peyotists as the author of the Gandy bill that had been introduced earlier into the U.S. House of Representatives to make possession of Peyote a federal offense. With the failure of this bill, Gandy turned his attention to his home state. He had a very experienced and capable ally: Gertrude Bonnin, the Yankton woman who made it a lifelong crusade to abolish Peyotism. The two of them orchestrated the process. In January legislation was introduced into the South Dakota House and Senate "to prohibit the traffic in and the possession of Peyote." During the debate on the bill Bonnin brought in twenty anti-Peyote Sioux to testify for the bill. No one testified against the bill. After this first reading, the bill was sent to the Committee on Food and Drugs. It recommended passage. The maximum punishment was a $500 fine and/or one year in jail. To no one's surprise, the bill passed easily: forty-one to one in the House, ninety-seven to zero in the Senate. It became law on 26 February 1923, when Governor William H. McMaster signed it. South Dakota had now criminalized the possession of Peyote. Eventually a total of fourteen western states would follow suit.[17]

In cases where Peyotists were arrested, it was not unusual for the charges to be dismissed or to be reversed on appeal. The attorney general of South Dakota, Buell F. Jones, tried a unique approach: he attempted to convince the secretary of state to void the Articles of Incorporation of the various Native American Churches and not to issue any new ones, because their purpose was to engage in an activity that was "illegal." This line of reasoning found no support.[18] In spite of positive developments for Peyote communities, opposition did not disappear. Some harassment continued, mostly in the form of confiscation of Peyote, because the U.S. Postal Service prohibited its passage through the mails. Nor did the Bureau of Indian Affairs stop its assault. In 1923 it issued yet another document attacking Peyotism: a 34-page typescript called "Peyote" that was sent to reservation officials, church groups, and nonprofit organizations concerned with Native Americans. It was very similar to the 1922 pamphlet. One interesting testimonial in the pamphlet is by R. E. L. Daniel, a BIA official from Oklahoma and soon to be the superintendent of the Yankton Agency. He wrote: "Its excessive use undoubtedly retards moral development and causes moral degeneracy . . . [and] produces general paralysis of the nervous system."[19]

By the mid-1920s the Yankton Peyotists were less concerned about state authorities, somewhat wary of reservation officials such as Superintendent Daniel, but very concerned about the growing missionary impact on the reservation. This was especially the case after Father Sylvester arrived; now three denominations (Catholic, Presbyterian, and Episcopalian) were strongly opposed to both traditional religion and the Native American Church.[20] The Catholic mission was not a direct threat to the existence of the Native American Church, but it was a severe irritant and threat to its growth. Father Sylvester's strategy was to paint the Peyote people with a very negative brush in order to make them look evil and in league with the devil. He wanted to prevent other Yanktons from joining the Peyote community by turning Peyote people into outcasts—or, to put it another way, to marginalize a group of people who were already within a marginalized group.

As described earlier, there had been a small number of Yankton Catholics since the first visit of Father De Smet in 1839. Lay leaders served the Catholic community on the reservation.

In 1918 the Benedictines assigned Father Sylvester to serve as an itinerant priest to ten missions on three reservations. His first major decision was to replace St. Paul's chapel with a larger facility. He purchased a church building in Wagner and had it moved thirteen miles to Marty. The old chapel functioned as a day school while a permanent school building was built. Once he was appointed as a permanent resident Father Sylvester's long-range plan was an extensive missionary complex with a large new church as the centerpiece of the mission. He began a fund-raising campaign and transformed the day school into a boarding school in 1924. In 1931 he added a secondary school, and two years later a three-story school building was completed that was in use until 1999. The Marty Mission became quite a large complex, eventually including thirty buildings and many acres of surrounding farm land. As the mission grew, so did the town of Marty. In 1928 a U.S. Post Office was established, with Father Sylvester as the first postmaster.[21]

In order to finance this growing operation, Father Sylvester built a print shop and published a monthly magazine called the *Little Bronzed Angel* (first issue June 1924). The bronzed angel was a smiling Indian child named "Little Dan," who had long black hair and wore a beaded vest. His photo adorned the masthead of the magazine. Father Sylvester developed an extensive nationwide mailing list of potential donors who received the magazine and appeal letters. One such appeal letter read: "My dear Friend, Our people here are the poorest of God's poor. In rags and tatters they live in wretched hovels, suffering from hunger and exposure."[22]

Father Sylvester worked very hard at fund-raising because it was the lifeblood of Marty Mission. Some of the fund-raising advice came from his friend Father Edward Flanagan, the founder of Boys Town. Father Sylvester also traveled to various cities to raise money. Chicago was one of his favorite sites. He took Indian children with him as fund-raising props. He would dress them in pseudo-Indian garb and have them sing, drum, and dance for potential donors. It is very ironic that at the boarding school children were not allowed to "speak Indian" and had to wear Anglo-style clothing, yet while fund-raising they wore "Indian" clothing with feathers on their heads and "tom-toms" in their hands. It is no less ironic that "Little Dan" is pictured with long hair, yet the boys in school were forbidden to have long hair.[23] Another way to raise money was for the Catholic women to make quilts for Father Sylvester to sell while on the fund-raising trips. Over the years hundreds of thousands of dollars were raised. Some of this money was used to purchase what had been reservation land from individual Yanktons who had received fee patents for their land.[24]

The funding supported Father Sylvester's dual missions of religious proselytization and vocational education. Both were based on instilling authority, discipline, frugality, self-restraint, and an Anglo-American work ethic. The regimen included daily communion, prayer, chapel every evening, and daily Bible instruction. Students were required to mix vocational instruction, religious instruction, and work. Having students work was an economic necessity for the school, but work was also to instill discipline. The students' pay was meager. Young students received three cents per week, older students fifty cents per week. They were expected to tithe one-third of their income. Father Sylvester was also able to build such a complex with limited resources because of the high unemployment on the reservation. Many Yanktons were hired as laborers for very low wages. Historian Gerald Wolff has described Father Sylvester's approach to American Indians as paternalistic in that he viewed them as childlike, only capable of manual labor. Rarely, if ever, did he allow the participation of Indians in positions of responsibility. Only after Father Sylvester's death in 1948 did St. Paul's High School add a college preparatory program with full-day classes. Unfortunately for many Yanktons, he saw American Indian religion in general, and Peyotism in particular, as a threat to his work. He usually referred to Peyotists as "medicine-eaters" or "peyote-eaters."[25]

Father Sylvester was not alone in these beliefs; Protestant missionaries held similar views. For example, in 1923 there was some debate about moving the Yankton Agency headquarters from Greenwood to Wagner. Reverend John P. Williamson, the Presbyterian missionary, immediately protested, requesting that the headquarters remain in Greenwood in order to maintain a "restraining influence" on the Yanktons, because without the superintendent local morals would be threatened and under the "cover of dances the most drunken and licentious orgies would take place."[26] The headquarters was not moved at this time.

In the 1920s, as in every other decade since the 1870s, church and state worked together, attempting to impose Anglo-American values on reservation communities. Aside from opposition from federal, state, and church officials, there were two sources of internal opposition to Peyotism on the reservation. Some members of the oldest generation of Yanktons, mostly full-bloods, remembered and valued—and sometimes still secretly practiced—the spiritual life of their parents and grandparents. Other people of this same generation, such as Grandma White Tallow and Chief Blue Cloud, were devout Catholics, following the example of Chief Struck by the Ree. Very few of the oldest generation became members of the Native American Church. The others in opposition to the Native American Church were members of the younger, generally less than full-blood generation that had been to boarding school or day school, belonged to a Christian denomination, spoke mostly English, had an acculturated lifestyle, and were active in Yankton politics. For example, in 1916 ninety-two Yanktons sent a petition to the U.S. Senate and the House of Representatives by way of the commissioner of Indian Affairs, supporting the passage of the anti-Peyote legislation being considered in Congress. It says: "All, the undersigned, members of the Yankton Sioux Temperance Union" petition the Congress to pass the Gandy bill to stop the "traffic in Peyote," adding that any delay in its passage would be a hindrance to the "civilization" of the Yankton people.[27] The existence of the petition reflects the continuing growth of Peyotism. In addition Gertrude and Raymond Bonnin were back living at least part of the time on the reservation. They became very active in local politics while continuing their campaign against Peyotism on the state and national level.

Yankton politics in the 1920s continued to be divisive. It was fueled by the endemic poverty that manifested itself in power struggles between factions. They struggled over representation on such issues as the tribal enrollment and land compensation cases. There was the potential to develop political unity over these cases, because everyone realized that speaking with one voice would assist their quest for financial compensation from the government over lost land, but achieving unity proved elusive. The specific claims involved the Red Pipestone Reservation in Minnesota and the Black Hills in South Dakota. These claims were not new, but they were brought to the forefront in 1920 when Congress authorized the United States Court of Claims to deal with Sioux land claims.[28] In 1921 the BIA prepared a final census roll of the Yankton population. This enrollment list would provide the basis for a per capita distribution of funds if the Court of Claims ruled in favor of the Yanktons, which made local politics more intense. Factions emerged, usually with the full-blood/mixed-blood dichotomy establishing a fault line. Underlying this factionalism was the economics of dwindling resources, with little hope for the future except for the possibility of financial compensation from a successful claim against the government. The Yanktons had an elected Business Committee and a Tribal Council. The Business Committee met, but factionalism and controversy ensued over who should represent the Yanktons in negotiations with the BIA. The committee debated the makeup of such a delegation, debated making additions to or deletions from the tribal census roll, and debated the parameters of the claims cases as well as who had the authority to sign a contract with a law firm to represent them. The situation was complex. People gathered, elected committees, and chose representatives; but others would not accept this, arguing that the process did not allow for sufficient participation. Some complained to the superintendent or petitioned the commissioner of Indian Affairs.

The complexity and interplay of economics and politics allowed for the merging of three issues: the power struggle between full-bloods and mixed-bloods, the controversy over the enrollment list, and the pursuit of the land cases. Many of the older full-bloods, without private or public school education or experience in politics, feared losing whatever influence they still possessed. Specifically, they worried about not receiving a fair share of the tribe's assets. Since the turn of the century, Yankton leadership had been passing to those who were the most acculturated, usually the mixed-bloods, who were almost all Christians. The full-bloods petitioned both the superintendent and the BIA to be allowed to send a delegation to Washington, D.C. In 1924 Superintendent Daniel reported on such a petition: "There is much dissatisfaction among the old full-bloods about the way certain mixed-bloods who pretend to have their interest at heart have as they say squandered contributions in misrepresenting them."[29] Daniel recommended against such a trip, suggesting that a more representative group be sent. The full-bloods wanted to go to Washington so that their viewpoints on the contentious issues would get a fair hearing. They did not believe they could get a fair hearing on the reservation, especially because the superintendent supported the most acculturated Yanktons.

In 1925 the Yanktons signed a contract with a Washington law firm to represent them in the Red Pipestone Reservation claim. The case goes back to the 1858 treaty and the establishment of the reservation. The Yanktons had been the caretakers of the red pipestone quarry. The site is sacred ground to all branches of the Sioux nation. The red stone that is used to make Sacred Pipes was mined here. The Lakotas, Dakotas, and Nakotas believe that the stone is sacred, because it is the flesh and blood of human ancestors. They tell a story of the great flood many ages ago. As the water rose, people fled to the mountaintops; but they could not escape the deluge and drowned. Their flesh, bones, and blood turned into the red pipestone. But not all had perished. In 1836 artist and explorer George Catlin was told: "While they were all drowning in a mass, a young woman, K-wap-tah-w, caught hold of the foot of a very large bird that was flying over, and was carried to the top of a high cliff, not far off, that was above the water. Here she had twins, and their father was War-Eagle, and her children have since peopled the earth." The site became well known to America after Catlin wrote about the great flood and the origin of the red pipestone in his books. He did an oil painting, *Pipe Stone Quarry*, of the reddish cliffs, depicting local people mining pipestone. Catlin sent samples back east. It was named catlinite in his honor. His writing inspired Henry Wadsworth Longfellow to write the poem "The Peace Pipe" as part of his *Song of Hiawatha* (1855). It was an ode to the power of the Great Spirit who gave the red pipestone to humanity. The Sioux today still tell the story of the great flood.[30]

Article 8 of the Treaty of 1858 stipulated that the Yanktons should have free and unrestricted use of the quarry. The Yanktons assumed it still belonged to them. The federal government believed that it had acquired the quarry and only guaranteed the Yanktons access to it. The government, thinking that it had control over the Pipestone Reservation, opened it up to non-Indian settlers. The Department of the Interior negotiated another agreement with the Yanktons in 1899. They agreed to give up all claims to the Pipestone Reservation except for a forty-acre track to be used for mining and camping. The government agreed never to sell the surrounding land and to pay the Yanktons $100,000. By a fourteen-vote margin, the Yanktons supported the agreement; however, the agreement died in a Senate committee after the senators were told that the government already owned the land. In 1910 Congress gave the Court of Claims jurisdiction in the case, but it did not resolve the dispute until it was given additional jurisdiction in 1920.[31] Resolution of the case now seemed possible; and with the growing debates over claims to the Black Hills, the full-bloods wanted their voices heard. A trip to Washington was the answer.

In March 1925 a group of Yanktons traveled to the nation's capital. Munn, Anderson and Munn, the law firm representing the Yanktons, hosted them. There were seven members of the delegation. Five made the trip from South Dakota: Moses Standing Bull, Hollowhorn, Simon Antelope, Ben Vandall, and David Simmons (half-brother of Gertrude Bonnin). The other two delegates, Gertrude and Raymond Bonnin, were already in Washington (Raymond was employed by Munn, Anderson and Munn). The Bonnins were leaders in the land claims cases. Gertrude Bonnin, a well-known author and political activist, was changing her politics at this time. She had moved away from assimilationist organizations such as the Indian Rights Association and was supporting John Collier's American Indian Defense Association. She worked to publicize the poor conditions on reservations and was now a critic of the BIA. Even with her support for the full-bloods and her support for keeping a strong reservation land base, however, she continued to be a vehement opponent of Peyotism.[32] The delegates arrived in Washington on 2 March; on 4 March they attended the inauguration of President Calvin Coolidge. Two days later, they were honored at a banquet at the Metropolitan Club, sponsored by Jennings C. Wise, the attorney who was handling the Yankton case. An impressive list of guests included Andrew W. Mellon, secretary of the treasury; John W. Weeks, secretary of war; Charles Burke, commissioner of Indian Affairs; General Nelson A. Miles; and foreign dignitaries, such as the ambassadors of Great Britain and Spain. James M. Beck, acting attorney general, gave the keynote address. A special souvenir program was printed and distributed to all in attendance.[33] It was an elaborate show of Washington pomp and ceremony.

On 9 March the delegation met with Edgar Meritt, assistant commissioner of Indian Affairs. The Yanktons challenged the enrollment of certain individuals, claiming that they were fraudulently added to the Yankton census. During the discussions both Hollowhorn and Moses Standing Bull (aged seventy and seventy-six, respectively) complained about the "old" Indians being taken advantage of by younger, "educated" Indians. Standing

Bull said: "We Indians are not able to read or write and our voice is strong. We may be able to talk loud—even sound like the roar of guns but it isn't recorded anywhere but you take these tricky young Indians—both the full-blood and the mixed-bloods—they get to work and write letters and I am fearful of things they say in those letters, because they can read and write well and that has more force than our words."[34] The seven delegates were promised that their concerns would be fully investigated.[35]

The following day the Yankton delegation visited the White House and was received by President Coolidge.[36] After a greeting, the delegation, the president, and some of his staff went outside to have a photograph taken. With the White House as a backdrop, twenty people lined up with the president. Some of the Yanktons donned "Indian garb." According to the Necklace/Primeaux family, Sam Necklace is in this photograph. A framed print of this photo adorned a wall in the home of Sam's niece, Auntie Pauline. Printed on the lower part of the photo is "Reception of the Sioux Indians—Dakota Delegation—President Coolidge, Washington, D.C. March 10, 1925." Both Auntie Pauline and Sam's grandson Asa said that Sam was in the photo. In fact, the photo is a family treasure that created some debate as to who should get it after Auntie Pauline died. After her death the photograph ended up in Arizona with a relative who confirmed to me that it was Sam Necklace. The problem with the family's version is that it cannot be confirmed from written sources. Many documents (such as the souvenir program from the banquet and the people reimbursed for travel expenses) list the Yankton delegates. Sam is not mentioned anywhere. In spite of the family's belief that Sam was part of the delegation, it is highly unlikely that he was there—yet how did Auntie Pauline acquire the photograph? Unfortunately, at this time there are no known photographs of Sam that could be used for comparison. Auntie Pauline said that she had no idea where the photo came from and had no knowledge of a trip to Washington, just that it had been hanging on her wall for many years.[37] This may be an unsolvable puzzle; yet it is a tribute to Sam's memory among his descendants that this photo is a treasured memento.

The enrollment issues discussed in Washington were urgent, because petitions for a settlement of the Red Pipestone Reservation were being filed. In June 1925 the U.S. Court of Claims reaffirmed the Yanktons' right to mine red pipestone but ruled that they should not receive compensation. Another petition was filed with the U.S. Supreme Court, asking it to review the Court of Claims decision. The high court ruled that the Yanktons were due compensation and sent the case back to the Court of Claims. In 1928 it ruled that the Yanktons were due $100,000, plus 6 percent interest, for a total of $328,558 or (based on a population of 1,953 and minus lawyers' fees) $151.99 per person. Each individual received a check for that amount.[38] The pipestone quarry issue was settled. The government designated the 624-acre site as a national park, named Pipestone National Monument. Today the Yanktons still quarry the red stone, but many Yanktons are not convinced that they should have lost control of this sacred ground.

Part of the urgency for the settlement of land claims was the terrible economic conditions. As mentioned earlier, the Yanktons had very little income; most people had lost their land, and few had any resources to fall back on. Poor health, problems with alcohol abuse, plus a terrible drought in 1925 that created severe food shortages the following winter added to the crisis. Very few Yanktons could support themselves by farming. A 1930 survey reported that 90 percent of the original reservation land had been lost.[39] Father Sylvester recorded much of this in his diary, especially in 1925 and 1926. He commented on poor housing, lack of jobs, hungry children, sickness, an "endless number of cases of destitution," and a five-year shortage of rain that he called "Sahara Desert weather." He also mentioned a letter that he had received in his diary (12 April 1926): "the Bishop of the Diocese has issued a letter ordering that the prayer for rain be said in every church." He made no comment about the irony of such a request while he was trying to stifle Yankton spiritual beliefs. Under these conditions it is not surprising that there was support to settle the land claim for compensation.[40]

THE GROWTH OF THE NATIVE AMERICAN CHURCH

During the 1920s Peyotism continued to expand throughout the West. Many factors contributed to this growth, such as the increasing ease of travel and communication. This allowed for more contact and reinforcement among Peyote communities, especially when facing opposition from state authorities. There was considerable cooperation, especially in South Dakota, when preparing articles of incorporation and sharing information on potential threats. It became quite common for people from different reservations to attend each other's Peyote services. Well-beaten paths linked the Winnebago, Yankton, Rosebud, and Pine Ridge Reservations. The same ease of travel facilitated proselytization. For example, someone like Oglala roadman Jim Blue Bird was able to travel widely, spreading knowledge about the Peyote faith. Many others did the same. In the 1920s Peyotism spread beyond Okla-homa and the southern and central Plains and into the northern Plains, into the Great Basin region of Utah and Nevada, and also into Arizona and Canada. The new groups adopting the Peyote religion included the Bannocks and Shoshones of Idaho; the Crees, Chippewas, Blackfoot, and Assiniboines of Montana; the Sioux of North Dakota; and the Chippewas, Crees, Blackfoot, and Sioux of Canada. Also affected were the Southern and Northern Paiutes and the Washos of the Great Basin. Peyotism also entered the Navajo Reser-vation, although not to a great extent at this time.[41]

The expansion of Peyotism also increased the demand for Peyote. The growing transportation network facilitated access to the "peyote gardens" in southern Texas and northern Mexico. As oil companies built roads, access to untouched peyote cacti became easier. A group of Mexicans and Mexican Americans, known as *peyoteros,* harvested and sold Peyote buttons wholesale to retail companies or traveled and sold them directly to Peyotists. The buttons could also be purchased by mail order. As early as 1909 the firm L. Villegas and Company of Laredo, Texas, was selling and shipping Peyote at $3.00 per thousand buttons. Upon receipt of the money, it guaranteed immediate shipment of any amount. In 1927 a *peyotero* from Oilton, Texas, traveled to Oklahoma with 38,000 Peyote buttons, which he sold for $2.00 per 1,000. More typically, in the 1920s Peyote was shipped by a number of Texas com-panies that sent many thousands of Peyote buttons to Oklahoma every year. It was shipped *en masse* to Oklahoma, because Peyote possession was legal in that state. Federal regulations prohibited the shipment of Peyote to states that had outlawed it, so many of the Peyote people, including the Yanktons, traveled to Oklahoma to purchase it.[42]

Another type of communication also facilitated the spread of Peyotism. Personal relationships developed among many young American Indians who attended boarding schools. After returning home, some of the students were attracted to Peyotism. They communicated and visited with old school friends. The influence of this group of young people, especially the graduates of the Carlisle Indian School and Haskell Institute in Kansas, was instrumental in creating a network of Peyotists. With these widespread contacts and oppor-tunities for proselytizing, the diffusion of the Peyote religion proceeded quite rapidly, as a unified complex that included theology, ritual, and an organiza-tional structure. All three of these elements melded with preexisting beliefs and structures. To the members of the Peyote communities it seemed to be a reinforcement or extension of traditional Native American spiritual values, not the introduction of something new. For the tribes of the Plains, Peyote itself was new; but it was introduced in a traditional way as a gift of God, sent to help in difficult times. The elements of the Peyote religion that paralleled traditional American Indian spirituality made the introduction of Peyotism possible. Theology and ritual are discussed below in the analysis of why a Yankton Peyote church emerged.

The initial introduction of Peyotism occurred on the individual or family level. This happened in one of two ways. Individuals would visit friends, relatives, or school contacts on other reservations and extol the virtues of the Peyote religion and then run a meeting for them. Or an individual from one reservation would travel to another reservation and learn about Peyote, as Charlie Jones did when he returned from the Winnebago Reservation and introduced Peyotism to the Yanktons. Once the Peyote religion was introduced, the development of the Peyote community was entirely local. There was the sense of being part of a wider Peyote world, especially after 1918, when virtually all Peyote communities took the name "Native American Church," but on the local level each community was autonomous. Peyotism spread with a relatively unified doctrine and ritual but with a decentralized organizational structure. Local groups chose their own leadership. Leaders emerged based on personal qualities such as integrity, spirituality, charisma, wisdom, ethical lifestyle, compassion, and commitment. This is similar to the way spiritual leadership emerged in many traditional Plains cultures. Beyond leadership, the local group developed its own structure under the requirements of state incorporation law. This meant elections, governance through bylaws, and dues, in addition to conducting prayer meetings, baptisms, marriages, ordinations, and funerals, without oversight or veto by a higher body. Peyotism functioned very well with a decentralized structure, in spite of some differences in doctrine and ritual in terms of the degree of Christian influence. The Native American Church groups had a basic theological unity based on the primacy of Peyote, which allowed individuals to feel that they were part of a nationwide community.

The Yanktons fit this pattern. In 1924 they joined with other South Dakota groups and incorporated as the Native American Church of South Dakota, yet they still remained a separate incorporated group. The pattern continued in 1944 when Peyotists in Oklahoma amended their articles of incorporation to become the Native American Church of the United States and then in 1955 became the Native American Church of North America. The Yanktons participated at all levels, taking leadership positions on the state and national level, but this did not infringe on local autonomy. The large state and national bodies created a sense of unity, but they mainly functioned as a defense against those trying to restrict or prohibit Peyote. These factors in the diffusion of Peyote are external and do not involve cosmological, doctrinal, or ritual issues, yet these are the real essentials in the spread of the Peyote religion.

The basic thesis of this work concerning the Yanktons and other Native Americans such as the Navajos (Diné) is that Peyotism spread because it was perceived as "Indian" religion. For example, James Tomchee, former president of the Native American Church of Navajoland, said in 1986 that "the way the peyote ceremony is practiced, I would say about 99 percent of whatever is taking place is basically Navajo."[43] It contained cosmological, theological, ceremonial, and ritual elements that paralleled traditional American Indian religious beliefs and practices. Peyotists believe it was developed by Indians for Indians and that it provided a bridge between the past and the present. When Peyotism entered a region, it was interpreted according to the traditional belief system and worldview and was vested with traditional meaning. It did not require a restructuring of cosmology. Peyote, viewed as a sacred or divine herb, was new; but the framework within which it existed was not new. Putting Peyote in a familiar cosmological framework allowed the Peyote religion to serve people's spiritual, aesthetic, and social needs.

In addition, becoming part of the Peyote community did not in the least weaken a person's identity as a Yankton, Winnebago, Kiowa, Omaha, Oglala, or member of another ethnic group. Peyotists would argue that it strengthened tribal identity while coping with a reservation environment that was a threat to people's identity. To be a Yankton and a Peyotist was reinforcing, not exclusive. The new elements such as Peyote itself and even the Christian elements that were absorbed into Peyotism were invested with values that resonated with the traditional meanings of life. An essentialist center of life was reinforced in a dynamic way to serve basic human needs. Not all Native Americans saw Peyotism in this light, but a significant number did accept it as an inherent part of the American Indian spiritual heritage.

PEYOTE AS MEDICINE

Many doctrinal and ritual elements were involved in the diffusion of Peyotism, but one factor was universal in its initial acceptance: Peyote as a medicine. This conclusion is not new, but it needs to be reiterated as a way of understanding the spread of Peyote. More than a century ago, James Mooney wrote that the Kiowas described Peyote as having medicinal properties. In 1914 anthropologist Paul Radin explained how John Rave promoted the curative power of Peyote as the way to attract Winnebago converts. In the 1930s ethnobotanist Richard Schultes and anthropologists Weston LaBarre and Omer Stewart reinforced this viewpoint. These three men were part of a new generation of young scholars who participated in Peyote meetings and interviewed Peyote people as part of their research. They saw healing as the essential element in the diffusion of Peyote. Schultes differed from the other two; he argued that Peyote was accepted as a curative in a pharmacological sense, while LaBarre and Stewart argued that Peyote was accepted as a curative in a spiritual sense. Stewart wrote that "first and foremost, the initial appeal to converts was for a cure." More recently, Ake Hultkrantz, a comparative religion scholar, wrote that with the prominence of health problems on the reservations healing was essential in the spread of Peyotism—though, he added, not as essential as the vision experience.[44]

Contemporary American Indian Peyotists who are authors or spokespersons (such as Leonard Crow Dog, Emerson Spider, or Vincent Catches) focus on the power of Peyote to heal.[45] If there is one dogma of the Peyote religion, it is that Peyote has curative power. The significance of this power is reflected in two sources: the Peyote origin narratives and more than a hundred years of testimonials by Peyote people. The origin narratives have many variants; but some of them tell of a voyage or quest, usually by a woman, to find a way to help the people who are suffering. During the quest the person finds or is given Peyote through divine intervention and ingests it, thereby becoming cured if ill, full if hungry, or finding the way home if lost. When back home the individual shares the "sacred herb" with the people, who are also healed or saved. They then begin to practice the Peyote religion.[46]

The power of Peyote to heal is revealed in literally hundreds of published and unpublished testimonials by people who claim they were healed. These testimonials are willingly shared and can be heard whenever Peyote people gather. The testimonials were also used to counter attacks on Peyotism and used when proselytizing as a way to attract new members. Healing is one of the most common reasons for having a Peyote meeting. In addition to attending the regular monthly meeting, an individual can request a special healing meeting, or, more typically, a family can sponsor a special meeting for the injured or ill person. The appeal of Peyote as a curative came at a time of physical and spiritual disequilibrium among many Native Americans. There was a decline of spiritual leadership and an increase in sickness and disease, including tuberculosis, trachoma, influenza, pneumonia, venereal disease, cancer, and the general ill health and malaise that go with poor nutrition and poverty. The most serious health problem, however, was the abuse of alcohol. Not many reservations escaped its scourge. Its impact was not only on the individual but also on the family and the community. Living conditions, unemployment, powerlessness, and idleness led to alcohol use, then to alcohol abuse, and then to alcohol addiction. Aside from using the law to prohibit alcohol on the reservations, there were no answers to this crisis—that is, until Peyotism began to diffuse throughout the West. Peyote was perceived as a generic curative; alcoholism was considered a sickness, so Peyote would be used to cure it. There are more testimonials about curing alcoholism than about other illnesses.

Because Peyote was introduced and accepted as a medicine, Peyote people across the country call it "medicine" when speaking English or use the generic word for medicine in their own language. In Lakota, Dakota, and Nakota Peyote is called *pežuta*. This means medicine and is the generic word for any substance that induces physical and/or spiritual healing. It is a powerful word as used in *pežuta wičaša* (medicine man) or *pežuta winyan* (medicine woman). The word *pežuta* implies much more than the English word "medicine." *Pežuta* explicitly means that physical healing and spiritual healing are integrated, because they take place together and are considered one and the same. The same is true of the Navajo word for Peyote, *azee* or medicine; like *pežuta*, the word is used for Peyote and for any substance with curative power.

If there is a second dogma in the Native American Church it is that the power to heal is a gift of God or the Great Spirit. Healing is not pharmacological; it is spiritual. Peyote is sacred, a gift from God or the body of God incarnate in plant form: thus its usage as a sacrament. American Indians have always taken a holistic approach to healing. Spirit, mind, and body are one; in fact one can only understand the power of Peyote to heal through a holistic interpretation.[47] Healing comes not only from the peyote cactus itself but also from participation in one's own healing through prayer and ritual, through the prayers of others, and finally through the power of the super- natural to heal. The beliefs about Peyote as a curative, in the American

Indian sense of the word "medicine," meant that it was accepted within the cosmological structure of their worldview. Peyote itself may have been new, but the structure and process were not. The tradition of healing in Native American cultures and the curative power of Peyote in the Native American Church are on the same cosmological plane. This helps explain the acceptance of the Peyote faith among many American Indians. One can be healed physically, but it can only occur through spiritual power.

This is where the tradition of healing in the prereservation era by medicine men or medicine women paralleled the process of healing in Peyotism: in both cases healing could only occur by spiritual means. Hultkrantz argues that curing is facilitated by Peyote being integrated with curative patterns already in existence. This viewpoint is reinforced by two recent studies of Peyotism as health care delivery systems among the Delawares of Oklahoma and the Navajos. On the basis of ethnographic and historical analysis, the authors concluded that the integration of religion and health care is an essential element of both Peyotism and traditional religion and that the significance of Peyote as a medicine is an essential factor in its acceptance and persistence. These conclusions reinforce the viewpoint of this study: that Peyotism and Yankton traditional religion have a common theological and cosmological basis.[48]

In analyzing Peyote as a medicine that cures alcoholism, there are three possible explanations as to why Peyote reduces or eliminates alcohol abuse. First, there may be pharmacological properties in Peyote that contribute to a physical cure. This has not been demonstrated. Second is the sociological/anthropological view of non–Native American scholars that becoming a member of a close-knit Peyote community gives one's life meaning and direction and that one's co-religionists expect abstinence as part of an ethical belief system—in other words, abstinence as a normative requirement of the Peyote religion.[49] Third is the viewpoint of members of the Native American Church that Peyote cures alcoholism through the power of God and that this is the only way a cure could occur. However one may view various interpretations, alcohol abuse has been greatly reduced among members of the Native American Church.

The purpose of this study is not a broad-spectrum analysis of the diffusion of Peyotism but a more specific analysis of its acceptance by a segment of the Yankton people. Previous sections of this study discuss when, where, and how Peyote spread and how it took roots on the Yankton Reservation.

Equally important, if not more so, is the question of why some Yanktons committed their lives to the Peyote way. We have looked at the impact of healing as one essential aspect in the diffusion of Peyote and can conclude that prereservation curative patterns parallel the curative patterns of Peyotism, thus making Peyote seem to be part of a traditional spiritual complex. This is also true for the Yankton culture, where healing was an essential element in the initial acceptance of Peyotism—specifically because the spiritual basis of healing did not change. Just as Wakan Tanka sent White Buffalo Calf Woman to the Sioux during difficult times, Wakan Tanka now sent Peyote and the Peyote religion. The peyote cactus was new, as the Sacred Pipe was at one time; but seeking and receiving help from the Great Spirit, who took pity on humans, was not new.

The number of Yanktons who participated in Peyotism has never been large. A realistic range, depending on the time frame, would be somewhere between 5 percent and 15 percent of the population. It would be difficult to develop a complete demographic profile of this group in the 1910s and 1920s, but some generalizations can be made. For the most part, the Peyote community consisted of full-bloods of the youngest or middle generation. They were born during the reservation era, with its boarding schools and allotment system. Their parents were reared in the prereservation or the early reservation days when a communal village life was still intact. For example, Sam Necklace's parents grew up in a communal environment, speaking Dakota. By the twentieth century the elder Yankton generation fell into one of two categories: those committed to a Christian denomination or those who were still holding onto the traditional religion based on the Sacred Pipe. Some practiced both. Full-bloods of the younger generation were educated in either government schools or denominational schools. Those who attended boarding school seemed particularly attracted to Peyotism. As full-bloods they grew up in homes where traditional social and cultural values were present; but the Yankton traditional religion had been under assault for several decades and not practiced except in the most rural areas of the reservation. The group least likely to become Peyotists was the younger generation of mixed-bloods. They also were educated in government schools or denominational schools; but given their mixed parentage they were more acculturated into the Anglo-American value structure. Most of them were active members of the Presbyterian, Catholic, or Episcopal churches on the reservation. Many of the mixed-bloods looked down on members of the Peyote religion.

They accepted the intense anti-Peyote propaganda that emanated from local officials and missionaries.

This also caused tension concerning sociopolitical and economic status on the reservation. As a result of being practicing Christians and living a more Anglo-American lifestyle, the mixed-bloods clearly had the advantage. This meant political favoritism from the superintendents on the reservation, who clearly privileged the "progressive," "civilized," or "better" Indians. One example (pointed out by Professor Hoover) is that Father Cook only allowed mixed-bloods into the Episcopal choir; and only those who were living an Anglo-American lifestyle had the opportunity for leadership positions within the church.[50] It also meant more economic advantage, as the few reservation jobs went to mixed-bloods. In contrast, the full-bloods felt more and more isolated throughout the 1920s and 1930s. They felt that their viewpoints and concerns were being ignored. Their response in the 1930s was more involvement in Yankton politics. Being part of the Peyote community was not conducive to improving one's socioeconomic and political status. The younger full-bloods who had been to school, who spoke, read, and wrote English and were conversant with the non-Indian world, were blocked from upward mobility on the reservation. They felt a sense of loss. As they reached middle age, very few became part of the leadership structure of the reservation. Socioeconomic and political status is an important variable, but one must be careful not to overstate its significance in the diffusion of Peyotism. Scholars must explain the historical environment in the diffusion of any cultural phenomenon; but when it comes to religion, historical variables such as social status provide only a partial answer. One still needs to explain why Peyotism became the religion of choice for many people.

SACRED COMMONALITIES

The viewpoint of this study is that Peyotism was accepted for its essential qualities as a body of spiritual beliefs that resonated with the prereservation spiritual belief structure. The idea that Peyotism is an American Indian religion is not new; but some have contended (for example, a recent study by Ake Hultkrantz) that Peyotism was "a new way of grasping and interpreting this [American Indian] tradition."[51] I would argue that Peyote was not a new way of grasping and interpreting traditional religion. The Yanktons accepted it because it fit the old way or traditional way of interpreting one's spiritual existence. This is another way of saying that the diffusion of Peyotism was facilitated by the large number of parallel ritual and structural elements as well as fitting within the traditional cosmological framework.[52] These conclusions concerning the diffusion of the Peyote religion came after considerable experience with the traditional Yankton religion and with several Yankton Peyote families. Before my experience (as discussed in the preface) I assumed that traditional American Indian religion and Peyotism were quite distinct, possibly having some overlap yet essentially different. My experiences with the Necklace/Primeaux families and their wider kinship network changed my viewpoint. I participated in many spiritual activities over a fifteen-year period. This included many Sweat Lodge ceremonies, Sun Dances, Vision Quests, and naming ceremonies as well as the ebb and flow of spirituality in everyday life. I also attended Peyote meetings. During these experiences I began to notice commonalities in ritual and symbolism and eventually to see that both religious systems were operating within the same theological structure.

The use of the Dakota language is an example of this commonality. Prayers and songs are sacred; the words are sacred. It is believed that the prayers are more efficacious if spoken or sung in Dakota. This is true for both traditional Yankton religion and Peyotism. That belief is not uncommon. It is the same with the Navajos: the Peyote people as well as the traditional spiritual leaders pray and sing in Navajo. The Yankton Peyote community used Dakota. Their prayers and songs were in Dakota, as was everyday conversation among themselves. The first generation of Yankton Peyotists grew up with Dakota as their first language. For example, Sam and Mary spoke Dakota and made it the language of their home. Their children were fluent Dakota speakers, as is their grandson Asa, who was reared in their home. The Peyote community helped preserve the Dakota language, reinforcing a Yankton Dakota identity within the Peyote community. I suspect (though I could not support it with statistics) that a higher percentage of Yankton Peyotists are fluent Dakota speakers than the percentage of Dakota speakers among all Yanktons. The practice of using Dakota in the spiritual life of the Peyote community parallels the use of Dakota in traditional Yankton spirituality.

In addition to this common use of language, there are many other parallels, such as the use of sacred foods and herbs. Sacred foods are used in Vision Quests and naming ceremonies. They are spiritual sustenance for sun dancers and special offerings to spirits to assist with healing. Sometimes sacred foods finalize a ceremony, as in the case of the Vision Quest. When a person returns from a Vision Quest, he or she is purified in a Sweat Lodge. Then, with family and friends and those who helped "put you out," sacred foods are offered in thanks and shared with all in attendance. Sacred foods are also part of the Peyote religion. In both spiritualities the actual use and symbolism of the sacred food are the same. Sam's grandson Asa makes the point, saying that Dakota sacred foods are used in Peyote meetings. In both cases the food is prepared and carried in by women. The foods are the same: water, corn, meat (buffalo if available), and fruit (*wožapi*, berry pudding). They are placed on the ground in a straight line, east to west, and then passed clockwise to each person, who swallows a small amount, recites *Mitakuye Oyasin* (for all my relations), and passes the food. In both cases the ritual preparation of the food is the same, as is the symbolic significance of the four foods. They represent all the elements of life that give spiritual sustenance and protection to everyone.

There are also parallels in the ceremonial functions of Peyote roadmen and traditional medicine men and women. Both guide people, leading them along the "right" path, praying for them and with them, and most importantly aiding in opening a communication channel to the supernatural in order to receive the requested assistance for oneself or others. This does not mean that there are no differences between the two. For example, medicine men and women possess secret knowledge for healing, which is not the case with a roadman; yet on the functional level they serve similar purposes. These spiritual leaders reinforce, in a material and abstract way, the belief that all things in the universe are related. Lakotas, Dakotas, and Nakotas express this belief in the prayer *Mitakuye Oyasin*. This prayer is used in all Yankton spiritual activities, including Peyotism, to conclude other prayers, to indicate the end of prayers, or when passing sacred food or the Sacred Pipe. Its utterance reflects in a microcosm the Yankton belief in the interrelated nature of the cosmos. As Yankton Peyotism emerged, it incorporated this traditional prayer.

Before continuing the discussion of commonalities between the two religions, I need to make several points. The first is that in spite of the many parallels there are significant differences. The Cross Fire way, for example, has incorporated elements of Christianity and eliminated the use of tobacco. There is no dancing in Peyotism, and the roadmen play a less significant role in healing than do the traditional medicine men and women. The Yanktons practice the Seven Sacred Rites of the Sioux, whereas Peyotism has one basic ceremony (though ritually complex) that lasts ten to twelve hours. The real issue is why Peyotism was accepted. As already stated, numerous commonalities made this possible. They made Peyotism seem "Indian"; they made Peyotism seem Dakota; and, specifically, they made Peyotism seem Ihanktonwan (Yankton). This was the essential core. It made Peyotism relevant, comfortable, and able to meet the spiritual, social, and aesthetic needs of a group of Yankton people.

THE SACRED CIRCLE

A further reinforcement of the commonality thesis is the symbolism of the sacred circle. It is ubiquitous in Yankton culture, as well as in all Lakota, Dakota, and Nakota groups, and in Peyotism. The circle in its literal usage and symbolic meaning pervades all spiritual beliefs and practices and is a metaphor for life. The circle represents the universe; it represents Wakan Tanka in that there is no beginning and no ending; as Vine Deloria, Jr., has written, "the circle was the emblem of eternity for the Sioux."[53] It symbolizes a universe where there is a primordial harmony and balance. The structure of the universe is re-created symbolically in ceremony and ritual. Virtually everything must reflect this circular unity. Within this universe there is motion; and in a cosmological sense the motion is considered clockwise—thus all spiritual activities must reflect this pattern. In the prereservation spirituality of the Yanktons, such as in the Sun Dance, the use of the circle as a symbol of the continuity of the universe is pervasive. The Sun Dance arbor is a large circle; the dancers move around the arbor in a clockwise direction. Virtually all of the ritual activities are conducted in a circular fashion, from dancing on all four sides of the sacred tree to the large circle of dancers praying during the piercing. After an individual is pierced, the head dancer leads that person clockwise around the circle and back to his or her original position. When the piercing thongs break through, the dancer is taken around the arbor, completing the circle. The creation of the circle begins on the opening morning of the Sun Dance. The head dancer leads the dancers around the outside of arbor, from the west side clockwise to the east side, in a semicircle, entering the arbor at the east gate. At the end of the fourth day the head dancer leads the dancers out of the arbor, through the east gate around the outside of the arbor to the west gate, thus completing the circle they began on the first day and officially ending the Sun Dance.

Similar symbolism is associated with the Sweat Lodge. The lodge is a domed shaped structure with a round base. The Sweat Lodge ceremony, one of the Seven Sacred Rites, is a purification ritual that is held before and after all other spiritual activities (such as before and after a Vision Quest) or can be held as a separate event. The essence of the Sweat Lodge is the pouring of water over hot stones (*inyan wakan*), creating steam, which along with prayer and song purifies and heals the participants. Inside the *inipi* everyone sits in a circle, and everything that takes place is done in a clockwise direction. This includes entering and leaving as well as the pattern of prayer: the person to the left of the entrance prays first, followed by the next person, and on around the circle. If there is a Sacred Pipe in the *inipi* it is passed clockwise. At the conclusion, everyone leaves in a clockwise direction and emerges spiritually cleansed and reborn. Because of its inherent power, the circle is used in a wide variety of ways. It is the shape of dream catchers and medicine wheels; it is the shape of drums; a circular motif is used in the logos of Native American nations, organizations, schools, and universities. Everyone recognizes the symbolism of the circle and its role in creating a spiritual environment for communication with the supernatural and a social environment for communication between people (i.e., talking circles). Leonard Crow Dog said: "Smoking in a circle we renew the sacred hoop of the nation"; Black Elk said the circle itself is sacred.[54]

The circle has virtually the same function in the Yankton Peyote community. A tipi with its round base is the choice structure for a Peyote meeting. Everyone sits in a circle inside, even when the meeting is held in a home or church building. During the long service, everything is passed clockwise around the circle, including the sacrament Peyote. It is first ingested by the roadman and then passed around the circle of participants. In a Half Moon service, tobacco is also passed around the circle. It is the same with other religious paraphernalia, such as the drum and drumstick. The roadman and chief drummer begin with four opening songs (prayers), then they pass the drum, the drumstick, the roadman's staff, and a small bundle of sage to the person on their left, who may choose to sing four songs, with the accompaniment of another person who plays the drum. The drum and staff continue to be passed around the circle until everyone has the opportunity to sing. The wooden staff (three to four feet long) is a very significant ceremonial object. The staff, similar in concept to the staff of a traditional holy person, represents the spiritual status of the roadman; but it is also a symbol of unity. The staff is passed around the circle, and everyone has the opportunity to sing while holding it. When the staff gets back to the roadman, it had been held or touched by everyone, completing the circle. The Peyote, the paraphernalia, and the songs continue around the circle until morning, when the sacred food is brought in and passed to each individual around the circle. As in the traditional spiritual ceremonies, the symbolism of the circle permeates Peyotism.

SACRED NUMBERS

Sacred numbers play a similar role in Yankton traditional culture and in Peyotism. Although there are a variety of sacred numbers, the most common are four and seven. The sacral nature of these numbers is widespread. Four is a sacred number in many American Indian cultures, and both numbers are sacred to all Lakota, Dakota, and Nakota groups. This parallel facilitated the acceptance of Peyotism. Four represents the sacred directions: west, north, east, and south. Seven represents the same four directions plus three additional directions: down for mother earth, upward to represent the universe or Wakan Tanka, and the center for all the people. Four and seven are also reflected in the overall structures of the Sioux people, who are divided into the Seven Council Fires, some of which are divided into seven bands and practice seven sacred rites, which include the four sacred foods. Four and seven are also significant in the ritual use of the Sacred Pipe. The pipe, widely used in various ceremonies, is the essential means of communication with the supernatural. When preparing a Sacred Pipe for prayer, one makes an offering of tobacco or *čanšaša* (inner bark of a dogwood or red willow tree) to the seven directions. This is done by holding a pinch of tobacco in one's fingers and offering it with a prayer toward the west then placing it in the pipe. The same pattern is followed for the other six directions. When this is completed, and with everyone sitting in a circle, the pipe is passed clockwise, with each individual taking four puffs and using one hand to draw the smoke over one's body, saying *Mitakuye Oyasin* and passing the pipe to the left around the circle until the tobacco is finished (this pattern may vary from group to group).

The Sweat Lodge ceremony also includes the numbers four and seven. After preparing the wood for the fire, each of the first seven rocks is placed on the wood in a prayerful manner. The first rock is offered with a prayer to one of the seven directions and placed on the fire. The next six rocks are offered to the other six directions and then placed on the fire. Additional rocks are added, and the fire is lit. When the rocks are red hot and the Sweat Lodge is ready, the first of the seven rocks is carried into the lodge. The person running the Sweat Lodge ceremony arranges each rock in a pattern that represents the sacred directions. Six more rocks are brought in, one at a time, and treated in the same manner. Throughout the Sweat Lodge ceremony the sacred numbers of four and seven are integrated into the ritual: for example, songs are sung in sets of four.

Like the symbolic power of the circle, the sacred numbers permeate the Sun Dance. Many of the Sun Dance rituals are patterned in sequences of four. An individual, family, or group that decides to sponsor a Sun Dance must hold the dance for four consecutive years. This is a significant commitment that must be made in order to increase the spiritual efficacy of the Sun Dance. In the same manner a Sun Dance chief makes a four-year commitment, as do the dancers, to participate in all four years. The Sun Dance itself lasts four days. The inside of the arbor reflects the significance of the four directions. Four openings serve as the entrances and exits to the Sun Dance circle, each facing one of the four directions and marked by two flags. In the center of the arbor is a sacred cottonwood tree that is carried in by the dancers and others. Considerable effort goes into finding an appropriate tree. After a tree is chosen, a spiritual leader, the dancers, and their supporters gather around the tree. They offer special prayers to the spirit of the tree and to the four directions before the sun dancers cut down the tree. Asking the life force of the tree for this sacrifice is dramatic but essential. When the tree is placed in a deep hole and stood up in the Sun Dance arbor, it becomes the center of the universe and symbolizes the linkage of the underground, the earth, and the sky. As the entourage carries the tree toward the arbor, it stops four times to pray. When the tree is placed in the ground, it is "fed" the four sacred foods. During the opening procession, as the dancers proceed around the arbor to the east entrance, they stop four times, face the sun, and give homage to Wakan Tanka. During the Sun Dance itself, sequences of four guide the dancers. They are positioned by the Sun Dance chief sequentially at each of the four directions, face the sacred tree, and dance and pray. Subsequent rounds of dancing follow the same pattern.

During the piercing rounds, when individual dancers are making their personal sacrifice, they pray to Wakan Tanka through the sacred tree. At the beginning of a piercing round the dancers form a circle around the tree. The dancer to be pierced approaches the tree, puts his or her hands on the tree and prays, then lies down on a bed of a sage. There are many ways of piercing, but the most common way for men is to have the chest or back pierced and for women the fleshy part of the upper arm. After the piercing a rope that is tied to the tree is tied around the piercing thongs. The dancer then goes back to his or her position in the circle and dances and prays while others are being pierced. When the piercing is complete, following the directions of the Sun Dance chief, those who are pierced approach the sacred tree, place their hands on the tree, pray, and then return to the circle. They do this four times. After the fourth prayer the dancers run from the tree. When the rope becomes taut, the piercing thongs break the skin. The personal sacrifice is complete. The dancer then circles the arbor, approaches the tree, and prays. The tree is connected to the universe; it reaches to Wakan Tanka.

During a 1999 Sun Dance at the home of Asa and Loretta Primeaux, Asa (who has diabetes, has had several strokes, and is blind and confined to a wheelchair) was there for four days. On the fourth day he was taken in his wheelchair inside the Sun Dance circle to the sacred tree. He placed the palm of his hand on the tree and prayed silently. Everyone could feel his whole being touching the sacred tree through his hand. For several minutes he held his hand to the tree, with tears streaming down his face.

At the end of each round of dancing, one of the dancers offers his or her Sacred Pipe to the singers to smoke. The dancer picks up the pipe from the altar then proceeds clockwise around the tree to the south-side opening. A person is chosen to receive the pipe. This is done in a very precise way. The dancer offers the pipe three times but pulls it back. On the fourth offering of the pipe, it is accepted. White Buffalo Calf Woman taught the Sioux this method of offering the Sacred Pipe.

The Vision Quest (*hanblečeya;* literally, crying for a vision) is another of the seven rites that involve sacred numbers. The term "Vision Quest," common in contemporary studies, is rarely if ever used by the Yanktons. The word "vision" is used frequently; but when referring to the *hanblečeya* people say "going out" or "going up on a hill." This refers to the solitary fasting for a day or sometimes two (sometimes four in the past). As with so much of Yankton spiritual life, personal sacrifice is involved. The Vision Quest is a sacred undertaking. After an offering of tobacco, a spiritual leader helps "put you out." It begins with purification in the Sweat Lodge. The individual is then taken to a solitary place for prayer, contemplation, and possibly a vision.

Upon his or her return, another Sweat Lodge ceremony is prepared, to share the experiences of the Vision Quest with others. Following the sweat, sacred foods are shared with those who fasted and their families and friends. Sacred numbers are involved as a form of protection while fasting. A person fasting is protected from the potential evil by eight tobacco ties, two for each of the four directions. Other protectors include an eagle plume and an additional 160 tobacco ties, made of eight colors. Four of the other colors represent the four directions. The tobacco ties are strung around the person, who is also cradling a Sacred Pipe in his or her arms. After a person is put in place and all the protective paraphernalia is properly arranged, the people who brought the fasters to the site sing the four directions song. The singers begin while facing west. The song asks for blessings and protection from the spirits of the west then continues by asking for the same thing from the other three directions. When the song is concluded, an elder or spiritual leader blows four series of four different-length notes on an eagle-bone whistle. Now it is almost dark. All the people except for those who are fasting leave; they will return the next day. Meanwhile the fasters spend the night in prayer, fearful of danger yet hoping for goodness and wisdom.[55]

The use of sacred numbers in traditional beliefs and ceremonies—from the division of the cosmos into the four directions to the four puffs on a Sacred Pipe—has counterparts in Yankton Peyotism, specifically the power of four and seven. According to Omer Stewart's "Peyote Element Distribution List," all Peyote groups in North America attach ritual significance to the number four.[56] The structure of the entire Peyote meeting reflects this significance. The cosmology is the same in that the four directions encompass a uniform and interdependent cosmos. Using four in a ritual pattern re-creates unity and balance and creates a path or a way, the Peyote way, for communication with the supernatural. The essential core of Peyotism is the ingestion of Peyote as a sacrament. It is a gift from Wakan Tanka: it teaches, it heals, it purifies, it blesses, it protects. Peyote takes central place on the altar. The half-moon or crescent-shaped altar, which is rebuilt for each service, is made of slightly moistened sand, which is shaped and patted down, with a groove or road along the top. This is the Peyote Road or the Peyote way. One's prayers travel this road. It also reflects the ethical and spiritual path of life that a Peyote person must follow. The roadman, as the name implies, helps guide people along this road. A very large Peyote button, called the Grandfather Peyote or Chief Peyote, is placed in the middle of the altar.

Sometimes in a Cross Fire service a Bible is placed on the altar (or next to it), with the Grandfather Peyote on top. During the course of a Peyote meeting, Peyote is passed around four times. The Peyote may be just the dried buttons; or dried buttons ground into a granular form and turned into an oatmeal-like consistency (with the addition of water), eaten with a spoon; or Peyote tea. As the Peyote comes around clockwise, each person may ingest four spoonfuls or take four sips of tea, praying while doing so. This is a sacred act. No one is allowed to pass between the Peyote and the fire, because it might interrupt the prayers. The entire night reflects the pattern of fours. There are four opening songs, four midnight songs, four morning songs, four quitting songs, and four sacred foods.

At the beginning of the meeting the roadman and the chief drummer sing four songs; the drum and staff are then passed to the left, and the next person sings four songs. The pattern continues around the circle until everyone has had the opportunity to sing four songs. At midnight there is a break. Water is brought in and passed around; then the roadman goes outside and blows the eagle-bone whistle toward the four directions. The number seven is used less often but is also significant. The drum used in Peyote music is about eight inches in diameter. It is covered with a drumhead that is fastened around the top of the kettle. Seven small stones are placed in the drumhead around the side of the drum. Each protruding stone serves as an anchor when tied to the others and around the drum. There are alternative interpretations of the meaning of the seven stones, yet all agree on the use of seven stones as a sacred symbol. For example, some Cross Fire people claim that the seven stones represent the seven Christian sacraments; some Sioux Half Moon Peyotists claim that they represent the Seven Council Fires. These commonalities in the use of sacred numbers add to our understanding of the acceptance of the Peyote faith.

SACRED PLANTS

Another significant commonality between Yankton traditional religion and Peyotism is the spiritual/medicinal use of plants. This is universal among American Indians, who believe that certain plants (just like certain animals) are imbued with the spiritual power to protect, purify, enlighten, or heal human beings when used in a prescribed manner. Many plants fit the criteria, but two in particular are used extensively by the Sioux: cedar (*Juniperus virginiana*) and sage (*Artemisia gnaphalodes*). The same is true for the tobacco, which is central to traditional beliefs; but in Peyotism it maintains its sacred quality only in the Half Moon way. It is not used in the Cross Fire services. Sage and cedar are used in all Yankton traditional spiritual ceremonies and are both used in Peyotism. The way they are used and the symbolism associated with their use are virtually the same in both spiritualities.

These plants are imbued by Wakan Tanka with power to help human beings. Cedar and sage have this power; they are *wakan* (sacred). They are used in two ways, as plants in themselves or as smoke or incense from burning them. Sage serves as a powerful protector throughout Yankton society. The smoke from a smoldering bundle of sage, when placed in an abalone shell, provides protection. It is employed as a sacred blessing for a marriage, a birth, a new home, a funeral, or another significant life event. Small bundles of sage are found today in people's homes, offices, or cars. Cedar is primarily used as incense when sprinkled on hot rocks or coals thrown into a fire. It did not take much observation to conclude that cedar and sage are used in the Sun Dance, Vision Quest, and Sweat Lodges in virtually the same manner as in Peyote meetings. During the Sun Dance sage and cedar are used throughout the four days of dancing. Both are essential to purify and protect the dancers. The dancers make crowns of sage to wear on their heads while dancing as well as wristlets and anklets of sage.[57] During the piercing the dancers lie on a bed of sage while the thongs and rope are attached. The wounds are cauterized with a mixture of sage and tobacco. Between rounds the dancers may be given sage tea. The purpose is not to quench their thirst but to give them additional spiritual protection. Sage not only protects but purifies. When a Sun Dancer offers his or her Sacred Pipe to one of the singers or an elder at the end of a round of dancing, that person must be purified. People take off their shoes, stand on sprigs of sage, and rub their hands with sage before receiving the pipe.

Cedar is used throughout the Sun Dance; like sage, it purifies, protects, blesses, and strengthens the dancers. During the Sun Dance all the spiritual paraphernalia and all the people are "cedared off," as almost everyone says (this is sometimes called "smudging"). The smoke from smoldering cedar is dispersed onto objects and people in order to purify and protect them. When the cedar smoke is brought near people, they pull the smoke toward themselves with their hands, trying to get as much smoke as possible to cover their bodies. Along with a Sun Dance chief and one or two head dancers (one male, one female if both are dancing), a fireman and a cedarman assist with the Sun Dance. The fireman is in charge of the sacred fire that burns for the full four days. It must not die out under any circumstances, or harm may come to the dancers. The cedarman is responsible for the cedaring-off of everything and everyone. A tin can with a handle is used to carry hot coals. The cedar is sprinkled on the coals, producing an incense effect of cedar smoke. A typical round of dancing includes the following uses of cedar. At the beginning of a round, hot coals are placed in a receptacle and sprinkled with cedar. As the dancers enter the Sun Dance arena they are cedared-off with the smoke, purifying themselves before they begin dancing. When the dancing starts, the hot coals and cedar are carried around the Sun Dance arbor, cedaring-off the four entrances, the Sacred Pipes resting on the altar, the buffalo skulls, and the sacred tree. The singers and the drum are cedared-off, as are all the people in attendance. During each round of dancing the cedar-man (always moving clockwise) goes from dancer to dancer, allowing them to cedar themselves. During the piercing rounds the cedar is used profusely to protect and strengthen the dancers who are undertaking the sacrifice of piercing.[58]

In Peyote meetings both sage and cedar play a central role. As in Yankton traditional religion, they purify, protect, bless, and strengthen. Four people conduct a Peyote meeting: a roadman, chief drummer, cedarman, and fire-man. The cedarman sits to the left of the roadman and has a bag of cedar. It is used as incense by sprinkling it on the fire in the center of the tipi. At the beginning of the meeting, just as at the beginning of the Sun Dance, the cedarman cedars-off all the paraphernalia that will be used throughout the night, including the Chief Peyote, drum, drumstick, gourd rattle, staff, eagle-bone whistle, and feather fans. Cedar is sprinkled on the fire, and each item is passed through the smoke. The same is true for all the participants, who purify themselves with the smoke when the cedar is sprinkled on the fire. During healing the roadman fans cedar smoke on the person, using his eagle-feather fan. Being in charge of the cedar is an important responsibility. The smoke helps carry the prayers skyward. The present chief priest of the Native American Church of South Dakota, Reverend Emerson Spider, Sr., has described the role of the cedarman: "The cedarman who takes care of the cedar throughout the night has to be a man who knows how to pray to the great creator. . . . Every time a person prays, he burns cedar. We use the cedar smoke as incense. . . . During our church services in the tipi we burn that

cedar whenever somebody prays, so that the smoke goes up. Our understanding is that we are making smoke signals to the Great Spirit so that he
will hear our prayers."[59]

Sage is used in the Peyote meetings as a purifier in the same way as in
Yankton traditional religion. At the beginning of a Peyote meeting a small
bundle of sage is passed around the circle of participants. Each person holds
the sage in his or her hands, lightly brushing the sage across the body as an
act of purification. If someone arrives late, the sage is passed to him or her
for the same purpose. Since Peyote is considered a holy sacrament, purification is an essential precursor to ingesting it. During the rounds of singing,
sage is passed around the circle with the drum and staff. Because the songs
are prayers, they will be more effective if sung while in a purified state. Emerson Spider makes the important point that sage is used in a "traditional way
of praying."[60]

THE VISION EXPERIENCE

Another significant commonality between Yankton traditional religion and
Peyotism is the experience of visions. The Yanktons are part of a wider Plains
culture complex where visions were and are an essential part of their spiritual
worldview. Scholars have debated whether the rapid diffusion of Peyotism
was facilitated by the existence of spiritual beliefs that included vision-seeking
practices such as the Sun Dance and the Vision Quest. Some scholars (Shonle,
LaBarre, Hultkrantz) have argued that Peyotism was primarily accepted
because Peyote produced visions. Most recently Gloria Young has suggested
that the rapid spread of Peyotism was because "Peyote facilitated visions."
She adds that curing was important but "was not essential." Other scholars
(Slotkin, Stewart, Hertzberg) have argued that the diffusion was influenced
by many factors, with visions being just one of them. Huston Smith clearly
articulates the viewpoint that Peyote as a gift of God is considered a curative,
and "it is not eaten to induce visions."[61] This is a complex issue, because
some American Indians without a vision-seeking tradition have accepted
Peyotism, while others with a vision-seeking tradition have not. In the case
of the Yanktons, and other Lakota, Dakota, and Nakota groups, there was
and is a universal vision-seeking tradition in their spiritual heritage; yet the
majority have not become Peyotists even through Peyotism was known to
them and probably practiced by some of their neighbors.

The diffusion of the Peyote faith did not follow a consistent pattern; it was quite differentiated and sporadic even within a particular group. In order to explain the diffusion of Peyotism, a wide range of religious, social, political and economic factors must be considered. Among the Yanktons, the parallel of vision experiences between traditional religion and Peyotism is clearly just one of the many factors leading to acceptance of Peyotism. Visions in Peyotism are important, as many testimonials indicate, but they were not the primary element. If the vision experience was the critical element in diffusion, then Peyotism would be more widespread among the Plains cultures. In the first half of the twentieth century there were only a few American Indian groups in the northern and southern Plains in which a majority of people were Peyotists. More analyses of diffusion on the microlevel are needed before a satisfactory macroanalysis can be considered tenable.

Another point to consider when assessing the role of the vision experience in diffusion is that most of the early Peyotists (as discussed earlier) were younger people, mostly full-bloods, with day-school or boarding-school experience. They grew up in the 1880s and 1890s, when the Sun Dance was outlawed and other spiritual practices were repressed. Traditional spiritual practices never totally disappeared; they were carried out in secret but with fewer participants and sometimes in a truncated form, such as a Sun Dance held indoors. The older generation, who grew up in the prereservation era or early in the reservation period when traditional spiritual practices were still common, did not become participants in the Peyote religion even though they had intimate knowledge of the significance of visions. The purpose of the vision experience is to seek communication with spirit beings or with Wakan Tanka. Visions may occur after ritual preparation that includes purification in a Sweat Lodge and fasting and prayer during a Sun Dance or Vision Quest. Visions are not limited to these experiences, however; they can occur at any time but are more common when one is spiritually prepared. One approaches the supernatural with humility and vulnerability as a pitiable human being who is seeking help and power in order to benefit one's family, people, or nation. The element of sacrifice (such as fasting) is essential in showing commitment and seriousness of purpose in seeking help from the spirit world. In a vision one might receive a message or a revelation that will help or protect one's people, guide one's path of life, or give the power to heal or lead in battle. The vision is a vehicle of communication with the sacred and can be experienced by both men and women.[62] The visions themselves are *wakan* (sacred). They may need to be interpreted by holy men or holy women. Some prominent examples of visions are Sitting Bull's vision before the Battle of Little Big Horn, Wovoka's vision and the establishment of the Ghost Dance movement, Crazy Horse's vision giving him a mission to fight and defend his people, and Black Elk's vision that led him to become a spiritual teacher.

The cosmological place of visions in the Peyote religion is similar to the role of visions in the Yankton traditional religion. Visions are a form of communication between humans and the spirit world. In Peyotism a humble, prayerful person seeks help and a response in the form of a vision. Peyote, as the sacrament, opens a channel (like the Sacred Pipe), making it possible to receive a vision or revelation; however, it should be reiterated that the power and knowledge one receives in a vision must be used for the collective good, not for personal gain. This is another commonality. The vision could offer a revelation for spiritual enlightenment or physical improvement or a revelation that might lead to change in one's own behavior or serve as a source of healing. A vision could help an individual to follow the Peyote road to a better spiritual life or to modify ritual practices to make them more effective, such as Sam Necklace's vision to create certain sacred markings in the ashes during a Peyote meeting. The fact that Peyote contains mild hallucinogenic substances should not be overstated. It may add power to the Peyote, but its true spiritual power is beyond the particular chemical properties of the peyote cactus. Few people in Peyote meetings have visions on a regular basis. Overall, visions play a less significant role in Peyotism than in Yankton traditional religion. It seems that the significance of the visions in Peyotism has declined throughout the twentieth century; today's Peyotists rarely mention them except when discussing origin narratives, founders, or ancestors. The vision element in Peyotism was just one more factor that contributed to the acceptance of the Peyote faith.

OTHER COMMONALITIES

There are other parallels between Peyotism and traditional religion, including the use of feathers, the eagle-bone whistle, the fire and fireplace as the center of the spiritual activities, and the central role of music, particularly the drum. Feathers, especially eagle feathers, have a powerful spiritual significance throughout the Plains cultures. The eagle, like the buffalo, is recognized as having spiritual power and has a special relationship with the Sioux people. It is not uncommon for eagles to appear in visions. There is no more powerful sight for sun dancers than to see eagles soaring above the Sun Dance arena. The eagles represent protection and strength; they carry special blessings for everyone as well as being messengers. In the prereservation era the Sioux believed that the spirit of the eagle presided over the tribal councils, hunters, war parties, and battles.[63] Highly prized, eagle feathers are sacred. They must never touch the ground or be defiled in any way and must be cared for and protected when not in use. Eagle feathers were used to make the great war bonnets of the Plains tribes and to adorn shields and lances; they were awarded for individual feats such as bravery and played a part in ritual and ceremony.

Today the Yanktons continue the widespread use of eagle feathers. During the Sun Dance, for example, dancers wear eagle feathers (men) or eagle plumes (women) on their sage crowns. The Sun Dance chief carries an eagle-wing feather fan that transmits power, wisdom, protection, and blessings from supernatural sources to everyone and everything involved with the Sun Dance. Other ritual uses of eagle feathers include the Vision Quest and naming ceremonies. When someone is fasting on a Vision Quest, an eagle feather is hung from a nearby juniper (cedar) bush in order to help ward off evil forces. During a naming ceremony an eagle feather or eagle plume is attached to the hair of the person receiving an Indian name. Receiving the eagle feather is an honor as well as an affirmation of status and identity.

The sacred nature of eagle feathers is also part of the Peyote faith, although the feathers of other birds are also used (e.g., hawks, scissortails, flickers, pheasants, macaws, and parrots). Birds symbolize the carrying of messages or prayers toward the sky. In addition to the eagle, the water bird is also highly venerated. It represents a generic waterfowl that most closely resembles the water turkey (*Anhinga anhinga*). Leonard Crow Dog says that "the greatest symbol of the Native American Church is the water bird."[64] The stylized bird, which is represented in virtually all Peyote art, has a long, slender neck, sleek wings, and elongated tail feathers. It is represented in swift flight, heading skyward and carrying prayers. The water-bird design is made into jewelry; it is sewn as an appliqué on women's shawls, men's vests, and pillows and painted on water buckets and appears in many paintings and prints as a symbol of the Peyote faith. The water bird appears in the logo of the Native American Church of North America.

The symbolism of the bird extends to feather fans, which have been in use since the inception of Peyotism. Various bird feathers are bound to a beaded handle, making a feather fan that is used throughout the Peyote service.[65] In virtually all Peyote communities an eagle-wing fan is used by the roadmen to fan cedar smoke onto the spiritual paraphernalia and the participants. A roadman's fan is especially significant in healing. The roadman waves the fan vigorously across the body of the ill person. With the ingestion of Peyote and the utterance of intense prayer, and in conjunction with the fan, the spiritual power of healing is transmitted to the individual. All Peyotists have their own feather fans. They are used throughout the Peyote service to draw cedar smoke toward oneself; but most importantly they offer spiritual protection and are used as an aid to prayer. When not singing or drumming, individuals sit quietly in prayer. The fan is held in front of one's face in order to avoid eye contact with other participants. This allows for full concentration while praying.

The sacral power of the eagle is also represented by the eagle-bone whistle, made from a hollow wing bone. The wing bone has a precisely cut single stop about one-inch from the end. It emits a high-pitched sound when one blows into the end. The most common use of the whistle is during the Sun Dance and Vision Quest. Sun dancers have eagle-bone whistles hanging around their necks. While dancing they hold the whistles in their teeth and blow them in unison with the drum and the singers. The whistle is adorned with an eagle plume (a small, soft, breast feather). According to Black Elk, the plumes are important because they are closest to the eagle's heart. He added that the whistle is the voice of the eagle and "our Grandfather, *Wakan Tanka*, always hears this, for you see it is really his own voice."[66] When an individual embarks on a Vision Quest, upon a hill or in a vision pit, a spiritual leader, family, and friends come along to help "put you out." They lay down a bed of sage, put up the four directions flags, and hang an eagle feather on a nearby bush. Everyone wishes the person well and tells him or her to be strong. Before leaving they sing the four directions song, which ends with the spiritual leader blowing the eagle-bone whistle while facing each of the four directions. The individual has all the necessary protections and now, alone, cradling the Sacred Pipe, is ready for a night (or nights) of fasting, prayer, and possible visions.

Roadmen in the Peyote religion have an eagle-bone whistle as part of their ceremonial paraphernalia. During a Peyote service the whistle plays a special role at midnight. At that time there is a break in the singing and drumming.

The drum and staff are returned to the roadman, who sings the midnight water song. A bucket of sacred water is brought into the tipi. It is blessed and passed clockwise to each participant. The midnight pause may also be a time for special prayers, or individuals may share their thoughts with everyone, or in a Cross Fire service a sermon may be delivered. The roadman then leaves the tipi and blows the eagle-bone whistle four times while facing each of the four cardinal directions.

Fire and fireplaces are also central to the Yankton traditional religion and Peyotism. Ceremonially they are the literal center; cosmologically they are the symbolic center. The fireplace is sacred, as expressed in the well-known term *očeti wakan* (sacred fireplace); the fireplace is the symbol of the Sioux nation, the Očeti Šakówin (Seven Council Fires). In Sioux tradition fire represents the power of Wakan Tanka, who gave the gift of fire-making to humans. This knowledge came in a vision many generations ago. The vision demonstrated how the heat of the sun could be turned into fire by rubbing two sticks together next to dry weeds. The message in the vision was that fire represents the Creator's power and is sacred and eternal, as Wakan Tanka is sacred and eternal.[67] Fire is essential in all ceremonies. The person who is responsible for the fire has an important duty to perform. The fire built to heat the rocks for the Sweat Lodge must be done in a precise way. When someone goes on a Vision Quest, a fire is started in the afternoon and must be maintained until the person returns. Representing the power of Wakan Tanka, it protects those on the Vision Quest; if the fire died out, harm could come to those who are fasting.

The significance of the fire can be illustrated by the four days of spiritual activities that take place on the Yankton Reservation on Asa and Loretta Primeaux's land each year in early June, just before the Sun Dance. During this time people may undertake a Vision Quest or participate in naming ceremonies and daily Sweat Lodge ceremonies. A sacred fire must be kept burning all four days. It is incumbent on all present to help with the fire, get firewood, and stay up to watch the fire. Even if there is a thunderstorm and downpour, the fire must not go out. In preparation for the Sun Dance, the Sun Dance chief asks someone to serve as the fire keeper. This person organizes the effort to collect the firewood and to help care for the fire over four days and nights. The fire keeper also prepares the Sweat Lodge and heats the rocks for the Sun Dancers, who must "sweat" before dancing at dawn and in the early evening after dancing. The fire is one of the essential elements of the Sun Dance, helping to create an environment so that Wakan Tanka will answer the prayers of the dancers.

The fire is the focus of the Peyote meeting and has been since the nineteenth century. It is located in the exact center of the tipi between the door (east) and the roadman (west). If a meeting is held in a home or building, a fire can be built on a platform or earthen bed; if that is not feasible, it is built outside, and hot coals are carried inside. The fireman is one of the four people who conduct a Peyote meeting. The role of the fireman is very difficult. Wood for an all-night fire must be gathered. This is not a casual undertaking: only certain woods can be used (such as ash or red elm), and they must be cut and split in a very specific manner in terms of length and diameter. The bark is also removed. The fireplace itself is very special to Peyote families. Many people speak of a family's particular fireplace, because it may include ritual elements handed down from previous generations or received in a vision. Also, the term "fireplace" is a metaphor for the type of Peyote service. One can refer to a roadman who runs a Cross Fire fireplace or a Half Moon fireplace. In this context "fireplace" means the fire, wood, coals and ashes, and altar as well as specific ceremonial practices.

The fireman prepares the inside of the tipi before the meeting begins, constructs the altar, then gets the wood ready for the fire by stacking it in a crisscrossed, V-shaped pattern, with the narrow end pointed west. The fire is started at the narrow end. The fireman must care for it the rest of the night, bringing in more wood and continually rearranging the burning wood to maintain the original shape so that hot coals and ashes build up in one area, where they can be formed into symbolic patterns. The fireman uses two sticks to shape the hot coals. The style of the design depends on the type of meeting that the roadman is conducting as well as the time, such as midnight or dawn. The ashes may be shaped into a heart, half-moon, star, eagle, water bird, or cross. For example, in the Half Moon way the cross may represent the four directions; in the Cross Fire way it may represent a Christian cross. Each of the designs has its own symbolic significance, but all have the same goal of harnessing power to send the prayers skyward.[68]

Music is an integral part of American Indian spiritual life, with the drum as the central feature. Among the Lakotas, Dakotas, and Nakotas the drum is used in most spiritual ceremonies as well in nonspiritual activities such as powwows. There are small hand-held drums for some activities, but the most widely used drum is a large bass-sized drum, thirty to thirty-six inches in diameter. The drum is sacred. Its construction, from choosing the wood for the frame to tanning the skin for the drumhead, is very elaborate. Before it is used in a ceremony such as the Sun Dance, it is blessed. It must be cared for and protected, usually with tobacco ties or with a sprinkling of tobacco on the drum. The sound of the drum represents the human heartbeat. Black Elk said that "the round form of the drum represents the whole universe, and its steady strong beat is the pulse, the heart throbbing at the center of the universe."[69] During the Sun Dance the drum and singers establish a rhythm for the dancers, helping them concentrate on their prayers throughout the four days of dancing. The drum aids in summoning the spirits that heal the afflicted, as if the voice of the drum was an offering to the spirits.[70]

Many factors play a part in healing ceremonies; but the one essential element in all healing is music in the form of songs accompanied by instruments, usually drums. The songs are prayers, and healing cannot take place without prayer. This is also true in Peyotism. The Peyote water drum is quite different from the traditional drum that is used at Sun Dances and powwows (see the photograph of a drum). The music is also quite different from traditional Sioux music; nevertheless the function and significance of the music and drum are similar. The Yanktons use a Peyote drum that is made from a three-legged cast iron kettle that contains water and is covered by an animal-skin drumhead. The water also affects the sound of the drum when it is tilted, which wets the drumhead and intensifies the sound. Not only is the Peyote drum higher-pitched than the traditional drum, but it is played more rapidly. The similarity between the two drums is their ritual and ceremonial role. The drum is at the center and represents the spirit of Peyote. Leonard Crow Dog says that it is the "Indian heart beat." Vincent Catches puts it another way: through the night the Peyote drum is the heartbeat of the meeting.[71]

The drumhead (usually deerskin) is tied onto the kettle before each meeting and removed at the end. The chief drummer has the responsibility of preparing the drum. This is an elaborate process, full of spiritual meaning. As noted, the drumhead is attached to the drum by seven stones and a long piece of rope. The rope is wrapped around the drum, forming the shape of a star on the bottom. This represents the morning star that one sees after a long night of prayer. It is the coming of a new day and thus spiritual renewal. According to Gerald Primeaux (great-grandson of Sam Necklace), his dad (Asa Primeaux) taught him that the drum represents mother earth. The seven stones represent the seven continents, and the four or seven pieces of charcoal that are added to the water in the drum represent the spirits of the deceased and those not yet born. The rope binds all things together. The drumbeat is the breathing of mother earth. In the morning after the Peyote service has ended, the chief drummer unties the drum; the water, now sacred, may be sipped and/or poured along the altar. Gerald said: "The altar is the road of life, so when they pour the water on it, it's like you're watering the earth so that growth comes from it, like in your mind, body, and spirit. Even mother earth itself. We need this water, everybody does. So when you pour it, it helps you get some of that goodness." Gerald added that these meanings came to his dad from "eating medicine in the ceremony."[72]

It is clear that the Peyote water drum represents the interrelatedness of all things on earth, an idea that reflects the Yankton traditional cosmology, as in *Mitakuye Oyasin*. This also represents another common feature of the drum: the sense of community that it creates in both Yankton traditional religion and Peyotism. The Peyote drum is played by one person at a time, whereas the traditional drum is played by any number of people together; but both types of drumming reflect the communal nature of the spiritual experiences. The Peyote drum is passed around the circle, giving each person the opportunity to drum and sing. The traditional drum is played collectively by a group of people sitting in a circle. In both cases the method of drumming re-creates the unity and continuity of the sacred circle.

In using the framework of common or parallel elements between Yankton traditional religion and Peyotism, it must be remembered that the Peyote religion was diffused as an established complex of belief, ceremony, and ritual. The Peyotists collectively or as individuals could add minor elements to the ritual, but the cosmological belief system and the overall ceremony remained intact. Thus the common elements in the two faiths were essential in making it relevant, comfortable, and able to fulfill the needs of certain people. The convergence between these religious complexes was on both a theological and ritual level. In addition the language remained the same. Individuals still referred to Wakan Tanka, closed prayers with *Mitakuye Oyasin,* and sang and prayed in Dakota.

Other commonalities also helped make Peyotism acceptable. For example, funeral services in both traditional religion and Peyotism are for one "who walked on," and everyone's prayers are for the departed one's spirit to have a successful journey; in both, some of the spiritual paraphernalia is buried with the deceased. There is a four-day mourning period followed by four annual memorial services. Honoring ceremonies are also common to both: special events to honor birthdays, graduations, returning veterans, elders, or any accomplishment. They offer thanks, recognizing the divine power that controls all. Another element essential to this discussion is the sense of community that was provided in the past by the *tiošpaye* (extended family), the band, and the village. By the 1920s bands were not functioning as corporate groups; but the *tiošpaye* remained a functional group, although weakened by scattered housing, children at boarding schools, and the growth of Christian denominations. Peyotism re-created community when community was in decline. It became a Peyote *tiošpaye*. This affected a person's identity as a Yankton Peyotist—some of the young men referred to themselves as the "peyote boys." People were no less Yanktons, but now they were also Peyotists. Within the Peyote community, Yankton or Dakota kinship terminology continued to be used. There was little distinction between blood kinship and fictive kinship (shirt-tail relatives, as I was told). The traditional respect for the elderly remained intact. They were referred to as grandpa or grandma and other adults as auntie or uncle or cousin for those of the same generation. In these areas there was considerable continuity.

In reviewing the literature on the history of Peyotism, as well as the Ghost Dance movement, one finds many theories and models that attempt to explain its origins and diffusion. These include acculturation theory, relative deprivation theory, nativistic movements, reformative movements, revitalization movements (divided into sacred and secular), and crisis cult theory, recently renamed crisis religion.[73] There are relevant elements in each of the paradigms. One could amass the necessary data from the Yankton historical experience to support at least several of these perspectives. Yet on closer examination they do not offer an interpretation that fully explains the Yankton experience in a holistic sense, as described in this chapter. Yes, the Yankton Sioux were relatively deprived, they were in crisis, and acculturation was a reality. These factors can be measured and compared with the models in a rationalistic manner. What is missing is the nature of the Peyote church itself. These theories analyze external phenomena; but by focusing on Peyotism itself and the Yankton traditional religion, one can gain an internal perspective that corresponds with the view of Yankton Peyotists that they accepted the Peyote religion for its intrinsic worth, relevance, and truth as a spiritual complex that meshed well with their spiritual roots. The conclusion to be reached is that Peyotism had so many commonalities with prereservation spirituality that it could provide a meaningful spiritual life that also satisfied social and aesthetic needs. The Peyote community acquired a degree of autonomy. Peyotism provided ecclesiastical and cultural autonomy when political and economic autonomy was not possible. This is not a proposal for a general hypothesis on the diffusion of the Peyote religion; it is simply a conclusion about Yankton Peyotism drawn from an ethnohistorical analysis as well as an ethnographic description based on field experience.

END OF THE 1920s

In the late 1920s life on the reservation was not improving. Jobs were scarce; there were health problems and poor nutrition; loss of land continued; and Yankton politics was rife with factionalism. The population, at 2,029 in 1930, was not growing. Only 62 percent of school-age children were in school (383 out of 619). The majority were in local public schools; the rest were in government boarding schools and mission schools.[74] Statistics indicate the changing structure of the population. The 1927 census shows that out of 2,022 people there were 404 full-bloods and 1,618 mixed-bloods (the majority of whom had less than half Yankton ancestry). This reality was a major cause of factionalism, discussed in the next chapter. There was, however, one important change. A reassessment of Peyote began in the late 1920s, as many federal policies toward Native Americans were being reviewed. Members of the Brookings Institution in Washington, D.C., undertook a study of the administration of Indian affairs. This massive study, known as the Meriam Report, appeared in 1928. It is a significant study in that it examined the terrible conditions that existed on the reservations. The data collected became the basis for its conclusion that serious reform was necessary. The report laid the groundwork for the reform of Indian policy in the 1930s. It included only a brief history of Peyotism and commented that the "Peyote Church" was flourishing and that there was no evidence that Peyote was a habit-forming drug. Although one part of the report referred to "peyote addiction," it did not call for the outlawing of Peyote.[75]

The high point of the anti-Peyote campaign had already passed. In 1924 Congress added a provision to the Indian appropriations bill that Peyote be included in the suppression of liquor traffic on the reservations; however, this was not enforceable, because Peyote possession had not been criminalized. From this time on, federal anti-Peyote agitation began to subside, as more and more people started to question whether Peyote was really harmful to one's health. There were now groups such as the American Indian Defense Association, led by John Collier, that defended Peyote usage on the basis of religious freedom. Other groups that were formerly part of the anti-Peyote forces, such as the Indian Rights Association, began to ignore it.[76] State laws at that time were not very effective in slowing the expansion of the Peyote religion. Between Oklahoma outlawing Peyote in 1899 (repealed in 1908) and Texas in 1937, fourteen states criminalized the possession of it. The states had no jurisdiction on reservations, but they could harass Peyotists and impede the transportation of Peyote. If states had any impact, it was to convince Peyote communities to incorporate. Provided that they followed proper procedures, there was no legal way that they could be denied state incorporation charters. At the same time the Peyote community on the Yankton Reservation faced less open hostility from Superintendent Daniel. At the end of the decade Peyote was rarely mentioned in his correspondence to Washington. He spent most of his time trying to encourage the Yanktons to become farmers on the Anglo-American family farm model. It was a losing proposition, because most of the land had already been sold; and much of what was left was leased to white farmers. Others did not have the financial resources to initiate a successful farming venture. In 1927 Superintendent Daniel listed only thirteen successful Yankton farming families in his agricultural report.[77]

By 1929 there were five incorporated Peyote groups in South Dakota. These communities had considerable contact with each other as well as with groups in other states. Cooperation was essential, as states were criminalizing Peyote. They shared information, attended each other's Peyote meetings, and generally supported each other. Almost all the groups in the United States adopted the name "Native American Church," giving them a sense of a broad-based unity and a basis for cooperation. In South Dakota members of the Peyote community on the Pine Ridge Reservation took a loose leadership role in the state. They incorporated in 1922 as the Native American Church of Allen [South Dakota] but renamed themselves the Native American Church of South Dakota in 1924. Leadership, however, did not mean control over other Peyote communities. Congregational autonomy was the norm, with each group selecting its own leadership, developing its own organizational structure, raising its own funds, and conducting its own internal activities, such as ordinations, baptisms, weddings, and funerals. The incorporated

Peyote groups in South Dakota began holding annual conventions, starting in 1922. Jim Blue Bird, the Lakota Peyotist, did much of the early communication and coordination work. The location of the convention rotated each year among the reservations. They had business meetings in the afternoon and Peyote meetings all night. The conventions were critical in maintaining statewide unity and developing a sense of community among the members (the Eightieth Annual Convention was held in 2002).

By the late 1920s the Yankton Native American Church operated on a business as usual routine. Peyote meetings were held regularly on the first Saturday of the month and at other times for special occasions or special needs. Secrecy was no longer a concern. Being part of the Peyote community was now public knowledge. For example, on various forms and applications Sam Necklace acknowledged his involvement with Peyotism. It is unclear when Sam became a roadman and started running Peyote meetings, but it was probably in the late 1910s or early 1920s. He was ordained as a priest in 1924, which meant he had been a roadman for at least several years. He continued as secretary, but other changes occurred. In 1926 Johnson Goodhouse, who had been chief priest since 1922, was replaced by Charles Iron Hawk. This may have been to give Goodhouse the opportunity to travel and proselytize. In 1926 he visited the Devil's Lake (Spirit Lake today) Reservation in North Dakota and Griswold, Manitoba, in order to spend time with the Canadian Sioux. In both places he ran meetings and helped establish the Native American Church. In 1928 Henry Blaine was elected chief priest. The following year, on 19 October 1929, Sam Necklace was chosen as chief priest of the Native American Church of Charles Mix County, a position he held for the rest of his life.[78]

Peyote meeting of the Yankton Native American Church, 1963, in honor of Adam Sitting Crow, Jr.'s fifth birthday. Adam, Sr., holding the cake; Joe Shields on the far left. Photo by Germaine Sitting Crow. From the author's collection.

Yankton Native American Church, 1994. Built in 1939, not used since the mid-1990s, and torn down in 2003. Photo by author.

Tipi belonging to Asa and Loretta Primeaux, used for Peyote meetings. Photo by author.

Mazanapi–Iron Necklace headstone, Yankton Reservation. Photo by author.

Sam Necklace headstone, Native American Church cemetery, Yankton Reservation. Photo by author.

Asa Primeaux, Sr., grandson of Sam and Mary Necklace, ca. 1990. Family photo.

Parnell Necklace (*right*)—grandson of Sam Necklace and master drum maker—and author, 2000. Photo by author.

Parnell Necklace and seven great-grandchildren of Sam and Mary Necklace, Powwow, Columbus, Ohio, 1997: Danny, Sam, Martina, Dakota, Moriah, Sage Baker, Kehala. Photo by author.

Peyote drum belonging to Gerald Primeaux, great-grandson of Sam and Mary Necklace, 1998. Photo by author.

Peyote motif pillow belonging to the Primeaux family, 1997. Photo by author.

Jennie Necklace Franklin, daughter of Sam and Mary Necklace and mother of Asa Primeaux, Sr., with granddaughters Jolene (*left*) and Janell, ca. 1976. Family photo.

Yankton Sioux Peyote Singers, Lake Andes, South Dakota, 1977: (*left to right*)
Francis Primeaux, Duane Shields, Joe Shields, Sr., Joe Abdo, Sr., Asa Primeaux,
Sr., Quentin Bruguier, Lorenzo Dion. Photo by Tony Issacs, courtesy of Indian
House, Taos, New Mexico.

Young generation of Yankton Peyotists, 2003. They are the sons and grandsons of those in the photo on page 192. *Left to right:* Lorenzo Dion, Jr., Larry Abdo, Jr., Paul Never Misses a Shot, Gerald Primeaux, Asa Primeaux, Jr., Tom Never Misses a Shot, Mike Primeaux, Jr. Photo by author.

CHAPTER SIX

Chief Priest
Sam Necklace and
the Native American
Church   1929–49

Peyote service in a tipi with a variety of religious
paraphernalia. Drawn by Asa Primeaux, Jr.

By the end of the 1920s there was an extensive Necklace *tiošpaye*. In 1930 Sam and Mary's household numbered five. Sam was forty-nine, Mary forty-five; Danny, Jennie, and Pearl, nineteen, sixteen, and eleven, respectively. Ben, the eldest son, lived nearby with his wife, Rosie, and one-year-old Gideon. Sam's mother, Margarette, was now seventy-two. His half-brother and closest friend, Amos, was now a widower with four children, ages nine through nineteen, living at home. Unfortunately, the life expectancy of Native Americans was still low; infant mortality was high. Sam and Mary lost another child. In 1935 Pearl, only sixteen years old, died from pneumonia. Ben's son Gideon died just after his second birthday. In 1934 Sam's mother died; she had been ill for several years with chronic heart problems.[1]

Sam's daughter, now Frances Necklace Gardner [Garner], lived in Bingham, Nebraska, with her husband and their three children, who were all enrolled members of the Yankton tribe. Sometime in the early 1930s they moved to Porcupine, South Dakota, on the Pine Ridge Reservation. The Yankton census of 1934 lists Porcupine as their residence. In 1937 Frances passed away from unknown causes. Her husband, Wilson, raised the three children. Frances is remembered with much affection in the family. Her brother Dan named one of his daughters after her.[2]

Sam and Mary's other children, Benedict, Daniel, and Jennie, spent most of the lives on the reservation, with the exception of periodic residences in other places where jobs were available. All three children were active members of the Native American Church, attending Peyote meetings with their parents. For a time Ben and Dan lived in the city of Yankton, South Dakota, where they were part of a small Peyote community. Ben was the first to marry; as just mentioned, his son Gideon died in 1931. Several years later, in 1936, his wife, Rosie, also died; they did not have any other children. In 1938 Ben married Sybil Eagle from the Sisseton Reservation. They had nine children and remained married until his death in 1964 at the age of fifty-seven. The other son, Daniel Baker Necklace (named after his father's oldest brother), married Josephine Primeaux from the Rosebud Reservation. The Primeauxs were a Peyote family. The marriage did not last, however; they divorced before having any children. In 1950 Dan married Katherine Sing from the Sisseton Reservation; they had ten children, with eight surviving into adulthood.

Sam and Mary's daughter Jennie (also with the middle name Baker) married Harry Primeaux, from the same extended family as her sister-in-law Josephine. In 1931 they had their only child, Asa. Jennie and Harry separated soon afterward; and with the exception of several years that Asa spent with his father on the Rosebud Reservation, he lived with his grandparents until adulthood. Jennie stayed with her parents for a short period and then married Josiah Franklin, a Yankton. They settled in a home on the top of the hill north of Greenwood. They had six children, four of whom survived into adulthood. Jennie remained close to her parents, especially her mother after her father died. Asa, however, continued to live with his grandparents even with his mother close by. Sam and Mary had seven children; four survived into adulthood. These three had twenty-eight children, and Sam's daughter Frances had three, making twenty-eight grandchildren. The majority of the grandchildren survived and had many children themselves. The Necklace *tiošpaye*, including in-laws such as the Primeaux and Rainbow families, numbers in the hundreds.[3]

The new decade also meant more responsibility for Sam. As chief priest of the Native American Church of Charles Mix County, he provided leadership in defending the Peyote community's rights in Yankton politics as well as defending the rights of the full-bloods who were losing influence in the political arena. Sam also spent time caring for members of the Peyote church, often traveled to other Peyote communities, and tried to meet the economic needs of his family in the midst of a terrible depression. The last twenty years of his life were defined by an intertwining of family, spirituality, and politics.[4]

THE DEPRESSION YEARS ON THE YANKTON RESERVATION

The four years of President Herbert Hoover's administration (1929–33) were grim for American Indians in spite of the fact that the Department of the Interior had some reform-minded officials who were being pressured by an increasing number of Americans calling for change. The Meriam Report was a model for reform. The main obstacle to meaningful change was the continued assumption that assimilation should be the goal of federal Indian policy. There were some improvements; for example, appropriations for food and clothing at government boarding schools were increased, and some of the corporal punishment of students was curtailed. Boarding school principals were now required to have college degrees, and several boarding schools were closed. Health-care appropriations also increased, but overall the Hoover administration took a cautious approach to change. Its efforts were miniscule compared with the great economic needs. On the eve of the election of Franklin D. Roosevelt, two-thirds of American Indians were landless. With a land base of 138 million acres in 1887, reservations accounted for only 52 million acres, and half of that was desert or semidesert. Historians are in universal agreement that federal Indian land policy "failed miserably" and that safeguarding Indian rights and land titles was not a governmental priority.[5]

The onset of the Depression was not immediately obvious on the Yankton Reservation, because economic conditions were already depressed. As the Depression wore on and the weather became more and more severe, however, the situation worsened with the fear of sporadic starvation. Per capita income dropped as the farming crisis grew and white farmers in the area were less able to employ seasonal Yankton workers. The summer of 1931 was extremely hot, dry, and windy, creating dust storms with dark clouds that hid the sun. Dust piled up everywhere, especially along fences and homes. Hordes of grasshoppers invaded the region. Virtually all crops and vegetation withered in the sun. Many cattle died. The next two years brought more heat and dryness. In June 1933 the grasshoppers returned. There was little that could be done; Father Sylvester of the Marty Mission gathered some of his parishioners for a procession through parched fields, reciting the rosary, sprinkling holy water on the fields, and imploring God to stop the grasshoppers.[6] The agency's annual economic report for 1933 outlined these harsh conditions. There were only 201 employed people on the reservation, many of them earning minimal wages. This affected housing and clothing. Out of 289 homes (144 were one- or two-room houses), 174 were listed in fair to poor condition, and 25 percent of the people were described as having inadequate clothing. In 1933, however, came the beginning of relief. The government started a biweekly distribution of staples, such as flour, sugar, and cheese. Father Sylvester opened a soup kitchen at the mission feeding 100 to 200 people daily.[7]

Not only were the summers insufferable, but the winters were not much better, with extreme cold and blizzards. Some described the winter of 1936 as the blizzard of the century.[8] Heating homes was difficult. Almost everyone had coal- or wood-burning stoves, but there was little coal to be distributed. Some people burned their furniture and wood from their front porches for heat. Many Yanktons remember the despair of these years. No one could forget the grasshoppers, the shortage of food, or the deaths of many horses. Some of these memories have been preserved. Cecil Provost put it well: "no rain, dust, grasshoppers—day after day." William O'Connor said the "times were deplorable."[9] The Marty Mission reopened its soup kitchen when necessary, and the government began to increase its supply of rations. In 1935 the government delivered several hundred mutton carcasses to help ease the food crisis. Even with the government aid there rarely was sufficient food. Some communal farming was tried, and there were small family gardens, but they were not enough. In the winter of 1936 Father Sylvester wrote to John Collier, seeking help for the reservation: "Indians here freezing and starving. Situation deplorable. . . . Indians burning their furniture." The following year several South Dakota newspapers reported on starvation on the Yankton Reservation, with headlines such as "Yankton Indians Starve."[10] The New Deal programs helped somewhat, but overall economic conditions did not improve.

President Roosevelt appointed Harold Ickes as secretary of the interior and John Collier as commissioner of Indian Affairs. These two men would reverse many of the government's Indian policies. Collier had been advocating the reform of federal Indian policy for years. His reforms were based on a new philosophical principle that replaced the assimilation model of the past half-century with a model based on cultural pluralism, including economic development, a degree of self-government, religious freedom, and cultural autonomy. Some called it the "Indian New Deal." Collier's first step was emergency relief to impoverished reservations. The Yanktons received direct relief with the distribution of food and surplus clothing. In March 1933 Congress established the Civilian Conservation Corps (CCC) to put the nation's unemployed to work. Some Yanktons went to Chamberlain, South Dakota, to work in an integrated CCC camp.[11]

This was not a satisfactory solution for the heavy unemployment. Secretary Ickes and Collier had Congress approve a separate administrative unit called CCC-ID (Indian Division) in order to set up work camps on reservations. The workers received a salary of $30 per month. By the summer of 1933 the camps were open, and thousands were put to work.[12] The Works Progress Administration (WPA), a New Deal program that provided work for people from all walks of life, sponsored some of the jobs. Both the CCC and WPA employed Yanktons. On the reservation they built the Song Hawk Dam and other smaller dams, springs were revitalized to provide water for cattle, and soil conservation projects were undertaken. Rebuilding roads and construction jobs at the new Indian hospital in Wagner also provided jobs. Over 80,000 American Indians were employed by the CCC-ID, 8,405 in South Dakota. The WPA employed several thousand more. These relief and rehabilitation programs did not solve the deep-seated economic problems, but they did provide jobs and much-needed income. These programs were essential to John Collier's vision, but his real goal was to move beyond relief to reform.[13]

The heart of John Collier's reforms was embodied in the Indian Reorganization Act (IRA), passed by Congress in June 1934. It established a variety of administrative programs that altered the federal relationship with American Indians. Its primary feature was to develop limited self-government on the reservations. In addition, the bill ended the allotment system, effectively stopping the loss of reservation land. Funds were also made available for community development, economic development, and loans for education. The IRA did not automatically apply to all reservations. Voters were asked to accept or reject reorganization under the new bill. The IRA received a mixed response, because it was a product of an Indian bureau that had developed and implemented many harmful policies over the last half-century. The vote on the IRA created tension and divisiveness. Each reservation had to vote several times. The first vote was to accept or reject reorganization, but it was not a simple majority vote. A majority of eligible voters had to vote no in order to reject the IRA. That meant that voters who stayed home had their votes counted as yes votes. This created considerable resentment, as reconsideration was prohibited. There were 174 Indian groups that voted approval of the IRA and 78 that rejected it. Upon approval, a tribal council was elected to draft a constitution that required approval by the secretary of the interior and ratification by a majority vote on each reservation. The IRA then allowed each reservation government to petition for a charter of incorporation, which also had to be ratified by the voters. With the approval of the charter the tribe became a corporation. Under this system the tribal council had the power to hire lawyers, to control the sale or lease of tribal land, and to enter into negotiations with the federal, state, and local governments. The IRA did not establish home rule or self-determination as it is understood today, but the reservations that accepted the IRA acquired limited power over local affairs.[14]

The debates over the IRA, both on and off the reservations, were intense. Off the reservations the debates were between those who advocated a continuation of the assimilation policies of the past and those who supported Collier's reforms. The antireform group included almost all the Christian missionaries. For example, the Catholic missions in South Dakota launched a negative campaign against John Collier and the IRA. Their attacks were circulated in letters and published in the *Little Bronzed Angel* and the *Catholic Sioux Herald*. They implied that John Collier was against religion and was promoting socialist if not communistic policies. They suggested that the very existence of Catholic schools was threatened by the passage of the IRA. Some long-time employees of the BIA also opposed the bill, arguing that it was a step backward and would revive the "blanket Indian" and perpetuate "tribalism." Those in support of the IRA were the reformers of the 1920s and 1930s who believed that government policies were bankrupt.[15]

On the reservations the debates were also intense, particularly in South Dakota, where they became an extension of the struggle between full-bloods and mixed-bloods. For the most part the full-bloods or traditionalists opposed the IRA; the mixed-bloods supported it. The full-bloods were suspicious of the federal government. They feared a loss of rights to a new tribal government. Those who had not sold their allotted land were afraid of confiscation of the land or loss of heirship rights. They feared that there was an underlying government agenda that was not in their best interests. Their suspicions were most intense against the mixed-bloods who supported the IRA. Many of the latter were landless, having sold their allotments and moved into the small towns in the area. Others were born after the allotment period and had not received any land. The full-bloods resented them for supposedly giving up their "Indian ways" and living an Anglo-American lifestyle. For their part, most of the mixed-bloods looked down on full-bloods for being unwilling or unable to be "progressive" and for clinging to "old ways." The mixed-bloods saw the IRA as an opportunity for upward mobility by gaining political and economic benefits through a local government system that had access to economic development funds. Prior to the IRA, the debate was over who should represent the tribe in negotiations with the government. Under the IRA, an elected tribal council would have certain political and economic prerogatives.[16] As the stakes increased, the intensity of the debate followed suit.

The debate over public issues was not new; it was a continuation of the political, economic, and cultural struggles that had been going on since the allotment system was instituted. As the Depression wore on and issues went unresolved, some Yanktons believed that a new tribal council was needed. A committee of nine, called the Claims Committee, was elected in 1924. It dealt with claims issues such as the Pipestone Quarry but did not involve itself in other reservation business. By 1931 four members of the committee had died; one resigned, leaving a committee of four, chaired by David Simmons. Many Yanktons felt that they were not well represented and wanted another election, because the remaining four members had not been reelected. In the summer of 1931 petitions were circulated calling for the election of a new tribal committee. Several Yanktons, including Sam Necklace, signed the petition, which was forwarded to the commissioner of Indian Affairs, who approved it and recommended that a constitution and bylaws be written.[17] He also pointed out that the constitution had to be approved by his office before the Yanktons could vote on it. The commissioner reminded C. C. Hickman, the superintendent of the Yankton Agency, that an elected tribal council served only in an advisory capacity to the commissioner and the superintendent; it could only act on issues that were submitted to it, and final action always rested with the Department of the Interior.[18]

In September 1931 a constitution and bylaws were drafted and sent to Washington for approval. The constitution was based on a dependency model; the Yanktons could take no action without federal approval. The commissioner's office approved the constitution, and the superintendent called a meeting of eligible voters to debate and vote on it. After a contentious meeting, the new constitution was approved by a vote of 230 to 125. The opposition was led by Raymond and Gertrude Bonnin and David Simmons (Gertrude's half-brother). They argued that there was a duly constituted tribal committee and that the Clement Smith faction would control the new committee. After the new constitution was approved, an election was held for nine members of a new Business Committee. Clement Smith was elected chairman. One important point concerning Yankton politics in the 1920s and especially in the 1931 election is that women began to participate in the petitioning process and as voters.[19]

The ratification of the constitution and the election of a tribal council did not settle the question of the old Claims Committee of 1924. It was unclear if it was defunct or if there were two committees. The new constitution did not address the issue. Commissioner Charles J. Rhoads responded to this dilemma by declaring that the Yanktons had two elected committees. The 1924 committee would be responsible for claims issues; the 1931 committee would serve as the Tribal Council. Many Yanktons believed that politics influenced the ruling to keep two committees. The Bonnin/Simmons faction struggled with the Clement Smith group, which had initiated the 1931 constitution. The Bonnins were well-known personalities in Washington and may have influenced the decision of the commissioner to keep the 1924 committee. Gertrude was president of the National Council of American Indians, and Raymond was executive secretary-treasurer. They used the organization letterhead to send lengthy letters; they also wrote to several members of Congress, asking them to intervene with Rhoads on their behalf. The Bonnins lived in Washington part of the year and knew Rhoads personally. He would not accept any negative reports about the Bonnins that were sent to him by Superintendent Hickman.[20]

The majority of the Yanktons were not happy with the decision. In April 1932 a new petition was sent to the BIA to "finally determine the selection of a new tribal business and claims committee" and readoption of a constitution and bylaws. The commissioner approved.[21] The Yanktons met on 22 September at the agency headquarters in Greenwood. James Irving was elected to serve as chair of the meeting, and David Ree nominated Sam Necklace to serve as secretary. Sam declined the nomination, saying that he wanted to take an active part in the proceedings. After considerable debate, they voted to abolish the 1924 committee. A new constitution was proposed, establishing a governing body called the Yankton Sioux Tribal Business and Claims Committee, made up of nine enrolled Yanktons serving two-year terms. The constitution was approved, which effectively decertified the 1931 constitution and the 1931 Business Committee. The floor was opened for nominations to the new committee. There were twenty-one nominations. Sam Necklace nominated Ben Vardall, a member of the Native American Church. Everyone voted for nine candidates, with the top nine who received the most votes becoming the new governing body. Vardall was not elected. Joseph Grabbingbear and Clement Smith received the most votes. On 5 October Commissioner Rhoads approved the new constitution and bylaws and certified the election.[22]

The Yanktons now had a new constitution and a new governing body; but in an ironic twist of events much of what seem settled became quite unsettled with the election of Franklin D. Roosevelt and the appointment of John Collier. The year 1933 was a watershed for the Yanktons. Not only was it the depth of the Depression, with hunger stalking the reservation, but other changes also occurred. On 1 April Superintendent Hickman was removed from office for his questionable role in Yankton politics. The Yankton Agency was also downgraded to a subagency and placed under the jurisdiction of the Rosebud Agency. The Yanktons now had an assistant superintendent who reported to Rosebud instead of directly to Washington. The change was ostensibly made for economic reasons, reducing the numbers of federal employees on the Yankton Reservation. It remained a subagency until 1967, when it was reestablished as an independent jurisdiction. As a subagency it received less consideration from the Rosebud superintendent.[23] Amidst these changes the Yanktons now had to decide whether to accept reorganization under the Indian Reorganization Act. In the fall the Yanktons began a series of meetings to debate their future. On 27 October 1934 they voted to accept in principle being organized under the IRA. Commissioner Collier sent them a congratulatory letter.[24] Voting to ratify an IRA constitution would be another matter.

A new IRA constitution was a product of the BIA, but each reservation could add amendments. The constitutions gave reservation governments more local autonomy. The guidelines, however, required approval of the constitution by the secretary of the interior, and any action taken under the new constitution was subject to review.[25] Meanwhile the Yanktons were preparing for an election of their tribal council, based on the 1932 constitution, which called for biennial elections. At a meeting in September there were twenty nominations from the floor for nine positions on the council. Amos Shields, a member of the Peyote community, nominated Sam Necklace. As in 1932,

Joe Grabbingbear and Clement Smith were the top vote getters. Sam did not fare well; he tied for fourteenth.[26]

In 1935 the Yanktons voted on the IRA constitution and bylaws; much to the surprise of the BIA, they rejected it by a vote of 299 to 187. The absentee ballots favored the constitution 57 to 1. The integrity of the absentee ballots was questioned, but they were not enough to change the result.[27] This meant that the Yanktons could not be organized under the IRA, which caused long-term confusion about the status of the tribe. They lost access to some federal benefits (it did not affect the CCC or WPA programs); they lost federal recognition of elected officials; and they gained the anger of John Collier. Attempting to rectify the situation, they submitted several new constitutions to Washington, but none were acceptable. For example, in December 1935 Gertrude and Raymond Bonnin prepared a new non-IRA constitution that gave the Yanktons more autonomy. They acquired over 300 signatures, including all the Necklaces, and forwarded it to Washington for approval; it was returned unapproved. There was also a group that continued to press for approval of an IRA constitution. The debates continued, but the deadlock remained. The Yanktons voted down another constitution in 1936. The two-year term of office was about to expire for the Yankton Business and Claims Committee, but the BIA would not approve the scheduling of a new election. The Yanktons did not have a duly elected governing body, but they went ahead anyway and conducted an unauthorized election. The same situation continued in 1938: the federal government would not approve an election, but the Yanktons nevertheless elected nine people to the Business and Claims Committee. Clarence Foreman became the new unauthorized chairman.[28] Collier wrote to Superintendent C. R. Whitlock of the Rosebud Agency, reminding him that the recently elected Yankton committee was not recognized by his office.[29]

With the absence of an authorized governing body there was a need for some type of administrative structure to coordinate federal relief and rehabilitation programs on the local level. The commissioner's office recommended that each of the three districts on the reservation (White Swan, Greenwood, and Chouteau Creek) elect a local rehabilitation committee. The town of Marty was later added as a fourth district. Each district elected three representatives to a local rehabilitation committee, with one member of each committee serving on a central rehabilitation committee that dealt directly with government officials. These committees were recognized by the BIA only in matters pertaining to federal rehabilitation programs.[30] This was the closest thing to a governing body that the Yanktons had.

Led by Clement Smith, 397 Yanktons signed a petition in 1939 in support of an amendment to the IRA that would exclude the Yanktons from its jurisdiction, allowing them to organize on their own. Collier testified against the amendment. He argued that the Yanktons would lose additional benefits if it passed. After hearing various sides on the amendment, the House Committee on Indian Affairs decided to take no action. In 1940 Clement Smith returned to Washington to testify again against the IRA. He said it "sets up the practice of communism." The chair of the House committee replied: "Frankly the Chair will state that he is of the opinion that the witness does not know what he is talking about."[31] The deadlock continued, but the BIA was clear about the significance of the Yankton decision to reject an IRA constitution. The political status of the Yanktons was outlined in a letter from William Zimmerman, assistant commissioner of Indian Affairs, to Superintendent Whitlock. Zimmerman reminded Whitlock that the tribal council headed by Clement Smith should not be recognized, as it was not a duly constituted tribal body. He added that "at the present time, there is no tribal council with whom the [Indian] Service can deal in effecting Rehabilitation agreements. . . . Terms of the Tribal Council elected in 1934 have expired and successors have not been chosen."[32] The lack of a recognized governing body continued until the Yanktons adopted a constitution in 1963. Meanwhile tribal business was conducted by calling special meetings, electing temporary chairs, and voting on issues by those in attendance.

The majority of reservation governments (including most of the Sioux) voted to accept an IRA constitution, but not the Yanktons. The debate over the IRA was influenced by many factors—some real, some imagined—including rumors, misinformation, misunderstandings, interference by so-called outsiders, Collier's abrasiveness, missionary involvement, and a number of competing factions, such as full-bloods versus mixed-bloods as well as old versus young. There was some realignment of the factions as groups came together to defeat the new constitution. The most harmful rumor was that under the new constitution the land of those who held allotted land would be confiscated and put under tribal control. It was many of the full-bloods, such as the Necklace family, who still held allotments and feared losing their land. They believed that the mixed-bloods favored the new constitution because it would increase their power by giving them more control over tribal resources. This was a very trying time. Many of the Yanktons interviewed in the 1960s and 1970s have vivid memories of the IRA turmoil. One, Bill O'Connor, said that anyone who was in favor of the IRA was accused of favoring it for personal gain. He also said that those opposed were called "Old Dealers" and those in favor were called "New Dealers." Others reported the same fear about losing land; some called the IRA "communistic." Some people feared that if you sold land or made it profitable the proceeds would come under tribal control, which of course meant the BIA.[33] The fact that BIA approval was required for certain actions taken by a tribal council convinced some that the government had no intention of allowing the Yanktons much autonomy. In the end there was too much opposition to the new constitution. Clement Smith, "unofficial" tribal chairman, originally supported the IRA but then campaigned against the new constitution. Raymond and Gertrude Bonnin worked hard to defeat the new constitution, finding support among the full-bloods and among the Peyote community.

Another significant factor that helped defeat the new constitution was that the missionaries on the reservations opposed the IRA from the beginning; in fact, they opposed virtually all of Collier's reform policies. All three denominations (Presbyterians, Episcopalians, and Catholics) advised their parishioners to vote against the constitution.[34] Father Sylvester was the main leader of the church opposition. He and the other missionaries did not consider the "Indian New Deal" to be reform; they considered it a retreat to "tribalism."[35] Father Sylvester wrote in the *Little Bronzed Angel* that "it would be a pity to encourage Indians to look upon certain things in his past as desirable." Four days after the election he received a letter of rebuke from Superintendent W. O. Roberts for his involvement in helping defeat the IRA constitution, especially sending some of his staff door to door to speak against it. A frustrated Roberts asked why he was so opposed to the constitution whereas Catholics on the Rosebud Reservation supported it.[36]

There is not a general consensus as to whether the Yanktons' decision to reject reorganization under the IRA hurt them in the long run. On the national level the debate still continues over John Collier's reforms. Some have argued that Collier was an assimilationist but took the long view that American Indian cultures needed to be nurtured and strengthened and only then assimilated into American society. The structure of IRA governments was styled after American models of government and did not take into account traditional people and traditional structures. It has also been pointed out that the power of the tribal councils was limited and major decisions required federal approval. Native American scholars such as Vine Deloria, Jr., however, have argued the positive side of the Indian New Deal.[37] Deloria contends that the real importance of John Collier's reform ideas lay in a conceptual shift away from the idea that reservations were delegated certain powers to the idea that reservations had inherent powers but that this conceptual shift did not bear fruit until the mid-1960s. He also argues that Collier's strongest reforms were in the economic area, not the political arena. Others have pointed to the end of the allotment system, the increase in the reservation land base, and the closing of boarding schools as positive reforms.[38] As for the Yanktons, it is unclear how the approval of an IRA constitution could have reversed the crushing economic problems of unemployment, poor housing, and an eroded land base. The Indian New Deal did, however, allow the Native American Church to operate in the open.

PEYOTISM AND SPIRITUAL AND CULTURAL AUTONOMY

Political and economic reform was essential to John Collier's "New Deal" for Indians, but of equal significance were his policies on religious freedom and respect and encouragement for American Indian culture. Collier espoused these views in the 1920s; when he became commissioner of Indian Affairs, he implemented them as federal policy. Within a year of taking office and before the passage of the IRA, he issued Bureau Circular #2970 (3 January 1934) to the superintendents of all reservations. The circular, titled *Indian Religious Freedom and Indian Culture*, is a clear statement of Collier's policies. He ordered all reservation officials to end interference with religious practices and cultural activities. This new policy included the Native American Church. Now, for the first time, the Peyote community could practice its faith without fear of federal harassment. The circular stated: "No interference with Indian religious life or ceremonial expression will hereafter be tolerated. The cultural liberty of Indians is in all respects to be considered equal to that of any non-Indian group. And it is desirable that Indians be bi-lingual, fluent and literate in the English language and fluent in their vital, beautiful and efficient native languages. The Indian arts and crafts are to be prized, nourished and honored."

The following year Congress enacted the Indian Arts and Crafts Act, another element in Collier's reform policy. It was part of his economic program, with the added goal of supporting the growth and development of the arts. Collier hoped to educate the public about American Indian art in order to develop a market. Funds were available to schools that were training Native American artists. Collier hoped that this would create income for the artists as well as encouraging the preservation of the arts. This was a drastic change in federal policy. Some of the artwork was exhibited at the San Francisco World's Fair in 1939 and at New York City's Museum of Modern Art in 1941. At the same time both the WPA and the Civil Works Administration employed Indian artists to decorate the walls of public buildings with murals, while others made rugs and pottery for BIA facilities. One example is Woody Crumbo (Creek-Potawatomi), a well-known Peyote artist, who was commissioned to paint murals in the Department of the Interior building. Interestingly, one of his murals is a Peyote painting that depicts a stylized water bird carrying prayers skyward after coming out of a tipi whose base is an extremely large Peyote button.[39]

These new policies protecting religious freedom and cultural autonomy were certainly beneficial to the Peyote community. The changes, however, did not mean that opposition to Peyotism ceased to exist. Some officials in the executive branch still supported assimilationist programs, while several members of Congress, hostile to Collier, attempted to repeal the Indian Reorganization Act. There was also opposition to the Peyote community on several reservations. The leadership of tribal councils was often made up of mixed-bloods with strong ties to Christian denominations. Many saw Peyotism and traditional American Indian religion as a step backward. For example, the members of the tribal council of the Rosebud Reservation passed a resolution requesting the attorney general of South Dakota to cancel the charter of the Native American Church of Rosebud, arguing that they should have jurisdiction over such a charter. They also passed an ordinance requiring Peyote roadmen and Yuwipi healers to apply for a license and pay a $5 annual fee in order to function as spiritual leaders. Licensing did not apply to Christians.

The most concentrated effort to fight Commissioner Collier's policies on religion and culture came from missionary groups on the reservations. On the Yankton Reservation all three Christian denominations opposed the new policies that would allow the open practice of the Peyote faith. Father Sylvester continued to lead the opposition. Changing federal policy and even the shifting public sentiment did not affect his views. In 1927 he wrote that he would, whenever possible, exhort the "medicine eaters" to abandon their evil ways, hoping that providence would allow these wayward people "to seek and find the truth."[40]

More than a decade later he was still using inflammatory language such as "paganism," "superstition," "drug-craving," and "immorality" when referring to the Peyote community. The only change was that he could now blame Commissioner Collier. Father Sylvester worked diligently to try to convince the Yanktons to vote against the IRA constitution. From the pulpit and in publications he fought the reforms. He argued that Peyotism threatened the long-range goals of Christianizing and "civilizing" American Indians. Many of his Yankton parishioners absorbed his negative views on Peyote people, seeing them as drug addicts, as nonprogressive, still practicing "paganism." Church publications carried the same message. As described earlier, the Marty Mission began publishing the *Little Bronzed Angel* in 1924 and the bilingual *Catholic Sioux Herald* in 1932. Both were published in the mission's print shop. The former had a national distribution; the latter was distributed mostly to Sioux reservations. Father Sylvester used these publications to attack the new reforms. Many clergy feared a revival of traditional religion and the expansion of Peyotism. There was open hostility directed at Collier. The *Little Bronzed Angel* referred to his reforms as a "revival of paganism."[41] *The Catholic Sioux Herald* also ran articles on Peyote. In 1935 an article appeared titled "Dakota Koska Peyote On Woyake" (A Young Dakota Man Tells All about Peyote). It was a testimonial on the evils of Peyote, claiming that Peyote gave a false sense of well-being and should be avoided. The article concluded with the statement that "the eating of medicine [Peyote] has no support from Jesus the Messiah, the Son of God."[42]

Others shared the view that Peyote caused serious physical disabilities. One of the missionaries, Father Louis J. Delahoyde, who arrived at the Marty Mission in 1936 and remained intermittently until 1949, told an interviewer that although Peyote "brought a measure of euphoria," its continued use brought "ultimate blindness." He also said that Sam Necklace was the leader of the Peyote group, calling him the "medicine man of the peyote church."[43] Other Catholic writers expressed similar views. Sister Mary Duratschek, writing a history of Catholic missions in South Dakota, took John Collier to task for tolerating the "Peyote-Cult and Yuwipi seances," because they are "fundamentally pagan." She also complained that there were no longer federal funds to support Christianizing Indian children.[44]

Father Sylvester's hostility toward Commissioner Collier went deeper than just the issue of religious freedom. He also had an intense animosity toward President Roosevelt and the New Deal. He argued that the Yanktons' opposition to the IRA constitution was due to a fear of communism and that the only way to combat communism was through private ownership of property. By 1939 Father Sylvester's writing became openly anti-Semitic. He tried to connect Jews, communism, and the Indian Reorganization Act. In an article titled "Yankton Reservation: New-Deal and Old-Deal" he pointed out that two Jews, Nathan Margold and Felix S. Cohen (lawyers who worked for the Department of the Interior), wrote the IRA constitutions. He added: "[T]hey [American Indians] have heard that Jews have been the cause of communism. Be it true or not, they know that to a considerable extent the Jews control the press, the radio and the movies. They are afraid."[45] Father Sylvester tried to connect Collier with atheism by claiming that his support for "pagan religion" was akin to "godlessness" and that the "Peyote Cult" was this "pagan religion." One of the people greatly admired by Father Sylvester was the anti-Semitic "radio priest" from Detroit, Father Charles Coughlin, who had become a national figure because of his nationwide Sunday afternoon radio broadcasts. Father Sylvester said the broadcasts were "for the benefit of millions who wish to listen."[46] Coughlin's speeches gave comfort to those Americans looking for scapegoats for America's economic problems and the coming war in Europe; his fiery broadcasts proclaimed the so-called Jewish conspiracy to be a major factor. Father Sylvester's admiration for Father Coughlin and his railing against the "Jewish conspiracy" was confirmed by Father Delahoyde.[47]

In 1940 Father Sylvester devoted most of two issues of the *Catholic Indian Herald* to Peyote. A long article titled "The Peyote Cult: A Superstition Destroying Like a Cancer the Life of the Indians Whilst the White Taxpayer Foots the Bill of Doctors and Undertakers" used old arguments from the 1910–20 era. The article revived the old unsigned anti-Peyote testimonials. It is unclear why this was dredged up in 1940. The only new argument was to try to provoke taxpayers into supporting a prohibition of Peyote, because their tax dollars were being wasted healing the sick and burying the dead: all from Peyote usage. Inflammatory language such as "cancerous growth," "craving," "his mind snaps," "sexual immorality," and "ready for the insane asylum" is used throughout the article. His conclusion was that Congress needed to be roused into action on Peyote or future historians would title the last chapter of Indian history "Peyote—Final Doom," because the incorporated Peyote church was a mask for legalized drug usage and profits for drug dealers.[48]

At that time there was no real possibility that federal law would prohibit Peyotism, but the Christian clergy could paint it in such a negative light that it would be difficult to attract new members. To a great extent this worked, as the Yankton Peyote community grew through marriage and birth rather than by attracting new members. One example of such a negative view of Peyote people came from Clarence Foreman, a longtime political leader of the Yanktons. He said that he opposed the Indian Reorganization Act because it allowed the Native American Church to function openly. He described Peyote as "a health-ruining drug" and said that he could tell a "peyote user" a hundred feet away because of the person's changed complexion. The members of the Peyote community were aware of this hostility and knew that others looked down upon them. Referring to the 1930s and 1940s, Selma Sully Walker said that some thought "we were a discredit to the tribe"; but she added that part of the reason for negative opinion was that some Peyote people were the poorest Yanktons, and some had questionable pasts, such as alcohol abuse.[49]

One reason that groups made little headway in the anti-Peyote campaign of the 1930s was Commissioner Collier. His influence was considerable when it came to defending the religious freedom of the Native American Church. In 1937 Senator Dennis Chavez of New Mexico, one of several senators who wanted to undo Collier's Indian New Deal, introduced a bill to prohibit the interstate transportation of Peyote (it was legal for private firms to ship Peyote or for individuals to carry it). Collier opposed the bill and orchestrated the effort to have it defeated. He brought in young scholars to testify against the Chavez bill. They included Weston LaBarre, who just finished a Ph.D. dissertation at Yale on the Peyote religion; Vincenzo Petrullo, who received a Ph.D. at the University of Pennsylvania and had his dissertation on Peyote published in 1934; and Richard Evans Schultes, a young botanist from Harvard. Well-known anthropologists such as Franz Boas and Alfred Kroeber sent written testimony against the bill. Unlike earlier congressional bills on Peyote, there was no concerted effort to support its passage; and with Collier's orchestrated plan to defeat it, it died quietly. That same year Collier used his influence to have the Department of Agriculture rescind its 1915 regulation prohibiting the importation of Peyote. In 1940 he was able to get the U.S. Postal Service to lift its 1917 ban on the shipment of Peyote through the mail service.[50]

Collier was aided in his defense of the Peyote religion not only by the testimony of the academic community but also by the new scholarship of the 1930s. At least four young scholars (LaBarre, Petrullo, Schultes, and Omer Stewart) were doing fieldwork with Peyote communities. All were participant observers: they not only interviewed Peyote people but attended Peyote meetings and partook of the "sacred herb." This gave them the authority to speak from experience. They were following in the footsteps of James Mooney, but with a difference. Mooney always testified against BIA policies; in the 1930s the young scholars testified and wrote in defense of BIA policies. Petrullo published the first book-length study of Peyote in the United States. It was a descriptive and historical account of Peyotism among the Delawares of Oklahoma. His fieldwork led him to the conclusion that there was no after-effect from ingesting Peyote; nor was it habit-forming.[51] Petrullo was recruited by Collier. After testifying against the Chavez bill, Petrullo wrote a very intriguing article on Peyote for *Indians at Work,* a BIA publication. He defended Peyotism as a way to repair the damage from previous federal policies that had reduced Native Americans to poverty and dependence. He saw Peyotism as the hope of the future. Petrullo wrote at length about how the chemical or physiological effect of Peyote is incidental and should not be seen as the reason for its use; he believed that Peyote's overall role was as a teacher, a unifier, and a purifier that reestablished harmony between God, the world, and the individual. He argued that the way to this spiritual unity was along the Peyote Road, because it was not just a religion but also a way of life and a full spiritual belief system.[52]

The value of Petrullo's analysis is that it is based on considerable fieldwork. The same is true with LaBarre and Schultes, who conducted their fieldwork in Oklahoma among the Kiowas. LaBarre began his work in 1935; and in 1936 they both spent the summer among Kiowa Peyotists. LaBarre was completing his dissertation, which was published in 1938 as *The Peyote Cult* (now in its fifth edition). It was the first broad study analyzing the historical, botanical, and ethnographic aspects of the Peyote religion. LaBarre became a highly respected scholar and used his professional reputation in the defense of Peyotism. In 1975 he wrote: "I have wholeheartedly, consistently and unequivocally defended the Native American Church as being, in culture-historical terms, a bona fide faith entitled to full Constitutional guarantee of religious freedom."[53] Richard Schultes became one of the world's leading botanists specializing in hallucinogenic plants, eventually becoming the director of the Botanical Museum at Harvard. He was important for the testimony he gave in Congress against the Chavez bill, but he was more important for both his scholarly and popular articles on Peyote. In 1937 he published "Peyote and the American Indian" in *Nature Magazine.* It was reprinted in the widely read *Literary Digest.* He reinforced the view that Peyote was not harmful and was not used habitually by American Indians.[54]

Omer Stewart began publishing on the Peyote religion in the late 1930s; like other Peyote scholars, he was an activist and a frequent courtroom witness. For more than fifty years he used his scholarship and his personal experience in the defense of Peyotism. In 1939 Stewart corresponded with John Collier, telling him that nothing unusual took place in the Peyote meetings he attended with the Washo-Northern Paiute people in Utah. Stewart went on to defend Peyote in the courtroom, in scholarly works, and in the media, including radio, magazines, and newspapers.[55] There would be other attacks on the Peyote religion and other attempts to restrict Peyote usage, sometimes by state legislatures, sometimes by tribal governments. Congress and the courts would again challenge Peyotism, but the climate concerning Peyotism changed in the 1930s. Future opposition would be sporadic. Never again would there be a broad-based effort aimed at the prohibition of Peyote. John Collier, in conjunction with the determined efforts of the Peyote community, helped bring about this change.

CHIEF PRIEST SAM NECKLACE AND THE YANKTON PEYOTE COMMUNITY

Though new federal policies reduced external pressures on the Yankton Peyote community, there were still local pressures that Sam Necklace had to confront. Throughout the remainder of his life, Sam was committed to protecting the Peyote community. This was not just a spiritual commitment but also a commitment to protect and support the community in social, political, and economic matters. During the Depression years Sam became embroiled in Yankton politics. As the large majority of the Peyotists were full-bloods, he became a leader of the full-bloods in their continuing struggle to maintain a voice in tribal affairs. The defeat of the IRA constitution was the major issue for the full-bloods, because many believed that it would reduce their role in tribal politics and threaten their already weakened economic base. This was not an issue that would disappear, because even after its initial defeat there were Yankton groups that tried to resurrect the IRA constitution.

Sam became chief priest in a way that was typical for leadership emerging in the Peyote community. He was a wayward young adult who changed his life after experiencing Peyote. This was followed by several years of active participation in the Peyote community as well as establishing himself as a responsible adult. Yankton roadman Quentin Bruguier said in an interview that one became a roadman or priest in the following pattern:

> You start at meetings using the Sacred Herb. You learn about life, you pray, you talk to God. You learn the stations, learn to burn cedar, take care of fire, take care of the drum, how to tie it, fix it. Then you become a leader or roadman. You pray for people, have funerals, baptismals, forgiveness for sin. Then when you learn the above you become a Priest—ordained. You are ordained by another Priest during a special meeting. As a priest, it is the highest calling, a strict life.[56]

After Sam was chosen as chief priest by the local Peyote community, he acquired many more responsibilities. He ran the official Peyote meetings, held on the first Saturday of each month. Until a church building was acquired, the services were held in people's homes. The Yanktons did not begin using tipis for their meetings until the 1960s. Sam was not the only one to run Peyote services. There were other Yankton roadmen who ran meetings in his absence or on their own when the need arose. Any member of the Peyote community could sponsor a meeting and request a roadman to run it. Sam, however, had broader clerical responsibilities, including weddings and funeral services and time spent caring for people who were in need or ill. His most significant role involved healing. This took place during a Peyote meeting. The healing process involved the ingestion of Peyote by the sick person and ministrations by the roadman or priest, accompanied by intense prayer and support from all in attendance, leading to communication with Wakan Tanka. On this spiritual level, healing may occur. Roadmen never took credit for healing; credit went to Peyote and the power of God. Baptisms and confirmations were also performed during Peyote services. Infants and new members were baptized; confirmations were for adults who had been baptized as infants and wanted to make a reaffirmation of their commitment. The chief priest also ordained other priests. For example, Sam ordained Amos Shields in 1935, John Claire in 1937, and Louie Stricker in 1939. It should be noted that baptisms, confirmations, and ordinations—of obvious Christian origin—only occur in the Cross Fire way. In the 1930s only the Cross Fire was practiced on the Yankton Reservation. The Half Moon did not come in until after World War II. According to his grandson Asa, Sam was also responsible for giving "Indian" names to many people. It was a busy life for Sam, with the responsibility of a ministry, the involvement with local politics, and the continuing struggle to provide economic sustenance for his family—a considerable task because there was no stipend associated with being a priest of the Native American Church.

Although Sam had an extremely busy and active life with the church, his family, and politics, he did not have the burden of running the business affairs of the church. As required under the state charter, there were administrative officers. Amidst the swirling debates over constitutions and the crisis of the depression, the church leadership, under president Henry Blaine and vice-president John Dragg, in 1933 began to debate amending the state charter. The amended charter may have been the result of the new atmosphere of reform under Commissioner Collier. It is virtually the same as the 1922 charter except for one significant change. As described in chapter 5, the 1922 state charter did not mention Peyote; the amended charter begins: "We, the church organization of the Peyote Church of Christ. . . ." This is important in the history of Yankton Peyotism, because for the first time Peyote as the central element of the church is articulated clearly, directly, and openly in a legal document. The administrative structure remained the same, except for two minor changes. In addition to the offices of president, vice-president, secretary, treasurer, Committee of Four, and chief priest, the position of priest was added and the Committee of Four became a Committee of Six. All officers and priests were elected biannually. In 1934 the amended charter was notarized and filed with South Dakota's secretary of state.

After Sam was ordained as chief priest, he wanted to acquire a church building and establish a Native American Church cemetery. In 1929 or 1930 someone, probably Johnson Goodhouse (one of the Native American Church founders), donated ten acres of land just north of the river road, several miles east of Greenwood.[57] As with many Peyote communities, a church cemetery was established. The first burial was that of Gideon Necklace, one of Sam and Mary's grandsons. Gideon was baptized by his grandfather when he was four months old; he passed away on 9 July 1930, when he was only sixteen months old. Since then Native American Church people have buried their family members in this cemetery. There are also a number of veterans buried there.[58]

In the late 1930s (possibly 1939) Sam acquired a building for a church. A small house located about ten miles away was donated by Emma Goodhouse Sitting Crow, daughter of Johnson and Ellen Goodhouse. Emma had married Louis Sitting Crow, uniting two Peyote families.[59] She had been baptized by Sam in 1937, and possibly the gift was a gesture of commitment to the Peyote community. The wooden frame house with a four-sided sloped roof was moved and set up with its door facing east. With some interior remodeling it was made into a one-room square structure approximately twenty-five feet by twenty-five feet.

Sam conducted Peyote meetings in this building for the rest of his life. He and Mary lived about two miles from the church (or one mile if they walked through the fields).[60] The inside of the church contained a pot-bellied stove; otherwise it was open space: everyone sat on the floor in a circle. On special occasions such as holidays, when many people attended church services, they had to form two circles. To add some comfort people sat on pillows or blankets. With a wooden floor on the inside, a fire was not feasible. A cloth serving as an altar was placed on the floor. The religious paraphernalia, including the "Chief Peyote," was placed on cloth. In front of the altar was an iron kettle. The fireman maintained the fire outside and periodically brought in hot coals that were placed in the kettle. The hot coals functioned as the fire. To celebrate the new building, an inaugural Peyote meeting was held. Everyone walked single file around the grounds while the church and the cemetery were blessed. The opening of the church was considered a very sacred event. Peyote people from all over the state attended the inauguration. The Sunday noon meal was a feast: the women of the church supplied a vast array of foods.[61]

Sam had a reputation for running very strict Peyote meetings. He required everyone to sit still and not go in and out while the service was in progress. He reminded people that they were there for only one reason: to pray and eat "medicine." Sam expected appropriate behavior, showing young people the proper way to sit. According to Clarence Rockboy, he did not want people to wear jewelry or women to wear makeup but wanted them to dress properly, which meant modestly. There should not be any showing-off of clothing or in singing style, he said: "just sing, just sing." He did not want any "fancy singing" or any competition between singers. Sam believed it was important to teach young people that the proper way to worship was with humility.[62]

Mary was a partner with Sam in his role as chief priest. She prepared the spiritual foods for Peyote meetings, naming ceremonies, and funeral services. She served as the morning water woman when Sam was running a Peyote meeting. Mary was also active with the Women's Committee, which raised money by making and selling star quilts, blankets, pillows, potholders with matching aprons, or almost any item the women could sew. They would hold sales on the church grounds and serve fry bread and soup. The funds were used to support the Native American Church and to help families who were experiencing hard times, having health problems, or mourning the loss of a family member.[63]

As part of his daily life, Sam spent extra time with young people, preaching self-reliance yet helping those in need.[64] One story that has been passed down is about Sam's impatience with long visits by relatives. Two relatives came to visit Sam and Mary and just stayed on. Eventually Sam threw them out, saying that they all had their own home and should go there.[65] Helping people in need was one thing, but helping those who would not help themselves was something else. Sam tried to work with young people by teaching them Peyote songs. He was noted as a fine singer. Almost everyone who knew him, including Clarence Rockboy and Joe Packard, praised his singing. As a teenager, Clarence remembers learning songs from "Uncle Sam." He recalls him saying, "Did you catch it, nephew, did you catch it?" (meaning did you learn the song).[66] Aside from practicing the songs with others, Quentin Bruguier pointed out that one also learns songs in Peyote meetings by listening, by taking Peyote, and by asking for God's help. Teaching young people the Peyote way was a preoccupation for Sam. This was particularly true with his grandson Asa, who was born (figuratively speaking if not literally) in the Peyote religion. Asa was born on 4 October 1931 and baptized by his grandfather five weeks later. Through his growing years Asa was very close to his grandparents. He said that his grandpa "was just like a father to me."[67]

Sam wanted the best education possible for his grandson. Asa remembers his grandpa going on and on about the importance of education and how education had helped him. At age six, Asa entered first grade at the government day school in Greenwood (the boarding school had been closed). After the third grade, Sam and Mary felt that Asa could get a better education in Catholic school. In 1933 Father Sylvester of the Marty Mission opened another elementary school in Greenwood. At first the classes were held in the small Catholic church; but in 1938 a frame school house was built for grades one to eight. St. John's was open to non-Catholics. At age ten Asa was enrolled for the 1941–42 school year. This was not a good year for him. He has very negative recollections. Of the thirty-one students in his class he was one of two students designated as "on trial" in his school record. His grades reflect a very difficult period. In interviews Asa said that it was a terrible year. He was caught speaking Dakota: the matrons would "sneak" around the playground trying to catch children speaking "Indian." He said that they took a razor strap and slapped his hands; then he had to bend over and was hit on the backside. He added that both nuns and matrons participated in something he called "a paddle wheel." He had to run the gauntlet, while each nun took a whack at his backside. At the end of the year his grandparents removed him and returned him to the government day school. Not long after this they moved to the city of Yankton, South Dakota.[68]

Everyone who knew Sam Necklace described him as having a strong personality. What left an impression on people was that he was a short man (five foot three or five foot four), somewhat slender, but with a very powerful presence. One person who knew Sam very well was Selma Sully Walker (1925–97). Selma knew the Necklace family through her father, John Sully, a member of the Native American Church and a roadman. She was also a childhood friend of Sam and Mary's grandson Asa (they called each other cousin). Selma grew up on the Yankton Reservation with the Peyote community and regularly attended Peyote meetings. She remembers being taught to have respect, if not awe, for spiritual leaders as a youth. She said that Grandpa Sam was "a very powerful man when he prayed: he prayed with a sincere manner, he was very dramatic."[69]

Selma recalls a Peyote meeting that she and her very ill mother attended. Her mother was lying on the floor, resting her head on a pillow. In a very strong voice, Grandpa Sam ordered her to get up. Selma recalls him saying, "I'm telling you Cora, niece, *toja,* don't lie there like that, get up, sit, walk outside." She got up immediately and began to walk around. Her mother soon began to feel better. Selma added that "he was the most powerful person I ever saw." This may sound like an extravagant statement, but not when you consider that Selma Walker was a prominent person in her own right as founder and director of the Native American Center of Central Ohio. Selma knew many eminent American Indian leaders throughout the country. Her comment is connected to another story she tells about Grandpa Sam. A young boy who had been playing in the river had drowned, and the body could not be found. Sam was called. He went out on the river in a boat. At one point he put his staff in the water and said the body is here; a diver went in and found the boy's body.[70]

Eunice Rainbow Dog Soldier also had vivid recollections of Sam Necklace. A life-long member of the Native American Church and a traditional Yankton woman, she made a point of saying that she was delivered by midwife Grandma White Tallow, a legendary figure in Yankton history. Grandma Eunice spoke very little English and was active in Peyotism and Yankton traditional religion. Even in her late seventies, she was still attending Sun

Dances in order to support her relatives who were dancing. She said that her father, Sam Dog Rainbow (b. 1868), was a medicine man and a Sun Dance chief. Others have confirmed that Sun Dances were held in secret on the Rainbow land (called Rainbow Paradise today). Her father did not become a Peyotist; but her two brothers, Harry and Alex, were the first Rainbows to join the Peyote community. Grandma Eunice had very fond memories of Sam. She said when she was young she had an illness that caused her to black out from time to time. Sam began to help her at Peyote meetings with sacred medicine and prayer. Eunice claimed that after a year she was cured and never had a reoccurrence the rest of her life. She also said that Sam came to her home to run meetings. Grandma Eunice's brother Harry Rainbow is the father of Loretta Rainbow Primeaux, who later married Sam's grandson Asa, uniting two more Peyote families. Asa and Loretta live on the Rainbow land. After Asa became a roadman, he conducted Peyote meetings in the same place that his grandfather had used forty to fifty years earlier.[71]

Healing was such an essential element of Peyotism that people traveled from other reservations seeking help. Joe Rockboy tells a story from the mid-1930s about a young man, Joseph Plays With Iron, who had a wife and children in Fort Thompson, South Dakota (Crow Creek Reservation), but was living on the Yankton Reservation with another woman. He began attending Sam Necklace's Peyote services. His name is listed in Sam Necklace's notebook as having been baptized by Sam on 23 June 1935. Through the power of Peyote, Plays With Iron realized the error of his ways and returned home to reconcile with his wife. He returned with his family to Greenwood, bringing his mother, who had been paralyzed from the waist down for twenty-five years. Plays With Iron hoped that with Sam's help and the healing power of Peyote, his mother would walk again. He sponsored four Peyote meetings for her. Three were held in Greenwood. For the fourth they returned to Fort Thompson, accompanied by several Yanktons. Joe Rockboy, who attended the services, said that she said she was able to walk after the fourth meeting. At that time she made a vow: she would spend her life praising the "sacred herb." Later, as life was going well for her, she forgot her vow and became paralyzed again. Her son then took her back to Peyote meetings, and eventually she was able to walk again. She lived a happy life until she passed away at an elderly age.[72]

These healing narratives are an essential part of Peyote history. They are told wherever Peyote people gather and are passed on from generation to generation. This particular narrative certainly adds to Sam's reputation as a priest, but its essential function is to express the power of God. A roadman or priest would never take personal credit for healing: Peyote is the healer; the roadman is the facilitator. From a lifetime of such experiences, Joe Rockboy philosophized on the meaning of Peyote in his life. "People run it down, but that's our salvation, that's the Indian Salvation, to use it for health, and anything you can think of. And the way I look at it, the way I feel about it, the herb is my protector, peyote is everything to me."[73]

Just as Peyote people traveled to the Yankton Reservation, Yanktons also traveled to other reservations. As chief priest, Sam traveled more than ever to other Peyote communities or to other places to help establish a Peyote church. For example, he traveled to the Sisseton Reservation to run meetings and help establish a Peyote community. He also traveled to the Winnebago, Rosebud, and Pine Ridge Reservations, where he was well known.[74] This was not unusual; Peyote people have regularly traveled back and forth to each other's communities since the early days of Peyotism. In many cases those who were highly respected as roadmen were invited to various reservations to run Peyote services. By the late 1930s the founding generation of Yankton Peyotists was aging, but most were still living and active in the church. Sam was almost sixty; even Grandpa Charlie Jones, in his late seventies, was still attending Peyote meetings. They were the grandparents of the younger, third generation of Peyotists. With infants and children being baptized throughout the 1930s and 1940s, the elders took special care of the children, giving them attention, love, and support as grandparents always had. Selma Sully Walker has vivid memories of Grandpa Charlie Jones. She remembers sitting on his lap, with him singing Peyote songs in her ear. She recalls him singing "*Pežuta yuta yo* . . . [To eat peyote . . .]." She considered him a sacred man. "He had a special sacredness that you could feel," she said. Teaching the children was the special role of the grandparents. This helped reinforce the Peyote community as a *tiošpaye*, especially because everyone used Dakota kinship terminology.[75]

One responsibility that the elders took upon themselves was to reinforce the sense of identity of the younger generation as Yanktons and as members of a Peyote community. An essential way of doing this was through Peyote music and language. The children learned by attending Peyote meetings, but they also learned directly from their grandparents at home. They taught the children how to sing Peyote songs, how to shake the gourd rattle, how to play the drum, and how to tie the drum. Language skills were reinforced, as they both spoke and sang Peyote songs in Dakota. This was important, because many of the children were in schools where only English was allowed. In the Necklace/Primeaux families, Peyote music was central to everyday life. Several were noted singers, as were other Yanktons—some with reputations extending beyond the reservation. Since the 1970s Yankton Peyotists have been recorded commercially and are popular with Peyote communities around the country. Their renown comes from their unique manner of harmonizing Peyote songs.[76]

It is difficult to imagine Peyotism without the music. The songs are prayers, which are central to spiritual life. It is sacred music. Music, prayers, and healing cannot function separately in Peyotism. Each element is part of an essential whole. The Peyote songs are not just an accompaniment to healing; they are, with Peyote, the core of healing. The songs as prayers are not elements in themselves but are vehicles for the journey along the Peyote Road. Learning the music at a young age is essential; excellence with song, drum, and rattle is one of the criteria to become a roadman. There are two sources for the songs. First, one can learn them from others. There is a valued tradition of passing songs from generation to generation as well as learning songs from other Peyote groups. Second, one can create them by inspiration, possibly aided by a vision. Either way they are gifts to be shared; there are no proprietary rights. Many singers have a large repertoire of songs: some of their own, some that they learned from others.

Peyote music has an extremely distinct style, easily distinguishable from the other types of American Indian music. Two people sing at one time, one singer using the gourd rattle, the other using the water drum. They sing sets of four songs that vary depending on whether they are opening songs, midnight songs, morning songs, or quitting songs. The roadman and chief drummer start with fixed opening songs. When they finish, the rattle, staff, and sage are passed to the person on their left, who asks someone to drum. The drum and drumstick are passed to that person. The lead singer, who is kneeling on both knees or sometimes on one knee, holds the staff and sage in the left hand and the rattle in the right. The other singer, who is already kneeling or sometimes sitting with legs crossed, holds the drum with the left hand. A single wooden drumstick is used. The drum is resting on the ground and is held at a slightly tilted angle, with four fingers on the side and the thumb on top. The thumb is used to apply pressure to the drumhead in order to affect timbre and pitch. At various times the drum is tilted so the water can keep the drumhead damp and taut. The rattle is made from a small pear-shaped gourd with a wooden handle, usually beaded, with a tuft of horsehair decorating the top; it symbolizes the soft tuft on the top of the peyote cactus. Peyote music sounds different from other Native American music because of the tempo of the drum. It is much faster: 120 to 150 beats per minute. This rapid tempo, kept up throughout the song, is accompanied by tense vocal delivery of rapidly repeated vocables. The combination of singers, drum, and rattle, all at the same speed, adds to the impression of rapid tempo.[77]

Peyote songs have two textual patterns: vocables and words and sentences in the vernacular. Sometimes words in English are added for the benefit of those not speaking the particular language. The vocables are ear-pleasing syllables that have spiritual significance but do not have a literal meaning. There are short vocables at the beginning and ending of a song. Some songs, called straight songs, are all vocables. Within the songs there is repetition of vocables and sentences in order to multiply the power of the prayer. An example of a line of vocable syllables from a Yankton song is *He ya no ho wi da he de yo wa.* The words in the Yankton Peyote songs have many common spiritual themes. The songs from the Cross Fire way have references to Wanikiya, Lakota or Dakota for Savior or Jesus. For example: "*He wanikiya ye yedo o do,* that's what the Savior said." Sometimes the English "Jesus" is used. There are references to the Savior in some Half Moon songs, although Christian elements are generally absent in their Peyote services. "Wakan Tanka" (God) is also used, especially in the Half Moon, as in "*Wa'ka ta'ka waonshia nai do,* God, you pity everyone."[78] The common themes of the songs include the sinful world, human weakness, individual sin, compassion from Wakan Tanka or Wanikiya, taking pity on human beings, giving strength, forgiveness, dawn is coming (new life), everlasting life, and the need for prayer. There are also references to Peyote: "Peyote, you have seen all the wrong things that I have done. In the name of Jesus, forgive me"; "Eat this peyote with God in mind, and you're going to live"; "I have taken your medicine, so God pity me"; "Peyote pity me. I am trying to be good."[79] Other examples from the Yankton songs: "To the end of life, I will be strong, and be praying with this Holy Medicine towards God," "I want to be in this Peyote Way of life with all my relations."[80]

The music itself is compelling—words cannot describe it. The combination of rapid tempo and repetition, with two accomplished musicians, makes the music vibrate throughout the tipi; echoes seem to reverberate from everywhere. When a particularly powerful set of songs has been sung, the Peyote people say it is not just the singers—it is the power of Peyote.[81]

From the mid to late 1930s the Yankton Peyote community was functioning reasonably well in the new atmosphere of religious toleration; but it was not thriving as well as it could because of the continuing economic stagnation, with little relief from the Depression. Federal programs helped, but they did not solve the underlying economic crisis on this or any other reservation. Hostility from the local Christian community and the endless politics of factions made things worse. All these circumstances affected the Necklace family and other Peyote families as they sought to lead meaningful spiritual lives, survive economically, and try to maintain a voice in Yankton politics.

Like many Yankton families, the Necklaces continued to have economic difficulties. Their economic survival was based on Sam earning wages, rental income from their allotted land, and subsistence gardening around the home, which was mostly Mary's responsibility. She raised a variety of vegetables in the garden, especially corn. One special type of white corn was used for spiritual food. Corncobs were saved for use in the pot-bellied stove. They were dipped in kerosene and used to start a fire. Other garden vegetables included squash, potatoes, tomatoes, onions, and string beans. The surplus was canned, and some items were dried. Chokecherry trees grew near the house. They had a chicken coop and a barn for the wagon and horses. Kerosene lamps provided light in the evening. There was no running water, and very few people had wells. Aside from the rainwater that they collected, the river and a few creeks were the only sources of water. They also collected all the wood they could find for cooking and heating, although coal was primarily used for heat. The river was a source of wood. Before the construction of the dams, upstream logging companies floated logs downstream. Some people along the bank would try to snag a log or two, let them dry out, cut them up, and take them home. The floating logs were also a dangerous amusement for teenagers, who sometimes tried to ride them. Asa remembers many trips in his grandfather's wagon to the river. They filled several wooden barrels with water; sometimes they fished and, with a little luck, brought home a tasty dinner.[82]

Sam Necklace was not able to earn a full-time income. Few Yanktons had full-time jobs. Some worked for the WPA or the CCC, but they were mostly younger men. Whether the Necklaces received any assistance from a New Deal program is unknown. Sam still worked as an interpreter. Joe Packard recalls: "I heard him interpret for some of the boys around here, and some of the white people, businessmen." Several people claim he worked for the tribe. He was not a regular employee of the tribe, but he may have worked as an interpreter when needed. This could not have brought in much money, if any, and could not be relied upon for income. He probably did interpreting and writing for individuals. He also earned some limited income by using his wagon to haul things or deliver goods. Upon occasion he still did seasonal work for local white farmers.[83] The difficulty in earning a living created considerable tension for the Necklace family. World War II did not increase the number of jobs on the reservation, but it did bring about a decline in the New Deal programs. Sometime in 1943 Sam and Mary decided to leave the reservation for the city of Yankton, South Dakota, where there was work. Meanwhile, as chief priest of the Native American Church, Sam was drawn more and more into Yankton politics.

For the people involved, local political issues were intense. For Sam this meant not just defending the rights of his church but also defending the rights and status of his generation. The full-bloods were declining in numbers and subsequently in status and influence. With excellent speaking skills and fluency in English and Dakota, Sam emerged as one of the leaders of the full-bloods. In 1932 the full-bloods began a campaign to have Superintendent Hickman removed from office. The petition was signed by 220 Yankton men and women and sent to Washington. The primary accusation against Hickman was unequal distribution of federal relief supplies during the dire conditions of drought and grasshopper infestation. They also protested against the tribal council, claiming it was a tool of Hickman. On this issue Gertrude and Raymond Bonnin and their supporters joined with the Peyote community in demanding his removal. Beneath the surface of the accusations was the fear of the loss of power by the full-bloods to the tribal council, made up of mixed-bloods. The petition states: "The action taken at said Council was not the expression of the tribe freely given but was the result of tyranny and domination exercised over them by two blue-eyed mixed-bloods who are practically white men without sympathy for the full-blood Indians."[84]

This issue had simmered for a long time. Sam Necklace felt that he must speak out, believing that the full-bloods were losing their birthright to people they considered traitors to the Yankton heritage. The intensity of emotion on this issue predates the New Deal and the debate over the IRA constitution. Aside from reaction to Hickman, their accusations were against two tribal council members who, they claimed, exercised dictatorial powers. These men were referred to as "the two blue-eyed so called Indians." The petitioners said the entire council was elected under the duress of poverty and the immediate need for relief and blamed Hickman for manipulating the electorate by his control of supplies. Their recommendation was not only to remove Hickman but also to abolish the Yankton Agency and make it a subagency. They argued that the reduced administrative costs would save tribal money. All the Necklaces signed the petition, including Sam's mother, then seventy-five years old. The petition was also signed by the Bonnins. In 1933 Gertrude Bonnin followed up the petition with a letter to the newly appointed John Collier. She asked him to decertify the 1932 election and abolish the tribal council.[85] It is unclear if the petition had any effect, because there was an investigation of Hickman already underway; but Hickman was removed from office. Collier would not, however, decertify the election and abolish the council.

As the debate over the Indian Reorganization Act and a new constitution emerged, the full-bloods again felt threatened and needed to organize themselves to defend their rights within the Yankton community. This is when Sam Necklace emerged in a leadership role, helping to create a political faction that included full-blood Peyotists and full-blood Christians such as the Bonnins and their supporters. It should be made clear that Sam did not become a major player in Yankton politics. Many discounted his views because he was a Peyotist, but he did attempt to mobilize people and fight against the increasing dominance of the mixed-bloods. In this sense he was a leading spokesperson of one political faction. It was a struggle that could not be won. Many of the mixed-bloods, now in their thirties and forties, were increasing their influence. In the period from 1890 to 1910 there were many marriages between whites and Yanktons, especially between white men and Yankton women. It was their offspring who were becoming a significant group in the 1930s. An analysis of the 1910 U.S. Census for Charles Mix County, which included the reservation, lists the percentage of "Indian and other blood" of each person, illustrating the large number of children from mixed-marriages.[86]

The cooperation between full-blood Peyotists and full-blood Christians on representation in Yankton politics did not lessen their mutual distrust. Gertrude Bonnin, for example, never ceased her efforts to prohibit the use and possession of Peyote. These struggles helped pull the members of the Yankton Peyote community closer together. Their only real allies were Peyotists on other reservations, who could offer moral support but could not really help their Yankton friends. The focus of this struggle for the full-bloods was to prevent the passage of an Indian Reorganization Act constitution. As noted, several groups kept proposing alternative constitutions, reinforcing the fears of the full-bloods concerning their rights to land and voice. What was particularly difficult was that the Yanktons did not have a duly elected tribal governing body reorganized by the BIA. Therefore individuals or groups seeking redress went through John Collier's office or through the U.S. Congress. Sam Necklace and others who were defending the rights of the full-bloods believed that there might be one potential ally: John Collier and a BIA that claimed it was defending religious freedom and cultural autonomy. This, however, was a complex situation, because the full-bloods mistrusted Collier, the IRA, and an IRA constitution on another level. Yet they would turn to Collier to try to protect and institutionalize their rights as full-bloods.

Land was the key issue. By 1938 the Yanktons had lost 90 percent of the original reservation, but the full-bloods owned much of the remaining 10 percent and wanted to protect it.[87] In several meetings of the so-called Tribal Council in 1937 and 1938, Sam Necklace asked the same question each time he spoke. It was the heart of the matter: who had power over the land? The following was recorded at one meeting. "Mr. Sam Baker [Necklace] was the first speaker and he confined his speech to asking but one question, and that was what authority, if any, has the Yankton Sioux Tribe over matters affecting the Tribe or its property."[88]

The strategy to defend the rights of the full-bloods was to try to institutionalize their rights in statutory form. The vehicle to achieve this end was to establish an organization for full-bloods. Sam Necklace became the chairman of a group called the Order of the Descendants of Real Americans. In 1939 Sam, as chairman, along with Joseph War Chief and the Reverend Charles W. Hare, sent a letter to Collier. It stated: "We are as active members of the Yankton Sioux Indians of full-blood do petition that you might give our resolution with a group of signers enclosed a just consideration . . . According to the Treaty of 1858 we feel as genuine Indians we should be given a chance to be heard in all deliberations." A resolution and a petition were sent with the letter. Necklace and the others proposed a unique approach to tribal government. Unfortunately for the full-bloods, it went unheeded. Their argument was that full-bloods were becoming fewer and fewer in number while mixed-bloods were increasing in number and were able to control and dominate the reservation, thus depriving the full-bloods of the rights and privileges guaranteed by the Treaty of 1858. The solution was to petition the commissioner of Indian Affairs and the U.S. Congress to recognize the entire full-blood membership as the official representatives of the Yankton Sioux. This would allow the "fast dwindling full-blooded members" to regain a voice in tribal decisions so that they could receive the benefits that were guaranteed by the government in return for the original concession of land. The resolution concluded with the statement that the government should not allow "our rights and powers to be usurped by the multitude of breeds of only fractional Indian blood."[89]

This was certainly very strong language; but it was not a proposal that the BIA would consider, because it was contrary to the types of constitutions that were part of the IRA. The petition was signed by eighty-seven full-bloods. The first three signatures were Peyotists Louie Stricker, Joshua Pretty Bull, and Sam B. Necklace. The people who signed the petition represented all the religious denominations on the reservation. The "resolution and petition" was notarized and sent to Commissioner Collier and Senators W. J. Bulow and Chan Gurney of South Dakota.[90] The assistant commissioner of Indian Affairs, William Zimmerman, wrote to Senator Bulow, saying that they could do nothing because they had an obligation to "other" Indians and that federal policy must be directed toward the whole.[91]

The full-bloods' voice would remain dim in Washington and in Yankton politics, but it would not be stifled. They continued to assert the viewpoint that as full-bloods they were guaranteed certain rights by the federal government. In January 1940 Sam Necklace wrote directly to secretary Harold Ickes, protesting a meeting of the tribal council that had been elected in 1932. He claimed that it was not a duly sanctioned meeting and protested the legality of the gathering. Under his signature, Sam listed his position as "Chairman, Order of the Descendants of Real Americans."[92] Others protested the same meeting by way of letters and petitions (which Sam also signed). Clement Smith, the tribal chairman from the 1932 election, now with a group called the Unity Organization, called for an election of delegates to represent the tribe in claims against the United States. Sam and others protested against the legality of the election of three people as representatives of the Yanktons. The petitioners asked the commissioner not to recognize the meeting or the election.[93]

After a few months the full-bloods had not received a reply to their resolution and petition. Sam wrote to Collier, complaining about the lack of a
response.[94] Finally, on 11 April 1940, Sam received a reply from one of Collier's
assistants. The answer was direct: "I am very much interested in your presen-
tation and while I sympathize with the full-blood people, I see no way in
which I can legally do what they ask."[95] He added that there was no authority
to remove mixed-bloods from the tribal rolls and recommended that when
the Yanktons finally got an approved constitution they could set up an advisory council of traditional people. The full-bloods did not like this response
but continued to seek ways in which they could maintain their influence.
Sam wrote again to Collier, this time insisting that full-bloods be represented
in any group that was going to Washington to represent the Yanktons in
claims cases. He suggested that a delegation of two or three full-bloods travel
to Washington, with expenses covered from tribal funds.[96] This proposal was
not accepted.

Meanwhile other Yanktons were having a change of heart about the 23
December meeting that had elected three people to a claims committee.
Another series of petitions ensued to accept the election. Sam Necklace had
originally supported the petition not to recognize the election of 23 December but now helped to circulate petitions to have the election validated by the
BIA. Over 300 people signed the new petition, including the Necklaces. Copies
were sent to Collier and Harold Ickes.[97] The change in attitude toward the 23
December election occurred when it became clear to many Yanktons that
they had no one to represent them in potential claims cases. This was a crucial
issue, because a successful claim could result in a much-needed distribution
of funds. The Yanktons needed a duly elected group to enter into negotiations and sign a contract with a law firm to represent them. They did not
want the BIA to select a law firm. Collier ignored the petition and refused to
recognize the election, but he did call for a new election for a claims committee.
He was not opposed to this committee; his concern was the BIA control over
the process of approving and certifying elections. With Collier's approval the
Yanktons could proceed with an election.

Sam Necklace and the full-bloods were concerned about this election.
They wanted to be represented but feared the process might leave them out.
The issue was whether representatives would be elected at-large or whether
each of the four voting districts would elect their own representatives as they

had with the rehabilitation committees. They feared that in voting by district a full-blood could not be elected; but in voting at-large they might be able to consolidate their vote and elect one of their own. Sam wrote to Collier, again stressing the discrimination against full-bloods, asking for an at-large election that he hoped would unify the tribe.[98] Whatever the structure of the election, the numbers were against the full-bloods. A census report (1 January 1943) indicated the decline in the number of the full-bloods. They accounted for 22 percent of the Yanktons, mixed-bloods for the other 78 percent. More telling was the birth rate. For the full-bloods it was 6/1,000 per year; for the mixed-bloods it was 36/1,000.[99]

Collier authorized an at-large election of three people to serve two years on a claims committee to represent the Yanktons in cases against the United States. The BIA and the Yanktons went through considerable effort to establish an election procedure that would satisfy everyone. Each of the four voting districts would elect three individuals to a local election committee, with the chairperson of each committee to serve on a Central Election Committee that would coordinate the election by designating polling places, preparing lists of eligible voters, and accepting nominations. A signed petition of twenty-five eligible voters could nominate any enrolled Yankton. The three nominees receiving the most votes would serve on the Claims Committee. Sam Necklace, Ben McBride, and Nick Frederick were elected to the Greenwood local election committee. The election was held on 24 August 1940; Clarence Foreman, Llewellyn Selwyn, and Charles W. Hare were elected.[100] Hare was from a full-blood family, but they were not Peyotists; they were Episcopalians. The committee members' first order of business was a trip to Washington to meet with BIA officials.

Throughout 1941 and the early war years the Central Rehabilitation Committee and the local counterparts continued to coordinate New Deal development projects, making some improvements on the land, putting some Yanktons to work, and providing additional relief. It was never enough, because the underlying economic malaise was so deep and had been present for so long that piecemeal projects provided only temporary support. Even Collier's so-called Chalk Rock Rehabilitation Colony failed. It was set up as a communal experiment, offering housing to some of the most needy Yanktons. The colony provided for communal gardening and canning and had a dairy and horse barn and a field to grow wheat, oats, corn, and hay. Unfortunately, the communal-style arrangement was a failure and did little to alleviate poverty.[101] For many Yanktons the economic situation was still grim. Annual income was lower than on neighboring reservations. For example, the Yankton per-capita income in 1938 was $108.43, compared to $150.50 and $170.31 for the Rosebud and Pine Ridge Reservations, respectively. They were also the lowest in income from direct relief and social security. There were still health problems too. Of the fifty-six deaths on the reservation over a three-year period (1936–38), sixteen were from tuberculosis, eleven from pneumonia. The number of Yanktons living on the reservation at this time was approximately fifteen hundred.[102] In addition, with the federal mobilization for the war, the relief and rehabilitation programs were curtailed. During the war there were actually fewer jobs on the reservation.

In 1943 members of the Rehabilitation Committee prepared a report for the BIA on reservation conditions, with suggestions for improvement. They saw the land as a key problem. Much of the 43,000 acres of land held by the Yanktons was fractionalized as a result of several generations of inheritance. Some people owned very small plots of land in widely scattered areas. The committee recommended land consolidation. Most housing was substandard. Many of the homes were in a deplorable condition, having been built earlier in the century. Some New Deal funds were available for home improvement, but they were insufficient to meet people's needs. There were still young families with no land and no home. They lived with relatives in crowded, unhealthy conditions. In all, it was a very negative analysis of reservation life. Subsequent reports by the BIA in 1944 and the Rehabilitation Committee in 1945 indicated no significant change in conditions.[103]

During the war years people began to move away, leaving about half of enrolled Yanktons living on the reservation. Sam and Mary Necklace and their grandson Asa were part of this exodus. The economic situation on the reservation reflected what was happening to the Necklace family. With Sam's increased involvement in Yankton politics and his continuing commitment to the Peyote church, he found he could not meet the economic needs of his family. In a sense this can serve as a commentary on the Indian New Deal. On the one hand, there was more religious freedom and cultural autonomy; but on the other hand, even with a few concessions to local self-government, the overall movement toward self-determination was minimal. The New Deal did not live up to Collier's pronouncements: economic development was slow and uneven. The Indian New Deal did, however, stabilize the reservation land base by ending the allotment system. New Deal policies can be credited with a certain amount of relief for the reservations but not a significant amount of rehabilitation. Unfortunately, poverty remained the norm on most reservations.

WORLD WAR II AND ITS AFTERMATH

World War II had a significant impact on Native Americans. Many volunteered for the military or were drafted; thousands left the reservation for jobs in wartime industries; and thousands of others remained on the reservations, doing their best to support the war effort. The war era was a watershed in Native American history. For better or worse the war accelerated change. It gave people who left the reservation a different perspective and outlook. It helped pull American Indians into the web of American life and also led to demands for better education and less tolerance of discrimination. Virtually all American Indians supported the war effort. There was the hope that a war with a democratic ideology could lead to more rights and opportunities. This would not occur for several decades, but the seeds of change were planted during the war years. More than 25,000 American Indians either volunteered or were drafted during World War II. They served in all theaters of the war, and many were awarded citations for battlefield valor. Most famous were the Navajo soldiers who became "code talkers" and used Navajo as the basis for a code to transmit messages. American Indian soldiers served in integrated units, in contrast to African Americans and Japanese Americans, who fought in segregated units. Five hundred and fifty American Indians gave their lives for the United States, including approximately one hundred Sioux, whose volunteer rate exceeded that of almost all other groups.[104] These veterans are still honored. There is not a reservation in America today that does not have a Memorial Day service for its veterans. They hold a special place of honor in all American Indian communities. Every Memorial Day members of the Yankton Peyote community hold a special prayer service for the veterans who are buried in their cemetery.

Many Yanktons enlisted in the military. Some saw combat. Other Yanktons left the reservation for war-related jobs. With the shortage of labor, some found seasonal agricultural work.[105] The Yanktons gave special consideration to their soldiers and veterans. When a young man left for war, family, friends, and relatives gathered for a blessing, a feast, and a round of long speeches by some of the elders. Sam Necklace's grandson Asa remembers when Percy Rainbow, a member of the Native American Church, left for military service. Sam held a Peyote meeting for him and helped prepare a protective medicine bundle for him to carry throughout the war. The bundle contained many sacred items, including a Peyote button.[106] This was not unusual. According to Jim Blue Bird and others, Peyotists carried a protective Peyote button with them while in the military service. Before soldiers left home, the local Peyote community held a special service; another was held upon their safe return. When someone died in battle, the family went through an elaborate and intense traditional mourning. In at least one instance, described by Paul Picotte, the relatives came into the home of the parents, taking many of their belongings to be given away as part of the mourning process. Many people gathered. A photograph of the deceased soldier was passed around to everyone to help share the grieving burden of the family.[107]

World War II was difficult for the Necklace family. Not only Sam and Mary but also their two sons Ben and Dan had a hard time surviving the harsh economic conditions on the reservation. Sometime in 1943 Sam and Mary made the decision to leave the reservation and move to Yankton, South Dakota. It was not a total move; they maintained their home on the reservation and returned frequently—particularly Sam, who went back to carry out his functions as chief priest. He returned at least once a month to run the regularly scheduled Peyote meeting at the church. Several years later both his sons moved to Yankton. It was a small town (7,709 population in 1950) in the midst of a large agricultural area, with light industry. As a town tied to the agricultural cycle it offered considerable seasonal work. Statistics on the number of American Indians living in Yankton are difficult to ascertain, because there was migration for summer work in food processing and construction. Some had year-long jobs at a box factory and in retail establishments and restaurants. There was a sizable group of American Indians, but it was a transient population. In the late 1950s one source put the number of American Indians at 269. Most were from the Yankton Reservation.[108]

Sam and Mary decided to move not only for the possibility of a job with a wartime labor shortage but also for the schools. They were unhappy with their grandson's education on the reservation and felt the public schools in Yankton were much better. Asa said that his grandfather wanted him to get an education that would help him deal with "modern ways."[109] Location and transportation were also crucial. The town of Yankton is about sixty miles east of the reservation, with direct rail service and bus lines to Wagner. Their home was about nine miles from Wagner.

There are several studies of the Indian population in the city of Yankton in the 1950s. We can assume that conditions in the 1940s, especially after the war was over, were not very different from those in the 1950s, except that the Indian population was smaller. Yankton did not have a segregated Indian neighborhood, but there was a clustering of families where low-cost housing was available. Life in Yankton was not easy. Discrimination was the norm. Jobs were hard to find except during seasonal labor shortages, because non-Indian employers preferred not to hire American Indians unless it was necessary to do so. Indian people were not welcome in many establishments such as restaurants. Life was unsettled, and social problems emerged as a result of cultural displacement and economic hardship. Alcohol abuse became a problem, as did confrontations with local law enforcement.[110]

One of the clusters of Indian families was on the eastern edge of Yankton. Sam and Mary were possibly the first Peyote family to move to Yankton. They found a small home to rent on the east side near Route 50. This area became the nucleus of a small group of Yankton Peyote families. Their grandson Asa asked me if I would like to see where they lived. We drove to the east side of Yankton on Route 50 and turned left on Burleigh Street, looking for 502. Much to Asa's surprise the three neighboring houses we were looking for were no longer there. It was a vacant lot. His two uncles, Ben and Dan, lived next door. He said it was a small, yellow two-bedroom house for him and his grandparents. By the 1950s there were six to eight Peyote families in the area.[111] Both Sam's grandson and niece said that he was able to find work at McDonalds, a combination grocery-department store located at the intersection of Pine and Third. It was six blocks from their home. Sam worked as a janitor but also helped butcher meat.[112] Asa began attending public school. It is unclear if Mary worked or not at this time. Some remember her washing dishes at a local restaurant, but it is not clear if this was in the 1940s or the 1950s, when she returned to Yankton as a widow to live with one of her sons.

Asa remembers most vividly the monthly trips he and his grandfather took back and forth to the reservation. Sometimes Mary went with them but not always, because it could be a difficult trip. On the first Saturday of the month they would leave Yankton in the morning and take either a Greyhound bus or the train to Wagner. From there they would usually walk along the dirt roads to the Native American Church. Sometimes they were able to get a ride, but usually they walked. Grandfather and grandson (now a teenager) walked together. Asa carried the luggage; Grandpa Sam carried his Peyote box (sometimes called a gourd box) in one hand and a long walking staff in the other. Asa remembers the trips with great reverence. He described these trips with his grandpa in great detail as he recently retraced the route they used to walk. They usually went directly to the church to begin preparing for that night's Peyote service. The next day, after the noon meal, they would go to the pink house and spend the night. On Monday morning they would head back to Wagner and return to Yankton. Selma Sully Walker remembers some of the occasions when Mary came back with Sam. She said that Grandma Mary treated this as a special occasion and always looked very nice at these meetings, because she would sew a new dress for herself.[113]

Sometime in 1946 or 1947 Sam started showing signs of illness. Perhaps he was feeling the early symptoms of tuberculosis. Because it can develop undetected, he may not have been aware of the infection. He was now in his mid-sixties. His hair (which he wore a little long) had turned white, and he was slightly stooped at the shoulders. His long hair was mentioned from time to time, because it was unusual. Most of the men in the Cross Fire way wore short hair, whereas some of the Half Moon men wore their hair "Indian style."[114] Sam began to receive a monthly old-age assistance check from the state of South Dakota in 1946. It is unclear if he continued to work. Sometime in 1947 they decided to return home. Their sojourn in Yankton was not a pleasant one but was necessary at the time. Their son Benedict remained there. They moved back to the pink house and restarted their lives on the reservation. Mary resumed her domestic routine, and Sam continued his calling as chief priest.

Back on the reservation the Necklaces found life still difficult. The population was declining, as young people were seeking opportunities elsewhere. Full-time work opportunities were rare; and the Yanktons still did not have a BIA-certified constitution or a governing body. There was, however, one area of the reservation where conditions were better. The White Swan region, located in the southwest corner of the reservation, was the center of a major controversy in the late 1940s and early 1950s, stemming from the federal government's decisions to build a series of dams along the Missouri River. In 1944 Congress passed the Flood Control Act, which authorized the U.S. Army Corps of Engineers and the Bureau of Reclamation to develop the

Pick-Sloan plan to build five huge earthen dams along the river in order to control flooding, improve water supplies, create hydroelectric power, and increase recreation opportunities. The subsequent flooding of land covered 350,000 acres, much of it reservation land. The communities located along the shoreline were destroyed. Approximately nine hundred Indian families lost their homes in North Dakota and South Dakota. The families along the river had no input into the Pick-Sloan plan. There were no negotiations, even though much of the land was held under treaty rights. Fort Randall Dam, named after the old military fort that once held Sitting Bull as a prisoner, was built on the Yankton Reservation near the While Swan community. The dam created Lake Francis Case, resulting in the inundation of White Swan by the Missouri River. The people were removed and scattered. Land and homes were lost, and their most sacred sites, the burial grounds of their ancestors, were flooded.

There was an even greater loss that could not be replaced. The White Swan community was a special place in the minds and hearts of many Yanktons, as it was the most traditional of all Yankton communities. The people of White Swan had resisted change. It was the region where prereservation spiritual ceremonies survived underground. The area had been settled for a long time, because it is a favorable location for hunting and fishing as well as having rich bottomland along the river. White Swan was the only reservation community that was somewhat self-sufficient.

Families in White Swan raised horses, cows, and chickens. They grew corn, oats, and hay; and almost every family had a vegetable garden. Then the Pick-Sloan plan emerged. The government used the power of eminent domain to remove the people. It was a forced land taking, and resettlement was involuntary. The residents scattered in different directions. The Army Corps of Engineers had the legal responsibility of removing the human remains from the local cemeteries and burial grounds. When the dam was completed, the water rose slowly, submerging what had been a cohesive community. The water covered some of the best farmland on the reservation, destroyed stands of trees, and eliminated an area that was rich in wildlife.[115]

The White Swan community was gone forever, but not the memory. It has lingered on with great sadness and a sense of loss. Ramona O'Connor, a Yankton who grew up in the White Swan community, has recently written about her painful memories: "Damages caused by the Dam touched every aspect of life. Physical losses could be measured but the psychological losses are still there. The people had a sacred attachment to their land. It gave them a comfortable environment with resources to sustain a way of life. These losses cannot be measured."[116]

The Yankton people lost 2,851 acres. The government compensation was $39.45 per acre. Each of the families forced to relocate received an average sum of $5,605 for the loss of their homes and land; however, no one was compensated for relocation costs at the time, putting an impossible financial strain on the families. The compensation was deposited in BIA trust accounts; and—given bureaucratic restrictions—the money was not immediately available.[117] It was not much compensation; but for the real loss of their community, no compensation would have been enough. Finally, as a sad postscript to this event, the Army Corps of Engineers did not fulfill its legal obligations. In December 1999 the controversy exploded again when low water and erosion revealed gravesites, skeletal remains, and coffin parts along the Missouri River where the White Swan community had been located. The Corps of Engineers had supposedly transferred all the remains to other cemeteries but obviously had not completed the job. The reaction has been outrage that such a sacrilege could have occurred. This incident has intensified the debate over federal policy and the protection of sacred sites. The Yankton people have received expressions of support from across the nation. There have been protests, prayers, and vigils. The Yanktons had to go to U.S. District Court to stop the Corps of Engineers from opening the dam and reflooding the area before the remains were removed. The exposed remains have been reburied, but the wounds that have been reopened will take a long time to heal. In 2002, after much protest and with support from Senator Tom Daschle, the U.S. Congress established a $23 million trust fund as compensation to the Yanktons for the loss of the White Swan land. The issue, however, is far from resolved. The Yanktons continue to accuse the Army Corps of Engineers of mishandling human remains and cultural objects. They are determined to stop this desecration. Individual Yanktons have stood in front of bulldozers to stop the work at the construction site; others have called for a tourist boycott of various historic venues in South Dakota. This confrontation is presently being adjudicated in Federal District Court.[118]

SAM NECKLACE: THE FINAL YEARS

During the last two years of his life Sam did not involve himself in Yankton politics as he had prior to leaving the reservation; however, he continued to serve the Peyote community as chief priest. He had help from other priests,

John Claire and Louie Stricker, who also ran Peyote meetings and helped care for the church building, the grounds, and the cemetery. In spite of his age and health problems Sam continued to travel. He made regular trips to the Sisseton and Devil's Lake Reservations to serve local Peyote communities and visit relatives. He attended Peyote meetings on the Rosebud, Pine Ridge, and Winnebago Reservations. He was well known to Peyotists throughout North and South Dakota and Nebraska. The Yankton Peyotists were still marginalized on the reservation. They were perceived as being part of a lower socioeconomic group. Although they no longer faced harassment or had to defend their right to exist, they did face a certain amount of avoidance by those Yanktons who belonged to one of the three major Christian communities on the reservation. Some did not take the Peyote religion seriously; others thought that Native American Church members attended meetings because Peyote was supposedly a "drug." Most social activities took place within the Peyote community. The women socialized with each other, including some communal activities such as quilting or volunteer work. The young people also socialized, resulting in marriages between Peyote families. A young Loretta Rainbow and her family regularly attended Peyote meetings run by Sam Necklace. She became friendly with Sam's grandson. Loretta and Asa eventually married, bringing together three Peyote families: the Necklaces, the Primeauxs, and the Rainbows. They function as a *tiošpaye* to this day.

Sam and Mary continued their close relationship. Mary went with Sam virtually everywhere, whether it was to the church or to travel to other reservations. Selma Walker remembers them together: "where Sam went, Mary just walked beside him, no matter what." Asa remembers them always walking together to and from church, carrying whatever they needed for the Peyote meetings.[119] Life at home followed its former routine. Mary resumed gardening, processing and drying foods for winter, and collecting things like chokecherries to be used for spiritual foods. She spent considerable time in the kitchen. She baked bread and always had a pot of soup on the stove. Her relatives remember her smoking almost all the time. Mary rolled her own, using her favorite Bull Durham tobacco. Sometimes she smoked Pall Malls. Her grandson Parnell described with amazement how his grandma could take a piece of the thin paper, pull out her tobacco, and very nimbly and quickly roll a cigarette. She let him try to roll one, but he could not get it right.[120] Grandpa Sam did not smoke. He still had his horses and wagon and made regular trips to the river for water, taking the youngsters with him to fill the water barrels and throw driftwood on the wagon. It is not known how Sam was feeling. He certainly slowed down, but at his age this was not unusual. He did not limit his travel. As described at the beginning of chapter 1, one day he was returning home after running a Peyote service in North Dakota. His family was with him. His grandson Asa said he did not seem sick at the time; he just "walked on" while sleeping in the car as the family was going home. When they realized he was dead, there was nothing they could do but continue home and make the necessary preparations. Grandpa Sam was sixty-eight years old. His death certificate lists his occupation as "Chief Priest" and the cause of death as tuberculosis.

The four-day wake and the memorial Peyote service were held on the Native American Church grounds. Two people who were interviewed went to the funeral. Both Joe Packard and Loretta Primeaux said that many people were there. They came from many reservations, as it was customary for people from various Peyote communities to pay respects. Sam had known many people, because he had traveled widely, serving many Peyote communities. The prayer service, which was very crowded, was run by Oliver Paul Spider, chief priest of the Native American Church of South Dakota. It was the first of four annual memorial services held for Sam. This is the customary way for the Peyote community to memorialize those who passed away and to pray for the spirit of the deceased as it journeys to its final destination. On the fourth day Sam was interred in the Native American Church cemetery.[121]

Meanwhile the family collected funds for a tombstone:

Rev. S. B. Necklace
Dec. 24, 1881
Sept. 20, 1949
Pyuta [sic] Yuta Yo Wiconi Ed
Ya Ekti Wanikiya Hi Ye Do
Married Mary Chinn
Feb. 12, 1906
Let Brotherly Love Continue
25 Years of Priesthood N.A.C
Church of Forgiveness

There are five tipis, the logo of the Native American Church, carved on the tombstone, which reads: "Through eating Peyote there is everlasting life, that's according to the Savior."[122]

Sam Necklace's estate was probated in 1953. He did not leave a will, so his estate, appraised at $3,332, was divided according to federal statute. Mary received six-eighteenths; his three children, Benedict, Daniel, and Jennie, each received three-eighteenths. The remainder was divided among his three grandchildren by his deceased daughter Frances, who was the child from the relationship Sam had just before he married Mary. The probate records list Frances's death in 1934. Her husband testified at the hearing, verifying that Frances was the mother of three children. Technically these children received the shares that would have gone to their mother. The husband testified that Frances's parents were Sam and this other woman.[123] Mary also testified. She was asked who Frances Necklace was. She answered, "It is not my daughter." In any case, Mary had raised her as a daughter. Some of the descendants were surprised to find out that Frances was not Mary's biological daughter. There was no stigma or label placed on Frances. She was simply a sister to Ben, Dan, and Jennie. During the probate hearings the State of South Dakota filed a motion to claim part of the estate for the old-age assistance provided for Sam. No details were recorded; but the hearing officer rejected the motion, saying that the estate was too small for such a claim.

In assessing the life of Sam Necklace we find a person who could function in both the Anglo and American Indian world but who made a conscious choice to function primarily in the latter. This is how he maintained his dignity and identity in a reservation system not conducive to positive reinforcement of a person's identity. One example is his use of language. In spite of his boarding school education and his proficiency in speaking, reading, and writing English, Sam chose to speak Dakota with the Peyote community and with his family. All his children and Asa, the one grandson he raised, spoke Dakota as a first language, only learning English after age five or six in school. The same was true with Mary: she also went to boarding school and spoke English, but at home she spoke Dakota. Several of her grandchildren said they do not remember her ever speaking English. Sam Necklace does not fit any of the various paradigms discussed in the literature, such as culture broker, negotiator of change, cultural mediator, intermediary, or political middleman.[124] He does fit a description of certain American Indians by Beatrice Medicine (Lakota): "those of us brought up within strong families (*tiošpaye*), with strong Lakota beliefs, are able to function in two worlds."[125] It should be pointed out again, however, that he chose to function primarily in an American Indian environment. Not only was Sam brought up in such an environment but he and Mary also maintained a similar environment for their family. They made a choice: they could function in both worlds, but they chose not to. They were not passive actors in the unfolding drama of reservation life. Sam decided to stay within the Yankton/Peyote milieu; only the reality of economic necessity made him compromise this value, but even as he sought temporary employment off the reservation he did his best to insulate the family unit from outside influences. When he encouraged education, he did not do so with the goal of assimilation but to foster the development of tools for survival in a hostile economic environment.

In Yankton politics Sam took a firm position from which he never wavered. He believed the full-blood Yanktons should be inheritors of the Yankton body politic. If that was not possible then he wanted to establish some way for their voice to be heard, for their perspective to be included in the political process. He helped establish an organization of full-bloods; through the use of petitions, verbal protest, and the full-blood vote, he hoped to stem the tide of change represented by the mixed-bloods. It was a losing battle for Grandpa Sam, but he persevered until the end of his life.

Sam Necklace is also responsible for helping to establish the Native American Church on the Yankton Reservation. Sam was not one of the founders. That credit goes to Charlie Jones, Johnson Goodhouse, and Charles Iron Hawk, who were active Peyotists before Sam; but Sam did join the church in its early years. He helped give it a permanent place in Yankton society. He played a key role in the incorporation of 1922 and as chief priest defended the rights of the Peyote community and helped put the church on a firm institutional foundation, which included the establishment of the church grounds, a cemetery, and a church building. The Peyote community today recognizes these contributions.

In an assessment of Sam Necklace's life one must conclude that his greatest contribution was the heritage and memory he left to his descendants. Even though he died in 1949, he is a living memory today, perpetuated by his grandchildren and great-grandchildren. A modest estimate of the number of great-grandchildren is approximately ninety-five. For example, as of 2003, Asa and Loretta Primeaux have thirty-two grandchildren. Sam's memory affects social, familial, and spiritual values. Many of his descendants are practicing Peyotists. Those who are roadmen have copied his style of altar and use his sacred markings. They know that this came to him in a vision, and they honor it as part of their heritage. In Peyote ceremonies today his great-grandsons Gerald and Asa Primeaux, Jr., tell the story of his vision and his sacred markings at the midnight break. This spiritual heritage has contributed to the continuity of his extended family. The same can be said of the impact of Sam and Mary Necklace on the social values that have been passed on to subsequent generations. As with many American Indian families, there is a tradition of passing down family history from generation to generation. Sam's grandson Asa said in an interview: "I heard from my grandfather who raised me, and he talked about his grandpa that did this and his great-grandpa down there, he did that. . . ."[126] This has reinforced the family's identity as Necklaces or Primeauxs and has also reinforced their identity as Yanktons.

This continuity was in the face of discontinuity and the economic dislocation. For example, almost all the descendants have a memory of Sam and Mary as being very strict when it came to individual behavior. Sam demanded proper behavior during Peyote meetings. Both Sam and Mary demanded that the young people honor their elders and behave in a proper way when in the presence of adults. One grandson, Bruce Iron Necklace, remembers his grandma not reprimanding the children who were misbehaving in front of adults but calling over his dad and saying: "What are you doing with those kids, aren't you teaching them how to be respectful, how to act around grown-ups?" He added that his grandpa was the same way.[127] This is another example of how the transmission of memory reinforces the family today. It gives the family strength, helps maintain continuity, and encourages the young generation to follow the "Indian way" and/or the "Peyote Road." Bruce Iron Necklace was born after his grandfather died, but he talked about his grandpa as if he knew him. Bruce and his wife, Katherine, have brought up their children with the memory of Grandpa Sam and Grandma Mary as part of their lives.

In 1982 another grandson, Parnell Necklace, held a naming ceremony for his son Danny. Danny's uncle and Parnell's cousin Asa Primeaux conducted the ceremony. Parnell, who made a tape recording of he event, asked Nancy Rockboy, who was attending the naming, to talk to everyone, especially the children, about the Necklace ancestors. Nancy was a member of the local Native American Church and the wife of roadman Joe Rockboy, who had recently passed away. She spoke in Dakota.

Sam and Mary Baker's grandchildren, like a rainbow, from them the grandchildren came. I can talk as far as I can remember. This man [Sam Necklace] is a churchman. He ran Peyote meetings. Some other ones run Peyote meetings, but they don't do it right, but this man is a strong member of the church, from there a generation came along. . . . He's quiet, he's a nice man, so everybody looks up to him and needs him. He loves his kids, his relations. All of his children and relations sit together and get along. . . . They want to know who are the grandparents, Sam and Mary, so I'm telling them, those are the grandparents, Sam and Mary, that's how the fourth generation got here [the great-grandchildren].[128]

The following year (1983) Parnell asked Asa to record on tape some of his knowledge of Yankton spiritual traditions and family history, so they could be passed on to the future generations of the family. Asa credits his grandparents and their ancestors for the family's spiritual heritage:

The reason I am living this way [spiritual life] and believe this way is in behalf of my grandparents. My grandparents on my mother's side, the Necklace clan. There were traditional people in there. Back there our great-great-grandfather was a medicine man, and this man was a natural blind. He was born blind. He had a power, he practiced that, he was a holy man. So that's where we came from, we're the offspring of our people, the Necklaces. . . . Our people were traditional people. They prayed that way, they had Sweat Lodges, Sacred Pipes, Indian names, they prayed that way. My cousin wanted me to say a little bit about our history, so it goes back that far to our great-great-grandfather to now his [Parnell's] little son. *Mitakuye Oyasin.*[129]

The memory of Sam and Mary is part of this multigeneration extended family. Their memory provides a path that some may choose not to follow, but for many in the family it provides a path rooted in the past. In 1985, when Parnell and Gracie Necklace had their second son, they named him Samuel after his great-grandfather.

CHAPTER SEVEN

The Peyote Road and Yankton Society

1949–PRESENT

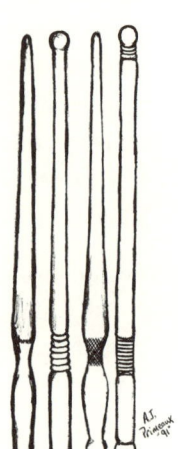

Peyote drumsticks. Drawn by Asa Primeaux, Jr.

After the passing of Sam Necklace, others in the church took up the mantle of leadership. The family lost its spiritual leader, but Mary, his wife, became the source of unity for the family. The life of the *tiošpaye* now revolved around her. Meanwhile people on the reservation had to face an onslaught of new federal policies that vacillated in the next few decades. From the reform-based Indian New Deal, to relocation and termination in the 1950s, to self-determination in the 1960s and 1970s, to the complex issues of sovereignty in the 1980s and 1990s stability has not been a cornerstone of either federal policy or reservation life. The changes in federal policy have been extreme, placing Indians at the mercy of changing policy initiatives; yet the pattern of inconsistency wrought a powerful reaction: American Indian determination to take their destiny into their own hands. This response produced a political, cultural, and social renaissance that continues to this day.

The Native American Church has continued its growth throughout the West. There is no official count of its members, but one recent estimate puts membership at 200,000, approximately 10 percent of the more than 2 million American Indians. Another estimate puts the number at 250,000. Since Peyotism is located primarily west of the Mississippi River, one can estimate that 20 to 25 percent of American Indians in this region are Peyotists.[1] On many occasions in the past half-century Peyotists have faced opposition from several states and from several members of Congress who wanted to regulate all use of Peyote as part of the war on drugs. The culmination occurred in 1990, when the United States Supreme Court ruled in *Employment Division of Oregon* v. *Smith* that the state of Oregon could apply its prohibition of Peyote to members of the Native American Church. The decision meant that sacramental use of Peyote was denied First Amendment protection. The *Smith* case sent shock waves through the Peyote community as well as other religious communities. It resulted in a nationwide mobilization, leading to the passage of the American Indian Religious Freedom Act Amendment (1994), returning First Amendment protection to the religious practices of the Native American Church.

During this era the Yankton people struggled through relocation and termination, initiated their own drive for self-determination, and participated in the cultural renaissance and the emergence of political activism. They also made strides in economic development with the establishment of a gaming casino. The Yankton Peyote community continued a slow but steady growth. The majority practiced the Cross Fire way, but there was a growing Half Moon group. Some differences of opinion arose as the Yankton Peyotists faced the resurgence of the open practice of Yankton traditional religion, including Sweat Lodge ceremonies, Sun Dances, and Vision Quests, all within the framework of the spirituality and centrality of the Sacred Pipe. The Necklace and Primeaux families grew in number, with the majority being active in the Peyote religion. Sam's grandson Asa became a roadman and an important person in his own right within the larger Peyote community. He is carrying on the traditions of his grandfather and certainly has been essential in passing on the memory of his grandfather to succeeding generations.

TERMINATION AND RELOCATION: THE YANKTONS IN THE 1950s

None of the federal government's attempts to solve economic problems on the reservations succeeded, as poverty remained endemic throughout the late 1940s. In fact one could argue that conditions were worsening, as Richard Clow has suggested, for the reservations in South Dakota. He points out that with the return of veterans and those who left for wartime jobs reservation conditions worsened as unemployment increased.[2] One solution advocated by several federal officials was to reduce the number of American Indians on the reservations. Thus relocation entered the vocabulary of the Department of the Interior. In 1950 President Harry Truman appointed Dillon S. Myer as commissioner of Indian Affairs. Myer, who had been the director of the

47ᵗʰ
ANNUAL CONVENTION
NATIVE AMERICAN CHURCH
OF
SOUTH DAKOTA

JUNE-17-18-19-20, 1971

Cover of Annual Convention Program (1971) of the Native American Church. The tipi is the church logo, with a Half Moon fireplace on the left and Cross Fire fireplace on the right, with a Peyote button placed on each altar.

agency responsible for the incarceration of 120,000 Japanese Americans during World War II, was an advocate of assimilation.

This set the stage for pursuing not only relocation of reservation Indians but also termination of reservations. The combination of relocation and termination was supposed to solve the "Indian problem" once and for all by assimilating Native Americans into the larger American society. Once the goals of termination became obvious, there was almost universal opposition by American Indians. The government encouraged individuals to participate in relocation programs by making promises of a better life, offering some travel and relocation money but not much else. The cities that were to receive the new residents were ill prepared to deal with the situation, particularly the degree of racial discrimination and prejudice that existed in many urban areas. Jobs were often difficult to find. Sometimes the only jobs were seasonal or, for women, in domestic service. Housing was a serious problem. The only available housing was in low-income areas. The children also had a difficult time in school, being a small minority in many schools. Relocation meant moving rural people to urban areas; it resulted in exchanging rural poverty for urban poverty. There were few successful relocations. Those nearby would go back and forth to their reservation. Others moved back permanently; but some stayed, becoming part of the inner-city poor.

Termination proceeded along with relocation. Congress terminated more than one hundred tribal groups. This ended federal trust protection, which meant that the land base would no longer have federal protection from those who wanted the land or access to the natural resources. It was not a coincidence that some of the groups chosen to be terminated had valuable resources on their land. For example, the Menominees of Wisconsin had to sell valuable land in order to survive after they were terminated. In California forty-one reservations were terminated. The new policy was an unmitigated disaster, but it did spark American Indians to organize, protest, and demand self-determination.[3]

In South Dakota the situation was the same. Sioux were relocated to South Dakota cities; some went to Sioux City, Iowa, or farther yet, to Minneapolis–St. Paul or Chicago. Some, such as later America Indian Movement (AIM) activists Russell Means and Ken Irwin, ended up in Cleveland. Individuals moved voluntarily but were influenced by promises of a better life. Local social service agencies were not prepared for this influx. As Clow notes, "by and large Sioux relocation was a calamitous reallocation of both resources and problems."[4] The impact on the Yanktons was not any different. Some government facilities on the reservation were abandoned or put up for sale. Several social services were curtailed, and the government day school in Greenwood was closed. The Yanktons, like others, were encouraged to relocate.[5]

The exodus of Yanktons to nearby cities began in the 1940s. Sam and Mary were part of this early movement. Many more would follow, eventually creating small Yankton communities in cities like Vermillion and Yankton. Yankton seemed like a town where one could find a job, and it was close enough for periodic visits to the reservation. By the late 1950s several hundred Yanktons had moved there. For the most part their goal of a better economic life was not fulfilled. As mentioned earlier, few employers would hire American Indians except for temporary employment; as a result most lived in substandard housing. The stress of life in Yankton resulted in increasing problems with alcohol and periodic problems with law enforcement. In a study of the sociocultural adjustment of American Indians in Yankton, Wesley R. Hurt documented these problems. He and his staff interviewed approximately fifty American Indians (mostly Yanktons) and drew the conclusion that adjustment to city life was unsuccessful. Very few could find full-time regular work. It was either part-time work or odd jobs. For example, Hurt says that one Yankton he interviewed "has done all kinds of common labor, such as working for Jensen Junkyard, lawn work, and snow shoveling. He has run ads once in a while for yard work." Housing was crowded, with families sometimes living together or taking in a boarder. Typical rent was thirty dollars a month. Some help was available from other sources, including old-age assistance from the state (averaging thirty-five dollars per month) and Aid to Dependent Children. The median school completion rate for American Indians in Yankton was ninth grade. When asked if they would prefer to return to the reservation if jobs were available, the majority answered yes. Many of the young men were frequently in trouble with the law, usually for public intoxication or disturbing the peace; some were arrested for hunting violations or vagrancy. There were few felony arrests. For most Yanktons their residence in the city was sporadic; some returned to the reservation or moved on to other cities. Only about 20 percent could be considered permanent residents.[6]

Problems continued back on the reservation, when people returned from Yankton or elsewhere. Some reservation residents, who had not left, felt that the returnees brought problems back with them. For example, Bessie Red Hawk, a Yankton elder, had an interesting comment on relocation. She said that some people go on relocation, spend the money they have, and come back with the bad habits they learned in the city.[7] She was right; not much good came out of relocation and termination.

MARY NECKLACE: THE LATER YEARS

After Sam passed away, Mary spent her remaining fourteen years alternating her residence between her children's homes and her home. She lived in Yankton with her son Ben, on the Yankton Reservation with her daughter Jennie, or in the summer months in the pink house, with extended visits by her son Dan and daughter-in-law Katherine, who lived on the Sisseton Reservation. In all three places grandchildren surrounded her. As a widow Mary rarely lived alone. She had a daily life integrated into her extended family. The grandchildren were now the central focus of her life. Being a grandmother was a traditional time-honored status among the Yanktons. That role was at the core of family and community life, fulfilling economic, social, and spiritual needs. Grandmothers are considered the inheritors of the tradition of White Buffalo Calf Woman: as caregivers, teachers, protectors, and disseminators of wisdom. The grandmothers specifically, and women in general, were essential to keeping the sacred circle whole. They represented mother earth. The grandmas were the link from the ancestors to future generations. They were also, along with the great-grandmothers, next to join with the Great Spirit in the afterlife. Holy women or medicine women were almost always grandmothers.[8] The Dakota word for grandmother is *unči;* it is also used as a term of respect when a younger person is addressing an elderly woman. One could argue that the role of the grandmothers in relationship to the grandchildren has become more significant in the last half-century. In earlier times the grandmas played a central role in child-rearing, but in a broader sense the children belonged to the entire community and were raised by the community. Today many in the community are dispersed, caught up in a fast lifestyle, facing societal pressures, divorce, and poverty. Under these circumstances many of the children belong to the grandmas.[9]

Grandma Mary (*unči* Mary) fulfilled this role, first by raising her grandson Asa, then by taking the responsibility for much of the everyday care of the other grandchildren. This included playing a major part in their spiritual and social development. She taught them the appropriate behavior around adults, from the use of kinship terminology to respect for elders: never sit when an older person is standing, allow older people to eat first, and never, never disobey an elder. She taught the children how to be a good relative. She also had a reputation for being strict—more so than Grandpa Sam. Her grandchildren could not conceive of disobeying her, not only out of fear of punishment but out of awe and respect. Today they speak of her very reverently. Much of her teaching was by example. Her granddaughters helped her prepare spiritual food. They learned about the proper way to prepare it and learned about its spiritual significance. Grandma Mary also helped organize giveaways. The grandmas, mothers, and daughters worked together to collect, make, and organize giveaway items and then prepare the food for the event. The children learned generosity and hospitality as basic social values. The children also saw the grandmas being honored (at a powwow with a special honor song and dance, for example, or at a birthday).

In 1991 the Necklace/Primeaux/Rainbow *tiošpaye* sponsored a four-day powwow. Grandma Eunice (Rainbow Dog Soldier) was honored as the eldest family member. More than one hundred people came into the dance arena, shook her hand, and lined up behind her to dance along with the honor song. Each year until she passed away (1994) she was honored on her birthday with prayers, spiritual food, speeches, and a feast, followed by a giveaway sponsored by her family. All the people who attended were given gifts to thank them for honoring Grandma Eunice.[10] The honoring of the elders is a powerful lesson for the children. The spiritual values that Grandma Mary imparted to the grandchildren were a mixture of traditional Sioux values and Native American Church teachings. From the latter the children were taught forgiveness, as the local Peyote faith was referred to as the "church of forgiveness." From their Yankton Sioux heritage the children learned never to commit the four cardinal sins: lying, jealousy, being two-faced, and hatred. The grandchildren of Mary and Sam teach these values to their children today.

One reason why Mary had such an impact on the grandchildren is that in her later years she lived with almost all of them in one place or another. In the city of Yankton Mary lived with Ben, Sybil, and their children in a small frame house on Burleigh Street next to the old house she and Sam had lived in. Their home was crowded with three adults and seven children, ages three to eighteen. Mary spent most of her time caring for the children. It is unclear if she worked. One relative, not living in Yankton, said she worked as a dishwasher in a restaurant. This is unlikely, given her age and responsibilities with the children. In 1960 she was interviewed for the Wesley Hurt research project. It was not an extensive interview; the notes were taken on the back page of someone else's interview. Mary reaffirmed that she was born on the Yankton Reservation and was a full-blood, went to Hope School in Springfield, South Dakota, and married Sam Necklace in the Tyndall County Courthouse. She added that she was baptized and confirmed in the Native American Church. She said she did not like the city—"too many drunkards"—and pointed out to the interviewer that she did not drink.[11]

On the reservation Mary stayed at home or with Jennie and her husband, Josiah, and four children. They lived in a large house between Greenwood and Marty. The house was always filled with people, as various other relatives stayed there from time to time. Sometimes Ben and Sybil and their children lived there. In either place Grandma Mary had plenty of household responsibilities. She baked bread daily and usually had soup cooking on the stove. Most of her time, however, was spent with the grandchildren. One granddaughter, Bernice Necklace, said that what she and the other kids loved most was jumping in bed with her *unči*. Mary stayed in the pink house during the warm weather. In the winter it would have been extremely difficult for her to heat the house. It was quite isolated and could not easily be reached in bad weather. Her son Dan and his family stayed with her during the summer months. Her daughter-in-law Katherine and grandson Bruce remember Mary as being quite busy cooking, sewing, and always working on a quilt. She still smoked (rolling her own), usually while she did something else. She carried a leather pouch at her waist that contained tobacco, rolling papers, and matches. With the help of her family she kept a small garden.

Mary also remained active in the Native American Church. She continued to attend meetings in the Greenwood church. Her grandson Asa, after returning from the Korean War in 1953, made a point of taking his grandma to the church and to visit the grave of Grandpa Sam. She usually went with Jennie, but sometimes they went as a family. It was important to Mary that her three children remained active members. Her daughter-in-law Katherine recalls attending various Peyote meetings when she and Dan and Ben and Sybil all went together. At that time Joe Shields was the roadman. Mary continued her work with the "Ladies' Aid" group, making quilts, fund-raising, and caring for the bedridden. Her life was full until the end.[12]

Mary Chinn Necklace died on 27 February 1963, at the age of seventy-seven. Her death certificate states: "[C]ause of death: Broncho Pneumonia. Interval between onset and death: 2 days." She passed away while living at Jennie's. Sometime in 1961 Grandma Mary, Ben, Sybil, and their children left Yankton and moved back to the reservation. Ben and Sybil found some work locally, and the children were enrolled in school. Mary's grandson Parnell Necklace has a vivid recollection of the events surrounding her passing. He was seventeen at the time. He describes his last conversation with her and her last hours. She was not feeling well and after school he checked on her:

I'm always checking to see how grandma was. We all stayed in that big house, Asa's mom's place, Jennie's house. The whole Necklace gang stayed there. I remember towards evening, my grandma called me over—I talked Indian then—she told me to come in the room. I went in there and she said, I'd like you to burn some stuff up. She said go start a fire outside. She gave me two or three matches. I started a fire outside and I came back in. She had a bunch of clothes—she said throw these in, make sure they're burnt-up. I said OK. So I burnt them all up. Then I came back in. She had a bunch of dollar bills, but they were bigger, you know. She said burn them up too. She took out four silver dollars. I'm giving you four of these, she said. She put them on the bed. These are yours, she said. I said OK. So I went out burned all the money up. Then I came back in. She had a bunch of papers, all crumbled up. She said burn 'em up next. I said OK. I burned them up. Then she said, watch the fire, make sure it burns down so you don't start a fire. I said OK.

So I was pushing live charcoals around with a stick. Then usually toward evening we listen to the Lone Ranger, that was one of the favorite programs in those days. I went and got a pail of water and splashed it all over the coals. Well, grandma, I said, I finished what you told me. She said good, now I'm ready. I said, boy, you're going someplace and not even taking anything. She said, I'm going to a good place. So I let it go at that. So I told Dad that. I said grandma said she's going someplace . . . she told me to burn all her clothes and papers. I showed him those four silver dollars: look what she gave me. He turned around, I heard him sobbing. I knew something was going on. Somebody told Aunt Jennie that, and you could just hear her crying. So I don't remember if we listened to the Lone Ranger that night or not, but I remember waking up and then a lot of commotion and they said grandma passed away. Somebody said it was Ash Wednesday in the morning. I don't even remember what I did with them silver dollars. That's about all I remember on grandma.[13]

Following the wake and the mourning period, Mary was laid to rest in the Native American Church cemetery next to her husband. Mary's memory has provided a legacy for the present relatives, especially as a role model for the girls and young women, and is still evoked. In 1982 at a naming ceremony for Danny Necklace, Nancy Rockboy spoke of Mary as a person who repre- sented love for all the relatives and for her church. She reminded the young people (Danny is a great-grandson of Sam and Mary) that they were the fourth generation and that the elders "teach them so that they can remember."[14] Like Grandpa Sam, Grandma Mary has given the family a memory that has become a source of values and identity rooted in both the Yankton Dakota and Native American Church traditions.

THE NATIVE AMERICAN CHURCH AND THE
CULTURAL RENAISSANCE: 1960s–1980s

Termination and relocation did not affect the growth of the Peyote religion. In fact relocation brought Peyote members to large urban areas such as San Francisco, Denver, and Los Angeles, where they formed local Peyote communities. The growth in the number of Peyotists was mainly among the Navajos, but there was also further expansion into the northern Plains, the Great Basin, Canada, and the Far West. For example, in the 1970s three Peyote groups incorporated in the state of Washington. Peyotism continued its expansion as a result of its theology and ritual, meeting the needs and having meaning for many American Indians. It was still perceived as an "Indian" religion. There is another very significant point: Peyotism as a theology, and the Peyote church as an institution, does not require individuals to give up other faiths. Professor Hoover has made this point about the Yanktons: Peyote, the Sacred Pipe, and the Cross are not mutually exclusive. They are different channels to the "same Great Spirit." Aberle points out the same thing about the Navajos: "many Navajo believe that they can follow traditional Navajo practices, attend Christian services, belong to Christian congregations, and attend Peyote meetings as members of the Native American Church."[15]

The major development in the history of Peyotism since World War II has been the widespread acceptance of Peyote among the Navajos. They number approximately 190,000, close to half of whom are practicing Peyotists. In March 1991 Robert Billy Whitehorse, president of the Native American Church of Navajoland, estimated that there were 80,000 Navajo Peyotists. At first the Navajos were slow to accept Peyotism, but then it spread rapidly. Its introduction onto the Navajo Reservation met with considerable resistance from missionaries, traditionalists, and Christian Navajos, who controlled the tribal council. In 1940 they passed a statute prohibiting the possession, use, or trafficking in Peyote. Commissioner Collier supported the statute on the grounds that it fell under the jurisdiction of the tribal council. Nevertheless there were Peyote roadmen from Oklahoma conducting prayer services in

Navajo country. In addition, some Navajos traveled to other reservations to attend Peyote services. Throughout the late 1940s and 1950s about a hundred Navajo Peyotists were arrested by reservation authorities each year. This sparked another national debate about Peyotism. In 1949 an article appeared in the *Journal of the American Medical Association* that severely condemned the Peyote religion. It cited no new research, only repeating old hearsay evidence from the 1920s on the ill effects of Peyote, but it did cause a reaction.[16] The BIA hired anthropologist David Aberle to make a thorough study of Navajo Peyotism. The result was *The Peyote Religion among the Navaho,* still the standard monograph on the subject. It also turned Professor Aberle into a lifelong defender of the Peyote religion.

The popular press became involved when *Time* magazine published the article "Button, Button . . . ," repeating the old orgy stories. They quoted one report: "Men hopped up with peyote are likely to grab the closest female, whatever age, kinfolk or not."[17] The sources for the *Time* story were Christian missionaries working on the Navajo Reservation. This brought an immediate response from the anthropological community, including Omer Stewart, who wrote:

> Sir: . . . Your article repeats a familiar pattern which has been recurring for over a half-century. Whenever the peyote cult has been accepted by another tribe, the local Indian Christian converts, wishing to please the missionaries, from whom they receive second-hand clothes and other handouts, report "sex orgies," "deaths," "insanity," etc. caused by peyote. No scientists have been able to discover these evils. I have checked dozens of such reports and found them all either pure fabrications or misrepresentations.[18]

A statement published in the journal *Science* that supported the Peyote faith followed. Five prominent anthropologists, including Omer Stewart, signed it. They protested the use of anti-Peyote propaganda, pointing out that all of them had attended Peyote meetings, had "partaken of the sacramental peyote," and did not witness anything unfavorable. They defended Peyotism as a religion and explained how the sacramental use of Peyote was the same as the sacramental use of wine. John Collier, now retired, also wrote in defense of Peyotism.[19]

Another young scholar who became an activist was anthropologist Sydney Slotkin of the University of Chicago, who did his fieldwork on Peyote among the Menominees. He went one step further than other anthropologists and became a member of the Native American Church of the United States. In 1954 he was elected to the Board of Trustees. He published both popular and scholarly works on Peyote, with articles appearing in *American Anthropologist, Saturday Review,* and *Time.* He also edited the *Quarterly Bulletin of the Native American Church* for three years. Although the *Quarterly Bulletin* had a short life, it marked an important milestone in the history of Peyotism. Its publication in 1955 coincided with the establishment of the Native American Church of North America. By the mid-1950s there were a significant number of Canadian Peyotists who had already incorporated as the Native American Church of Canada. The purpose of a broader-based organization and a new publication (it was mimeographed and mailed free of charge) was to coordinate efforts to defend Peyotism. In developing communication among Peyote communities, President Allen P. Dale made it clear that belonging to this organization did not preclude organizing on a tribal, county, or state level. Nor did the larger body have a parochial theological agenda in support of one style of Peyote worship over another. President Dale said the only goal is to "protect our way of worship."[20]

Slotkin's major work, *The Peyote Religion,* is a history of the legal status of the Peyote religion and includes a valuable review of federal and state legislative and administrative policies. He also describes the organizational structure of the Native American Church. This is a scholarly work, but it is written by a church member and has been referred to by LaBarre as a "manual for peyotists." Slotkin and his contemporaries Stewart and LaBarre are part of a small group of activist anthropologists who throughout the twentieth century defended the Peyote religion in popular and scholarly writing and as expert witnesses in court cases and legislative hearings.[21]

In the mid-1950s, under the leadership of the Native American Church of North America, President Frank Takes Gun (Crow) took an active role defending Navajo Peyotists. The American Civil Liberties Union (ACLU) also defended them. Meanwhile a court case emerged in California that had great significance for the Navajos. In 1962 Jack Woody and two other Navajos were arrested in Needles, California, for the use and possession of Peyote during a religious service. They were indicted, tried, and found guilty. The ACLU took their case and appealed it up to the California Supreme Court. In *People v. Woody et al.* (1964) the California court reversed the convictions by applying the First Amendment and protecting the right of Native American Church members to use or possess Peyote for religious purposes.[22] In 1967 the Navajo Tribal Council reversed the 1940 statute by passing a Navajo human rights bill that included religious freedom. The use of Peyote on the reservation by members of the Native American Church was decriminalized. Under the new statute, Peyotism continued to expand and flourish. There are two major Navajo Peyote groups. In the northern Four Corners area are Peyotists who are affiliated with the Native American Church of North America; and in the southern Window Rock area is the Native American Church of Navajoland, which has remained independent. The majority of the Navajo Peyotists follow the Half Moon way, although a significant number are Cross Fire. Some traditional Navajos still do not support the Peyote religion, but the Peyotists do not accept this viewpoint. According to Aberle, the "Peyotists refer to themselves as traditionalists and respecters of Navajo ceremonies."[23]

There has been considerable contact between Navajo and Yankton Peyotists. Some have traveled back and forth, and roadmen from each group have run Peyote meetings on the other's reservation. Asa Primeaux has served as a roadman on the Navajo reservation; and Leo Harvey, a Navajo from the Window Rock area, has been a roadman on the Yankton Reservation. A very fruitful collaboration has taken place in Peyote music. Navajo/Yankton Peyote songs have been commercially produced and are very popular around the country (see the discography in the bibliography).

During the termination and relocation era the Yankton Peyote church grew slightly in numbers. As the overall Yankton population grew, the membership of the church increased proportionally. By this time almost the entire membership had been born into Peyote families. There were some new members but not many. No proselytizing took place on the local level. The struggle was to keep the young people involved. One estimate is that there were approximately five hundred members of the church during this period, less than 10 percent of the Yankton population (including members who lived both on and off the reservation). For example, one of the larger Peyote families, the Bruguier *tiošpaye*, numbered about seventy people.[24]

After Sam Necklace passed away, the church continued to function as it had in the past. Louie Stricker (1898–1974) served as chief priest and John Claire (1898–1966), also a priest, shared leadership. Joe Rockboy, Joe Shields, Sr., Nelson Dragg, and Victor Kutena served as roadmen. They still held their monthly meeting at the church in Greenwood and were following the Cross

Fire way. The inside walls of the church were adorned with poster art that reflected the Cross Fire absorption of Christian elements, especially the integration of Jesus as Savior and the Son of God, into Peyote beliefs. The poster art included a framed print of Leonardo da Vinci's *Last Supper;* a print of a bleeding heart motif of Jesus with open hands, showing the wounds of the crucifixion; and a print of Joseph, Mary, and Jesus, with Mary seated holding the infant Jesus on her lap. Another print of an 1840s-style Christian poster reflected the struggle between the wages of sin and evil and the forces of righteousness, with insets around the outside illustrating competing scenes of good and evil. The center reprints *The Lord's Prayer.* This poster may have been displayed because of the line "and forgive us our debts as we forgive our debtors." The Yankton Peyote church has always been called the "church of forgiveness."

A print of the painting *Catherine Tekawitha: Lily of the Mohawk* also hung on the wall. She is kneeling before a wooden cross in prayer. Kateri Tekawitha (ca. 1656–80), baptized by Jesuit missionaries in 1676, joined the Society of the Holy Family and took a vow of chastity. In spite of physical disabilities and abuse she persevered in her beliefs and her spiritual mission. Upon her death at age twenty-four, it was reported that the pockmarks on her face from a childhood smallpox infection had miraculously disappeared. After her interment, Christian Indians began visiting her grave. Many of those who prayed there claimed that their prayers had been answered. Over the years her stature has grown. In 1980, the 300th anniversary of her death, she was beatified by the Catholic Church, the last step before sainthood. She will become the first Native American to be declared a saint by the Catholic Church. It is interesting to note that Tekawitha is a significant symbol for several religious communities. In addition to the display of her image in the Native American Church, the Catholic mission on the reservation also used Tekawitha as a symbol to attract Yanktons to Catholicism.[25] It is unclear how long the artworks had been hanging in the church. Some remember them from the 1950s, but no one knows who put them up or when. To some people it seems that they have "always" been there.[26]

In the 1950s the church building was in good condition. It was painted white on the outside and light blue inside. The floor was covered with checkered linoleum, and curtains covered the windows. A 1963 photograph shows an American flag hanging on the west wall. The photo was taken the morning after a Peyote meeting; it pictures Adam Sitting Crow, Sr., holding a birthday cake with a five-year-old Adam, Jr. Joe Shields, Sr., is sitting in the background. John Claire was the roadman for the service.[27]

The church functioned as an incorporated body, held business meetings on the Sunday after the monthly prayer meeting, and used *Robert's Rules of Order* to conduct business. Peyote meetings were also held on Christmas, Easter, and Memorial Day. During Lent weekly prayer meetings were held at the church. The monthly meetings helped to bond the Peyote community. Many of those off the reservation returned for the monthly gathering. The church was a focal point for the community. Those who did not have cars had horses and wagons; some arrived early, and some stayed on a day to two longer. In addition to the spiritual activities, there was much socializing. The adults spent time together before and after the Sunday noon meal. The children played, running foot races, climbing trees, or playing softball. Some of the adults pitched horseshoes.

The young men, called "peyote boys," had a fast-pitch softball team. They played other Yankton teams on Sunday afternoons in the towns of Lake Andes, Greenwood, and Marty. The "peyote boys" played very competitive softball, because it was more than a game to them. The pitcher was Leonard Bruguier, the present director of the Institute of American Indian Studies at the University of South Dakota. He said it was more than softball because their spiritual beliefs were involved. Many people still viewed Peyote as a drug and looked down on Peyotists. Bruguier said they were so competitive because they had something to prove. They had stayed up all night and eaten Peyote and "yet could still perform physically and mentally." Some of the players on the other teams drank alcohol on Saturday nights and had Sunday hangovers, so by winning softball games the "peyote boys" could prove that there was no negative effect from Peyote and in doing so reaffirm their way of life.[28]

Activities such as softball were important in building social bonds among the youth. The young women also had activities that kept them involved with the church. They helped adult women prepare for the Sunday noon meal and did volunteer work for the church. They helped with the sewing of items worn or taken into Peyote meetings, making shawls with embroidered Peyote symbols such as a water bird or tipi and embroidering similar symbols on pillows or on vests that their fathers, husbands, or brothers wore during church services. The young boys spent time learning Peyote songs and drumming, sometimes learning the songs from their fathers or uncles; or the young people would just gather, tie a drum, and begin to sing for practice or for enjoyment. This was quite common: without tape recorders, the only way to learn was to listen to someone else and then practice until they had it right. Some young men became apprentices. They spent time with a roadman, learning the ritual, acquiring the necessary paraphernalia, and attending as many Peyote meetings as possible. Eventually they might be asked to "poke fire"—that is, to serve as the fireman for a Peyote service. After quite a few years of learning, and earning the respect of others, someone would sponsor a Peyote meeting and ask an individual to be the roadman. It was quite a responsibility, but he would humbly accept the invitation to serve the community.

As the Yankton Peyote community developed in the early 1950s, it was involved with neighboring Peyote groups for spiritual activities but not yet involved with the Native American Church of the United States. The Yankton Peyotists were not members and did not participate in the annual conferences; nor did other South Dakota Peyotists. Almost all of the national officers were from Oklahoma, and the early conferences were held there. After 1955, when they changed their name to the Native American Church of North America and began to hold conferences outside of Oklahoma and deal directly with broader issues, the Yanktons began to participate. Under the initiative of Louie Stricker they became part of the larger group. Several of the conferences were held in South Dakota; and Clarence Rockboy, a Yankton Peyotist, served as an officer in the international organization. In 1976 Yankton roadman Neulan Dion became president of the Native American Church of South Dakota.

In addition to the Peyote community on the reservation, there was a Yankton Peyote community in the city of Yankton. As mentioned earlier, many Yanktons left the reservation in the 1950s. They did not particularly enjoy life in the city; but being part of a local Peyote community helped, and they could easily travel back and forth to the reservation. In Wesley Hurt's research in Yankton, he collected the names and ages of children in school as well as the ages and education of the adults. He also conducted in-depth interviews with fifty individuals; six were members of the Yankton Peyote community. At one time or another in the 1950s and 1960s some members of the following Peyote families lived in the city of Yankton: Bruguier, Dion, Dog Soldier, Dragg, Kezena, Necklace, Primeaux, Rainbow, Rockboy, Shields, Sitting Crow, and Sully. There was a regular exodus of the Peyotists to the reservation to attend the monthly Peyote service at the church in Greenwood. Rail service no longer was available, but some people now had cars.

They would pile as many people into a car as possible for the 75-mile trip. Some of those interviewed mentioned that Melvin Bruguier, a roadman, was the local Peyote leader in Yankton. Emma and Nelson Dragg, longtime Peyote people, were interviewed, though they said little about the Native American Church. The interviewer wrote: "Stricker is a priest, John Claire is leader, Dragg is a helper of Melvin Bruguier, a leader."[29]

Daniel Dion, from the White Swan community, was also interviewed. He said when he was young he was a drinker and a gambler. He developed arthritis in one hand, affecting normal usage. He went to medical doctors, but they could do nothing to help him. In 1952 Dion began attending Peyote meetings; eventually, after taking the "sacred herb," his arthritis disappeared, and he regained normal usage of his hand. He remained with the church, eventually becoming a roadman. He told the interviewer that he was in the city of Yankton working while his wife and eight children were living on the reservation. Dion added that he could not support them if he remained at home. The best he could do was $5 a day working for white farmers, but off the reservation he had a good job in an alfalfa mill. Daniel Dion was one of many in the Dion family who became active in the Native American Church. Others, including his son Lorenzo Dion, Sr., Lorenzo Dion, Jr., and Neulan Dion, Sr., became roadmen; and Neulan Dion, Jr., in addition to being a roadman, is a well-known singer. A younger member of the Dion family, Shane Paterson, is a Peyotist and a follower of the Yankton traditional religion. He runs Peyote meetings, conducts Sweat Lodge ceremonies, and is a Sun Dance chief.[30]

During the interview Dan Dion described some elements of Peyotism. Of all the interviews, he was the only one to do so. He said that the "church had four principles: Baptism, Marriage, Confirmation, Forgiveness of Sin." He made a drawing of his fireplace (altar) on the interviewer's notes. It was horseshoe shaped, with a cross and a heart inside. Dion said that the former represents salvation and the latter, love. It was a Cross Fire–style fireplace, but he called it a "New Way" fireplace. Dion concluded with the comment that since joining the church he has not returned to drinking.[31]

The Dions and the other Peyote families in Yankton lived in the same neighborhood on the east side and socialized with each other. In the interviews several people said that they did not face any exclusion or hostility from other Native Americans but that their socializing with each other was an extension of reservation patterns, having common spiritual interests and kinship ties. It was the same with the young people, who "hung out" together. Leonard Bruguier, who lived many years in Yankton and graduated from Yankton High School, remembers many times after school when the guys would gather in someone's home, tie a drum, and practice Peyote songs. He also mentioned that some Peyote people also belonged to Christian denominations, as noted earlier. He said that on weekends when people did not attend a Peyote meeting it was not unusual for them to attend either an Episcopal or Catholic church. In the case of his immediate family, it was the Episcopal church.[32]

In 1961 Lloyd Bach, a graduate student at the University of South Dakota, wrote a master's thesis on Peyotism. Part of his research included attending a Yankton Peyote meeting and interviewing as many members as possible. The purpose of the research was to analyze speech and auditory changes during a Peyote meeting. It was conducted under the auspices of the Speech and Hearing Clinic at USD; however, it was anthropologist Dr. Robert Hall, director of the Institute of American Indian Studies, who introduced Bach to the Peyote community. The personal data he collected and the interviews he recorded provide a cross section of a group of Peyotists at a given time. Bach prepared a questionnaire. He was interested in why each individual was a member of the Peyote faith. Bach attended a Cross Fire meeting in the church in Greenwood on 15 April 1961 and interviewed thirty people; he identified them by initials only but included their age, education, and occupation. All thirty were male; twenty were Yanktons, two Winnebagos, three Santees, two Omahas, and three Oglala Lakotas. The average age was 38.5; the youngest was 24, the oldest 65. The average school completion was tenth grade, but the group included four college students, four in trade schools, and two who had no schooling. It was evenly divided between those who went to public schools and those who went to BIA schools. In listing their occupation, nine said farm workers; two, construction workers; three, laborers; one, truck driver; one, store clerk; two, unemployed; and eight, students. All thirty were members of the Native American Church; 10.8 years was the average length of adult membership, with a range from 3 to 30 years. Bach also pointed out that the Peyote service was conducted in the Dakota language.

The individual reasons for being members varied, including family connections, such as "my folks were members." Several said that Peyotism is "all Indian" or the "real Indian religion," but most cited the healing power of

Peyote, particularly as a cure for alcoholism. One Omaha in attendance said that "it suits the Indian's religious traditions best." In order to gain a better understanding of the Yankton Peyotists, it is instructive to read the verbatim answers they gave as to why they participated in the Native American Church:

- At first my brother talked me into going, then I went because it made me feel so good, inside and out.
- My little girl was sick and my cousin told me the peyote would help her. I took her to a meeting and they prayed for her. They gave me peyote to eat and to pray with. The Road Chief took her and held her up before the Peyote Father. They gave her peyote tea to drink. She started to look and act better right away and she soon was well again.
- I took part to help solve my problem. I drank too much and would get into fights and trouble.
- I was going to a white man's church here—in Greenwood. There was a lot I didn't understand. A lot of fussing around. Then this started up. Someone brought in peyote again and more of us went to those meetings. They were all Indian. We got along good and get good help from God so I keep going.
- My son got this peyote from his friends. He eats some and goes to the meetings. He wants me to go. No one can tell me what is right before, but peyote can and so I keep going—to get help, to know about God and Peyote Spirit.
- He [my father] couldn't understand the value of some of the doings in the white man's churches. He heard about the new religion called peyote. . . . God gave us peyote and we should make good use of it.
- This is the one true Indian Religion. We stick together and want to keep it. We haven't much else left of our old ways. The white men who are against peyote try to stop us. They can't prove anything is wrong and us Indians get so much help from it.
- My mother was very sick—the doctors couldn't help her. These friends came and wanted to do something for her. They wanted to give her peyote. She tried it. The first time she got better. They took her to more meetings. Pretty soon she could walk. I thought that looked good so I tried it myself. I use it mostly for sickness.
- I was drunk and no one could make me stop. All I made went into drink and my family had it bad. Then another fellow told me to take peyote and

to come to the meetings. He got help so I thought I would try it once. The peyote helps make you think different. The others pray and talk and all help each other. So now I go to all the meetings. I can work and not drink.

- I have a family and I think they should have some religion. This is the only truly Indian Religion. We are Christian as much as anybody. Jesus Christ is in the Spirit of Peyote. We worship Him and He helps us to do right. God is the Great Spirit and takes care of us if we believe in Him.

- I have been sick for a long time. The doctors didn't seem to get any place and besides it was too expensive. I had some friends that used peyote. They kept after me to come to a meeting so I went to please them. They gave me a lot of peyote to eat and I was very sick in the stomach. They prayed and talked. This sickness kept getting worse until pretty soon it all came up. Then I felt better. The spiritual part of the ceremony taught me how to live and the peyote is helping my health.

- Good Indian religion. Help when sick.

- I started because my mother wanted me to. It helped my folks when they were sick and didn't have anything to eat. The members of the Church brought them peyote and food. Peyote makes people have brotherly love like that. Then I went to other churches but I liked this one best. Indians work together to help each other. I think peyote was sent to us by God, so we should use it.

- Because it is the true Indian Religion and the white man should not try to take it away. The white men fight and get drunk when they come out of their church. Indians pray and help each other. The Peyote Spirit given to us to help us. God sent it and poor Indians need help.

- It is the true religion of the Indian. The power from peyote has spiritual effects. We get help in sickness from this green herb given to us by God. It does for us what the wine and bread does for the white men.

- It is the way I worship the Great Spirit God. When I am sick it is the best medicine.

- Drink was getting the best of me and I couldn't keep a job. A fellow that had tried peyote told me to try it.

- It helped me when I was sick. God gave the Indians peyote so they should use it and be thankful.

- It is our religion. We are members of the Native American Church. Peyote has been a big help to the Indians when everything else changed. They find happiness in the meetings helping each other and praying for help through the Spirit of Peyote.

- It is a way of life. It is the best religion that the Indians have.[33]

Bach's introduction to the Yankton Peyote community by Dr. Hall was not an isolated occurrence. It was part of an effort by the Institute of American Indian Studies to study and support the Native American Church. The institute, established in 1955, is dedicated to the preservation, study, and teaching of American Indian culture. It established the South Dakota Oral History Center, now one of the largest oral history collections in the United States. The collection includes the American Indian Research Project (AIRP), which contains over 1,900 interviews. In 1958 the institute entered the debate on Peyotism. Director William Cape wrote to the dean of the School Medicine at USD and suggested a study of the effect of Peyote on the individual.[34] This was followed up by an invitation to Dr. F. E. Kelsey of the Department of Physiology and Pharmacology to undertake the study. The research was published in the *South Dakota Journal of Medicine and Pharmacy*. It concluded that Peyote was not a narcotic and that "there is not evidence of drug tolerance or withdrawal symptoms characteristic of true narcotics."[35] The institute produced 3,000 reprints of the article and distributed them free of charge. When the supply was exhausted, it produced several hundred mimeographed copies.[36] The institute began publishing its *News Report* in 1959. It disseminated information on the institute's activities as well as the activities of South Dakota's Indian population, including the Native American Church. That was the beginning of a long relationship between the institute and the Native American Church, particularly the Yankton Peyote community. This included Professor Herbert Hoover, who was a personal friend of roadman Joe Rockboy and a longtime supporter of the Peyote religion. The present director of the institute, Leonard Bruguier, is a Yankton Sioux and a lifelong member of the Native American Church.

The institute's interest in Peyotism coincided with the attempt by the Peyote community to have the South Dakota legislature rescind the 1923 law prohibiting the use, possession, or transportation of Peyote. The institute and the Yankton Native American Church worked together to change the law. In 1959 a group of Yanktons sent the South Dakota legislature a copy of a bill to decriminalize the sacramental use of Peyote. The state was not enforcing the 1923 law; yet it could begin to do so, since Peyote was defined as an illegal drug. This meant working in coordination with all the South Dakota Peyote groups. In 1960 there were fifteen Peyote communities in South Dakota. Part of their strategy to become effective in lobbying the state legislature was to strengthen themselves by joining the national Peyote group. At a special meeting in 1959 the Native American Church of South Dakota passed a resolution, proclaiming its affiliation with the Native American Church of North America. The resolution, which stated that "it now becomes necessary to form ourselves into a more united organization for religious freedom," was notarized and filed with the secretary of state.[37]

In June 1960 the Native American Church of South Dakota held its Thirty-eighth Annual Convention on the Yankton Reservation. The main topic at the business meeting was coordinating efforts to change the 1923 statute. The institute's director, Dr. Hall, was in attendance, as was state senator J. E. Lehman.[38] Both men spoke at the business meeting about lobbying strategies. Frank Takes Gun, president of the Native American Church of North America, was also in attendance.[39] Following the convention Dr. Hall worked with Yankton Peyotist Francis V. Weston in developing information for the lobbying effort. Weston was designated to represent the Native American Church of South Dakota as a liaison to the state legislature. Dr. Hall was very proactive in his support. He sent Weston all the information he could find showing that Peyote was not harmful. Hall asked Weston to supply him with 1,000 Peyote buttons so he could give some to the University of South Dakota's medical school and send some to the National Institute of Health in Washington, D.C.[40] Hall also sent a lengthy letter to the state Legislative Research Council, supporting the Peyotists' viewpoint and arguing that the legal protection for the sacramental use of Peyote is long overdue.[41]

As a result of these activities the Yankton Peyotists became much more active in the statewide organization. At the Fortieth Annual Convention, Clarence Rockboy was elected secretary and Melvin Bruguier was elected as a trustee. They also continued to lobby the state legislature.[42] The lobbying efforts, however, made little headway until national events put the issue of Peyote back in the news. In December 1963 there was another attempt to pass federal legislation to regulate Peyote as a narcotic. House Bill 1488 was introduced, but immediate opposition arose; and by mid-1964 the bill was dead. In its continuing activist role the Institute of American Indian Studies lobbied against HB 1488. It sent letters of opposition to South Dakota's two senators, George McGovern and Karl Mundt, and House representative E. Y.

Berry.[43] In the same year the California Supreme Court in the *Woody* case gave legal protection to the sacramental use of Peyote. These events contributed to the revival of the Peyote issue in the state legislature. In 1968 the earlier statures prohibiting Peyote were repealed, effectively decriminalizing the use and possession of Peyote by members of the Native American Church. Like other states, South Dakota maintained its prohibition of Peyote usage by non–Native Americans.

While the Peyote community was struggling with the state of South Dakota, the larger Yankton community was again discussing an issue that had been unsettled since the 1930s: a constitution and a governing body. The Yanktons still had the constitution of 1932 (which had been ratified by the BIA) but did not have a recognized governing body, because they had not organized under the Indian Reorganization Act. In the late 1950s discussions were initiated on establishing a governing body. The debate was provoked by the continuing poor conditions on the reservation, particularly the substandard housing. The Yanktons also believed that as a subagency they were a "stepchild" to the Rosebud Agency and did not get equal treatment by BIA officials. Many believed that the tribe had lost rights and federal aid by not being organized under an IRA constitution.

In 1958 a meeting was held in Wagner. The Yankton voters who were present elected an ad hoc tribal council, with William O'Connor serving as chair. The first issue was whether they should adopt a new constitution or amend the 1932 constitution. In 1961 a constitutional committee was elected to draft a new constitution; but after consulting with attorneys they decided to amend the 1932 constitution. In July 1962 the Yanktons in general council adopted the amended constitution; and in April 1963, after making several changes, the BIA approved it. The following September the Yanktons held an election for a nine-member governing committee. Percy Archambeau was elected chair.[44] The official name of the governing body is the Yankton Sioux Tribal Business and Claims Committee. Membership in the tribe, or the "Living Yankton Sioux Indian Tribal Roll" as it was called, required an individual to have "one-quarter degree Yankton Sioux blood" and not be enrolled elsewhere. The amended constitution was not strong. Tribal funds were under BIA control, and all contracts required BIA approval; there was no real local judicial power. One section, crucial to many Yanktons, was the guarantee that any land belonging to a member of the tribe, as either allotted land or inherited land, would remain under control of the owner. The Yanktons are still governed by this constitution today.[45]

The adoption of the 1963 constitution occurred at the beginning of a major period of change for the Native American population. As a result of American Indian protests and the changing political and cultural climate of the 1960s, the policy of self-determination replaced relocation and termination. The first significant protest was at the American Indian Chicago Conference in 1961. The almost five hundred delegates in attendance produced a "Declaration of Indian Purpose" demanding an end to termination. The Chicago conference was followed by the establishment of the National Indian Youth Council, an activist group committed to advancing self-determination by insisting that American Indians should be a part of the policy-making process. President John F. Kennedy and the Secretary of the Interior Stewart Udall slowed the termination programs of the Eisenhower administration and established economic development as their primary goal, but they did not reject termination as a policy. President Lyndon Johnson, with Udall continuing as secretary of the interior, expanded economic development programs for the reservations with the help of the Economic Opportunity Act (1964) and the War on Poverty. This was the first time that a significant amount of federal funds flowed to the reservations. It was also Johnson and Udall who finally repudiated the termination policy. Under Presidents Johnson, Richard Nixon, Gerald Ford, and Jimmy Carter, self-determination meant continuing the trust relationship between the federal government and tribal governments but transferring the control of some federal programs to reservation governments.

The movement toward self-determination was supported by Senators Edward (Ted) Kennedy and Robert F. Kennedy, who said the conditions on the reservations are a "national tragedy." The Senate subcommittee's report "Indian Education: A National Tragedy" endorsed self-determination and helped awaken the nation to the plight of American Indians. The title of *Time* magazine's cover story on 9 February 1970 reflected the changing climate: "The American Indian: Goodbye to Tonto." The inside story depicted the attitudes of "The Angry American Indian."

More important, however, were the thousands of American Indians from all across the country who were committed to making self-determination and sovereignty a reality. They organized, protested, and marched; they risked their lives so that the lives of others might improve. They protested against BIA policies, uncooperative and restrictive state governments, harassment by city police departments, and conservative tribal leadership on some reservations. The cutting edge of American Indian activism was the American Indian Movement, founded in Minneapolis/St. Paul in 1968, in order to protest the harassment and brutality by the police against local Indians. Living in Minneapolis at the time was Sam and Mary's grandson Asa; he and Leonard Crow Dog became spiritual advisors to AIM in its early days. Protests and struggles emerged across the nation, including the occupation of Alcatraz Island (1969–71), the Trail of Broken Treaties march on Washington (1972), and the occupation of Wounded Knee (1973). The intensity of the protests and the support they received from segments of the American public helped convince Congress to agree to the transfer of control of some federal programs to reservation governments. In the 1970s AIM focused on pressuring the government to honor treaties and to recognize the sovereign rights of reservation governments. The key element was the participation of American Indians throughout the process of planning, decision-making, developing, and controlling reservation governance.[46]

Out of the movement for self-determination emerged the American Indian cultural renaissance—or, to put in it another way, the renaissance was the cultural component of self-determination. Native American communities from coast to coast participated in this cultural revival. AIM was the most outspoken group supporting traditional cultural and spiritual practices and traditional leadership. The explosion of the cultural renaissance showed that in spite of years of assimilation policies there was still a strong sense of identity in American Indian communities. The renaissance included all the arts: fiction, poetry, painting, sculpture, music, dance, and drama. It is especially significant that the renaissance included a revival of traditional arts and crafts, such as basket making, pottery, sand painting, beadwork, porcupine quillwork, wood carving (flutes, totem poles, masks), drum making, leather work, spinning and weaving textiles, feather work, jewelry, and stonework (pipe bowls, Inuit sculpture).

The most public expression of the cultural renaissance was the powwow. These gatherings had not disappeared during the era of assimilation; but they were infrequent until the late 1960s, when American Indian communities, from the remotest rural reservation to major urban areas, began to sponsor them. By the mid-1990s there were almost a thousand powwows a year across the country. They brought people together to socialize, to celebrate, to share, to drum, to sing, and to dance; they also included prayers, honoring ceremonies, and giveaways. This amazing phenomenon demonstrated that decades of cultural repression had not destroyed the roots of American Indian cultures. The powwows are also a reflection of the flowering of the arts. In addition to the drumming, singing, and dancing, there is the beauty of the dancer's regalia. Each person's attire is distinct, either made by the dancer or handed down from generation to generation: elaborate feather work for bustles, roaches (head pieces), and fans; leatherwork for moccasins, leggings, vests, and dresses; and sewing for ribbon shirts and dresses. With the addition of appliqués, bells, jingles, and beadwork, the powwow regalia is a striking example of the creative power of the cultural renaissance. Historians may look back and identify the powwow as the defining symbol of late twentieth century Native America.

As mentioned above, the cultural renaissance had a significant impact on all areas of American Indian life, including the Native American Church. One result was spreading knowledge of the Peyote religion to the American public; another was the impact of the explosion of the arts on Peyote art. The public's increasing awareness of Peyotism was not a favorable development, as the youth culture of America—hippies, yippies, and flower children—learned about the hallucinogenic properties of Peyote. This caused intense concern within the Peyote community: many young people sought access to Peyote and began trespassing on the Peyote gardens in Texas or trying to buy it from a variety of sources. State and federal agencies became concerned and began to revisit the Peyote issue. In 1966 Peyote was added to the Drug Abuse Control Act as a controlled substance, although an exemption was made for its use by American Indians in spiritual ceremonies. In 1967 the Texas legislature made possession of Peyote illegal. Since Texas was the only area where a significant number of the cacti grew in the United States, this caused an outcry from the Peyote community. Texas repealed the blanket prohibition in 1969 and allowed for use of Peyote by American Indians, requiring individuals to be at least one-quarter Indian and have proof of membership in the Native American Church.[47]

The interest of American youth in Peyote goes back to the early 1950s, when members of the Beat Generation, so-called Beatniks such as Jack Kerouac, Allen Ginsberg, and William Burroughs, began experimenting with Peyote. All three had spent time in Mexico, where they had easy access to Peyote. What gave Peyote its notoriety in the 1950s was the publication of Aldous

Huxley's *The Doors of Perception* (1954). Huxley was already a cult hero to the Beats for his *Brave New World* (1946). The Beat Generation greeted his new book with great enthusiasm. Huxley reported on his experiments with Peyote and tried to convince his readers that Peyote could open the doors of human consciousness and prepare the way to reach a mystical state. More and more of the Beat group began seeking out this cactus. Ginsberg claimed that he wrote poetry after eating Peyote. This small group of writers popularized Peyote to others of their generation. For example, in Ginsberg's famous poem "Howl" (1956), he mentions Peyote. This poem was recited at poetry readings across the country.[48] In 1959 a long poem/essay by Jack Green entitled "Peyote" appeared in a local New York City publication called *the newspaper*. It began by saying that "peyote is one of the most beautiful things that ever happened to me." The following year it received a wide readership when it was reprinted in a Beat anthology. In 1962 William Burroughs included his Peyote experience in *Naked Lunch*.[49]

Members of the Beat Generation were certainly familiar with Peyote, but they were a small subculture with limited influence on the wider American youth culture. This would change in the mid-1960s, when the emerging counterculture turned to the Beat writers, especially Kerouac and Ginsberg, for inspiration. The significance of the Beat Generation in this context is that their writings helped introduce youth of the 1960s to hallucinogenic drugs in general and to Peyote in particular, with its active ingredient mescaline.

Counterculture youth began reading Huxley's *Doors of Perception* when the rock group the Doors made it known that their name came from Huxley's book. As the counterculture became cognizant of Peyote, this became an issue for state and federal authorities and a crisis for members of the Peyote community, who feared another attempt to outlaw their sacrament. The growing knowledge of Peyote also created other problems. One was the concern about the supply of Peyote. It was not widely available, because its growth area was limited and the Mexican government prohibited its export. The future of peyote cacti was a concern as more and more people sought Peyote buttons. A second concern that emerged at this time was whether non-Indians should be allowed to participate in Peyote services and partake of the holy sacrament. There is a very definite split between those who believe that Peyote is a gift from God to American Indians for their exclusive use and those who believe it is a gift from God to American Indians but to be shared with all humanity. The debate over this contentious issue continues today. By the end of the 1960s federal policy allowed for the religious use of Peyote by Native Americans; and most states had a similar exemption. Nevertheless members of the Peyote community were very uneasy, always fearful that governmental policies could change and restrictions might be placed on their spiritual practices.

The political activism, the powwows, and the cultural renaissance were accompanied by a similar revival of American Indian spiritual ceremonies. Traditional religion had declined but had not disappeared. As on the Yankton Reservation, it had gone underground. In the late 1960s it emerged into the open. Prior to this time there were few visible signs of Yankton traditional religion. One did not see any Sweat Lodges; nor were there any publicly announced Sun Dances. If someone prayed with a Sacred Pipe, it was kept a secret within the family. This was due in part to fear of condemnation; in addition, many Yanktons were members of Christian denominations and had little interest in traditional religion. There were no openly acknowledged medicine men or women. If someone desired traditional healing as in a Yuwipi ceremony, a healer had to be brought in from elsewhere. Several decades later this has changed. There are many Sweat Lodges on the reservation; Sun Dances are held every summer; people go out fasting; there is traditional healing; and many pipe carriers try to live their lives honoring the Sacred Pipe.

The revival of traditional spirituality in terms of both beliefs and practices has two origins. It was partially a response to the external influences of the cultural renaissance of the 1960s. The activism that permeated the movement toward self-determination led many to conclude that the heart of an American Indian revival was its spiritual heritage. Many young people became more involved as part of a concerted effort consciously to reject decades of assimilation. Many of the sun dancers and participants in other ceremonies were members of the younger generation. A chapter of AIM was established on the Yankton Reservation in 1971; and some of the Native American Church people became members. Neulan Dion was the chairperson of the local chapter, and Asa Primeaux served as a spokesperson for AIM, explaining its principles and goals and trying to get support from the Yankton people. AIM promoted the Yankton traditional religion and the Native American Church. To some people, AIM was threatening. The superintendent of the Yankton Agency, Charles Smith, wrote a column in the *Sioux Messenger*, condemning AIM.[50] In 1972 AIM sponsored a powwow, inviting all Yanktons to attend. It included a special drum night to teach traditional songs to young people.[51] AIM, with activists such as Leonard Crow Dog (who was frequently on the Yankton Reservation), was calling for a revival of traditional American Indian spirituality.

The second source for the cultural revival on the Yankton reservation was internal. Traditional spirituality had never died. Some families, especially the full-bloods in rural areas, continued traditional spiritual practices. Other families did not engage in traditional religion but had memories of parents, grandparents, or relatives who did. Some elements of an earlier era continued above ground, such as kinship terminology, the making of relatives (*hunka dowanpi*), giveaways, naming ceremonies, and patterns of mourning. There were occasional local powwows, and some Yanktons traveled to other reservations for powwows and ceremonies. Those families with a recent heritage of traditional religion now felt comfortable practicing their beliefs openly as a matter of pride. They felt no need for secrecy, because there was little chance of ridicule and no opposition from federal authorities. Some Yanktons did not choose to participate in the religious revival. Some who saw themselves as devout Christians did not take part; others saw it as radical in conjunction with AIM and threatening to the political status quo.

The revival of Yankton traditional spiritual practices created a dilemma for the members of the Native American Church. It was the first significant doctrinal struggle since the early debates on the role of Christianity in Peyotism. Peyotists saw themselves as having a "traditional" religion but not necessarily with the specifics involved in the Seven Sacred Rites of the Sioux. Many Peyotists, especially the Cross Fire group, also called themselves Christians. A split ensued as the Yankton traditional religion expanded and some Peyotists were drawn to its ceremonies. With the revival of the use of the Sacred Pipe, the question arose as to whether a Sacred Pipe could be brought into a Peyote service as well as the larger issue: could a Peyotist also be a believer in the Sacred Pipe? There were two camps on this issue. The Half Moon group claimed there was no conflict: an individual could do both, because they were complementary, two ways to the same spirit. The Cross Fire group, with some exceptions, argued that the two spiritualities together would create conflict and should not function side by side.

Emerson Spider, Sr. (Oglala), the head priest of the Native American Church of South Dakota, clearly articulates the Cross Fire perspective: "[A]s we came along, we put the peace pipe away and in place of it we now use the Bible."[52] The differences in viewpoint reflect the degree of Christian elements in Peyotism. The debate, however, is within the framework of the basic theological premise of Peyotism: the primacy of Peyote as the Holy Sacrament from which all knowledge emanates. The debate was contained within this context. For example, Emerson Spider said that it is through Peyote that "we would find Christ" and that his grandfather, his father, and he himself had found Christ through Peyote.[53] Conversely, the revival of Yankton traditional religion gave support to those Peyotists who wanted to reduce or eliminate Christian elements in the Peyote ceremony. Some Cross Fire people began practicing the Half Moon way, particularly the Primeaux/Necklace family, led by Asa Primeaux. This meant discontinuing the use of the Bible in Peyote meetings and reintroducing tobacco as a sacred substance to be used in prayer.[54] The Cross Fire way, however, continued to be the predominant style of worship on the Yankton Reservation.

Several of the Yankton Peyotists became pipe carriers and active participants in traditional spiritual practices. The earliest were Joe Rockboy and Adam Sitting Crow, Neulan Dion, Sr., and Asa Primeaux. Their wives, Nancy War Rockboy, Germaine Sitting Crow, and Loretta Rainbow Primeaux, were active partners in sharing traditional religious practices and the Native American Church. Germaine Sitting Crow, for example, an active member of the Native American Church since the late 1940s, was also a sun dancer. These women, and others, were a major force in transmitting spiritual values from one generation to the next. They saw no conflict, only reinforcement, incorporating the Sweat Lodge, the Sun Dance, and the Sacred Pipe into their cosmology. They believed it was fully compatible with Peyotism in general and the Half Moon specifically. It was also not a coincidence that those whose spirituality included Peyote and the Pipe were almost all fluent in Dakota, having grown up in traditional-style families.[55]

The two spiritualities were not integrated (that is, combining elements from both to create something new). They were practiced side by side, at different times, in different circumstances. For example, starting in 1990, the Primeaux family sponsored a Sun Dance at their home, called Rainbow Paradise after Loretta Primeaux's maiden name, Rainbow. This is part of a two-week "spiritual conference." It is a period of extensive spiritual activities that begins with four days of Sweat Lodge ceremonies, Vision Quests, naming ceremonies, pipe ceremonies, and purification of the sun dancers. It also includes getting ready for the Sun Dance by preparing the arbor, building Sweat Lodges for the sun dancers, and getting wood and rocks for the sweat ceremonies and the sacred fire. On several occasions a Peyote meeting was held following the Sun Dance. Some of the sun dancers attended the Peyote meeting, while Peyotists who did not attend the Sun Dance came for the Peyote service. The ceremony and ritual of the Sun Dance and the Peyote meeting were not integrated but coexisted, functioning side by side in one extended family during this period of spiritual activities.[56]

The Yanktons who practiced both spiritualities also had support from outside the reservation, particularly from the Rosebud Reservation, where the traditional groups had always been stronger. The most important were Leonard Crow Dog and before him his father, Henry. Both were traditional medicine men as well as roadmen in the Native American Church and were well known to the Yanktons. Crow Dog is a very strong supporter of both spiritualities. He said: "I see nothing wrong with holding on to my Lakota beliefs, while at the same time, I also practice the peyote way."[57] Another source of support was Charles Kills Enemy, (Yankton/Sičangu Lakota) from Rosebud. He was active in both spiritualities and saw them as fully compatible.

An example that reflects the relationship between Sacred Pipe and Peyote and ties it to the cultural renaissance and the activism of AIM is from a 1972 radio program at the University of South Dakota called *Radio Oyate.* It was a panel discussion that included Leonard Crow Dog, Neulan Dion, Asa Primeaux, and Adam Sitting Crow. All were pipe carriers as well as members of the Native American Church, and three were active members of AIM. They argued that traditional religion and Peyotism combined with political activism were necessary for the continuing development of American Indian culture and the revival of traditional spirituality. This would create the unity that was necessary to succeed in the struggle against the federal government, with its long history of broken promises. All four panelists expressed strong support for AIM. The radio program ended with a selection of Peyote music.[58] This panel discussion is an excellent barometer of the attitudes of those who saw traditional American Indian religions and the Peyote religion as part of the same spiritual heritage.

Individuals such as Adam Sitting Crow, Joe Rockboy, and Charles Kills Enemy were very significant in bringing traditional spiritual practices out into the open, setting examples for others to follow. Professor Hoover has said of these men: "They resurfaced with something that was strictly nineteenth century."[59] Hoover witnessed some of these changes in the late 1960s and early 1970s. He was a personal friend of Joe Rockboy and Charles Kills

Enemy, who both asked if they could run spiritual ceremonies on his land outside of Vermillion. Hoover has retold these experiences as a participant in the events: "I have two churches [on my land]. I have a Sweat [Lodge] that is active, run by Charles Kills Enemy, and I have a Peyote fireplace belonging to Joe Rockboy. I always played that role as a host and as a sponsor."[60] Hoover and Rockboy spent considerable time together. Rockboy shared his opinions about who was really knowledgeable and whom he respected in the Peyote community. He mentioned Joe Shields, "a man who descends from Samuel B. Necklace as the priest of this congregation." We trusted him as the Catholics trust the pope, he added. Others that he respected for their depth of knowledge about the spiritual ways of the Native American Church were Quentin Bruguier, Asa Primeaux, Neulan Dion, Sr., and Clarence Rockboy (his son).[61]

Sam's grandson Asa followed the path taken by Joe Rockboy in practicing the ways of the Sacred Pipe and the Native American Church. As described throughout this study, the Necklace/Primeaux *tiošpaye* was totally committed to Peyotism. In the early 1970s, however, Asa began moving himself and his family toward the Yankton traditional religion. In 1970 he returned from Minneapolis to the reservation, where he and his wife, Loretta, eventually moved out onto the land of the Rainbow family. Through his in-laws, the Rainbows, he began attending "sweats" and went fasting. He recalls his first experience. "In 1972 I went fasting right out here; that man, my grandpa [kinship term], Steve Poorman brought this man, this man is going to pray for you, so he prayed. His name is Alfred Stands. He took the pipe that I was going fasting with and he prayed. So they got it ready for me. They left me out here, so after it got dark, all these things happen right here." Asa built a Sweat Lodge in the back of his home and began the process of acquiring spiritual knowledge. He spent the next seven years learning. Either Poorman or Stands would run "sweats" for him. Asa said, "He'll start the fire and get the sweat ready and then he conducts it, all them years, that's all I used it for, I never sat down to run it until 1979. I went to Crow Dog [Henry, father of Leonard Crow Dog], the old man says go ahead. That's when I started running sweats." He adds:

That's how I got started. I couldn't run sweats for seven years, until I knew all the songs, all that; each year I went fasting, for songs and all that prayer. Here in 1979 I went to sleep, a man came to me. He said I'm your grandfather, he said, my name is spider man, Iktomi. He said now it's time for you to go ahead, run sweats, he said. So I woke up, I told my wife. We got ready and drove over to Henry's [Crow Dog's], and I told him. Good, he said. He took the pipe that I took and he smoked it and he said we're going to have a sweat here for you, he said. I stayed there all day; that evening they run me two sweats. He said go on, so I come back and I've been running sweats from that time until now.

Asa also discussed how his sixteen months in the Korean War played a role in his spiritual development. He said that during the seven years he did not touch the wood or rocks or build a sweat fire. He added:

> I wasn't capable, I wasn't eligible to touch wood because I figure, I took myself as a sinner. I went to Korea and I killed them Koreans over there with a gun. I shot them. I got blood on me. . . . They trained me to kill, so I done that, I was an assistant machine gunner. I know I shot a lot of them so I have to go through all this, seven years. Keep forgiving, forgive, forgive, forgive, that's what the spirit was saying. Here this dream comes in for me to run the sweats.

Since that time, he said, "I follow the traditional ways, you call the red road. During that time I learned many things. I went fasting right here, right where I live now. I fasted for a vision, you call Vision Quest, and that very first experience that I had I learned the sounds of the spirits, and then I understood." Asa went on to describe his first vision experience:

> So through what I experienced, they showed me some colors. Here after they showed me a way you call it, the spider altar, in there they shown me seven colors, that's red, white, blue, green, yellow, black, polka dot, and in there there's red, red represents the west, they say our red men, these things that I talked about the ghosts, the spirits, they call them day-walkers. You can't see them, you can't hear them, but from the time daylight comes until the sun goes down toward the west, so the red represents the west, along with the grandfathers [spirits] because they went that way. They can turn around and come back with a storm, say a rainstorm or a tornado and lightning and thunder. And the white represents north. You see there's a grandfather over there he's got white hair, he's dressed in white all the time and they say his four seasons of the year spring, summer, fall, winter. At wintertime, this grandfather can take care of us, so that he can have pity for our children, grandchildren, that's grandpa winter, they call him, it's white, white repre-

sents north. And then we have blue and that represents the sky. When you look up you see blue, and that's where the grandfathers are, the flying creatures are up there, so you pray to them. And they also got green and the green represents mother earth. Say within the four seasons, the spring, mother earth makes everything green, it all comes from mother earth, so green represents mother earth. And then we have yellow. We have yellow that represents the east. Say in the morning you get up real early you see an eagle flying east, in between the dawn and the sunrise, in between these, there is always yellow vision they see over east, so yellow represents the east, it represents the eagles. Then we have black, black represents the south, that's where the warm air comes from. Our grandfathers, our grandsisters, they say they come from the south spiritually and when we call them they also bring warm air, they bring everything warm from the south and black represents our grandfathers, grandmothers, the relatives, so black represents that. And then the polka dot, black with white dots, polka dots, that represents the spider people, the spider clan. The spider was here at the beginning of creation ever since the human being, the red man was created, the spider people were created also. So that's why the black material with polka dots, that represents the spider people. So these are things that I know, I learned it through my own fasting. So that's what he wanted to know and then in there where I make my altar, I put some sand down and I make a circle, inside the circle I mark four directions. It's a medicine wheel. In there are some markings that go there, there's a circle, a star, a lightning mark, and also a turtle, [it] represents the people of knowledge and wisdom. So these things are there in that altar, around that altar are ninety-one tobacco ties. Fifty red, twenty-five black, sixteen polka dot. So that's the way I pray with the pipe. That's one of the things I've learned on my own.[62]

For some the combination of traditional ceremonies and Peyotism was troubling. Certain Yanktons who were totally committed to Peyotism believed one should not mix spiritualities. Others took a more ecumenical approach and believed Yankton traditional religion and Peyotism were compatible and that both were part of their spiritual heritage. Kills Enemy, a traditional Sioux holy man, was also a devout Catholic and a supporter of the Native American Church. Hoover tells a great story about him. They were driving in his truck in Vermillion when they pulled behind a car with a bumper sticker showing a hand with the index finger pointing upward. It was a religious message indicating that there was only one way to God and that was through

Jesus Christ. Kills Enemy began to laugh. Hoover wondered what he was laughing at. When he looked over, Kills Enemy was holding up three fingers, obviously meaning that there were three ways to God: Christianity, the Sacred Pipe, and Peyote.[63]

The cultural renaissance stimulated both an explosion of the arts and a revival of traditional religion. This was a nationwide phenomenon, but on the Sioux reservations it was particularly pronounced, as a greater and greater number of people participated in the revival of traditional religion. This religious revival corresponded with the revival of the arts, which can be explained by the nature of American Indian art and spirituality. The two are integrated. They function together inside the cosmological framework of American Indian societies. This is especially true of Peyote art; it is religious art, created exclusively by members of the Peyote community, produced for ceremonial usage and inspired by spiritual experiences. It is not made to be collected, displayed, or sold, although it may be made to be given as a gift. This art is to be used in a spiritual setting. When it is not in use, it is stored away; when it is no longer useful or is worn out, it is discarded. One rarely sees Peyote paraphernalia on display in the home of a Peyote family. The term "Peyote religious art," the title of a recent book, is redundant, because Peyote art is inherently religious. This is not meant as a criticism; it is a way to make the point that all Peyote art is religious. Religion and art are inseparably intertwined in Peyote theology. Although there is Peyote art that is not used in Peyote meetings, it is still religious in nature. Since earlier in the century, various Native American Church artists have produced paintings and drawings that express spiritual values and use Peyote symbolism. The same is true with Peyote-inspired jewelry; it may be worn to a Peyote meeting, but it can also be worn as an everyday item.

Daniel Swan points out that Peyote art is a distinct genre of American Indian art.[64] It is historically and stylistically unique and encompasses a wide range of media, using specific iconic features that represent elements of Peyote theology. Peyote art takes a wide variety of forms, including painting and drawing; beadwork; jewelry; appliqué work on shawls, vests, and pillows; carving on drumsticks, roadmen's staffs, and Peyote boxes (sometimes called gourd boxes); and painted motifs on Peyote boxes, rattles, and water buckets. The buckets are particularly beautiful examples of painting sacred symbols on a utilitarian item that is used to carry water into a Peyote meeting.

The artwork described above can be divided into items that are made for ritual use and items such as paintings that are not used or displayed in a Peyote meeting. Regardless of the particular function, all reflect distinctive Peyote iconography. The most ubiquitous symbols are the Peyote button, the tipi, and the water bird. They appear on almost all art forms and represent the essential core of Peyotism: the Peyote button is the sacrament, the tipi is the house of prayer, and the water bird carries prayers skyward. Other common symbols include water drums, drumsticks, gourd rattles, feather fans, fire and ashes, altars, roadmen's staffs, eagle-bone whistles, spiritual food, sage, cedar, and various birds. The iconography of the Cross Fire way also integrates Christian symbols such as crosses, hearts, and images of Christ. For example, a roadman's staff may have a cross carved on top or incised on the side. Another example is the painting *Indian Religion* by Tennyson Eckiwaudah (Comanche), which depicts Jesus emerging from the top of a tipi that contains silhouetted Peyotists in prayer.[65] These symbols communicate and reinforce Peyote spiritual ideas and values.

Objects created for specific ritual use hold a special place for all Peyotists: they are sacred. After they are made, they must be blessed in a Peyote meeting and are blessed each time they are used. The blessing is a purification process where the item, such as the roadman's staff, is cedared-off or smudged by passing it through the smoke of smoldering cedar. It may also be rubbed with sage as part of its purification. The same is true with the water drum. Before tying the skin to the drum, a prayer is said. After the drum is tied, it is purified in the same manner. It becomes sacred, as does the water inside the drum. When the drum is untied, some participants sip the water to receive a special blessing. The remainder is poured along the altar. The prayers that have passed through the holy water create harmony among the participants, as the altar is the holy road that all should follow.[66]

Another form of sacred art that is essential to Peyote meetings is the creation of symbols with the ashes from the fire. This is an ephemeral art form, created and re-created throughout the night. It is one of the fireman's functions. He uses two pieces of firewood to shape the hot ashes into a meaningful design such as an eagle, water bird, star, or cross (see chapter 5 for details). The symbols act as empowering agents, giving strength to the prayers by creating a more efficacious environment for the answering of those prayers.

Peyote art that is not used in ritual is still considered spiritual but not with the same degree of sacredness as the items used in Peyote services. This includes jewelry, such as bracelets, rings, tie or scarf slides, tie clasps, belt buckles, and earrings. These are worn as aesthetic pieces as well as symbols of one's beliefs. Swan's study illustrates the wide variety of Peyote art. It also shows how Peyote art is integrated into the belief structure of Peyotism, connecting aesthetics and theology. The nonritual art also includes a significant amount of two-dimensional art that is not used in ritual. Paintings, drawings, and murals have become significant since the 1930s.

Most of the Peyote art that is used in ritual is three-dimensional and emerged with the origins of the Peyote religion. As the religion diffused through the Southern Plains, the ritual items accompanied the ceremony. They were mentioned in the early literature. James Mooney, for example, describes a 1890s Kiowa painted gourd rattle. Early photographs also show the ritual paraphernalia. In the early 1890s Silverhorn (Kiowa) produced the earliest Peyote drawings in his ledger books. In the following decades he produced other drawings and paintings, using Peyote motifs. Other painters, all Peyotists, include Carl Sweezy, Earnest Spybuck, Monroe Tsatoke, Stephen Mopope, and Archie Black Owl. Several of them had formal training and were professional artists.[67] In the 1930s there was a great expansion of American Indian arts, including Peyote art, encouraged by the establishment of Dorothy Dunn's art studio at the Santa Fe Indian School, the Indian Arts and Crafts Board established by Congress in 1935, and the New Deal's Federal Arts Project, which put American Indians to work producing arts and crafts. One example is Peyotist Woody Crumbo, who painted a Peyote mural on a wall in the Department of the Interior. The culmination of this expansion in the arts was the showing of American Indian art at the Golden Gate International Exposition in San Francisco (1939) and the very well publicized exhibit at New York's Museum of Modern Art in 1941, which included a Peyote work, *Bird in Flight,* by Kiowa painter Monroe Tsatoke. This may be the first showing of a Peyote painting at a major exhibition. The painting depicts a stylized water bird carrying prayers upward. On each wing there is a Peyote button, and the back of the bird is decorated with a feather fan.[68]

In the late 1960s and throughout the 1970s Peyote art became more recognized as a American Indian art form. As the renaissance in Native American arts expanded and museums began exhibiting more American Indian art, they started to include Peyote art. One example was an exhibit of Southern Plains art at the Southern Plains Indian Museum, in Anadarko, Oklahoma, in 1969. The exhibit traveled to eight other sites in South Dakota and Montana. Of the fifty-seven items in the exhibition catalog, eighteen were Peyote artworks. They included an oil on canvas by Tennyson Eckiwaudah, titled the *Native American Church: Peyote Religion.* There were two tempera works on mat board; six Peyote feather fans; four gourd rattles, all with carved and beaded handles; a silver water-bird pin; and two beaded pendants with water-bird motifs. All the works were by Kiowa and Comanche artists whose art had been produced in the 1960s. This is an important point: using the contemporary works of Peyote artists rather than mounting an exhibit of items that were in storage or in an anthropological collection.[69]

There was an increase in the production of Peyote art as well as an expansion of the types of art produced. The production of ritual instruments for use in prayer grew in conjunction with the rise in the number of Peyotists. These items did not enter the Native American arts market. It was extremely rare to find a ritual item for sale.[70] Nonritual Peyote art, however, was produced in ever increasing quantities. First, there were more Peyotists to produce such works, as well as more Peyotists and non-Peyotists who desired such items as paintings, drawings, and original prints. Some were reproduced as posters, sponsored by individual artists, by various local or national organizations, or sometimes by commercial enterprises. A large amount of silver jewelry displaying Peyote symbolism was produced, as well as beadwork with Peyote motifs made into a variety of items such as pendants or medallions, bolo ties, belts, moccasins, earrings, and hairpieces. This type of nonritual Peyote art continued to expand in the 1970s and 1980s. Peyote art began to adorn the covers of record albums, cassettes, and CDs. One could find printed Peyote symbols on pillows, shawls, and T-shirts.

In spite of the increase in the production of nonritual Peyote art, the various works, both two-dimensional and three-dimensional, reflect the inner beliefs of Peyotism. They were made by the artist as a representation of these beliefs and values. One example is the drawing at the beginning of chapter 6. It is a pencil drawing by Asa Primeaux, Jr., a great-grandson of Sam and Mary Necklace. The tipi, the official logo of the Native American Church of North America, is resting on an oversized Peyote button. The size reflects the primacy of Peyote, and, as the foundation for the tipi, it symbolizes Peyote as the foundation of the religion. Because Peyote services are held at night with a large fire in the center of the tipi, the participants are silhouetted when seen through the tipi canvas. Many artists try to capture this effect. On the left of the drawing is a water drum and drumstick; on the right, starting from the top, is the roadman's staff, a gourd rattle with a fringed handle, an eagle feather, an eagle-bone whistle, and a cedar bag. Above the tipi are two water birds that carry prayers to Wakan Tanka. The drawing represents the Half

Moon way, as there are no Christian symbols such as one might find in a Cross Fire drawing.

Within the past thirty years several Yankton Peyotists have become well-known artists. F. Dennis Lessard mentions Clarence Rockboy, Joe Abdo, and Neulan Dion, Sr., as being exceptionally talented in producing ritual items.[71] Clarence Rockboy and his father, Joe, are especially well known for their beadwork. Some of their beaded feather fans and gourd rattles are in museum collections.[72] Several years ago Clarence Rockboy was honored as the annual recipient of South Dakota's Living Indian Treasure Award in recognition of his contributions to American Indian art. The large majority of Peyotists are highly skilled artists, singers, and musicians. They make their own religious paraphernalia and their own musical instruments, and they create their own music and compose their own songs. One grows up learning these skills. It is not just that Peyote art and everyday life are integrated but that Peyote art and spirituality are integrated. The function of all Peyote art produced for ritual purposes is prayer; they are instruments of prayer that facilitate communication with the supernatural world.

The utilitarian nature of the items produced for use in the Native American Church does not mean they are devoid of aesthetic principles. They are constructed and decorated with the aesthetic criteria that best enhance the symbols that express the theology of Peyotism. Using traditional Peyote aesthetics evokes a sense of beauty through the use of symmetry, balance, and patterns of color. Much of the iconography, such as the water bird, is stylized. The primacy of Peyote is demonstrated by its centralized position in paintings and drawings. Form and function are also integrated. For example, the top of a gourd rattle is decorated with horsehair. It provides balance to the fringed handle and gives the rattle a sense of symmetry; in addition, the horsehair represents the small white tuft that is found on the top of freshly harvested Peyote buttons. Form and function are one, as the design of the rattle, the sound of the rattle, and the prayers it accompanies glorify Peyote, the "sacred herb." The gourd rattle epitomizes the ritual use of Peyote art: the integration of aesthetics, iconography, and spirituality.

As the renaissance in the arts and the revival of traditional religion expanded in the 1970s, concerns emerged regarding the parameters of religious freedom. The congressional response to these concerns, after considerable protest and lobbying, was the passage of the American Indian Religious Freedom Act of 1978. The bill guaranteed federal protection for the right of American Indians to the free exercise of religion. It described religious freedom as an inherent right of American Indians to practice their traditional beliefs without fear of interference or harassment and reaffirmed access to sacred sites as well as the use and possession of sacred objects. The law was also intended to protect the rights of the Peyote community to possess and use Peyote. Some argued that the bill was primarily a policy statement and a series of recommendations without the necessary enforcement machinery and as such was unsatisfactory. As a result some groups began working for a stronger bill.

RELIGIOUS FREEDOM AND THE STRUGGLE FOR SOVEREIGNTY

From an American Indian perspective the logical culmination of the movement toward self-determination is sovereignty. In the 1980s the term "sovereignty" became commonplace in the American Indian lexicon. It meant that tribal governments would be attempting to gain more and more control over reservation life as an inherent right. This would be accomplished by asserting and upholding treaty rights and by using the courts to define, defend, and expand legal jurisdiction. In addition to control of the land, there are water rights, control of natural resources, and the right to create corporations. Sovereignty as an extension of self-determination also includes control of schools, social services, taxation, the establishment of gaming casinos, administering justice through tribal courts, and police jurisdiction in various areas. Tribal governments have the right to determine their own membership, establish election procedures, control zoning, and issue hunting and fishing licenses for reservation land.[73] The concept of sovereignty rests on the doctrine of Diminished Tribal Sovereignty. Indian nations did not relinquish all sovereign rights in their relations with the United States government. There are certain powers that are part of an inherent sovereignty, not delegated by Congress, that have never been extinguished. In the *United States v. Wheeler* (1978) the Supreme Court stated that Native Americans do not have "full attributes of sovereignty . . . but they have not given up full sovereignty."[74]

The issue of tribal jurisdiction over tribal members is not in dispute; what is in dispute are the jurisdictional rights of tribal governments over nontribal members who live, work, or own a business on reservation land. For example, the right of a tribal government to tax a nontribal business on reservation land is a controversial issue. Many non-Indians are very resentful of any tribal jurisdiction over them. A significant reaction to the increasing sovereign rights of reservation governments has been a backlash against American Indians that seeks to reduce Native American sovereignty or altogether eliminate it. The greater the power or perceived power that American Indians have, the greater the resentment and the more severe the backlash. As American Indians acquire more political and economic power, they are increasingly able to assert sovereign rights. The backlash has led to attacks on American Indian interests such as casinos. A number of anti-Indian organizations have emerged in states such as Montana, Wyoming, Washington, and Idaho; and anti-Indian feeling is high in Wisconsin, North Dakota, and South Dakota. The backlash is fueled by non-Indians who have economic interests on reservation land and resent reservation governments that have the power of taxation, and it has also exacerbated the conflict between reservation governments and state and local governments.

This conflict is not new. It is well established in American law that reservations are free from state jurisdiction; but the tension is growing as reservation governments are increasing in power and wealth and have become more aggressive in asserting their rights. States resent not being able to tax the gaming casinos or to tax cigarettes and gasoline sold on reservations. There are also jurisdictional disputes on nontrust lands located within reservation boundaries, particularly on reservations with a significant amount of allotted land owned by non-Indians. This is a major problem on the Yankton Reservation, creating much anger and mistrust. Elements of the anti-Indian backlash (which includes some state and local governments) are lobbying Congress to restrict the jurisdictions of reservation governments.

The relationship with the federal government is also complex. The government-to-government concept is well established, though not always followed in practice. In 1983 President Ronald Reagan declared he would deal with American Indians government to government. This was part of his "new federalism" as it was applied to Indian policy. Budget cuts during the Reagan years, however, were devastating to the reservations, as social, educational, and health programs were greatly curtailed. Presidents George Bush and Bill Clinton restored some of the budget cuts and reaffirmed the government-to-government relationship. Prior to 1871, when treaties were negotiated, the relationship was nation to nation in theory. Out of this historic experience came limited sovereignty—that is, tribal governments retained some inherent sovereign rights, and the federal government had certain trust responsibilities. These responsibilities grew out of the treaty era, when trust responsibility meant fulfilling treaty obligations and establishing federal policy in the best interests of American Indians. Again, these were theoretical obligations of the federal government; more often than not they were ignored. The trust responsibility means protecting the land base, protecting fiscal stability, managing the trust funds, and ensuring the general welfare through education and health care. Because the federal government does not recognize reservations as sovereign nations but does recognize them as governments with certain sovereign rights (limited sovereignty), there are always gray areas that require adjudication by federal courts. This means there is an inevitable clash between the trust responsibility and the doctrine of limited sovereignty.

A crucial area for the establishment of sovereignty is education. Since 1976 the Yanktons have controlled their own education system. Since the close of the government school in Greenwood, there has not been a federal school on the reservation. Yankton families sent their children either to local public schools or to Marty Indian School, a Catholic institution. In 1976 the church turned the school over to the Yankton government. St. Paul's church, the rectory, the convent, and the cemetery remained under Benedictine jurisdiction, but the school and the surrounding property came under Yankton control. It is still called Marty Indian School, contains an elementary, middle school, and high school, and is run by a locally elected school board. The Yanktons also opened a community college in 1994. Marty Indian School has added Dakota language and Yankton history to the curriculum, and it has an Indian Studies Department. At the same time, the Yankton government moved its headquarters from Greenwood to Marty, making Marty the administrative and educational center of the reservation. The new tribal headquarters had once been a church building. In 1998 the Catholic Church issued an official apology to the Yankton people for past harsh disciplinary practices in its school. The apology came during a Good Friday mass at St. Paul's church and was also printed in the church bulletin. During the mass the Stations of the Cross were observed at various church and tribal buildings, where the apology was repeated at each station. The apology asked for "forgiveness from those who have been wounded and injured." A spokesperson for the church said the apology was part of a healing process for the church and the Yankton community.[75]

Religious freedom is also a major issue in the struggle for self-determination and sovereignty. American Indians insist that religious freedom must include control of sacred sites and burial grounds, access to and protection of sacred sites on federal land, the repatriation of human remains and sacred objects, and continued access to sacred items such as Peyote and eagle feathers. The members of the Peyote community believe that the future of their religion is tied to the future of American Indian religious freedom. These concerns made the year 1990 a watershed for religious freedom issues. First, the U.S. Congress passed legislation to protect human remains, burial sites, and sacred objects. Second, the Supreme Court narrowed the free exercise clause of the First Amendment in regard to the use of Peyote by American Indians. The legislation was a response to the century-long history of American museums, universities, and historical societies collecting, storing, and displaying hundreds of thousands of skeletal remains and funerary objects. The protection of human remains and sacred objects is a religious freedom issue, as is the repatriation and reburial of those remains. After a considerable lobbying effort by American Indian groups such as the Native American Rights Fund, Congress passed and President Bush signed the Native American Graves Protection and Repatriation Act. The law requires federal agencies and private museums and universities receiving federal funds to inventory their collection of human remains, associated funerary objects, sacred objects, and objects of cultural patrimony and notify the tribes of origin and return the remains and objects if requested. The law has caused resentment among some archaeologists and curators; but most institutions, after an initial reluctance, have begun the complicated process of repatriation.

The second event was the Supreme Court decision in *Employment Division, Department of Human Resources of Oregon v. Smith*. With the passage of the American Indian Religious Freedom Act in 1978, the Peyote community was less concerned about state and federal interference in its religion than at any time in the twentieth century. Most states had exemptions for religious use of Peyote; therefore it came as somewhat of a jolt in 1984 when two employees were fired from their jobs for the ceremonial use of Peyote. This jolt turned into utter shock and dismay in 1990, when the U.S. Supreme Court upheld the right of the state of Oregon to refuse to exempt the ceremonial use of Peyote by Native Americans from its drug abuse statutes. This decision created a firestorm of protest that led to new legislation in 1993 and 1994.

Alfred L. Smith, an American Indian and a member of the Native American Church, and Galen Black, a non-Indian, worked for a private drug and alcohol treatment center in Portland, Oregon. Their employer had a non-drug-usage policy for employees; after it was learned that Smith and Black had participated in the sacramental ingestion of Peyote in Native American Church services, they were fired. When they applied for unemployment insurance compensation, the Oregon Employment Division turned them down, ruling that they were fired for misconduct in using an illegal drug, because the possession of Peyote was a felony.[76]

Smith and Black filed a lawsuit against the Employment Division, claiming that they were protected by the free exercise of religion clause of the First Amendment; thus they should receive unemployment compensation. The Oregon Court of Appeals reversed the denial of unemployment compensation, and the Oregon Supreme Court affirmed the decision. The Oregon Employment Division then appealed to the U.S. Supreme Court. It vacated the judgment and remanded the case back to the Oregon Supreme Court, which ruled state law did not exempt Peyote but that the statute as applied to the plaintiffs violated their First Amendment right to the free exercise of religion. *Oregon v. Smith* went back to the U.S. Supreme Court to determine if the free exercise clause of the First Amendment protected a person's religious use of Peyote from a state's criminal prosecution. The court voted 6–3 against the two Peyotists, denying them unemployment compensation and upholding Oregon's statute prohibiting all use of Peyote. The decision also reversed the Oregon Supreme Court's finding that Smith and Black's constitutional rights were violated.[77]

The court's decision meant that any state could repeal the statutes that exempted the use of Peyote for religious purposes—or, to put it another way, states could totally ban the use of Peyote without violating the First Amendment rights of American Indians. This narrowed the free exercise of religion clause by allowing states to restrict a religious practice. The court decision also abandoned the "compelling state interest" test that is usually applied in such cases. This doctrine means that a certain activity can be prohibited for the good of the state or the general population if the court can demonstrate that the activity does harm to the larger group. In *Smith* the court did not argue that Peyote was harmful, or demonstrate that the religious use of Peyote would harm the citizens of Oregon, or cite any connection between Peyote use and the trafficking in illegal drugs. The court declared that Oregon had the right to control Peyote, even if it restricted the free exercise of religion of two of its citizens.[78]

The *Smith* case provoked outrage from many quarters. It was seen as a threat to religious freedom, with the failure to cite the compelling state interest doctrine and the narrowing of the free exercise clause of the First Amendment. Protest against *Smith* came from the left and right. Both the *Washington Post* and the *National Review* criticized the decision. Two scholars wrote: "For United States citizens who are members of the Native American Church, the Bill of Rights is dead."[79] Fearing that the Supreme Court would not uphold the rights of Smith and Black, in the days before the decision was announced, Smith had sent a letter to many Peyotists around the country, asking for unity and support during this crisis.[80] This was the initial step in organizing protest. Once the decision was announced, public protest emerged. The only recourse to a Supreme Court decision was legislative relief in the form of a bill guaranteeing that the free exercise clause of the First Amendment would be applied to members of the Native American Church; otherwise states would have a patchwork of statutes: some exempting Peyote, others prosecuting for possession of it. This was an impossible situation, creating a legal quagmire for the Native American Church. The answer was to organize, publicize, create coalitions, and lobby Congress for legislative relief. In Congress a bipartisan effort was launched to consider relief from the *Smith* decision. Some members of Congress had two concerns: the weakening of the compelling state interest doctrine when applied to a First Amendment case and the denial of the right to the free exercise of religion by Peyotists.

Outside of Congress, Reuben A. Snake, Jr., took the leadership role and created a coalition to overturn *Smith*. Snake was a nationally known, highly respected leader. He was the former chair of the Winnebago Nation of Nebraska, past president of the National Council of American Indians, and a lifelong Peyotist and roadman in the Native American Church. Snake created a national coalition of more than a hundred organizations, including religious and environmental groups, Native American organizations, reservation governments, and most of the incorporated Peyote churches (such as the Native American Church of South Dakota). The coalition, called the Native American Religious Freedom Project, became the lobbying arm of the Native American Church. In 1992 Senator Daniel Inouye (D-Hawaii), chair of the Native American Affairs subcommittee, called for congressional hearings.[81] Meanwhile there was an important development in Oregon. On 24 June 1991 the state legislature passed a bill permitting the sacramental use of Peyote by Native Americans. This brought relief to Peyote groups in Oregon, but it did not affect the Supreme Court's *Smith* decision.

As part of the effort to gain legislature relief from the *Smith* case, the Native American Religious Freedom Project mailed out information packets to law-makers, journalists, and scholars in late 1991. It contained documents on the history of the ceremonial use of Peyote, a summary of the draft legislation, and copies of newspaper articles, columns, and editorials as well as statements of support by Reuben Snake and Senator Inouye and a letter of support for new legislation by the chief administrator of the Drug Enforcement Administration of the Justice Department. It included copies of articles from law journals and copies of resolutions of support from various organizations such as the National Council of Churches, the American Anthropological Association, and the Arizona and New Mexico legislatures. There was quite a powerful letter from Robert B. Whitehorse, president of the Native American Church of Navajoland, to the Supreme Court Justices, outlining the spiritual signifi-cance of Peyote and summarizing the Peyote origin narrative of the Navajos. This lengthy information packet proved quite helpful in building support for the new legislation.[82]

In an attempt to influence public opinion and to educate lawmakers, Reuben Snake (with the support of his organization) produced a sixty-minute documentary film, *The Peyote Road: Ancient Religion In Contemporary Crisis.* The film, released in 1993, was an appeal to Congress to pass the necessary leg-islation to protect the Peyote religion; it summarizes the *Smith* case, includes an interview with Alfred Smith, and reviews the history of Peyotism, with a focus on Peyote as an ancient sacrament, comparable to bread and wine in Christianity. In addition the film reviews the history of discrimination against Peyotists, contains interviews with male and female members of the Native American Church, and includes a description of a Peyote ceremony and expla-nations of the religious paraphernalia used. The film ends with a memorial "to the ancestors who passed this way of worship through the generations" and is dedicated to the memory of anthropologist Omer Stewart.

Overall, *Peyote Road* is an excellent film. It takes a historical approach, looking at a century of Peyotism and interspersing the development of the church with the attempts to prohibit Peyote. The film uses scholars such as Vine Deloria, Jr., to review the history of the Peyote religion. The historic view is balanced by an analysis of contemporary problems, giving one the sense of crisis for the Native American Church since the *Smith* decision and exploring the actions needed to protect religious freedom. The film also includes examples of Peyote art and Peyote music. This award-winning film is significant for two reasons. First, it was part of the struggle for religious freedom and the effort to promote new legislature to protect the Native American Church. It demonstrates how activism, mobilization, and coalition-building can influence public policy. Second, the film is important as a historic document. There are important interviews with Peyotists and analyses of Peyote ceremonies and symbolism, often illustrated by historic and contemporary photographs and film footage.[83] Sadly, Reuben Snake, the producer of the film and the organizer of the coalition, passed away before he could see the fruits of his labor. He not only left an important film but brought together a coalition that lobbied successfully for new legislation. Senator Inouye delivered a speech on the floor of the Senate in his memory.[84]

The *Smith* decision led to two pieces of legislation. The court's failure to apply the compelling state interest doctrine to the Peyote case worried many legislators, legal scholars, and a wide range of religious organizations. Without the application of this doctrine, it would be possible for state legislators to outlaw a specific religious practice without having to demonstrate it was contrary to state interests. Members of both houses of Congress introduced and passed the Religious Freedom Restoration Act of 1993, which required the application of the compelling state interest test to future First Amendment cases. This would guarantee the free exercise of religious practices unless a clear danger to society could be demonstrated. As important as this legislation was, it did not specifically address the Peyote issue. This came about in mid-1994, when a bill was introduced in Congress that dealt with the free exercise of religion aspect of the *Smith* decision, including the issue of sacred sites, religious use of eagle feathers, religious rights of American Indian prisoners, and the use of Peyote. Some believed the bill was too broad; therefore a narrower bill that only dealt with the Peyote issue was introduced as an amendment to the American Indian Religious Freedom Act of 1978. The new legislation states that "the use, possession, or transportation of peyote by an Indian for bona fide traditional ceremonial purposes in connection with the practice of a traditional Indian religion is lawful, and shall not be prohibited by the United States or any state." The bill had widespread support and passed the House and the Senate by a unanimous voice vote. On 6 October 1994 President Clinton signed it into law. The bill effectively overturned the Supreme Court's *Smith* decision by giving full legal protection for the sacramental use of Peyote.[85] Subsequently the Pentagon issued a ruling giving American Indians in the military who are members of the Native American Church the right to use Peyote as a sacrament. This ended another chapter in the long history of the struggle of the Native American Church for its constitutional right to the free exercise of religion.

THE YANKTON PEYOTE COMMUNITY

In the last two decades of the twentieth century the Yankton Peyotists shared the benefits and the tribulations of reservation life with the other Yanktons. As of 2002 official enrollment was 7,616, with about half living on the reservation or adjacent to it; however, many of the others, living in the towns and cities of South Dakota, frequently return home for family, cultural, and spiritual activities. Members of the Yankton Peyote community have been active at home and in state and national organizations, practicing their faith and defending their church. They have participated in various national campaigns to defend Native American religious freedom, including the *Smith* case. At home the Yanktons are facing a series of complex issues. The most serious is a jurisdictional dispute with state and local authorities, which threatens to disestablish the reservation. Even with a growing middle class, numerous professional people, and a gaming casino, economic problems still plague the reservation. The Yankton Sioux Housing Authority has put considerable effort into upgrading the housing, but there are still many people who live in substandard homes, who are unemployed or underemployed and suffer corresponding social problems. Local agencies have been established to deal with the problems, but with mixed results. The typical everyday concern is earning a living, paying the bills, and taking care of the children. The Yankton government continues to look for opportunities for economic development. A successful recycling center provides jobs and sufficient income to make trash collection pay for itself. There are plans to develop tourism, expand the casino, and develop a revolving loan fund for tribal members to start small businesses.

The most successful economic development venture has been the casino. In the early 1980s the Yanktons established a bingo hall at an abandoned U.S. radar station on reservation land near Fort Randall Dam. Bingo was played three days a week. In the late 1980s, as court decisions and the Indian Gaming Regulatory Act (1988) made it possible for reservations to establish gaming parlors, and coupled with the budget cuts by the Reagan administration, tribal governments began establishing casinos on reservations. The Yanktons decided, after considerable debate, to turn the bingo hall into a casino. Some of the elders and spiritual leaders opposed gambling on religious grounds and questioned the morality of gambling as a source of income for the tribe. Some also questioned the wisdom of selling alcohol at the casino. The younger leadership took a pragmatic view and saw the casino as providing income for the tribe and jobs for individuals. With unemployment very high, and with no alternatives, the pragmatic view prevailed. A Yankton Gaming Commission was established, and the casino opened for business in 1991. It contains a restaurant, a lounge, a gift shop, and a 58-room hotel; a travel plaza with a convenience store was added several years later. Of the 350 employees (as of February 2002), 70 percent are Yanktons, 10 percent are other American Indians, and 20 percent are non-Indians. The casino is not the answer to the Yanktons' long-range economic stability, but it has provided significant revenue to support various reservation programs and salaries for Yankton families.

Amid change and flux, there is one constant: religion is still central to the lives of most Yanktons. In addition to a small Peyote community, more people than at any time in the past hundred years are participating in traditional religious ceremonies. Sweat Lodges are common, as well as Sun Dances, Vision Quests, and Sacred Pipe ceremonies. The local Episcopal, Presbyterian, and Catholic churches still have considerable membership. Some people participate in both traditional and Christian religious services. To most Yanktons today, of whatever denomination, religion defines the core of their lives. Reinforcing the religious revival is the continuing cultural revival. Many people produce arts and crafts, and many are talented musicians, singers, and dancers. There are large annual powwows, one sponsored by the Yankton government, another by the casino. The tribe has established a small buffalo herd with plans for further expansion. Rebuilding a buffalo herd has given everyone a feeling of optimism by reinforcing a sense of connection to the past. In today's Yankton society a rich cultural and spiritual life coexists with serious economic problems. In spite of 150 years of hardship the official logo of the Yankton nation reads: "Land of the Friendly People of the Seven Council Fires." The *Y* in *YS* (Yankton Sioux) is shaped like a Sacred Pipe, a reflection of their spiritual roots.

Economic problems abound, but the most threatening problem the Yankton people face today is a jurisdictional dispute with the state and local governments that could result in the disestablishment of all or part of the reservation. In 1992 a waste management firm planned to build a facility on land that was owned by non-Indians but was originally part of the Yankton Reservation. With concerns over jurisdiction and worries over the safety of nearby drinking water, the Yanktons went to court in 1994. At issue in *Yankton Sioux Tribe v. Matt Gaffey* was whether stiff federal Environmental Protection Agency (EPA) guidelines would apply to the building of the facility if it was deemed Indian land or if weaker state guidelines would apply if it was deemed non-Indian land. As the case went to court, local townships and the state of South Dakota joined in as a third party on the side of the waste management firm, calling for the disestablishment of the Yankton Reservation. The state argued that it was disestablished in 1894 when the Yanktons sold 168,000 of their 430,000 acres to the federal government (see chapter 3). The Yanktons argued that the agreement for the sale of the land also upheld the Treaty of 1858 and reaffirmed the legal status of the tribe. Both state and federal courts heard the case, but they rendered differing opinions. In January 1998 the U.S. Supreme Court, in *South Dakota v. Yankton Sioux Tribe,* declared that the 168,000 acres of land "ceded" in 1894 was now under the jurisdiction of the state of South Dakota. The court did not rule on the remaining 220,000 acres of allotted land that was once held under fee simple title by individual Yanktons but had been sold to white farmers. The remaining acreage (approximately 40,000) was still under tribal jurisdiction.

In August 1999 the U.S. Eighth Circuit Court of Appeals ruled that the 220,000 acres of the 260,000 total were no longer under tribal jurisdiction and that Congress in 1894 did not disestablish the reservation but did diminish its size. The status of the remaining 40,000 acres is still unsettled. After the Eighth Circuit opinion was released, both sides petitioned the U.S. Supreme Court to rehear the case. The Yanktons want jurisdiction reestablished over the whole 260,000 acres; the state claims that the actual amount of tribally owned land is one square mile (640 acres). The U.S. Attorney's office filed a brief with the Supreme Court supporting the Yankton position on jurisdiction. In June 2000 the Supreme Court remanded the case back to the Eighth Circuit Court of Appeals for a rehearing. The immediate impact has been the expansion of local law enforcement jurisdiction over what was Indian land, resulting in confrontations, accusations, and considerable tension. Mark Barnett, the attorney general of South Dakota, is quoted as saying that the case is about "power and revenue."[86]

In the midst of the jurisdictional disputes the Yankton people made history in 1999 by electing Madonna Archambeau as tribal chairperson. She is the first woman to lead the Yankton nation, receiving 55 percent of the vote. The election also ousted seven of nine incumbents from the Tribal Business and Claims Committee, the Yanktons' governing body. This occurred after a year of political turmoil, which, according to *Indian Country Today*, involved allegations of misappropriation of tribal and casino funds, intimidation, and nepotism.[87] Archambeau is not new to politics. She has served on the Business and Claims Committee in the past. According to some, her election bodes well for the future, because she brings stability to the political process. She was reelected in 2001 and again in 2003.

Archambeau's victories may be a reflection of a growing role for women in Yankton politics. In 1985 a group of women established the Native American Community Board to develop a voice on issues of health, education, and economic development. They incorporated as a nonprofit organization in 1986; and in 1988 the board established the Native American Women's Health Education Resource Center in the town of Lake Andes. Its first program, "Women and Children in Alcohol," focused on fetal alcohol syndrome. Over the years its programs have grown and now include reproductive rights, health screening, diabetic nutrition, cancer prevention, AIDS prevention, and community organizing and leadership. It also publishes a newsletter, *Wicozanni Wowapi* (Health News). In 1991, after considerable controversy and a zoning battle, the center opened a shelter for women. The Women's Lodge, as it is called, offers protection for women and their children. It has a hotline service and provides counseling, legal advocacy, and medical attention.[88] The resource center and the shelter emerged to fill a need: women and children, particularly those in difficult economic circumstances, required health or social services and had nowhere to turn in times of domestic crisis.

In 1994, responding to some of the same needs but offering an alternative solution, a group of Yankton women organized by Faith Spotted Eagle reestablished the Braveheart Women's Society. It offered women cultural and spiritual solutions to social and domestic problems. The society began as a healing retreat in the Black Hills as part of a fetal alcohol syndrome prevention program. The original Bravehearts were Yankton women in the prereservation era who brought back the dead and wounded from the battlefield. Today's Bravehearts bring back or rescue young women from "emotional death" by awakening the health of their mind, body, and spirit. The Braveheart Society is rooted in traditional values and seeks to revive and transmit those values to a younger generation by developing a nurturing and mentoring relationship between mature women and young women. The young women are instructed in the Dakota language; they are also taught traditional healing, the valuing of children as *wakan* (sacred), and how to maintain wellness by reestablishing the sacred circle. In order to accomplish these goals the Braveheart women have revived the women's coming of age ceremony (Išnati Awiča Dowan). This was one of the Sioux's Seven Sacred Rites.

In 1998 the ceremony was held in a public setting for the first time in more than one hundred years. It was one of the spiritual ceremonies outlawed by the U.S. government; some Yankton families, however, had continued it in secret. The Braveheart women, many of whom are elders, use this opportunity to instruct the young women in the responsibilities of life. On a spiritual level, by prayer, song, and instruction, they establish a connection with their roots through an understanding of the significance of White Buffalo Calf Woman. The broad goal is to assist young women in the transition to adulthood by developing a strong sense of personal identity and a sense of place in Yankton society. The specific goals are to help young women to avoid alcohol and drug abuse, domestic violence, sexual abuse, and exploitation and, if a woman is victimized by physical and emotional abuse, to rebuild her self-esteem and a sense of worth so that she can regain control over her life. The philosophical basis of the Bravehearts is that strong women create strong societies.[89]

In the last quarter of the twentieth century and early twenty-first century the goal of creating a strong society (as the Braveheart women are attempting to do) has been a central unifying theme of the spiritual, cultural, and social activities of the Yankton people. A strong society means the reestablishment of the sacred circle: the symbolic representation of wholeness. Black Elk said: "In the old days when we were a strong and happy people, all our power came to us from the sacred hoop of the nation, and so long as the hoop was unbroken the people flourished."[90] During 150 years of reservation life the people did not flourish. The goal of reestablishing the sacred hoop is central to all spiritual life on the reservation, whether it is the Yankton traditional religion, Christianity, Peyotism, or some combination of the three. The members of the Yankton Peyote community believe that through their spiritual values and practices they can reestablish and reinforce the sacred hoop and create a strong society. Their major concern is the existence of impediments to the re-creation of the sacred circle, such as governmental policies, laws, or actions that threaten religious freedom. These impediments included "Operation Eagle" in the 1980s and, with the *Smith* decision in the early 1990s, the fear that South Dakota could join Oregon in criminalizing the religious use of Peyote.

In the early 1980s members of the Native American Church as well as other American Indians were subjected to a sting operation ordered by U.S. secretary of the interior James Watt. Dubbed "Operation Eagle," it was supposedly aimed at the illegal trafficking in eagle feathers, wings, and claws. It is legal for American Indians to possess eagle parts for religious purposes but illegal for non-Indians. Federal agents posed as collectors and offered large amounts of cash for religious items that contained eagle parts. Those Indians who succumbed to the sting were arrested, tried, convicted, and jailed. Those who were approached by undercover agents were living in areas that had a 50–75 percent unemployment rate and were having trouble supporting their families. The operation produced expressions of outrage that such a sting— some called it entrapment—was aimed at poor people. Yankton Sioux tribal chairman Larry Courneyor and spiritual leader Leonard Crow Dog from the Rosebud Reservation openly condemned the operation. Some of the victims who were members of the Native American Church believed that they were targeted because of their religious beliefs. Several Yankton Peyotists targeted by the sting operation were arrested and spent time in federal prison. Watt himself fueled part of the outrage. He participated in the massive budget cuts of the Reagan administration and was considered anti-Indian when he was quoted as making derogatory comments about tribal governments and reservation life. Secretary Watt may not have been actively involved in anti-Indian organizations, but his words and actions gave comfort to those who wanted to curtail self-determination and sovereignty. Many wondered why a secretary of the interior would target impoverished American Indians for a sting operation, particularly members of the Native American Church.[91]

As mentioned earlier, the *Smith* case sent shock waves through the Peyote community. The Yanktons were concerned about its impact on the state of South Dakota. The state had no jurisdiction on the reservation, but there was concern about travel to other reservations and the transportation of Peyote into the state. South Dakota exempted the religious use of Peyote in its criminal code in the 1960s, but a national change of climate, initiated by the *Smith* case, could affect the attitudes of South Dakota lawmakers. This obviously did not happen, but people were worried in 1990, especially on the heels of Operation Eagle. Feelings of anxiety about the future were rampant. For many people the *Smith* case was not an isolated phenomenon but part of the overall struggle for First Amendment protection.

Many of the Yankton Peyotists supported political activism in the struggle for religious freedom. One Yankton who combined the effort to protect the use of Peyote with other religious freedom issues was Asa Primeaux, the grandson of Sam and Mary Necklace. His work in these areas, combined with his spiritual activities, reflects the heritage of his grandfather. Asa was brought up to protect and to teach these God-given ways, as he would say. For a period of about ten years (1985 to 1995), Asa traveled throughout the country. He spoke at universities, was a keynote speaker at conferences, participated in public forums, gave interviews to the media, and lobbied for religious freedom legislation. In Ohio he pursued the issue of religious rights for American Indians in prison; he was the first spiritual leader to conduct a Sacred Pipe ceremony in an Ohio penitentiary at Orient State Prison. He and others, such as the state's American Indian organizations, lobbied the state legislature to protect burial sites (particularly Ohio's famous mounds) from both professional archaeologists and grave robbers. In the late 1980s he worked with state senator Dick Schafrath (former Cleveland Browns football star) to develop legislation to prevent desecration of graves and public display of human remains.[92] Asa also conducted a number of reburial ceremonies for American Indian remains that had been on display or in private hands. He combined these activities with his role as spiritual mentor to many of central Ohio's Native Americans: he established several Sweat Lodges, prepared people for Vision Quests, held naming ceremonies, and blessed people's homes. Asa also conducted many traditional healing ceremonies.

Sometimes spiritual activities blended with political issues, such as holding Sacred Pipe ceremonies in Ohio state parks that are considered sacred sites, including Blackhand Gorge, Flint Ridge, and Circle Mound (all near Newark, Ohio) and the world-famous Serpent Mound in southern Ohio. These places are of particular significance, because Dakota oral tradition posits an eastern location as an early homeland (see chapter 1). Asa believes that it was at Flint Ridge that Wakan Tanka gave his Dakota ancestors the gift of fire. Archaeologists and developers threatened some of these sites. For example, a country club wanted to expand its facilities at the expense of near-by ancient mounds. As significant as these concerns were, Asa's primary concern was the new threat to the Peyote religion that his grandparents had taught him. This was deeply personal; it was his faith and the faith of his family.[93]

Ever since Smith and Black had been fired and denied unemployment compensation for participating in the Peyote religion, the Peyote community had watched with anxiety the unfolding court cases. In 1989 concern accelerated as the Supreme Court prepared to hear the case. In November Asa and his grandson Mark Welsh traveled to Washington, D.C. Asa said, "I am going to Washington to make a testimony for our Indian religion."[94] He also said that he was defending the faith of his grandparents. He met with Smith and Black's lawyers and spoke with Smith. About five hundred Peyotists traveled to Washington; each morning and evening they gathered in circles, burnt cedar, and prayed.[95] After the *Smith* decision went against the Peyote community, Asa considered developing a coalition to coordinate the reaction to the decision. He named it the Sacred Peyote Way of Life Coalition. It did not progress beyond the discussion stage, as Asa was experiencing health problems and others such as Reuben Snake were putting together a national coalition.[96]

While dealing with the issues of government restrictions and the ever-present fear that some misdirected antidrug war would put new prohibitions on Peyote, people also focused on several related issues. In the last twenty years there has been a concern about the supply of Peyote. As a result of increased demand from a growing church membership and decreased supplies, the price has gone up considerably. In the 1950s the cost for a thousand dried Peyote buttons ranged from $12 to $20; today the cost is approximately $175 to $200 per thousand. The supply is dwindling: all known growing areas of the peyote cacti in Texas are on private property, and some landowners are reluctant to allow full access to them. One answer to the supply problem is to reduce the amount of Peyote consumed during religious services; however, this supply issue has reopened a debate with roots that go back to the 1960s concerning the participation of non-Indians in Peyote services.

A closely related issue is membership for non-Indians. Not surprisingly, this is a hotly debated topic with practical implications and theological overtones. More non-Indian attendees means more pressure on supplies. If non-Indian participation increases, some fear that lawmakers may revisit the Peyote issue, particularly in Texas, the nation's major region for the peyote cactus, where the harvesting and sale of Peyote is licensed and controlled by the Texas Department of Public Safety. The cultivation of Peyote is not an option at this point. Cultivating the cactus is illegal, but it would be a costly endeavor even if it was decriminalized for members of the Native American Church. One possibility, though it is not very likely to be successful, is to lobby for the importation of Peyote from Mexico, where it is more abundant.[97] Another concern is that in several states a Native American who supplies Peyote to a non-Indian, even in a religious service, may be in legal jeopardy. One

solution that some Peyote groups follow is to allow non-Indians to participate in the religious service but not to partake of the sacred herb.

This concern over the supply has exacerbated the theological debate about
the will of God in giving the gift of Peyote. Is this gift, with its power to heal
and to teach, just for American Indians or is it to be shared with all humanity?
Each view has its adherents. That debate is not separate from the overall
debate about the future of American Indian cultures and the fear of their dilu-
tion through homogenization and Anglicization. The same debate is going on
over the issue of whether non-Indians should be allowed to participate in the
Sun Dance. In South Dakota, including the Yankton Reservation, these same
issues are causing concern.

In the past twenty to thirty years changes have occurred in the Yankton
Peyote community. For example, there has been less centralization of the
Peyote community around the church in Greenwood. No religious services
have been held in the old church building. They are held around the reservation at various people's homes, where tipis are set up for the prayer meeting.
There are several reasons for this change. The church was in poor physical
condition; it was sixty years old, virtually beyond repair, and impossible to
heat in winter. Another factor is today's mobility: people all have cars and
can easily gather anywhere. Years ago the church ground, with its central
location, was a gathering place for the community, where people arrived
much earlier and stayed longer. Today the church grounds are still used. The
cemetery is well taken care of and is still the main burial ground for the Peyote
community. On some occasions, such as Memorial Day or Easter, a tipi is
erected next to the old church to hold Peyote services there. Someone (either
a priest or roadman) has been in charge of the church grounds since Sam
Necklace died: first John Claire and Louie Stricker, then Joe Rockboy and Joe
Shields, and recently the late Neulan Dion, Sr. In 2003 the old church was
torn down. The Peyote community is debating the feasibility of building a
new church.

The decentralized location of Peyote meetings involves issues other than
the physical condition of the church. Differences of opinion emerged over
the role of the Yankton traditional religion in the Peyote community as the
revival of traditional spirituality took place. Some of the Peyotists, as noted
above, were participants in traditional religious ceremonies.[98] As roadmen
they began to reduce the Christian elements in the Peyote meetings they ran.
Asa Primeaux and his extended family eventually stopped running Cross

Fire meetings and began practicing the Half Moon way, eliminating virtually all Christian references and reintroducing the use of tobacco. As Sacred Pipe ceremonies became more common, as more Sweat Lodges were built, and as the Sun Dance was revived, some of the Peyote people began to participate. They did not leave the Peyote faith they participated in both. They did not see any incompatibility in worshiping with the Sacred Pipe and Peyote; in fact, they believed the two reinforced each other, as they came from the same spiritual source. Other members of the Peyote community did not accept the growing influence of traditional religion. They wanted to maintain the Cross Fire way, with its Christian elements. One result was that people began to sponsor Peyote meetings at private homes. The meeting was run according to the wishes of the sponsor and the roadman who ran the meeting.

An important point about this issue is that it did not develop into a pattern of exclusion. People attended each other's Peyote services, regardless of whether it was Half Moon or Cross Fire. The official monthly prayer service of the Native American Church of Charles Mix County may be held at an individual's home, but everyone is welcome to attend. In spite of the differences, everyone agrees on one point: the primacy of Peyote.

The national debate over who should be allowed to participate in Peyote services and partake of the holy sacrament is also an issue within the Native American Church of South Dakota. As mentioned above, both viewpoints have their defenders. The issue was debated in 1999 at the Seventy-seventh Annual Convention, held at Rainbow Paradise, the home of Asa and Loretta Primeaux. At one of the business meetings the issue was raised when several members wanted to ban non-Indians from partaking of the holy sacrament. Their arguments were less theological and more practical, concerning the supply of Peyote and worry that authorities might revisit the exemption on Peyote as a controlled substance if non-Indians participated. This was not settled, although at this convention it was agreed to allow the sponsors to have the final word.[99]

From the family's perspective, having the convention on their home grounds brings the history of Sam Necklace and Yankton Peyotism full-circle. At this exact location Sam Necklace conducted Peyote services sponsored by the Rainbow family. Now, with his grandson married into the Rainbow family, the Native American Church of South Dakota is honoring Asa for his lifelong commitment to the Peyote faith. Loretta served as hostess for the convention, and many of the family members participated in the activities. Jackie Never

Misses a Shot wrote a dedication to Rainbow Paradise, calling it a place "where the sun dancer dances, searching for the answer to his prayers; of the Peyote man seeking a vision while under the influence of our sacred medicine" (appendix II). The five-day gathering included daily business meetings and three nightly Peyote services. President S. Scott American Horse presided over the convention, and Reverend Emerson Spider, Sr., high priest of the Native American Church of South Dakota, was the presiding spiritual leader. Reverend Spider, who calls his church the Native American Church of Jesus Christ, believes that Peyotism and Lakota, Dakota, and Nakota traditional religion should not mix, meaning that Peyote people should not participate in traditional ceremonies.[100] In an interview in 1999, however, he indicated that he had changed some of his earlier views. He said that at one time he did not believe in the Sun Dance, but now he prays before Sun Dances and prays for the sun dancers. Like Asa Primeaux, Reverend Spider was literally born into the Peyote religion. He told me very proudly that Albert Hensley, the legendary Winnebago Peyote leader, baptized him into the Native American Church (he said that he was too young to remember the baptism). William Black, a Peyote leader in the 1920s, was his grandfather. Reverend Spider added that his mentor was Jim Blue Bird (Lakota), one of the early advocates of introducing Christianity into Peyotism.

On the issue of inclusion Reverend Spider is an advocate of the view that Peyote is a gift to all humanity. He clearly stated his point of view in the same interview and then reiterated it during a Peyote service he conducted on the last night of the convention. He said that he opposes those who want the Peyote religion exclusively for American Indians. His argument is based on the belief that God is love, and in understanding God's love for people of all races a church cannot exclude anyone and still call itself a church. Reverend Spider believes that anyone who wants to enjoy the spiritual benefits of the "sacred herb" should be allowed to do so. He took out a well-worn New Testament reader titled *New Life Study Testament* and read his favorite passage aloud. It was Corinthians I:13, with the message that charity is the greatest gift of all.[101] Even though Reverend Spider and Asa Primeaux disagree on the compatibility of Peyotism and traditional religion and belong to different persuasions of the Peyote faith, they agree on the issue of inclusion. For many years Asa has taught that the ways of God are for all people. In his teachings he emphasizes the prayer *Mitakuye Oyasin*, for all my relations, meaning that all living things are related as part of God's creation. He said that excluding people from God's ways is against God's will. Asa extends his belief in inclusion to both traditional American Indian spirituality and Peyotism.[102]

Reverend Spider also commented on the differences between the Half Moon and Cross Fire way as well as the differences in ceremony from reservation to reservation. He said that he does not view this as a problem and actually sees the two coming closer together. When he conducted the Peyote meeting at the convention, he combined the Half Moon and Cross Fire, out of respect for all present. He made tobacco available to anyone who wanted to use it for prayer—something that would not occur in a Cross Fire service. Reverend Spider said that God does not judge you by your beliefs: God judges you by your actions. Since Peyotists from all over South Dakota were invited, the printed program proclaimed unity and stated that the convention would be conducted by both Half Moon and Cross Fire fireplaces; therefore "let us all unite in prayer so our sacred medicine, Peyote, can flourish and be abundant to us." The dedication of the annual convention to Asa, the grandson of Sam and Mary Necklace, is testimony to the spiritual heritage bequeathed to him. Loretta sponsored the second Peyote meeting for her husband. Roadman Willard Bruguier conducted the service. He and others offered special prayers for Asa. In spite of his poor health, he attended all the Peyote services at the convention.

The Peyote faith is not widespread among the Yanktons; but where it exists it is stable and has deep roots going back to Charlie Jones and the early years of struggle to establish the faith and to build the church as an institution. The Necklace, Primeaux, and Rainbow families, along with other equally important families, helped establish the Peyote religion for coming generations. The spiritual roots planted by Sam and Mary have borne fruit in their many descendants who are active members of the Native American Church and participants in Yankton traditional religion. For example, many of the family members are Sun Dancers, go on Vision Quests, and have "sweats" on a regular basis. Grandpa Sam and Grandma Mary are a living memory, as each new generation learns about them from the previous generation. Loretta also sponsored the Peyote service held on the first night of the convention for her thirty-one grandchildren. They are Sam and Mary's great-great-grandchildren. Their first great-great-great grandchild, Tawny Fool Bull, was born in 2000 and represents the firstborn of the sixth generation of this Peyote family and the firstborn of the eighth generation that began with Iron Necklace. On 21 April 2001 she was baptized into the Native American

Church, continuing a tradition of integrating the children into the Peyote faith. Her grandfather, Willard Fool Bull, a roadman from the Rosebud Reservation, conducted the service.

Throughout the generations the children have been integrated into the family's cultural and spiritual activities. As mentioned earlier, each year the family sponsors a "spiritual conference," which includes daily Sweat Lodge ceremonies, naming ceremonies, Vision Quests, and a Sun Dance.[103] The children are involved; they attend "sweats," some of the teenagers are sun dancers, and many of them help with the work of getting rocks and firewood and repairing the Sun Dance arbor. The relatives come from near and far to attend these spiritual activities.

The grandchildren are integrated into the spiritual and cultural life of the family and the larger Yankton society not just during this two-week period but throughout the year. Very early in life their identity as members of the Necklace/Primeaux *tiošpaye*, as Peyotists, and as members of the Yankton nation is well established. From early childhood on they participate in all the cultural and spiritual activities. They are taught to follow the Peyote Road and to live according to God's teachings and follow the footsteps of their ancestors. For example, they are brought into the Sweat Lodge as infants. All the children have a traditional naming ceremony and are honored as they pass from one stage of life to another. For instance, when the children graduate from eighth grade or from high school they are honored with a special Peyote service. One such invitation reads:

> 8th Grade Graduate—Marty Indian School
> You are cordially invited to attend a
> Graduation Prayer Service in honor of Deanna Charity Fool Bull
> On Saturday, June 8 and Sunday June 9, 1996
> At Mr. and Mrs. Asa & Loretta Primeaux, Sr., Residence: Marty, SD
> N.A.C. Prayer Service Conducted by: Asa Primeaux, Jr.

Deanna is part of the fifth generation, the great-great-granddaughter of Sam and Mary Necklace and the daughter of Edith Primeaux Fool Bull. By the time the children reach adulthood they have been honored many times.

One of the most obvious inheritances is Peyote music. Yankton Sioux Peyotists have always been known as exceptional singers, including the Necklaces, Primeauxs, Rainbows, Dions, Abdos, Bruguiers, Rockboys, Shields, and others. The music was transmitted from generation to generation; with hours and hours of practice, and a commitment to a deeply held faith, a tradition of excellence prevailed. The Yanktons were well-known singers in South Dakota and Nebraska (among the Winnebagos and Omahas); they received national attention in the 1970s, however, with the issuing of fifteen albums and/or cassettes of Yankton Peyote songs. Eight of the albums were Yankton Peyote songs featuring a variety of singers; a ninth featured Joe Shields and his son Duane. (As a tribute to the quality of the music, volumes 1–4 were reissued in 2003.) The six others were titled *Asa Primeaux and Sons*. These releases made Asa and his sons recognized for their harmonized style of singing. Asa had learned to sing and drum from his grandfather and his father, Harry Primeaux, who also had a reputation as an excellent singer.

When Asa married Loretta Rainbow, three Peyote families were joined: the Necklaces on the maternal side, the Primeauxs on the paternal side, and the Rainbows as in-laws. This union of families produced a next generation of Peyote singers who have received national renown. Gerald Primeaux, Asa and Loretta's son, has produced several CDs. His first, *Primeaux-Dion: Yankton Sioux Peyote Songs, In Loving Memory,* was nominated as a finalist for the 2000 Native American Music Awards: Best Traditional Recording category. Gerald has followed with two more CDs, *Yankton Sioux Peyote Songs* and *Songs of Prayer for Life.* Following in the footsteps of his father, Gerald has become a roadman in the Native American Church and is also active in Yankton traditional religion. He runs Sweat Lodge ceremonies and is a sun dancer. His brother Asa, Jr., has followed a similar path, as did their younger brother Mike, now deceased. Asa and Loretta's five daughters—Edith, Jolene, Sylvia, Tina, and Jennifer—are equally active in the families' spirituality and are rearing their children to follow along the same path.

In 2001 Verdell Primeaux and Johnny Mike (Navajo) astonished many people in the music world when their *Bless the People: Harmonized Peyote Songs* won the Grammy Award in the Native American Music category. Verdell Primeaux is the son of Francis Primeaux (Asa's brother), also a well-known singer. Not surprisingly, both Gerald and Verdell have credited their family for their success. Both have built on the family tradition of harmonized Peyote songs that was developed by their fathers, uncles, and grandfather.

In 1991 the Máza Napin Tiošpaye (Iron Necklace extended family) sponsored a two-day powwow at the home of Asa and Loretta. Invitations were printed, and an arbor was built and decorated with streamers. It was a traditional powwow that served as a family reunion, although everyone on the

Yankton Reservation was welcome to attend. Hundreds of people came, including many dancers and singers. This festive event brought the descendants of Sam and Mary Necklace together.

The families described here have not escaped the trials and tribulations of life. Tension and disagreements, exacerbated by severe economic problems, are a part of family life on the reservation. Yet on another level there is a sense of primacy in establishing spiritual and cultural values as the essential focus of everyday life. The grandchildren are taught that these are the ways of the ancestors that will provide them with a meaningful existence. In 1983 Asa said to some of his relatives concerning his life and heritage that "living this way, and believing this way, is in behalf of my grandparents."[104] The entire family shares this heritage and continues to follow the Peyote Road in the manner of Sam and Mary Necklace.

Epilogue

Samuel B Necklace

Chairman, Full-blood Organization

Signature of Sam Necklace on a letter to John Collier,
commissioner of Indian Affairs.

Sam and Mary Necklace have left a valuable legacy to their descendants.
They have bequeathed a collective memory of spiritual and cultural values
for subsequent generations, the so-called Seventh Generation. They lived
through an era in the early decades of the twentieth century when preserv-
ing tradition was difficult. They were, however, able to carve out a niche for
themselves within the Yankton Peyote community, where they developed
cultural and spiritual agency in spite of the economic deprivation, political
disfranchisement, and religious repression. The story of the Necklace family
is the continuation of this heritage. The memory of Sam and Mary has
helped mold the future of a large *tiošpaye* or extended family. Many of their
grandchildren and great-grandchildren are active Peyotists, some are roadmen, and their grandson Asa has provided spiritual sustenance to many
American Indian communities. The descendants of Sam and Mary have
married into other Peyote families, fusing long traditions of commitment to
the Peyote Road. The family is now in its fifth generation following the
Peyote way. Contemporary family members are nationally known as Peyote
singers. Verdell Primeaux is a Grammy Award winner in traditional Native
American music, and his cousin Gerald Primeaux now has three CDs, with
one nominated for a Native American Music Award. With the recent popularity of Peyote music and the reputation of the Primeaux family as singers,
the records and cassettes of the 1970s are being reissued as CDs by Indian
House.

The spiritual legacy has manifested itself not only in the imprint of Peyotism on the family but in the active role of many family members in the Yankton traditional spirituality. The large majority are pipe carriers, have been given "Indian names," regularly attend "sweats," go out fasting, and in spite of the economic stresses of life have persevered in following the "red road." Many members of the family, both male and female, are Sun Dancers. Asa and Loretta sponsored twelve Sun Dances from 1990 to 2002. Many of the dancers are family members. Many family members also follow the powwow circuit as dancers or as drum groups or as both. For example, Parnell Necklace, grandson of Sam and Mary, and his two sons and daughter have drummed at powwows throughout the United States and Europe. They are known as the Maza Napin Singers. They have also performed in several European countries.

Another significant point is that even those grandchildren who were too young to remember Grandpa Sam and those born after he died still make reference to him. Sam and Mary are living memories. Their grandchildren have used them as role models in raising their own families and thus contributing to the family's sense of identity. Asa has been mostly responsible for transmitting the memory of his grandfather to his children and grandchildren, now the fifth generation of a Peyote family. Whether speaking of Peyotism or of Yankton traditional spirituality, there is always the refrain of this came from "my grandpa." Credit is given to parents and grandparents during Peyote services and for Peyote songs. For example, Gerald Primeaux thanks his family members on his latest recording for passing along their songs to him.

The study of Yankton Peyotism brings forth an interesting question concerning Peyotism and Pan-Indianism. Wherever Pan-Indianism or so-called intertribal religious movements are analyzed, the Native American Church is included in the discussion. In fact some people, such as Hazel Hertzberg, have argued that Peyotism is the essence of Pan-Indianism. She wrote that the Peyote faith was the "pan-Indianism of the reservation."[1] While it is true that there is a significant Pan-Indian dimension to Peyotism in that individuals from any American Indian group may participate and become members, travel to each other's reservations and pray together, socialize, and share the same faith, it does not follow that they are "Pan-Indian." There is no diminution of one's ethnic identity as one participates in the Peyote faith.

In 1955 James H. Howard, in defining Pan-Indianism, posited the idea that Peyotism was contributing to a nontribal Indian culture.[2] Are his assertions valid fifty years later? Has Peyotism helped to produce a "generic Indian"? If we examined the large number of Navajo Peyotists in the last sixty years, would we find them less Navajo? I think not. The same is true in South Dakota among the Sioux in general and the Yanktons in particular. Only a brief time with Lakota Peyotists will indicate this is not happening. It certainly has not happened to the Yankton Peyotists, either Cross Fire or Half Moon. There is still a powerful Ihanktonwan identity (as well as a Dakota identity). I would argue that Yankton Peyotism has actually reinforced a Yankton identity, because they believe Peyotism is rooted in their past and has many parallels with a traditional cosmology and belief system, as has been shown in this study. The use of the Dakota language among the Yanktons has declined in the past fifty years; but where it is surviving some of the credit goes to the Peyote community. Part of this parallel emerged into the open in the late 1960s, as a number of Peyotists played a major role in reviving Yankton traditional spirituality. A comparable occurrence took place on the Rosebud Reservation, with Leonard Crow Dog espousing Peyotism and Lakota traditional spirituality at the same time. On the Yankton Reservation this again reinforced an Ihanktonwan identity. Scholars should certainly continue to look at Peyotism from a Pan-Indian perspective, but without a mindset that assumes an expanding Peyotism will produce a "generic Indian."

The expansion of Peyotism to approximately 250,000 American Indians, along with the explosion of the cultural renaissance, has actually worked to strengthen ethnic identities, as the revival of the arts and the movement toward a fuller sovereignty have an ethnic base and a reservation homeland. The members of the Necklace/Primeaux family have a strong sense of their Yankton heritage. Their involvement with the Native American Church was within the framework of Yankton society, as indicated by their use of Dakota. The family memory, however, predates Sam Necklace, and goes back to Mazanapin (Iron Necklace) and Hintunkasanwin, both born in the prereservation era and perceived as the family's founders. One branch of the family has taken Iron Necklace as its surname. It is Sam and Mary, however, who are the living memory for this family. They married when Yankton Peyotism was emerging. The Necklace commitment to Peyotism and the Yankton Native American Church grew stronger together. With the power of Peyote, God's gift to them, they developed powerful spiritual roots that they bequeathed to coming generations.

Afterword

On Monday, 2 June 2003, Asa Primeaux, Sr., passed away. It was not unexpected. He had been ill for several years, but that did not lessen the feelings of sadness and loss. I had hoped that he could touch and feel this book about his grandparents and his cherished Peyote faith. He was blind the last years of his life and always touched and smelled whatever came into his hands; he could tell the type of wood from its smell. It is the passing of an era for the Primeaux/Necklace *tiošpaye*. Asa was the spiritual leader of the family as well as spiritual mentor to many others around the country. He ministered to many hundreds of people: running "sweats," conducting naming ceremonies, preparing people for Vision Quests, performing marriage and funeral services, conducting various healing ceremonies, and organizing and running Sun Dances. As a roadman, he also conducted literally hundreds of Peyote services around the country.

Asa played a role beyond serving as a spiritual mentor to family, friends, and those in need through his practice of Yankton traditional spirituality and his lifelong commitment to the Native American Church. He believed and practiced both faiths, side by side, seeing them as mutually reinforcing, with roots in the same traditional past. Asa's spiritual beliefs were similar to those of his lifelong friend Leonard Crow Dog. He was also supported and assisted by his wife, Loretta, of the Rainbow family, who were both traditional people and Peyote people. Asa and Loretta's children and grandchildren are following these same spiritual paths.

The funeral, consisting of the traditional four days of mourning, was conducted to reflect Asa's life: it included both Yankton/Dakota and Peyote funerary practices. The Sweat Lodge behind the house was dismantled, and a new one erected. Sweats were held each night. His body was laid out in the home, as many people came to pay their respects and offer prayers for his spiritual journey. On Wednesday some of the young members of the Yankton Peyote church came and sang a series of Peyote mourning songs, honoring Asa and praying for his spirit. On Thursday Leonard Crow Dog arrived. He gave a long oration on Asa's life, their friendship, their travels, and on how he and Asa, whom he called *tahanši* (cousin), introduced Peyote people to the Sweat Lodge. He closed with a traditional Lakota prayer for Asa's spirit.

A Peyote memorial service was held on Friday night; it began at 7:30 p.m. and ended at 8:00 a.m. A special caboose was added to the tipi to accommodate a large number of people. Leonard Crow Dog served as roadman. Arlen Lightfoot (Oto), former president of the Native American Church of North America, was cedarman; Lorenzo Duane Shields (Yankton), chief drummer; and Terry Fool Bull (Sičangu-Lakota), fireman. The long service included many songs, prayers, and eulogies for Asa. It was conducted in the Half Moon style, as Asa would have liked it. Many family members and friends attended, including many of the younger generation of Yankton Peyotists, such as Neulan Dion, Jr., the present chairperson of the Yankton Native American Church, and Larry Abdo, Jr., the vice-chair. It was the young members of the church who did all the work in putting up the tipi and preparing for the memorial service (see the photograph of the young generation of Yankton Peyotists). The Peyote community came together to honor Asa and to help and support the family.

Asa was in every sense his grandfather's grandson. His grandparents raised him in the Peyote faith. Asa was baptized by his grandfather when he was three months old and given the name Pejuta Hokšina (Medicine Boy). Asa credited his grandparents with all he knew. At his grandfather's gravesite in 1991 we began to discuss ideas for this book. At midnight during the Peyote service, as a special recognition of Asa's spiritual beliefs, the fireman made a series of sacred patterns in the ashes. These were the same markings that Asa used, which came to his grandfather in a vision many years ago. It is fitting that Asa is buried within thirty feet of his grandfather and grandmother in the Native American Church cemetery in Greenwood.

With the passing of Asa, a circle has been completed. As described in the text Asa and his two brothers, Paul George and Francis, made a commitment to hold a series of three Sun Dance cycles of four years each. After the first four-year cycle, Paul George walked on. Later, during the second four-year cycle, Francis walked on. Now almost exactly a year after the last Sun Dance of the last cycle of Sun Dances, Asa has walked on; the circle is completed.

Although the circle is complete, it continues in another way. Asa represents continuity within the traditional American Indian concept of the Seven Generations, which means that each generation is responsible for transmitting spiritual and cultural values to the next generation. Asa fit this model: the values of his grandparents have been transmitted to his children and grandchildren.

Mitakuye Oyasin

Notebook of Sam Necklace

In 1922, as the Yankton Peyotists debated incorporation and a constitution, Sam Necklace began keeping a notebook. As the first secretary of the Native American Church of Charles Mix County, he recorded business meetings, listing officials, committees, and bylaws. This notebook is the only known documentary source on the internal developments of the early church. It includes a handwritten constitution before it was submitted to the state for incorporation. As chief priest, Sam Necklace listed his duties, such as recording births and baptisms.

ARTICLES OF INCORPORATION

We, the church organization of the peyote church of christ [*sic*], having heretofore associated ourselves together as a religious, benevolent and church association under the laws of the State of South Dakota, and for the purpose of organization and having a charter issued to us by the proper State authorities therefor [*sic*] under the name "Native American Church," and by which name we certify the following bylaws of our association, duly and regularly adopted by us.

ARTICLE I

The name of this organization shall be and remain "Native American Church."

ARTICLE II

The purpose of the corporation is to foster and promote the christian religious belief of the Sioux Indians of South Dakota, and all Indians within the United States, recognizing, adopting, continuing and using the peyote for Sacramental and religious purposes, and teaching the scriptures, morality, kindly charity, right living, to cultivate a spirit of self respect, brotherly love and union among all the American Indians, with the right to buy, sell, own and care for property for the use and purposes of conducting religious services and performing duties of charity, and all business pertaining thereto.

ARTICLE III

The central place of business of this corporation is the city of Wagner, Charles Mix County, South Dakota.

ARTICLE IV

The principal and regular officers of the association shall be a president, Vice-president, Secretary, Treasurer, and a committee of Six. All to be elected by the members of this association at a meeting held at the end of two years. Officers shall hold their office until their successors are elected and accept the office.

ARTICLE V

The term for which this corporation shall exist is a perpetual term.

ARTICLE VI

The President, Vice-president and the committee of six shall constitute the governing board of trustees with full power to transact the business authorized by the membership. It shall be the duty of the president to preside on all occasions, and when absent to be represented by the Vice-president in the capacity of acting president. The secretary shall have charge of all records and keep a complete record of all meetings and transactions of the church and membership. The treasurer shall have custody of all money and shall pay it out upon the order of the president and secretary.

ARTICLE VII

The corporation shall have no capital stock, but it is authorized to levy assessments, to be determined at a regular meeting of which notice shall be given.

ARTICLE VIII

The present officers are:— Johnson Goodhouse, president; Charely [sic] Iron Hawk, Vice-president; Samuel B. Necklace, Secretary; Henry Wind Shooter, Treasurer. The committee of six are:— Amos Shields, Joshua Pretty Bull, Not Afraid of Pawnee, George Circle Fool, Wm. J. Eaglethunder, Francis Little Stallion.

This constitution shall be signed by the President, Vice-president, Treasurer, Secretary and the Chairman of the committee of six to be present when the same is acknowledged. Johnson Goodhouse, Charely Iron Hawk, Samuel B. Necklace, Amos Shields, and Joshua Pretty Bull.

The church organization of the Native American Church was made in the year of our Lord 1922 on Oct. 7th.
Officers of the Native American Church are:

Johnson Goodhouse—President
Chas Iron Hawk—Vice President
Samuel B. Necklace—Secretary
Henry Wind Shooter—Treasurer
Committee of six:
Amos Shields—Chairman
Joshua Pretty Bull
Not Afraid of Pawnee
Wm. J. Eaglethunder
Francis Little Stallion
George Circle Fool

The charter was issued to us Nov. 28th, 1922.

Johnson Goodhouse was elected, President of the Native American Church was appointed to have charge of the charter, on Nov. 28th 1922.

Johnson was elected to be Chief Priest, to conduct all prayer meetings for the Native American Church on June 3rd 1923.

The Native American Church to have their prayer meetings first Saturday of each month regular.

The annual dues shall be $1.25 each year, this must be paid from each member or adult.

On July 4th 1923 the Chief Priest was given the privilege of making his own stick [staff] and other things that is needed for the church.

On Jan 1st 1925 the women decided to have women's aid in order to help carry on the work for the church, elect their officers.

Ellen Goodhouse—President
Amelia Medicine Horn—Secretary
Annie Wahechunka—Treasurer
Emma Sitting Crow—Collector

On Aug 8th 1926 the Native American Church elected new officers for the next two years and are—

Chas Iron Hawk—President
Herbert Johnson—Vice President
Samuel B. Necklace—Secretary
Mary Red Hawk—Treasurer
Committee of Four;
Howard Red Hawk—Chairman
Victor Kutena
Joshua Pretty Bull
Not Afraid Of Pawnee

On Aug 8th 1926 Chas Iron Hawk was elected to be Chief Priest to conduct all monthly meetings for the Native American Church.

On Jan 8th 1928 Henry Blaine was elected to be Chief Priest to conduct all monthly prayer meeting for Native American Church.

On Oct 19ᵗʰ 1929, Samuel B. Necklace was ordained to be Chief Priest to conduct all prayer meetings for the Native American Church.

On July 14ᵗʰ, 1923. There will be no loan made to anyone out of Native American Church fund or Treasurer.

To have some respect for our church there will be no smoking in the home where the prayer meeting is to be held.

Aug 8ᵗʰ 1926. Officers of the women aid or Society.

Elaine Red Hawk—President
Mary Blaine—Vice President
Mary C. Necklace—Secretary
Eunice Blaine—Treasurer
Belle K. Johnson—Seamstress

On Jan 18ᵗʰ 1934. The certificate of amendment was issued to us.

On Feb 3ʳᵈ 1935, Amos Shields was ordained to be priest of the Native American Church.

On June 6ᵗʰ 1937 John Claire was ordained to the office, for Priest.

On Aug 17ᵗʰ 1935, Two nights Prayer meeting was held at Fort Thompson S. Dak. by the members of Native American Church of Greenwood S. Dak.

On April 9ᵗʰ 1939. Israel Louis Stricker was ordained to be a leader of the Native American Church.

The church organization of Native American Church, Oct 7ᵗʰ 1922. Names of all that are Baptized. "Christ took upon him the nature of man, he died for the whole human race, without respect of persons; equally for all," and Written by, Sam B. Necklace Chief Priest.

Josephine Iron Hawk
Baptized—Aug 9ᵗʰ 1925
Born—June 14ᵗʰ 1925

Father—Chas Iron Hawk
Mother—Virginia Iron Hawk
By Johnson Goodhouse Chief Priest

Verdelia Sitting Crow
Baptized—Dec 6th 1925
Born—Oct 18th 1925
Father—Louis Sitting Crow
Mother—Emma Sitting Crow
By Johnson Goodhouse

Marvin Moses Cole
Baptized—Sept 4th 1927
Born—Aug 9th 1927
Father—Robert Cole
Mother—Amelia Cole
By Chas Iron Hawk

Gideon Necklace
Baptized—Aug 5, 1928
Born—June 14th 1928
Father—Benedict Necklace
Mother—Rose M. Necklace
By Henry Blaine-Chief Priest

Elisa Shields
Baptized—Sept 4, 1927
Born—Aug 9, 1927
Father—Amos Shields
Mother—Sophie Shields
By Chas Iron Hawk

Helen Iron Hawk
Baptized—Oct 7, 1928
Born—
Father—Chas Iron Hawk
Mother—Virginia Iron Hawk
By Henry Blaine. Chief Priest

Vernice Sitting Crow
Baptized—Oct 7th 1928

Born—Aug 18th 1928
Father—Louis Sitting Crow
Mother—Emma Sitting Crow
By Henry Blaine

Charely Iron Hawk
Baptized—April 7, 1929
Born—May 1882
Father—
Mother—
By Henry Blaine Chief Priest

Louis Sitting Crow
Baptized—June 23 1929
Born—Aug 15th 1904
Father—Adam Sitting Crow
Mother—Helen Sitting Crow
By Chas Spotted Eagle. Priest

Amos Shields
Baptized—June 23, 1929
Born—April 20th 1890
Father—Ezekiel Shields
Mother—Louise Shields
By Chas Spot. Priest

Herbert Johnson
Baptized—June 23rd 1929
Born—
Father—Wakute
Mother—Marpiya
By Chas Spotted Eagle, Priest

Annie Shields
Baptized—June 23rd 1929
Born—Dec 12th 1898
Father—Louis Oka

Mother—Josephine Oka
By Chas Spot. Priest

Belle Johnson
Baptized—June 23rd 1929
Born—
Father—Dennis Me. Kittean
Mother—Ellen R. Kittean
By Chas Spotted Eagle, Priest

Rosie Shields
Baptized—June 23rd 1929
Born—Dec 25th 1924
Father—Amos Shields
Mother—Annie Shields
By

Marvin Amos Johnson
Baptized—July 14th 1928
Born—
Father—Herbert Johnson
Mother—
By

Mary Avis Johnson
Baptized—July 14th 1929
Born—
Father—Samuel Weston
Mother—Sarah Weston
By

David Henry Stricker
Baptized—Feb 3rd 1935
Born—
Father—Israel Louis Stricker
Mother—Cecilia Stricker
By Sam B. Necklace, Chief Priest

Dolan Cecilia Campbell
Baptized—Dec 25th 1936
Born—Sept 25th 1936
Father—Joseph Campbell
Mother—Lorena Campbell
By Sam B. Necklace, Chief Priest

Asa Primeaux
Baptized—Nov 14th 1931
Born—Oct 4th 1931
Father—Harry Primeaux
Mother—Jeanie Primeaux
By Sam B. Necklace. Chief Priest

Were confirm
Easter Sunday April 9, 1939.
Ward Dion.
By Sam B. Necklace

was Baptized April 9, 1939
Easter Sunday
Nelson Dragg
By Sam B. Necklace

confirm
Verdelia Sitting Crow.
April 9th 1939
By Sam B. Necklace,

Ordain to be a Leader
Israel Louis Stricker
April 9th 1939. Easter sunday
By Sam B. Necklace, Chief Priest.

Peter, Sam, B. Necklace
Baptized—
Born—Dec 27th 1800 [sic]

Father—Peter Necklace
Mother—Margaret Necklace
By Charely Iron Hawk, Chief Priest

Viola Louise Shields
Baptized—Jan 13th 1934
Born—Jan 4th 1934
Father—Amos Shields
Mother—Annie Oka Shields
By Sam B. Necklace, Chief Priest

Harry Henry Blaine
Baptized—
Born—
Father—
Mother—
By Chas Iron Hawk, Chief Priest

Margaret Mary Blaine
Baptized—
Born—
Father—
Mother—
By Chas Iron Hawk, Chief Priest

Buckley Pamani
Baptized—June 23rd 1935
Born—
Father—
Mother—
By Sam B. Necklace Chief Priest

Joseph Plays With Iron
Baptized—June 23, 1935
Born—
Father—Thomas Plays With Iron
Mother—Anna Plays With Iron
By Sam B. Necklace. Chief Priest

James Blaine
Baptized—April 12th 1936
Born—
Father—
Mother—
By Sam B. Necklace, Chief Priest

Jesse Big Eagle
Baptized—Aug 30th 1936
Born—
Father—Peter Big Eagle
Mother—Helen Big Eagle
By Sam B. Necklace. Chief Priest.

Irene Josephine Necklace
Baptized—Sept 6th 1936
Born—July 8th 1916
Father—David Primeaux
Mother—Amy Roubeaux
By Sam B. Necklace, Chief Priest

Mable Mary Necklace
Baptized—Sept 6th 1936
Born—Aug 25th
Father—Eli Chinn
Mother—Mary Chinn
By Sam B. Necklace, Chief Priest

Elizabeth Dorothy Johnson
Baptized—Sept 5th 1937
Born—July 31st 1937
Father—Amos Johnson
Mother—Rosie D. Johnson
By Sam B. Necklace, Chief Priest

Emma Good House
Baptized—Dec 5th 1937

Born—July 7th 1902
Father—Johnson Good House
Mother—Ellen Good House
By Sam B. Necklace, Chief Priest

Lucinda Ellen Good House
Baptized—Dec 5th 1937
Born—
Father—
Mother—
By Sam B. Necklace, Chief Priest

Joseph Campbell
Baptized—Dec 12th 1937
Born—
Father—Sam Abda
Mother—
By Sam B. Necklace, Chief Priest

Lorena Campbell
Baptized—Dec 12th 1937
Born—Aug 2th, 1905
Father—David Stricker, Sr.
Mother—
By Sam B. Necklace, Chief Priest

Jeanie Virginia Iron Hawk
Baptized—Nov 28th 1937
Born—
Father—James Blaine
Mother—
By Sam B. Necklace, Chief Priest

Herbert Cook, Jr.
Baptized—March 27th 1938
Born—Feb 18th 1913
Father—Herbert Cook, Sr.

Mother—
By Sam B. Necklace, Chief Priest

John Claire
Baptized—April 3rd 1938
Born—July 2nd 1899
Father—
Mother—
By

Minnie Claire
Baptized—April 3rd 1938
Born—
Father—
Mother—Louise Weston
By Sam B. Necklace, Chief Priest

Francis Nathan Primeaux
Baptized—March 1st 1938
Born—May 12th 1938 [sic]
Father—Harry Primeaux
Mother—Elaine Primeaux
By Sam B. Necklace

Elaine Primeaux
Baptized—May 1st 1938
Born—Jan 26th
Father—Howard Red Hawk
Mother—Mary Red Hawk
By Sam B. Necklace, Chief Priest

Harry Primeaux
Baptized—May 1st 1938
Born—March 26th 1912
Father—Mitchell Primeaux
Mother—Amelia Primeaux
By Sam B. Necklace, Chief Priest

Israel Louis Stricker
Baptized—May 13th 1938
Born—Dec 25th 1899
Father—David Stricker
Mother—
By Sam B. Necklace, Chief Priest

Cecilia Stricker
Baptized—May 13th 1938
Born—1905
Father—Alex Horn Eagle
Mother—
By Sam B. Necklace, Chief Priest

Blanche Stricker
Baptized—May 13th 1938
Born—Jan 18th 1924
Father—Israel Louis Stricker
Mother—Cecilia Stricker
By Sam B. Necklace

Virgel Nathan Stricker
Baptized—May 22, 1938
Born—Sept 20th 1932
Father—Israel Louie Stricker
Mother—Cecilia Stricker
By Sam B. Necklace, Chief Priest

James Williams, Jr.
Baptized—Oct 9th 1938
Born—Sept 25th 1887
Father—James Williams, Sr.
Mother—
By Sam B. Necklace, Chief Priest

Mary Williams
Baptized—Oct 9th 1938

Born—May 24th 1898
Father—
Mother—
By Sam B. Necklace, Chief Priest

Harvey Williams
Baptized—Oct 9th 1938
Born—March 13th
Father—James Williams, Jr.
Mother—Mary Williams
By Sam B. Necklace, Chief Priest

Vivian Williams
Baptized—Oct 9th 1938
Born—Feb 29th
Father—James Williams, Jr.
Mother—Mary Williams
By Sam B. Necklace, Chief Priest

Noral Williams
Baptized—Oct 9th 1938
Born—March 26th 1926
Father—James Williams, Jr.
Mother—Mary Williams
By Sam B. Necklace, Chief Priest

Kenneth Williams
Baptized—Oct 9th 1938
Born—Feb 27th 1931
Father—James Williams, Jr.
Mother—Mary Williams
By Sam B. Necklace, Chief Priest

Fredrick Ben Necklace
Baptized—Oct 30th 1938
Born—April 29th 1907
Father—Sam B. Necklace
Mother—Mary C. Necklace

Raymond Dan Necklace
Baptized—Oct 30th 1938
Born—March 9th, 1911
Father—Sam B. Necklace
Mother—Mary C. Necklace

Beulah Grace Stricker
Baptized—Dec 25th 1938
Born—June 29th 1938
Father—Israel Louis Stricker
Mother—Cecilia Stricker
By Sam B. Necklace, Chief Priest

Mary Stone Man
Baptized—Jan 1st 1938
Born—May 21st 1899
Father—John Atana
Mother—Virginia Atana
By John Claire, Priest

Charely Arthur Stone Man
Baptized—Jan 1st 1939
Born—July 18th 1926
Father—James Stone Man
Mother—Mary Stone Man
By John Claire, Priest

Celice Ellen Sitting Crow
Baptized—
Born—
Father—Louie Sitting Crow
Mother—Emma Sitting Crow
By John Claire, Priest

Donald Williams
Baptized—
Born—May 4th 1934

Father—James Williams, Jr.
Mother—Mary Williams
By John Claire, Priest

George Primeaux
Baptized—June 5th 1938
Born—Mar. 28th 1907
Father—Mitchell Primeaux
Mother—Lucy Primeaux
By Samuel B. Necklace, Chief Priest

Golden May Campbell
Baptized—June 5th 1938
Born—June 5th
Father—Joseph Campbell
Mother—Lorena Campbell
By Sam B. Necklace, Chief Priest

Nave Joseph Campbell
Baptized—June 5th 1938
Born—
Father—Joseph Campbell
Mother—Lorena Campbell
By Samuel B. Necklace, Chief Priest

Leona Johnson
Baptized—June 5th 1938
Born—June 11th 1935
Father—Marvin A. Johnson
Mother—Rose D. Johnson
By Samuel B. Necklace, Chief Priest

Lucy Cook
Baptized—Jan 8th 1939—
Born—
Father—Charely Green Crow
Mother—Susan Green Crow
By Sam B. Necklace, Chief Priest

Abraham Grant
Baptized—Jan 8th 1939
Born—May 2nd 1890
Father—
Mother—
By Sam B. Necklace, Chief Priest

Lucy Claire
Baptized—Feb 5th 1939
Born—
Father—
Mother—
By Samuel B. Necklace, Chief Priest

Soloman St. Cloud
Baptized—Mar. 5th 1939
Born—
Father—
Mother—Annie St. Cloud
By Sam B. Necklace, Chief Priest

Nelson Dragg
Baptized—April 9th 1939—Easter
   Sunday
Born—
Father—John Dragg
Mother—Emily Dragg
By Sam b. Necklace, Chief Priest

Timothy Henry Stricker
Baptized—Jan 12th 1940
Born—Jan 12th 1940 [sic]
Father—Israel Louis Stricker
Mother—Cecilia Stricker
By Samuel B. Necklace, Chief Priest

Emma Rechinda Necklace
Baptized—March 10th 1940

Born—June 20th 1939
Father—Fredrick Ben Necklace
Mother—Martina Sibel Necklace
By Sam B. Necklace, Chief Priest

Adolph Adam Sitting Crow
Baptized—
Born—
Father—Louie Sitting Crow
Mother—Emma G. Dragg
By Sam B. Necklace, Chief Priest

Adam George Circle Fool
Baptized—Mar. 24th 1940
Born—
Father—
Mother—
By Sam B. Necklace, Chief Priest

Frank Junior Drappeau
Baptized—Mar. 24th 1940
Born—
Father—Frank Drapeau
Mother—Susan Drapeau
By Sam B. Necklace, Chief Priest

Helen Sarah Pretty Bull
Baptized—April 7th 1940
Born—June 25th 1890
Father—
Mother—
By

Joshua Pretty Bull
Baptized—Jan 5th 1941
Born—July 3rd 1883
Father—

Mother—
By Matthew Bro Of All, Chief Priest

Genevive Emily Dragg
Baptized—Nov 2nd 1940
Born—Oct 7th 1940
Father—Alfred Dragg
Mother—Ethel Dragg
By Sam B. Necklace, Chief Priest

Moses Heart Lance
Baptized—July 5th 1942
Born—July 22nd 1911
Father—William Lance
Mother—Kate R.F. Lance
By Samuel B. Necklace, Chief Priest

Agnes Florence Ree
Baptized—Jan 3rd 1943
Born—
Father—
Mother—
By Sam B. Necklace, Chief Priest

Doris Celeoda Shields
Baptized—Jan 3rd 1943
Born—Jan 3rd 1943 [sic]
Father—Joseph Shields
Mother—Rena Shields
By Sam B. Necklace, Chief Priest

Issac Wayne Primeaux
Baptized—
Born—
Father—
Mother—
By Sam B. Necklace, Chief Priest

Clarence Homer Rockboy
Baptized—Aug 29, 1948
Born—April 22, 1933
Father—Joseph Rockboy
Mother—Eliza Little Bird
By Samuel B. Necklace, High Priest

Darrell Joseph Rockboy
Baptized—
Born—March 29th 1940
Father—Joseph Rockboy
Mother—Cleothilda Big Eagle
By Samuel B. Necklace, High Priest

Phillis Mae Johnson
Baptized—Sept 5, 1948
Born—Dec 27, 1948 [sic]
Father—Amos Johnson
Mother—Rose Johnson
By Sam B. Necklace, High Priest

Amy Marie Cole
Baptized—
Born—
Father—Robert Cole
Mother—Amelia Cole
By

Confirmation

Julia J. McBride, March 19th 1939
Emma Dragg, Witness

Noah Dion, April 3rd 1939

Vera Sitting Crow, Jan. 15th 1939

Frank Eli

Alfred Dragg

Nelson Dragg

Ward Dion, April 9th 1939—Easter
   Sunday

Verdalia Sitting Crow, April 9th
   1939—Easter Sunday
All done by Sam B. Necklace, Chief
   Priest

Vernice Sitting Crow

Rose Shields, Feb 4th 1940
By Amos Shields, Priest

Noble Blaine, Jan 14th 1934
Louie Stricker—Witness

Geo Circle Fool, Feb 11th 1934

Joshua Pretty Bull—April 7th, 1940

John Sully
Done by John Claire, Priest

Frank Weston
Done by John Claire, Priest

Alex Rainbow
Done by Sam B. Necklace, High
   Priest [*sic*]

Victor Kutena
Done by Amos Shields, Chief Priest

Eliza Kutena
Done by Amos Shields, Chief Priest

Program: 77th Annual Convention of the Native American Church of South Dakota, 1999

In 1999 the Native American Church of South Dakota held its Seventy-seventh Annual Convention on the Yankton Reservation. The convention site was on the land of Asa and Loretta Primeaux. The convention was dedicated to Asa in recognition of his lifelong commitment to Peyotism. The program lists the day-to-day activities such as business meetings in the afternoon and Peyote prayer services at night (conducted in both the Half Moon and Cross Fire manner). It also lists the leaders and the major participants and lends insights into the values and beliefs of the Native American Church of South Dakota.

NATIVE AMERICAN CHURCH OF SOUTH DAKOTA, INC.
77th Annual Convention
June 23–27, 1999

S. Scott American Horse, President   Jackie Never Misses A Shot, Secretary
Arlen Lightfoot, Vice President   Ethel R. Red Bear, Treasurer
Joseph Isham Jr., Sergeant-At-Arms

INTRODUCTION/WELCOME

The Native American Church of South Dakota, Inc., requests the honor of your presence at our 77th Annual Convention.

This year we will convene at the Primeaux Residence known as "Rainbow Paradise" 3 miles north of Marty, South Dakota. This conference is dedicated to Mr. Asa Primeaux Sr. (Pejuta Hoksina), hosted by Mrs. Loretta Primeaux.

Mr. Asa Primeaux Sr., a firm believer and advocate for our "Divine Herb" Peyote (Sacred Medicine), dedicated himself wholeheartedly to our Native American Church. Although he has endured many trials and tribulations—his physical setback and recent loss of his son, Michael Harry Primeaux—he still maintains his faith in our Native American Church.

Today, the Native American Church of South Dakota, Inc., acknowledges and recognizes Mr. Asa Primeaux Sr., for his struggles, efforts and accomplishments for our "Divine Herb" Peyote.

RAINBOW PARADISE
By J. Never Misses A Shot

Colors of red, orange, yellow, green, turquoise, blue and purple, the colors of the rainbow after a rain, shining down on the Paradise where the sun dancer dances, searching for the answer to his prayers; of the Peyote man seeking a vision while under the influence of our sacred medicine. Peyote, singing praises of thanks to the best of the Peyote drum, the heart beat of Mother Earth. High up above Rainbow Paradise, flies the Sacred Eagle, bringing blessings of good health—physically, mentally, spiritually and emotionally—to all who are participating in this glorious event. Rainbow Paradise, the place where Pejuta Hoksina, his family, and a great many relatives call his home.

—Dedicated to Asa Primeaux Sr. (Pejuta Hoksina)

Topic of discussion and agenda items will be announced prior to the business sessions. Camping sites and water will be available. This Conference will be conducted by both Half-moon and Cross-fire fireplaces. Let us all unite in prayer so our sacred medicine, Peyote, can flourish and be abundant to us. Master of Ceremonies: Rev. William Richards. Security and Patrol: Gerald Primeaux Sr., Tyrone Primeaux, Asa Primeaux Jr., and Neulan Dion Jr.

JUNE 23, 1999
ENCAMPMENT DAY

Morning devoted to activities. Anyone having any questions should contact Gerald Primeaux Sr., or Edith Fool Bull. Anyone wishing to volunteer their assistance in cooking or security should contact Gerald Primeaux Sr., or Loretta Primeaux.

Lunch and supper will be provided by the hostess.

Evening prayer services for the grandchildren of Loretta Primeaux will commence with Mr. And Mrs. Arlen Light Foot Sr., sponsored by Mrs. Loretta Primeaux.

JUNE 24, 1999

8:00 a.m.   Flags will be raised at this time in Memory of all deceased veterans.

A special tribute to the late Rev. Neulan Dion Sr., the leading flag throughout the Conference. Rev. Dion was our former President of the NAC of South Dakota, Inc. He was our spokesman, leader, confidante, mentor, etc., to many of the relatives all over. He is sadly missed today.

Other deceased veterans being honored are as follows:

Martha American Horse	Abel Iron Rope Sr.	John Never Misses A Shot
Richard Fool Bull	Sam Dion	Buckley Gage Pomani
John Weasel Bear	Melvin Bruguier Sr.	Adam Eagle Feather
Charles Arthur Stoneman Sr.	Virgil Stricker	Chester Blue Horse Sr.
Frances Primeaux Sr.	Narcisse Irons	Daniel Fool Bull

10:00 a.m. President American Horse will open the 77th Annual N.A.C. Conference with four songs and a prayer by Vice-President Arlen Light Foot Sr.
Welcome Address—Mrs. Loretta Primeaux
12:00 p.m. Recess—Breakfast and lunch will be provided by the Primeaux family.
1:00 p.m.   Guest Speaker: TBA
2:00 p.m.   Officers Report
4:30 p.m.   Retiring of National Ensigns
Supper provided by the hostess.

Evening prayer services will commence honoring Mr. Asa Primeaux Sr. (Pejuta Hoksina) sponsored by Mrs. Loretta Primeaux and children. Conducted by Mr. and Mrs. Willard Bruguier Sr.

JUNE 25, 1999

8:00 a.m.   Raising of Colors

10:00 a.m. Guest Speaker: TBA
12:00 p.m. Recess—Breakfast and lunch will be provided by Mrs. Loretta
               Primeaux and family
1:00 p.m. Resumption of Business Agenda: TBA
4:30 p.m. Supper Break—Provided by Mrs. Sherry Holland
5:00 p.m. Retiring of Colors

Evening prayer services will commence honoring of Mr. Bryan Becenti, 12th grade graduate of Tohatchi, New Mexico. Sponsored by Mrs. Sherry Holland, conducted by Mr. and Mrs. Cleveland Never Misses A Shot.

JUNE 26, 1999
8:00 a.m. Raising of Colors
9:00 a.m. Guest Speaker
10:00 a.m. Resumption of Business Session New Business
12:00 a.m. Recess—Breakfast and lunch provided by Mrs. Sherry Holland
1:00 p.m. Clergymen's Conference Women's Auxiliary
4:30 p.m. Supper Break—Provided by the hostess
5:00 p.m. Retiring of Colors

Evening prayer services will commence with Rev. Emerson Spider Sr. Sponsored by the officers and members.

JUNE 27, 1999
8:00 a.m. Raising of Colors
10:00 a.m. Business Session will resume (If warranted.)
12:00 p.m. Recess—Breakfast and lunch will be provided by officers, members
               and Mr. Eddie Etsitty in honor of Mrs. Loretta Primeaux

In the p.m., This Conference will conclude with the retirement of our National Ensigns and all members joining hands, forming a Circle Of Life, with a prayer to the Father, Son, and Holy Spirit. Amen.

So until next year, may the Great Spirit abide with you, guide and bless you all accordingly.

TAPS

Day is done, gone the sun, from the lake, from the hill, from the sky, all is well, safely rest. God is nigh. Thanks and praise for our days, 'neath the sky, as we go this we know, God is nigh.

Arlen Light Foot Sr., Chet Stoneman Sr., Quentin Bruguier Jr., Mike Neal Sr., and Gerald Primeaux Sr., will be in charge of all the flag ceremonies.

OLD GLORY

The symbol of freedom, freedom to sing the songs of praises to the sacred drum beat and the rattle of the sacred gourd. The color of Red—symbol for the blood, that was shed for numerous of wars. The color of White—symbol of virtue, innocence, pure and free as the spirit of our creator. The color Blue—symbol of the sky, where our sacred Eagle soars.

Old Glory—the symbol of freedom. Freedom to pray to the Great Spirit for courage, guidance and blessings of good health.

Old Glory—the symbol of freedom for men and women who sacrificed their lives so we may live in peace and harmony.

Old Glory—a symbol of freedom where all men are equal.

—By J. Never Misses A Shot

WOPILA TANKA

We, the Native American Church of South Dakota, Inc., take this opportunity to thank the hostess, Mrs. Loretta Primeaux, and all those caring individuals who have contributed their time, labor or donations to make this Conference possible. May the Great Spirit bestow his blessings upon them and their families.

Congratulations to all the Native American Church youth who have graduated from Head Start, 8th grade, 12th grade and college. They are the future of our Native American Church.

A "SPECIAL THANKS" to all our veterans who take care of all our flag ceremonies.

Notes

ABBREVIATIONS

AIRP   American Indian Research Project, University of South Dakota
ARCIA Annual Report, Commissioner of Indian Affairs
BIA   Bureau of Indian Affairs
CCF   Central Classified Files
CIA   Commissioner of Indian Affairs
IAIS   Institute of American Indian Studies, University of South Dakota
NA   National Archives, Washington, D.C.
NAKC   National Archives, Kansas City
RA   Richardson Archives, University of South Dakota
RG   Record Group, National Archives
USD   University of South Dakota

PREFACE

1. Steinhard, "Introduction"; McCall, *African in Time–Perspective,* 76–77; Vansina, *Oral Tradition;* Vansina, *Oral Tradition as History;* Henige, *Oral Historiography.* Henige's work is a significant revision of the use of oral data. Vansina's second book on oral tradition is a major revision of his first study.

2. Asa Primeaux, Sr., interview by author, 20 September 1991.

3. Ella C. Deloria, "Some Notes on the Yankton," 3.

4. Joe Packard, interview by author, 5 October 1991.

5. Werbner, *Tears of the Dead.*

6. Asa also invited four Capital University faculty members to spend several weeks at his home in order to learn about American Indian culture. After he received

an honorary degree, family and friends honored him with a special Peyote religious service.

7. Ake Hultkrantz, the well-known scholar of comparative religion, uses the term "traditional Indian religion."

CHAPTER ONE. THE SIOUX

1. Asa Primeaux, Sr., interview by author, 11 May 1992; Parnell Necklace, interview by author, 30 October 1991.

2. Parks and Rankin, "Siouan Languages," 104–105; Swanton, "Siouan Tribes and the Ohio Valley"; Foster, "Language and the Culture History of North America," 100–101; Hollow and Parks, "Studies in Plains Linguistics," 69–70, 76–77; Goddard, "The Classification of the Native Languages of North America."

3. For a thorough review of the literature and oral traditions concerning Sioux origins, see Bruguier, "The Yankton Sioux Tribe," 7–14; Parks and Rankin, "Siouan Languages," 100, mention that the Dhegihas have oral traditions linking them to the lower Ohio Valley.

4. Hare, "The Yankton Indians," 321.

5. Swanton, "Siouan Tribes," 49. Also see Bruguier, "Yankton Sioux," 23–24, for further discussion of migration patterns from the east coast and the Ohio River Valley.

6. Paul Picotte, interview by Richard Loder, Summer 1969, AIRP; Deloria, *Speaking of Indians*, 8.

7. Bruguier, "Yankton Sioux," 69–78; Powers, *Oglala Religion*, 5, 16–17; Armstrong, *From Sea unto Sea*, map 21 (1719), map 24 (1752); DeMallie, "Sioux until 1850," 722–32. This includes a 1697 map showing the same divisions, as well as DeMallie's thorough analysis of Sioux villages at the end of the seventeenth century.

8. Bruguier, "Yankton Sioux," 19–20; Powers, *Oglala Religion*, 16–17; Woolworth, *Sioux Indians III*, 8; DeMallie, "Sioux until 1850," 727–32.

9. DeMallie, "Sioux until 1850," 727–32; DeMallie and Parks, eds., *Sioux Indian Religion* (editors' introduction), 6; Powers, *Oglala Religion*, 11–14; Grobsmith, *Lakota of the Rosebud*, 6–8; Hoover, *The Yankton Sioux*, 14; Woolworth, *Sioux Indians III*, 7–8; Howard, "The Dakota or Sioux Tribe," 3; Hassrick, *The Sioux*, 3–6.

10. DeMallie, "Sioux until 1850," 725; Hoover, *Yankton Sioux*, 14; Hoover, "Arikara, Sioux, and Government Farmers," 28–30; Howard, "The Dakota or Sioux Tribe," 4–6; Woolworth, *Sioux Indians III*, 9–24; Bruguier, "Yankton Sioux," 43–44. See Bruguier for a review of gender roles in Sioux society, 46–50. For the economic life of the eastern Sioux, see Anderson, *Kinsmen of Another Kind*, 1–28.

11. DeMallie, "Sioux until 1850," 724–25.

12. Hassrick, *The Sioux*, 63; Robinson, "A History of the Dakota or Sioux Indians," 20; Woolworth, *Sioux Indians III*, 15; Anderson, "Early Dakota Migration and Intertribal Wars," 17.

13. Anderson, "Early Dakota Migration," 18–26.

14. DeMallie, "Sioux until 1850," 727; Hoover, *Yankton Sioux*, 14; Bruguier, "Yankton Sioux," 16–17; Hassrick, *The Sioux*, 65. Hassrick's view of Sioux expansion also takes account of multifaceted causation.

15. Bruguier, "Yankton Sioux," 97–98; DeMallie, "Sioux until 1850," 727, 731–35, 748, map on 719; Anderson, *Kinsmen of Another Kind*, 2; Abel, ed., *Tabeau's Narrative of Loisel's Expedition to the Upper Missouri*, 122–23.

16. Bruguier, "Yankton Sioux," 16–17; Powers, *Oglala Religion*, 5; Hoover, *Yankton Sioux*, 11. Douglas Parks claims that the translation of the word "Sioux" as snake or enemy is a misrepresentation. There are many variations in the transliteration of the Ojibwa and French term for the Sioux. For a thorough synonymy, see DeMallie, "Sioux until 1850," 749–50 (Parks is the author of this section).

17. John Wesley Powell, "Note by the Director," in Riggs, *A Dakota-English Dictionary*, xi; Powers, *Oglala Religion*, 6–9; Foster, "Language and the Culture History of North America," 101; Hollow and Parks, "Studies in Plains Linguistics," 69–76; Riggs, *Dakota Grammar, Texts, and Ethnography*, 177–78, 185–86, 178n1. Riggs's 1852 work was reprinted posthumously in two parts. The dictionary section was expanded and published in 1890 and reprinted in 1992. The grammar section of the 1852 work was expanded with the addition of some Lakota terms, published in 1893, and reprinted in 1973.

18. DeMallie and Parks, "Editors's Introduction," in DeMallie and Parks, *Sioux Indian Religion*, 7; DeMallie, "Sioux until 1850," 750; Agnes Picotte, "Editorial Notes," in Deloria, *Speaking of Indians*, 15, supports the view that the Yanktons at one time spoke Nakota and called themselves Nakotas.

19. Carolyn I. Schommer, "Foreword to the Reprint Edition," in Riggs, *A Dakota-English Dictionary*, v.

20. Konnie LeMay, "Sisseton-Wahpeton First to Drop 'Sioux' from Name," *Indian Country Today*, 27 October 1993, B1–2.

21. DeMallie, "Sioux until 1850," 727; Bruguier, "Yankton Sioux," 101; Hassrick, *The Sioux*, 69–70. For a traditional version of how the Sioux acquired the horse, see Black Elk's account in DeMallie, ed., *The Sixth Grandfather*, 314–16.

22. See Powers, *Oglala Religion*, 45–47, for an analysis of the meaning of *wakan*.

23. Bruguier, "Yankton Sioux," 99; Haines, *The Buffalo*, 42–43, 63.

24. Bruguier, "Yankton Sioux," 100–101; Hassrick, *The Sioux*, 90–91.

25. Haines, *The Buffalo*, 25–27.

26. Bruguier, "Yankton Sioux," 46–47.

27. Brown, *The Sacred Pipe*, 17–19.

28. Haines, *The Buffalo*, 25–27.

29. White, "The Winning of the West," 330; Haines, *The Buffalo*, 115–17; Bruguier, "Yankton Sioux," 83–110. Bruguier includes an overall analysis of the impact of iron trade goods and the introduction of the horse.

30. Looking Horse, "The Sacred Pipe in Modern Life," 68–73; Thomas, "A Sioux Medicine Bundle."

31. Looking Horse, "The Sacred Pipe," 68–69.

32. Ibid., 73.

33. Brown, *The Sacred Pipe*, 5–6. For a critical assessment of the teachings of Black Elk, see Rice, *Black Elk's Story.*

34. Brown, *The Sacred Pipe*, 7.

35. Ibid., 72.

36. Ibid., 68–100; Amiotte, "The Lakota Sun Dance"; Powers, *Oglala Religion*, 95–100. Part of this account is based on personal experience. In 1988 and 1989 I attended Sun Dances sponsored by Paul George Godfrey on the Rosebud Reservation. From 1990 to 2002 I attended Sun Dances on the Yankton Reservation sponsored by Asa and Loretta Primeaux. I participated as a Sun Dancer and served as a fireman or cedarman at the other Sun Dances.

37. Brown, *The Sacred Pipe*, 116–26; Deloria, *Speaking of Indians*, 43–44; Powers, *Oglala Religion*, 101.

38. Powers, *Yuwipi*, for an analysis of the interrelationships among the Sweat Lodge ceremony, the Vision Quest, and the Yuwipi.

39. Haines, *The Buffalo*, 191, 205–206; Smits, "The Frontier Army and the Destruction of the Buffalo," 319–20.

40. Smits, "Frontier Army," 314–15, 332–38 (quotations on 337).

41. Grinnell, "The Last of the Buffalo," 286.

CHAPTER TWO. THE IHANKTONWAN (YANKTON) NATION

1. Woolworth, *Sioux Indians III*, 31–35; DeMallie, "Sioux until 1850," 724.

2. DeMallie, "Sioux until 1850," 727, 731; Hoover, *Yankton Sioux*, 25; Woolworth, *Sioux Indians III*, 31–35; Bruguier, "Yankton Sioux," 81.

3. Hoover, *Yankton Sioux*, 25.

4. Howard, "The Dakota or Sioux Tribe," 290.

5. Ibid., 320.

6. Sometimes July is called *mdokeèokawi* or midsummer moon.

7. Howard, "The Dakota or Sioux Tribe," 282, 290–91, 301; Woolworth, *Sioux Indians III*, 24–26; Cutright, *Lewis and Clark*, 91.

8. Bruguier, "Yankton Sioux," 81; Sansom-Flood, *Lessons from Chouteau Creek*, 16; Woolworth, *Sioux Indians III*, 21–25, 35; Howard, "Dakota or Sioux Tribe," 291, 303.

9. Hoover, "Arikara, Sioux, and Government Farmers," 29–30; Howard, "Dakota or Sioux Tribe," 291–92; Woolworth, *Sioux Indians III, Report on the Yankton*, 35; DeMallie, "Yankton and Yanktonai," 779; Hare, "The Yankton Indians," 322. In 1912 Hare gave a speech in which he referred to this era as an idyllic period in Yankton history. He called it "an ideal age where children were brought up to respect proper values."

10. Bruguier, "Yankton Sioux," 114–18; Schilz and Schilz, "Beads, Bangles and Buffalo Robes"; Hoover, *Yankton Sioux*, 26; Woolworth, *Sioux Indians III*, 30–36.

11. Bruguier, "Yankton Sioux," 115–16; Sansom-Flood, *Lessons from Chouteau Creek*, 17–18; Woolworth, *Report on the Yankton*, 37–43.

12. Ronda, *Lewis and Clark among the Indians*, 255.

13. Ibid., 23–26; Bruguier, "Yankton Sioux," 123–25; Lewis and Clark, *History of the Lewis and Clark Expedition*, 1:92–93 (references from reprint edition).

14. Ronda, *Lewis and Clark*, 25–26; Woolworth, *Sioux Indians III*, 45–49, 53; Howard, "Dakota or Sioux Tribe," 287.

15. Lewis and Clark, *History of the Lewis and Clark Expedition*, 1:91.

16. Ibid., 85–88.

17. Sansom-Flood, *Lessons from Chouteau Creek*, 23; Paulson, *Sioux Collections*, 202 (Rockboy quotation); Bruguier, "Yankton Sioux," 122–24.

18. Asa Primeaux, Sr., interview by author, 20 September 1991.

19. Cutright, *Lewis and Clark*, 73–74; Lewis and Clark, *History of the Lewis and Clark Expedition*, 1:94–95; Bruguier, "Yankton Sioux," 125.

20. Bruguier, "Yankton Sioux," 293 (all the Yankton-U.S. treaties are reprinted on 292–319); and Sansom-Flood et al., *Remember Your Relatives*, 1:52–57, 2:95–107.

21. Paulson, "Federal Indian Policy and the Dakota Indians," 294–307; Hoover, *Yankton Sioux*, 27; Bruguier, "Yankton Sioux," 136–140, 304–308; Sansom-Flood and Bernie, *Remember Your Relatives*, 1:13; Howard, "Dakota or Sioux Tribe," 287–88; Woolworth, *Sioux Indians III*, 87–99.

22. Prucha, *The Great Father* (1995), 164–65, 1227–29. The federal government has not been consistent in its terminology for the Bureau of Indian Affairs. Over the years it has used "Office of Indian Affairs," "Bureau of Indian Affairs," and "Indian Service" interchangeably. This study follows the practice of the National Archives and Records Administration and uses "Bureau of Indian Affairs (BIA)" when referring to either government records or the government's administrative unit for Indian affairs. In 1947 "Bureau of Indian Affairs" became the official name.

23. Bruguier, "Yankton Sioux," 145, 311 (Treaty of 1837); Sansom-Flood and Bernie, *Remember Your Relatives*, 1:13; Paulson, "Federal Indian Policy," 307–308.

24. Hoover, *Yankton Sioux*, 26–28; Bruguier, "Yankton Sioux," 146; Woolworth, *Sioux Indians III*, 124–36.

25. "Digest of Reports of the Indian Commissioner 1815 through 1852," 501–502. The $5,000 in goods is also mentioned in the digest for 1846 (486).

26. Woolworth, *Sioux Indians III*, 227–29; Howard, "Dakota or Sioux Tribe," 289.

27. DeMallie, "Yankton and Yanktonai," 777; Bruguier, "Yankton Sioux," 147–49; Prucha, *Great Father*, 343–44.

28. Sansom-Flood and Bernie, *Remember Your Relatives*, 1:1–2; Dr. Leonard R. Bruguier (Tashunka Hinzi, Buckskin Horse), present-day Yankton historian and director of the Institute of American Indian Studies, USD, is a direct descendant of Theophile Bruguier and one of War Eagle's daughters.

29. Riggs, *A Dakota-English Dictionary*, 160n1.

30. Yankton Census, 1887, Indian Census Rolls, RG 75, National Archives (NA Microfilm Publication M595, Roll 680); Hoover, *Yankton Sioux*, 106–107; Bruguier, "Yankton Sioux," 177; Dorsey, "Siouan Sociology," 217–18; DeMallie, "Sioux until 1850," 740–42, gives a thorough listing of Yankton bands from extant sources.

31. Utley and Washburn, *Indian Wars,* 185–86; Woolworth, *Sioux Indians III,* 173–75; Hoover, *Yankton Sioux,* 16, 29–30; DeMallie, "Yankton and Yanktonai," 779.

32. Woolworth, *Report on the Yankton,* 178–79.

33. Ibid., 188; Sansom-Flood and Bernie, *Remember Your Relatives,* vol. 1; Sansom-Flood, *Lessons from Chouteau Creek,* 13–15, 19–20, 31–34; Bruguier, "Yankton Sioux," 158, 315–19.

34. Howard, "Dakota or Sioux Tribe," 389; Woolworth, *Sioux Indians III,* 188–89; Sansom-Flood and Bernie, *Remember Your Relatives,* 1:17.

35. Ibid., 1:5–6, 9–13, 19, 2:14; Woolworth, *Report on the Yankton,* 192–96.

36. Sansom-Flood, *Lessons from Chouteau Creek,* 22.

37. ARCIA, 1859: 121–27.

38. Bruguier, "Yankton Sioux," 155–56.

39. Hoover, *Yankton Sioux,* 40–41.

CHAPTER THREE. SAM NECKLACE AND RESERVATION LIFE

1. Yankton Census, 1887; Hoover, *Yankton Sioux,* 31–35; Bruguier, "Yankton Sioux," 179–83; ARCIA, 1859: 128.

2. Howard, "Dakota or Sioux Tribe," 282; Bruguier, "Yankton Sioux," 178–79, 189.

3. Hoover, *Yankton Sioux,* 33; Sansom-Flood, *Lessons from Chouteau Creek,* 39–52; Sansom-Flood et al., *Remember Your Relatives,* 2:1–5; Bruguier, "Yankton Sioux," 196–218; ARCIA, 1866: 180–85.

4. Utley and Washburn, *Indian Wars,* 202–204; Hoover, *Yankton Sioux,* 16; Sansom-Flood, *Lessons from Chouteau Creek,* 53–58; Bruguier, "Yankton Sioux," 200–206.

5. Paul Picotte, interview by Joseph Cash, 16 August 1968, AIRP.

6. ARCIA, 1873: 322, 333, 369; 1874: 400, 410; Hoover, *Yankton Sioux,* 36; DeMallie, "Yankton and Yanktonai," 779–80.

7. ARCIA, 1873: 323, 369; 1875: 472.

8. ARCIA, 1873: 303, 323–24, 369; 1874: 346–47, 401, 434; 1875: 472; Hoover, *Yankton Sioux,* 36.

9. Barton, *John P. Williamson,* 125–26.

10. Ibid., 124–36, 174; Hoover, *Yankton Sioux,* 41–44; Bruguier, "Yankton Sioux," 223–24; Sansom-Flood et al., *Remember Your Relatives,* 2:14–19.

11. Woodruff, "Episcopal Mission," 558–59, 578; Hoover, *Yankton Sioux,* 42–43; Bruguier, "Yankton Sioux," 224–28.

12. Howe, *Life and Labors of Bishop Hare,* 51–52, 92; Woodruff, "Episcopal Mission," 578; ARCIA, 1873: 323, 369; 1874: 418–19; 1875: 471.

13. Suttmiller, "A History of St. Paul's Indian School at Marty, South Dakota," 1–14; Duratschek, *Crusading along Sioux Trails,* 40–51, 275; Bruguier, "Yankton Sioux," 222–23; Hoover, *Yankton Sioux,* 44.

14. Prucha, *Great Father,* 503.

15. Ibid., 501–27.

16. Lewis, "Reservation Leadership and the Progressive-Traditional Dichotomy," 125.

17. Cook-Lynn, "A Monograph of a Peyote Singer"; Abdo et al., *Yankton Sioux Peyote Songs*. See discography. As a result of ill health, in his last years Asa no longer served as a roadman; but he continued to attend Peyote meetings.

18. Asa Primeaux, Sr., taped recording of naming ceremony for Daniel Necklace, 15 August 1982.

19. 53rd Congress, 2nd Session, Senate, Ex. Document 27, 18 January 1894, 47; 56th Congress, 1st Session, House of Representatives, Doc. No. 535, 26 March 1900, 27–29.

20. Register of Yankton Families, 1900, Yankton Agency, Box 32, RG 75, NAKC. The original and microfilm are available.

21. Farming and Grazing Lease, Peter Baker Necklace, CCF, Yankton, 1907–39, Box 126, RG 75, NA.

22. Sansom-Flood et al., *Remember Your Relatives*, 2:49.

23. Weeks, "Humanity and Reform," 180–84.

24. Quoted in ibid., 185.

25. McDonnell, *The Dispossession of the American Indian, 1887–1934*, 2; Weeks, "Humanity and Reform," 185–87.

26. McDonnell, *Dispossession*, 124.

27. Bruguier, "Yankton Sioux," 254.

28. These photographs can be found in Hoover, *Yankton Sioux*, 32; Sansom-Flood et al., *Remember Your Relatives*, 1:4, 2:30.

29. Hoover, *Yankton Sioux*, 35–40.

30. Cecil Provost, interview by Joseph Cash, 19 August 1968, AIRP; Paul Picotte, interview by Joseph Cash, 16 August 1968, AIRP.

31. ARCIA, 1887: 59; 1888: 68–71; McDonnell, *Dispossession*, 20–22; Hoover, *Yankton Sioux*, 39; Sansom-Flood et al., *Remember Your Relatives*, 2:27.

32. The report of the commissioners, the agreement, the minutes of the negotiations, individual testimony, and the signatures were entered into the *Congressional Record*. Report of the Yankton Indian Commission, 53rd Congress, 2nd Session, Senate, Ex. Doc. No. 27, 18 January 1894, 1–101.

33. Ibid., 30–32.

34. Harwood, "Opening the Yankton Reservation to Settlement," 381; The poster can be found in Frazier, ed., *Many Nations*, 67.

35. Sansom-Flood et al., *Remember Your Relatives*, 2:39–41; reprint of the Agreement of 1892, 101–107.

36. Report of the Yankton Indian Commission, 47.

37. Ibid., 16.

38. Sansom-Flood et al., *Remember Your Relatives*, 2:11, 23; Pupils in St. Paul's School, Yankton Dakota, Folder 7 (Negative No. 54,535), National Anthropological Archives, Washington, D.C.

39. Zitkala-Ša, *Old Indian Legends*; Zitkala-Ša, *American Indian Stories*.

40. Zitkala-Ša, *American Indian Stories,* 55–56. This originally appeared as "The School Days of an Indian Girl."

41. Ibid., 62–63.

42. Adams, "From Bullets to Boarding Schools," 222–33.

43. ARCIA, 1884: 106; 1885: 284.

44. Joe Rockboy, interview by Herbert Hoover, 19 February 1975, AIRP.

45. David Zephier, Sr., "Memorandum for the Commissioner," 9 April 1906, Yankton Sioux, RG 75, NA, IAIS.

46. Paul Picotte, interview by Richard Loder, 15 July 1969, AIRP; Woodruff, "Episcopal Mission," 580, mentions Anna M. Baker; Affidavit of Samuel Baker or Samuel Baker Necklace, 26 March 1917, CCF, Yankton, Box 95, RG 75, NA.

47. Annual Narrative Reports, Flandreau Indian School, RG 75, NA, Micro Series 1011, Roll 42; 1902 Report Card, Attendance Registers, Box 2, Flandreau Indian School, RG 75, NAKC.

48. Mae Eastman, interview by Vince Pratt, 28 July 1971, AIRP; Lottie Good Thunder, interview by Vince Pratt, 11 August 1971, AIRP; Cornelia Eller, interview by Herbert Hoover, Summer 1972, AIRP; Mildred Stinson, interview by M. Edward McGaa, Spring 1968, AIRP; Fred Eastman, interview by M. Edward McGaa, Spring 1968, AIRP.

49. Attendance Registers, Enrollment Registers, Flandreau Indian School, RG 75, NAKC; Annual Narrative Reports, Flandreau Indian School, RG 75, NA, Micro Series 1011, Roll 42.

50. Woodruff, "Episcopal Mission," 563–79; Howe, *Life and Labors of Bishop Hare,* 97–98.

51. ARCIA, 1901: 379; 1911: 77.

52. ARCIA, 1898, "Report of Missionary," 291–92.

53. ARCIA, 1899, "Report of Missionary," 350.

54. Paul Picotte, interview by Joseph Cash, 16 August 1968, AIRP.

55. Hoover, *Yankton Sioux,* 46; ARCIA, 1898: 289; 1909: 3.

56. ARCIA, 1901: 377; 1902: 350.

57. Prucha, *Great Father,* 672; McDonnell, *Dispossession,* 60–62.

58. McDonnell, *Dispossession,* 70.

59. Hoover, *Yankton Sioux,* 46–47, 52–53; Hoover, "Yankton Sioux Experience in the Great Indian Depression, 1900–1930," 62–63; DeMallie, "Yankton and Yanktonai," 790–91.

60. Yankton Census, 1900.

61. Asa Primeaux, Sr., interview by author, 20 September 1991.

62. The treaty monument has never met with universal approbation. Today it is not particularly popular with the Yanktons, but it is a tourist attraction and is marked on official South Dakota maps. I would like to thank Professor Herbert T. Hoover for sharing information on the Monument Society. The photograph taken at the monument site is in Sansom-Flood et al., *Remember Your Relatives,* 2:67. The Monument Society material is in CCF, Yankton, Box 1, RG 75, NA.

63. Supt. James Staley to BIA, Petition enclosure, 18 April 1902; Thomas Ryan to BIA, 5 August 1902, Yankton Sioux, RG 75, NA, IAIS.

CHAPTER FOUR. THE PEYOTE RELIGION

1. Hoover, *Yankton Sioux,* 39.
2. Deloria, "Some Notes on the Yankton," 5. This article contains a photograph of the inside of the store.
3. Pauline Necklace Kezena, interview by author, 17 September 1991.
4. Asa Primeaux, Sr., interview by author, 20 September 1991.
5. Felix T. Brunot, et al to CIA, 1908 [*sic*], Box 1, Folder 1, Yankton: 1908–28, Tribal Rights and Enrollment Committee, RG 75, Richardson Archive, University of South Dakota (RA). The Richardson Archive has a limited collection of photocopied documents on the Yankton from Record Group 75, National Archives, Washington, D.C.
6. Petition to BIA, n.d., Box 2, Folder 9, Yankton: 1907–31, Land Sales and Allotments, RG 75, RA; Valentine to William Bean et al, Yankton Indians, 13 May 1910.
7. Ibid., Estep to CIA, 21 January 1910; Valentine to Estep, 4 February 1910.
8. Ibid., Estep to Valentine, 7 March 1910; Estep to Valentine, 23 April 1910.
9. Ibid., Petition to CIA, 25 April 1910.
10. Second Assistant CIA to Leech, 24 May 1912, Box 2, Folder 4, Yankton 1912, Tribal Councils, Organizations, RG 75, RA.
11. Ibid., Leech to CIA, 10 May 1912.
12. Paul Picotte, interview by Joseph Cash, 16 August 1968, AIRP, USD.
13. McDonnell, *Dispossession,* 55.
14. Ibid., 88–89; Prucha, *Great Father,* 875–76.
15. McDonnell, *Dispossession,* 93, 103; Prucha, *Great Father,* 875–77.
16. ARCIA, 1907: 67, 77; 1908: 63.
17. ARCIA, 1909: 3; 1911: 197.
18. ARCIA, 1913: 113; McDonnell, *Dispossession,* 93, 142*n*25.
19. Samuel Baker Necklace, Farming and Grazing Lease, 4 December 1913, CCF, Yankton, Box 126, RG 75, NA; Peter Baker Necklace, Farming and Grazing Lease, 2 April 1914; Foot Necklace, Farming and Grazing Lease, 7 March 1914; Heirs of Iron Necklace, Farming and Grazing Lease, 16 January 1914; Charlie Jones, Farming and Grazing Lease, 18 December 1913.
20. ARCIA, 1915: 94–95.
21. McDowell, *Dispossession,* 93, 102; Prucha, *Great Father,* 879–84.
22. McDowell, *Dispossession,* 97.
23. Ibid., 96; Hoxie, *The Final Promise,* 180–81.
24. "A Ritual of Citizenship."
25. "Indian Ritual Admission to Citizenship," in Lane and Wall, *The Letters of Franklin K. Lane,* 208–10.

26. "A Ritual of Citizenship," 162.

27. Lane to George Wickersham, 17 May 1916, in Lane and Wall, *Letters of Franklin K. Lane*, 207.

28. Supt. Leech to Lane, 21 June 1916; Felix Brunot et al. to Lane, 27 July 1916, quoted in McDonnell, *Dispossession,* 101.

29. McDonnell, *Dispossession,* 101; Evan G. Boyd, Special Officer to H. A. Larson, Chief Special Officer, 10 April 1916, Records of Law and Order Section, Box 1, RG 75, NA. Boyd wrote that "there seems to be an organized bunch in every town that is laying for the Indian, to give him liquor and get what they have in trade or money."

30. ARCIA, 1919: 83; Hoover, "Yankton Sioux Experience."

31. Walter Runke to William Johnson, 30 March 1911, CCF, 1907–39, Liquor Traffic, Box 3, RG 75, NA.

32. Superintendents' Annual Narrative and Statistical Reports, Yankton Agency, 1911, RG 75, NA (Microfilm Publication M 1011, roll 72). Annual Narratives follow the fiscal year, 30 June to 30 June (henceforth Superintendents' Annual Narrative).

33. Yankton Agency to Office of Indian Affairs, 7 April 1900, 26 November 1900, CCF, Yankton, RG 75, NA. I would like to thank Professor Hoover of the University of South Dakota for making documents relevant to Charlie Jones available to me.

34. A. W. Leech to CIA, 10 February 1912, CCF, Yankton, RG 75, NA.

35. Statement signed by Charles Jones, 12 February 1912, CCF, Yankton, RG 75, NA.

36. F. H. Abbott, Assistant CIA to Leech, 8 March 1912, CCF, Yankton, RG 75, NA.

37. Superintendents' Annual Narrative, 1913, roll 72.

38. Report of S. A. M. Young, 18 April 1914, CCF, Yankton, Box 7, RG 75, NA; E. B. Merritt, Assistant Commissioner of Indian Affairs to Young, 6 May 1914.

39. Leech to Henry Larson, Chief Special Officer, 13 November 1916, Correspondence of Chief Special Officer, Records of Law and Order Section, Box 1, RG 75, NA; David A. Richardson, M.D., to Leech, 10 November 1916.

40. "Statement of Mr. Charles Jones, with reference to the use of peyote among the Sioux Indians," enclosed in Leach to Larson, n.d.

41. Asa Primeaux, Sr., interview by author, 4 May 1991.

42. Pauline Necklace Kezena, interview by author, 17 September 1991.

43. Eunice Rainbow Dog Soldier, interview by author, 17 September 1991.

44. Clarence Rockboy, interview by author, 25 November 1991.

45. Abdo et al., *Yankton Sioux Peyote Songs*, vol. 1, IH 4371 and 4371C (cassette). The seven Yankton singers are Joe Abdo, Sr., Quentin Bruguier, Lorenzo Dion, Asa Primeaux, Sr., Francis Primeaux, Duane Shields, and Joseph Shields, Sr. Reissued in 2003 in CD format by Indian House.

46. Louie Stricker, interview by Omer C. Stewart, 1972, Stewart Papers.

47. "Statement of Mr. Charles Jones, with reference to the use of peyote."

48. Asa Primeaux, Sr., interview by author, 4 May 1991. In sworn testimony concerning his land, Sam Necklace said he was in Oklahoma in 1916.

49. ARCIA, 1905: Part 1, Winnebago, 253.

50. Quentin Bruguier, interview by author, 6 June 1993. I attended a Peyote meeting with John Decora just before he passed away. We spent several hours discussing the long relationship between Winnebago and Yankton Peyotists. Louie Stricker, interview by Omer C. Stewart, 1972, discusses the early relationship with the Winnebagos.

51. For additional insights into the Peyote religion during its early years, see Radin, ed., *Autobiography of a Winnebago Indian*. This is the autobiography of Sam Blowsnake, whose pseudonym is Crashing Thunder. Reissued in an expanded version in 1926 as Radin, ed., *Crashing Thunder*. Also see Blowsnake (Sam's brother), in Radin, "Personal Reminiscences of a Winnebago Indian," and their sister, in Lurie, ed., *Mountain Wolf Woman, Sister of Crashing Thunder*. There is additional autobiographical material in Radin, *The Winnebago Tribe*, which includes the autobiographies of John Rave, Albert Hensley, and Jesse Clay. The Wisconsin Winnebagos today call themselves the Ho-Chunks; however, throughout the twentieth century they were referred to as the Winnebagos. For consistency with the sources, I use the name "Winnebago," except when using it in a contemporary sense.

52. Stewart, *Peyote Religion*, 144–45.

53. Rave quoted in Radin, *The Winnebago Tribe*, 389, 393.

54. Ibid., 391; Radin, "A Sketch of the Peyote Cult of the Winnebago," 5–12; LaBarre, *Peyote Cult*, 121.

55. Radin, *Autobiography of a Winnebago Indian*, 55n153.

56. Albert Hensley to CIA [Francis Leupp], 9 October 1908, Correspondence of the Chief Special Officer, Records of Law and Order Section, Box 1, RG 75, NA; Stewart, *Peyote Religion*, 230.

57. Stewart, *Peyote Religion*, 230; Slotkin, *The Peyote Religion*, 60.

58. Stewart, *Peyote Religion*, 149–51, 167; LaBarre, *Peyote Cult*, 162–65.

59. Anderson, *Peyote*, 44–45 (2nd ed.); LaBarre, *Peyote Cult*, 73–74, 164–65; Radin, *Winnebago Tribe*, 394–97, 400, 411–12; Radin, "Sketch of the Peyote Cult," 10–11.

60. Hensley quoted in Radin, *Winnebago Tribe*, 140.

61. Ibid., 420; Radin, "Sketch of the Peyote Cult," 11, 17–18.

62. William E. Johnson to CIA, 4 May 1908, Correspondence of Chief Special Officer, Records of Law and Order Section, Box 1, RG 75, NA; Johnson to Superintendents, 10 June 1909, CCF, Liquor Traffic, 1907–1939, Box 3, RG 75, NA; Stewart, *Peyote Religion*, 131–36.

63. Johnson to CIA, 11 September 1909; Radin, *Winnebago Tribe*, 415.

64. Radin, *Winnebago Tribe*, 417; LaBarre, *Peyote Cult*, 121; Stewart, *Peyote Religion*, 158–59.

65. Stewart, *Peyote Religion*, 161; LaBarre, *Peyote Cult*, 121; Radin, *Winnebago Tribe*, 417.

66. Hurt, "Factors in the Persistence of Peyote in the Northern Plains," 18.

67. For an in-depth view of contemporary Winnebago Peyotism, see Noah White, interview by Herbert Hoover, 25 June 1970, AIRP; Sterling Snake, interview by Herbert Hoover, 29 July 1970, AIRP; also see Hoover, "Interview: Noah White."

Sections of the Noah White and Sterling Snake interviews are also in Cash and Hoover, eds., *To Be An Indian,* 30–38.

68. Radin, *Winnebago Tribe,* 74.

69. Stewart, *Peyote Religion,* 3–4; Anderson, *Peyote,* 168–71, 176 (see chapter 8 for a botanical history of peyote).

70. Boyd, "Pictographic Evidence of Peyotism in Lower Pecos, Texas Archaic," 232, 244; Stewart, *Peyote Religion,* 8, 17. For the Huichol Indians, see Furst, *People of the Peyote.*

71. Kelsey, "The Pharmacology of Peyote"; Stewart, *Peyote Religion,* 3–4; Anderson, *Peyote,* 133–52.

72. Aberle, *Peyote Religion among the Navaho,* xli.

73. Mooney, "Peyote," 237; Schultes, "Peyote and Plants Confused with It," 61–88; Stewart, *Peyote Religion,* 4–7; Anderson, *Peyote,* 32–33, 163.

74. Slotkin, "Peyotism, 1521–1891," 204–207.

75. Quoted in Stewart, *Peyote Religion,* 19.

76. Stewart, *Peyote Religion,* 18–21; Anderson, *Peyote,* 4–11; Slotkin, "Peyotism, 1521–1891," 208.

77. Stewart, *Peyote Religion,* 20–24.

78. Ibid., 20–26, 30–31; Slotkin, "Peyotism: 1521–1891," 209; Anderson, *Peyote,* 24.

79. Stewart, *Peyote Religion,* 30–34. This section is a summary of Stewart's analysis of the transitional stage of Peyotism.

80. Moses, *The Indian Man,* 60; Stewart, *Peyote Religion,* 34–36.

81. Mooney, "The Mescal Plant and Ceremony," 7; Smith and Snake, eds., *One Nation under God,* 24.

82. Mooney, "Mescal Plant and Ceremony," 7–8.

83. Johnson to CIA, 4 May 1908, Correspondence of the Chief Special Officer, Law and Order Section, Box 1, RG 75, NA.

84. Stewart, *Peyote Religion,* 47–57; Slotkin, *Peyote Religion,* 34; LaBarre, *Peyote Cult,* 122.

85. Stewart, *Peyote Religion,* 58–62, includes a discussion of the sources concerning the Lipan Apaches.

86. Ibid., 41–42; LaBarre, *Peyote Cult,* 42, discusses some of the differences.

87. The best study of the Ghost Dance movement is still Mooney, *Ghost Dance Religion and the Sioux Outbreak.* Also see Kehoe, *The Ghost Dance.*

88. "Peyotists at Carlisle," Omer Stewart Papers, Box 65, Leaders and Indian Schools; Stewart, "The Peyote Religion and the Ghost Dance," 27–29; Stewart, *Peyote Religion,* 66–67; Hertzberg, *The Search for an American Indian Identity,* 13–15.

89. Stewart, *Peyote Religion,* 68–75; Hagan, *Quanah Parker,* 36–61, 116–19.

90. Swan, *Peyote Religious Art,* 30–31; Swan, "Early Osage Peyotism," 53–59; Wiedman, "Big and Little Moon Peyotism as Health Care Delivery Systems," 374–75; Anderson, *Peyote,* 44–45; Stewart, *Peyote Religion,* 88–90, contains Wilson's conversion experience as told to his nephew; LaBarre, *Peyote Cult,* 151–61, and diagram of a Half Moon altar, 44.

91. Stewart, *Peyote Religion*, 79; Howard, "Half Moon Way," 1–21.

92. Hodge, ed., *Handbook of American Indians North of Mexico*, 959. The photograph, in a larger format, is reprinted in Stewart, *Peyote Religion*, 85.

93. Stewart, *Peyote Religion*, 91–92.

94. Swan, *Peyote Religious Art*, 34–35; Wiedman, "Big and Little Moon Peyotism," 374–75; Newberne, *Peyote*, 33–36.

95. LaBarre, *Peyote Cult*, 113; Stewart, *Peyote Religion*, 97.

96. Newberne, *Peyote*, 33–36; Stewart, *Peyote Religion*, 148–209; Slotkin, *Peyote Religion*, 36–40.

97. Stewart, *Peyote Religion*, 87–88, 175–81; Stahl, "The Peyote Religion and the Sioux to 1945"; Hurt, "Factors in the Persistence of Peyote"; Crow Dog and Erdoes, *Crow Dog*, 94.

98. Superintendents' Annual Narrative, 1916, roll 173. Also see 1914, 1917, rolls 172, 173.

99. Ibid., 1914, roll 172.

100. Yankton Census, 1918; Newberne, *Peyote*, 26–36; Larson to CIA, 8 December 1916, Records of Law and Order Section, Box 1, RG 75, NA; Larson to CIA, 18 December 1916.

101. E. B. Meritt to Superintendents, 28 March 1919, Circular No. 1522, Peyote, CCF, 1907–39, Liquor Traffic, Box 2. Copies of the responses of the Yankton Agency personnel can be found in Omer Stewart Papers, Box 43. The originals are in CCF, 1907–39, Liquor Traffic, RG 75, NA.

102. Superintendents' Annual Narrative, 1920, roll 173; Hoover, *Yankton Sioux*, 56.

103. Superintendents' Annual Narrative, 1918, roll 173.

104. Ibid., 1920.

105. Joe Packard, interview by author, 16 September 1991, AIRP.

106. Sansom-Flood et al., *Remember Your Relatives*, 2:71.

107. Hoover, *Yankton Sioux*, 52.

108. Superintendents' Annual Narrative, 1911, roll 172. There is a photograph of a Yankton dancehall in Sansom-Flood et al., *Remember Your Relatives*, 2:58.

109. ARCIA, 1906: 16–23; 1913: 10; 1915: 23–26; Fair Programs: "First Annual Sioux Indian Fair, Greenwood, S.D., 1913," "Second Annual Yankton Sioux Fair, 1914," CCF, Yankton, Box 1, RG 75, NA.

110. Fair Programs: "First Annual Sioux Indian Fair, Greenwood, S.D., 1913," "Second Annual Yankton Sioux Fair, 1914"; Leech to CIA, 11 October 1912, CCF, Yankton, Box 1, RG 75, NA; Leech to CIA, 4 November 1912; Leech to CIA, 6 October 1913; Cato Sells to Leech, 24 October 1913; Sells to Homer Redlightning, 24 October 1913; Leech to CIA, 17 December 1914; Sells to Redlightning, 12 January 1915.

111. ARCIA, 1914: 23; Hoover, *Yankton Sioux*, 55–57; Maroukis, "Yankton Sioux Tribal Fairs"; "Agricultural Reports to Bureau of Indian Affairs, 1913–1922," Yankton Sioux, Box 3, RG 75, RA.

112. Joe Packard, interview by author, 5 October 1991, AIRP.

113. Daniel to CIA, 2 July 1925, Box 2, Law and Order, RG 75, RA.

114. ARCIA, 1924: 13–14.

115. Hoover, "Yankton Sioux Experience," 53–69.

116. Stewart, *Peyote Religion*, 181.

117. Brumble, *American Indian Autobiography*, 118–46, contains an analysis of Sam Blowsnake's and Albert Hensley's autobiographies, including their conversion experience.

118. Yankton Census, 1900–1906, 1928; Pauline Necklace Kezena, interview by author, 17 September 1991; Asa Primeaux, Sr., interview by author, 20 September 1991. Auntie Pauline was in a position to know a great deal about her uncle Sam's life. For a period in the late 1920s to early 1930s, she lived with Sam, Mary, and Frances. When she enrolled at Flandreau Indian School, her uncle Sam was listed as her legal guardian.

119. Yankton Census, 1906, 1907.

120. Mary Chinn Baker to R. J. Taylor, December 1907, CCF, Yankton, Box 86, RG 75, NA; Taylor to CIA, 29 January 1908: Acting Commissioner Valentine to Mary Chinn Baker, 7 February 1908; Mary Chinn to Taylor, CCF, Yankton, Box 88; Taylor to CIA, 28 January 1909; Chief Clerk, Office of Indian Affairs to Mary Chinn, 8 February 1909.

121. Katherine Sing Necklace, interview by author, 1 October 1992. In order to respect the privacy of those involved I have not used last names.

122. Report of S. A. M. Young, Supervisor, Yankton Agency Schools, December 1912, CCF, Yankton, Box 8, RG 75, NA; BIA to Secretary of the Interior, 8 March 1916, CCF, Yankton, Box 94, RG 75, NA; Patent in Fee Report, Samuel B. Necklace, 8 February 1916, CCF, Yankton, Box 95, RG 75, NA.

123. Sworn statements of Samuel N. Baker, Yankton Agency, 26 February 1917, 20 March 1917, 25 March 1917, CCF, Yankton, Box 95, RG 75, NA; Application for a Patent in Fee, Samuel Baker, 3 May 1920, CCF, Yankton, Box 104, RG 75, NA; Report on Application for a Patent in Fee, Samuel Baker, 4 June 1920; Sells to Superintendent Yankton Agency, 9 August 1920.

124. Joe Packard, interview by author, 16 September 1991, AIRP; Pauline Necklace Kezena, interview by author, 17 September 1991.

125. Asa Primeaux, Sr., interview by author, 20 September 1991.

126. Ibid.

127. Ibid.

128. Asa Primeaux, Sr., interview by author, 4 May 1991; Asa Primeaux, Jr., interview by author, 8 June 1996; Eunice Rainbow Dog Soldier, interview by author, 17 September 1991. Auntie Eunice confirmed Sam's altar. I have chosen not to describe the markings within the altar, because they belong to the spiritual legacy of Sam Necklace's descendants and not to the public domain.

129. Asa Primeaux, Sr., interview by author, 4 May 1991; Asa Primeaux, Jr., interview by author, 8 June 1996. During a later interview Asa, Sr., reiterated the description and significance of the markings (30 January 1992).

130. Howard, "Half Moon Way," 5; Shonle, "Peyote, the Giver of Visions," 69; Catches, "Native American Church," 18.

131. Stewart, *Peyote Religion*, 223–24; LaBarre, *Peyote Cult*, 168–69, 294; Slotkin, *Peyote Religion*, 58, 135*n*11, 136*n*15. Slotkin reviews the arguments used by Peyotists to show parallels with Christianity, 65–77.

132. Stewart, *Peyote Religion*, 217; Slotkin, *Peyote Religion*, 53–54; Welsh, "Peyote—An Insidious Evil"; Seymour, "Peyote Worship."

133. Welch, "Zitkala-Ša," 84–85, 137–41; Stewart, *Peyote Religion*, 198–200, 221; Slotkin, *Peyote Religion*, 58; LaBarre, *Peyote Cult*, 169; Willard, "The First Amendment, Anglo-Conformity and American Indian Religious Freedom," 26–30.

134. Mooney, "Mescal Plant and Ceremony"; Mooney, "Peyote," 237; Moses, *The Indian Man*, 57–60, 182–84, 200–203.

135. Congress, House, Subcommittee of the Committee on Indian Affairs, Peyote Hearings, HR 2614, 65th Congress 2nd Sess. pt. 1, 21–25 February; pt. 2, 23 March 1918; Stewart, *Peyote Religion*, 218–22; Willard, "First Amendment," 26–32; Welsh, "Zitkala-Ša," 140; Moses, *The Indian Man*, 200–203.

136. Stewart, *Peyote Religion*, 222–25; Willard, "First Amendment," 34–35; Slotkin, *Peyote Religion*, 55, 58. For correspondence concerning Mooney's involvement in the incorporation of the Native American Church and his removal from Oklahoma, see Slotkin, *Peyote Religion*, 136–37*n*18 and *n*19.

137. Stewart, *Peyote Religion*, 221; Willard, "First Amendment," 34–35; Slotkin, *Peyote Religion*, 55.

138. Welch, "Zitkala-Ša," 168–69.

139. Meritt, *Concerning Peyote.*

140. Slotkin, *Peyote Religion*, 56; Stewart, *Peyote Religion*, 226–27; Stewart, "Peyote and the Law," 47–48.

141. Welch, "Zitkala-Ša," 47; Stewart, "Gertrude Simmons Bonnin."

CHAPTER FIVE. THE NATIVE AMERICAN CHURCH OF CHARLES MIX COUNTY

1. ARCIA, 1922: 20

2. Ibid.

3. Stewart, *Peyote Religion*, 227.

4. Ibid., 226–27.

5. Newberne, *Peyote*, 8, 11.

6. Ibid., 13.

7. Ibid., 22.

8. Stewart, *Peyote Religion*, 230; Slotkin, *Peyote Religion*, 61.

9. Notebook of Sam Necklace, Institute of American Indian Studies, USD. I am using the capitalization and spelling in the notebook.

10. Copies of incorporation papers are available from the secretary of state, South Dakota.

11. Stewart, *Peyote Religion*, 230.

12. Eunice Rainbow Dog Soldier, interview by author, 17 September 1991.

13. Notebook of Sam Necklace.

14. Clarence Rockboy, interview by author, 25 November 1991.

15. Joseph Shields, Sr., interview, 1976, record notes, in Abdo et al., *Yankton Sioux Peyote Songs*, Indian House, IH 4371C.

16. Quentin Bruguier, interview by author, 6 June 1993.

17. *State of South Dakota: Proceedings of the Senate*, 103, 106, 109, 127; *State of South Dakota: Proceedings of the House of Representatives*, 110–11, 130, 143; Stewart, *Peyote Religion*, 227–28; Slotkin, *Peyote Religion*, 56.

18. Stewart, "Peyote and the Law," 47–49; *State of South Dakota: Biennial Report of the Attorney General, 1923–1924*, 86–89.

19. U.S. Office of Indian Affairs, "Peyote" (mimeograph).

20. Hoover, *Yankton Sioux*, 44–45.

21. Carson, *Blackrobe for the Yankton Sioux*, 1–5, 90–91; Suttmiller, "History of St. Paul's," 15–27; Wolff, "Father Sylvester Eisenman and Marty Mission," 360–64; Zens, "The Education Work of the Catholic Church among the Indians of South Dakota from the Beginning to 1935," 340–41; Hoover, *Yankton Sioux*, 44–45. Mother Katherine Drexel of Philadelphia was a major benefactor to Father Sylvester.

22. Eisenman Papers, Sample Letter, 26 April 1923, Folder 1, RA.

23. Wolff, "Father Sylvester," 365–77; Carson, *Blackrobe*, 122–45, see 134 and 141 for photographs of the Indian children on fund-raising trips. Carson is Father Sylvester's sister.

24. Grace Picotte, interview by Herbert Hoover, 7 July 1973, AIRP, discusses quilts and fund-raising. In 1926 there were at least three land purchases made in Father Sylvester's name. See Receipt for Patents and Transmit Patents, CCF, Yankton, Box 109, RG 75, NA.

25. Wolff, "Father Sylvester," 372–74, 388–89; Suttmiller, "History of St. Paul's," 78–79; "With the Medicine Eaters," *Little Bronzed Angel* 3:12 (May 1927).

26. Williamson to Burke, 23 February 1923, Yankton, Box 2, RG 75, RA.

27. Petitioners to CIA, 14 March 1916, CCF, Yankton, Liquor Traffic, Box 4, RG 75, NA; Leech to CIA, 17 March 1916; Meritt, Assistant CIA to Leech, 28 March 1916.

28. Hoover, "Yankton Sioux Experience," 64.

29. Daniel to CIA, 21 February 1924, CCF, Yankton, RG 75, IAIS.

30. Catlin, *Letters and Notes on the Manners, Customs, and Conditions of the North American Indians*, 2:168, plate 270; For contemporary narratives of the great flood and the origin of the red pipestone, see Crow Dog and Erdoes, *Crow Dog*, 134–35; Lame Deer and Erdoes, *Lame Deer*, 236.

31. Hoover, "Yankton Sioux Tribal Claims," 128–30; Corbett, "The Red Pipestone Quarry," 108–13.

32. Welch, "Zitkala-Ša," 177–94; Jennings Wise to Burke, 24 April 1924, CCF, Yankton, Box 14, RG 75, NA. Wise wrote to Burke informing him that Bonnin was employed by his firm working on the case *Yankton Sioux* v. *United States*.

33. Souvenir Program, IAIS. The program includes a brief historical sketch of the Yanktons and a list of all the guests.

34. Hearing before E. B. Meritt, Assistant CIA of Indian Affairs, 9 March 1925, CCF, Yankton, RG 75, IAIS, USD.

35. Burke to Daniel, 10 March 1925, CCF, Yankton, Box 1, Tribal Rights-Enrollment, RG 75, RA; Burke to John Edwards, Assistant Secretary of the Interior, 10 March 1925, CCF, Yankton, Box 14, RG 75, NA; Daniel to Burke, 20 March 1925.

36. Burke to Daniel, 9 March 1925, CCF, Yankton, RG 75, IAIS, USD. There is a postscript on bottom of this letter: "March 10, P.S. Today the delegation were [*sic*] at the White House and were received by the President."

37. Pauline Necklace Kezena, interview by author, 17 September 1991. I have not been able to locate a photograph of Sam Necklace. I examined the collection of Yankton photographs at the National Anthropological Archives. Several of the Necklace/Primeaux relatives have also been trying to locate photos.

38. Hoover, "Yankton Sioux Tribal Claims," 130–31.

39. Hoover, *Yankton Sioux*, 56; Hoover, "Yankton Sioux Experience," 66–67.

40. Father Sylvester Eisenman, "Diary, 1913–1934," RA; Superintendents' Annual Narratives, 1924, 1925, 1926; Leech to CIA, 17 February 1921, Yankton, Law and Order, Box 2, RG 75, RA; Daniel to CIA, 25 March 1924. Almost all the letters and reports mention alcohol problems.

41. Stewart, *Peyote Religion*, chapters 9 and 10.

42. L. Villegas to F. Skillman, Broken Bough, Neb., 5 April 1909, CCF, Liquor Traffic, 1907–39, Box 3, RG 75, NA; Morgan, "Man, Plant, and Religion," 84–95.

43. This is not a new viewpoint. It has been expressed by LaBarre, *Peyote Cult*, 166; Hertzberg, *Search for an American Indian Identity*, 283; Stewart, *Peyote Religion*, 331; Tomchee is quoted in Davies, *Healing Ways*, 181.

44. Mooney, "Mescal Plant and Ceremony," 9; Radin, "Sketch of the Peyote Cult of the Winnebago," 12; Schultes, "The Appeal of Peyote (Lophophora Williamsii) as a Medicine"; Stewart, *Peyote Religion*, 248; LaBarre, *Peyote Cult*, 58, 85; Hultkrantz, *Attraction of Peyote*, 105.

45. Crow Dog and Erdoes, *Crow Dog*, 91–113; Spider, "The Native American Church of Jesus Christ," 189–210; Catches, "Native American Church."

46. Vecsey, *Imagine Ourselves Richly*, 153–81, contains an analysis of many Peyote origin narratives.

47. Hultkrantz, *Attraction of Peyote*, 103.

48. Ibid., 103–104; Wiedman, "Big and Little Moon Peyotism," 377–84; Davies, *Healing Ways*.

49. Hultkrantz, *Attraction of Peyote*, 107–108.

50. Hoover, *Yankton Sioux*, 100–101.

51. Hultkrantz, *Attraction of Peyote*, 165.

52. These ideas were first presented as "The Introduction of Peyote among the Yankton Sioux," Department of History Workshop, Ohio State University, 29 November 1994.

53. Deloria, *Singing for a Spirit*, 33.

54. Crow Dog and Erdoes, *Crow Dog*, 137; DeMallie, *Sixth Grandfather*, 80–81.

55. The ritual details of a Vision Quest vary from one group to another. The descriptions here are based on the Vision Quest practices of the Necklace/Primeaux family. Also see the teachings of Black Elk for the broader significance of the Vision Quest among the Sioux. For an overview of the Vision Quest tradition on the Plains, see Irwin, *The Dream Seekers*.

56. Stewart, *Peyote Religion*, 354.

57. Photographing a spiritual activity such as a Sun Dance is considered very inappropriate; nevertheless some photographs of the Sun Dance have been published: Crow Dog and Erdoes, *Crow Dog*; Powers, *Oglala Religion*; Grobsmith, *Lakota of the Rosebud*.

58. As with other ceremonies, the ritual details of a Sun Dance vary from place to place and Sun Dance chief to Sun Dance chief. This description of the use of cedar is based on my experiences at Sun Dances.

59. Spider, "The Native American Church of Jesus Christ," 200–201.

60. Ibid., 201–202.

61. Shonle, "Peyote, the Giver of Visions"; LaBarre, *Peyote Cult*; Hultkrantz wrote that "the visions primarily facilitated the diffusion of Peyote on the Plains," *Attraction of Peyote*, 117; Young, "Intertribal Religious Movements," 1005; Slotkin, *Peyote Religion*; Stewart, *Peyote Religion*; Hertzberg, *Search for an American Indian Identity*; Smith and Snake, *One Nation under God*, 173.

62. On the power of women to communicate with the supernatural, see St. Pierre and Long Soldier, *Walking in the Sacred Manner*, 17–35.

63. Walker, *Lakota Belief and Ritual*, 103, 122.

64. Crow Dog and Erdoes, *Crow Dog*, 100.

65. For examples of feather fans, see Swan, *Peyote Religious Art*, 40–43.

66. Brown, *Sacred Pipe*, 71.

67. Ibid., 32; DeMallie, *Sixth Grandfather*, 311.

68. Crow Dog and Erdoes, *Crow Dog*, 102–103; Spider, "The Native American Church of Jesus Christ," 201.

69. Brown, *Sacred Pipe*, 69.

70. DeMallie, *Sixth Grandfather*, 237.

71. Crow Dog and Erdoes, *Crow Dog*, 98–99; Catches, "Native American Church," 20.

72. Gerald Primeaux, interview by author, 8 June 2002.

73. Hultkrantz, *Attraction of Peyote*, 84. For a discussion of these paradigms, see the "classification of social movements" in Aberle, *Peyote Religion among the Navaho*, 315–33. Hultkrantz also discusses many of the theories of diffusion.

74. ARCIA, 1930: 47, 54.

75. Meriam, *Problem of Indian Administration*, 222, 629. For an analysis of the Meriam Report, see Prucha, *Great Father*, 808–12, 836–38.

76. Hertzberg, *Search for an American Indian Identity*, 275–76.

77. Daniel to CIA, 23 May 1927, CCF, Yankton, Extension Service, Box 4, RG 75, RA.

78. Notebook of Sam Necklace.

CHAPTER SIX. CHIEF PRIEST SAM NECKLACE AND THE NATIVE AMERICAN CHURCH

1. Yankton Census, 1930, 1934, 1937. Some data come from probate records and death certificates.

2. Yankton Census, 1930, 1934, 1937. There is some confusion concerning Frances's married name. The Yankton census up to 1930 lists "Warner" as her name. The 1934 Yankton-Rosebud census records her name as "Gardner. "The probate hearing (1952) upon her father's death lists "Garner." She did not divorce and remarry. At the probate hearing her husband, Wilson, testified that he was the husband and the father of the three children. The last names of the three children also changed from the earlier census to the later one. The only viable explanation at this point is a transcription error or some type of bureaucratic mix-up, as administrative responsibility for the Yankton Reservation was transferred to the Rosebud Agency in 1933.

3. Yankton Census, 1930, 1934, 1937. Death certificates and probate records were also used.

4. Prucha, *Great Father*, 926–30.

5. Ibid., 895; McDonnell, *Dispossession*, 122.

6. *Little Bronzed Angel* 9:6 (September 1933); Joe Packard, interview by author, 16 September 1991, AIRP.

7. Clow, "Tribal Populations in Transition, 365–67; Eisenman, "History of the Mission," and Eisenman, "Diary," 1931–34, Sylvester Eisenman Papers; *Little Bronzed Angel* 6:12 (May 1931); *Catholic Sioux Herald* 2:12 (1933); "Economic and Social Survey of the Yankton Indian Reservation for 1933," CCF, Rosebud, Economic and Social Survey, RG 75, NAKC.

8. *Little Bronzed Angel* 12:2 (February 1936).

9. Cecil Provost, interview by Joseph Cash, 19 August 1968, AIRP; William O'Connor, interview by Joseph Cash, 27 August 1968, AIRP. For more personal recollections of the Depression, see Cash and Hoover, *To Be an Indian.*

10. Sylvester Eisenman to Collier, 22 January 1936, Eisenman Papers, Folder 5, Correspondence, RA; *Yankton Press,* 20 July 1937. There are newspaper clippings among the Eisenman papers.

11. Hoover, *Yankton Sioux,* 59.

12. Bromert, "The Sioux and the Indian—CCC," 344–47.

13. Ibid., 348–50, 355; Hoover, *Yankton Sioux,* 59–60; Prucha, *Great Father,* 946–47; Paul Picotte, interview by Joseph Cash, 16 August 1968, AIRP.

14. Prucha, *Great Father,* 957–63; Deloria and Lytle, *The Nations Within,* 141–45.

15. Deloria, *Speaking of Indians,* 141–45; Iverson, *"We Are Still Here,"* 91–93; Prucha, *Great Father,* 959–63.

16. Bromert, "The Sioux and the Indian—CCC," 342–43; Bromert, "Sioux Rehabilitation Colonies," 45.

17. Petition to CIA, 8 July 1931, CCF, Yankton, 1931–32, Box 3, RA.

18. Ibid., Rhoads to Superintendent Hickman, 3 August 1931; Constitution and Bylaws in Hickman to Rhoads, 1 September 1931.

19. Minutes of the General Tribal Council of the Yankton Sioux Indians of South Dakota, held at Greenwood, South Dakota, 28 September 1931, CCF, Yankton, Box 3, RG 75, RA; Welch, "Zitkala-Ša," 214–15.

20. Welch, "Zitkala-Ša," 216–17; R. Bonnin to Rhoads, 21 September 1931, CCF, Yankton, Box 3, RG 75, RA; R. Bonnin to Rhoads, 7 October 1931; Senator Frazier to Rhoads, 6 October 1931.

21. Rhoads to Yankton Indians, 28 March 1932, CCF, Yankton, Box 3, RG 75, RA; Petition to CIA, 23 May 1932.

22. Constitution and Bylaws of the Yankton Sioux Tribal Business and Claims Committee, 22 September 1932, CCF, Yankton, Box 3, RG 75, RA; Rhoads to Hickman, 5 October 1932.

23. Hoover, *Yankton Sioux*, 58.

24. Collier to Indians of the Yankton Reservation, 5 November 1934, CCF, [Rosebud], Yankton, Box 4, RG 75, RA. After 1933 much of the Yankton archival material is under the Rosebud Agency. In the Richardson Archives this material is catalogued under the Yanktons.

25. "Constitution and Bylaws of the Yankton Sioux Tribe," in Ben Reifel, Field Agent to CIA, 23 September 1935, CCF, Yankton, Box 3, RA.

26. Minutes of the Tribal Council, 22 September 1934, CCF, Yankton, Box 3, RG 75, RA.

27. "Certification of Rejection," Supt. Roberts, 23 November 1935, CCF, Yankton, Box 3, RG 75, RA.

28. Clement Smith to Claude Whitlock, 16 December 1938, CCF, Yankton, Box 4, RG 75, RA.

29. Collier to Whitlock, 18 February 1939, CCF, Yankton, Box 4, RG 75, RA.

30. William Zimmerman, Assistant CIA to Whitlock, 21 April 1937, CCF, Rosebud, Box 4, RG 75, RA; Whitlock to Collier, 24 September 1937. These letters are with the Rosebud Agency material in the Richardson Archive.

31. Deloria and Lytle, *Nations Within*, 178–80.

32. Zimmerman to Whitlock, 21 April 1937, CCF, Yankton, Box 3, RG 75, RA.

33. William O'Connor, interview by Joseph Cash, 27 August 1968, AIRP; Percy Archambeau, interview by Joseph Cash, 19 August 1968, AIRP; Norbert Picotte, interview by Herbert Hoover, 3 February 1978, AIRP.

34. Cecil Provost, interview by Joseph Cash, 19 August 1968, AIRP.

35. Father Louis J. Delahoyde, interview by Gerald Wolff, 15 March 1974, South Dakota Oral History Project.

36. *Little Bronzed Angel* 10:5 (May 1935); Roberts to Father Sylvester Eisenman, 27 November 1935, CCF, Yankton, Box 3, RG 75, RA.

37. Some of the studies critical of the Indian New Deal are reviewed by Deloria and Lytle, *Nations Within*, 186–88.

38. Ibid., 188–90; Iverson, *"We Are Still Here,"* 102; Prucha, *Great Father,* remains a standard reference on Native Americans and the New Deal.

39. Prucha, *Great Father,* 947, 973–76, illustration on 65.

40. *Little Bronzed Angel* 3:12 (May 1927).

41. *Little Bronzed Angel* 10:5 (May 1935); 12:2 (February 1936).

42. *Catholic Sioux Herald* 4:8 (15 April 1935): 4. I would like to thank Professor Jerome Kills Small of the University of South Dakota for the translation.

43. Father Louis J. Delahoyde, interview by Gerald Wolff, 15 March 1974, South Dakota Oral History Project, USD.

44. Duratschek, *Crusading along Sioux Trails,* 37–38.

45. *Catholic Sioux Herald* 8:5 (March 1937): 7.

46. *Catholic Sioux Herald* 9:15 (1 August 1940): 5.

47. Father Louis J. Delahoyde, interview by Gerald Wolff, 15 March 1974.

48. *Catholic Indian Herald* 9:15 (1 August 1940); 9:16 (15 August 1940). The *Catholic Sioux Herald* was renamed in 1940.

49. Clarence Foreman, interview by Joseph Cash, 26 August 1968, AIRP; Selma Sully Walker, interview by author, 16 August 1994, AIRP.

50. Slotkin, *Peyote Religion,* 55; Stewart, *Peyote Religion,* 237–238.

51. Petrullo, *The Diabolic Root,* 6. This is the first monograph on Peyote published in the United States; however, it is predated by Alexandre Rouhier, *La plante qui fait les yeux émerveilles--Le Peyotl.*

52. Petrullo, "Peyotism as an Emergent Indian Culture."

53. LaBarre, *Peyote Cult,* xii.

54. Schultes, "Peyote and the American Indian"; Schultes, "Appeal of Peyote," 698–715.

55. Stewart to Collier, 5 August 1939, CCF, 1907–39, Liquor Traffic, Box 4, RG 75, NA. Stewart, a former Mormon, says that the Mormons were "very perturbed" at the expansion of Peyotism because it threatened proselytizing among American Indians.

56. Quentin Bruguier, interview by author, 6 June 1993.

57. Germaine Sitting Crow, interview by author, 28 October 1991.

58. Asa Primeaux, Sr., interview by author, 16 September 1991. This interview took place as Asa and I walked through the cemetery.

59. Germaine Sitting Crow, interview by author, 29 October 1991. Emma Goodhouse Sitting Crow is Germaine's mother-in-law.

60. Asa Primeaux, Sr., interview by author, 16 September 1991; Clarence Rockboy, interview by author, 25 November 1991. Clarence, born in 1933, told me that he had been attending this church since he was a child.

61. Selma Sully Walker, interview by author, 16 August 1994, AIRP. Selma and her dad attended the inaugural Peyote service.

62. Clarence Rockboy, interview by author, 25 November 1991; Loretta Rainbow Primeaux, interview by author, 10 June 1997. Dressing properly means dressing well. Men wear slacks and dress shirts; women wear long dresses and cover their shoulders with a shawl.

63. Germaine Sitting Crow, interview by author, 29 October 1991; Selma Sully Walker, interview by author, 16 August 1994, AIRP.

64. Joe Packard, interview by author, 16 September 1991, AIRP.

65. Selma Sully Walker, interview by author, 16 August 1994, AIRP.

66. Clarence Rockboy, interview by author, 25 November 1991; Quentin Bruguier, interview by author, 6 June 1993.

67. Asa Primeaux, Sr., interview by author, 20 September 1991.

68. Eisenman Papers: Rosters, Greenwood School, RA; Asa Primeaux, Sr., interview by author, 20 September 1991.

69. Selma was enrolled at the Sisseton Reservation through her mother but lived on the Yankton Reservation with her father until she married in 1950. Her mother and stepfather were also Peyotists.

70. Selma Sully Walker, interview by author, 16 August 1994, AIRP. It was through Selma that I met Asa Primeaux. He was in Columbus helping Selma at the Indian Center as a spiritual advisor to the local American Indian community.

71. Eunice Rainbow Dog Soldier, interview by author, 17 September 1991; Loretta Rainbow Primeaux, interview by author, 10 June 1997. Loretta Primeaux was the interpreter for me when I interviewed Grandma Eunice.

72. Joe Rockboy, interview by Herbert Hoover, 18 December 1972, AIRP.

73. Ibid.

74. Selma Sully Walker, interview by author, 16 August 1994, AIRP. Throughout my many interviews with Asa, he discussed the frequent travels of his grandfather.

75. Ibid.

76. See the bibliography for Yankton Peyote music. There is also a significant collection of Yankton Peyote music in the Oral History Center, USD.

77. McAllester, *Peyote Music,* 65–80.

78. Cook-Lynn, "Monograph of a Peyote Singer," 13–15 (includes five Yankton Peyote songs that are transcribed and translated into English).

79. These references are from the record notes to Abdo et al., *Yankton Sioux Peyote Songs,* vols. 1–4, and Shields et al., *Yankton Sioux Peyote Songs,* vols. 5–8. The translations were made by Reverend Joseph Shields, Sr.

80. Primeaux and Dion, *Primeaux-Dion: Yankton Sioux Peyote Songs,* record notes. Translations by Gerald and Loretta Primeaux.

81. McAllester, *Peyote Music,* 56–57, 78–88 (nine Dakota Peyote songs are transcribed); Cook-Lynn, "Monograph of a Peyote Singer," 13–15; Merriam and d'Azevedo, "Washo Peyote Songs."

82. For everyday life on the Yankton Reservation during the 1940s, see Dudley, *Choteau Creek.*

83. Joe Packard, interview by author, 16 September 1991, AIRP; Selma Sully Walker, interview by author, 16 August 1994, AIRP.

84. Petition to Senator Lynn J. Frazier, Senate Investigating Committee, 3 December 1932, CCF, Yankton, Box 8, RG 75, NA. Frazier forwarded the petition to the BIA.

85. Bonnin to Collier, 3 August 1933, CCF, Yankton, RG 75, NA, IAIS.

86. Thirteenth Census of the United States. South Dakota: Campbell and Charles Mix County. Microfilm Series 1624, roll 1,478, NA.

87. "Yankton Project Plan for Land Acquisition," 1938, CCF, Rosebud, Box 229, RG 75, NA. Of the original 430,405 acres of Yankton land, the tribe or tribal members held title to 45,200 acres. Non-Indians owned 385,205 acres of the original acreage. The Department of the Interior purchased 2,500 acres for the tribe and was contemplating the acquisition of an additional 3,300 acres that would be distributed to landless Yanktons.

88. Raymond Bonnin to Superintendent Whitlock, 1 January 1938, CCF, Rosebud, Box 4, RG 75, RA.

89. Sam Necklace, Chairman, et al. to John Collier, 29 December 1939, CCF, Rosebud, Box 4, RG 75, RA.

90. "Resolution and Petition," December 1939, CCF, Rosebud, Box 4, RG 75, RA.

91. Ibid., Zimmerman to Bulow, 10 February 1940; Gurney to CIA, 2 February 1940.

92. Necklace to Harold Ickes, January 1940 [sic], CCF, Yankton, Box 14, RG 75, NA.

93. Charles Picotte, to Collier, 2 March 1940, CCF, Yankton, Box 14, RG 75, NA.

94. Necklace to Collier, 23 February 1940, CCF, Rosebud, Box 4, RG 75, RA.

95. Fred H. Daiker, Assistant to the Commissioner to Sam Necklace, 11 April 1940, CCF, Rosebud, Box 4, RG 75, RA.

96. Necklace to Collier, 20 April 1940, CCF, Yankton, Box 14, RG 75, NA.

97. "Yankton Sioux Petition" to Collier and Ickes, 23 March 1940, CCF, Yankton, Box 14, RG 75, NA.

98. Necklace to Collier, 18 May 1940, CCF, Yankton, Box 14, RG 75, NA. Necklace signed this letter "Chairman, Full-blood Organization."

99. "Economic and Social Survey and Programs, Yankton Reservation," CCF, Rosebud, RG 75, NA.

100. "Preliminary Notice of Election," 20 June 1940, "Memorandum," Central Election Committee, 11 July 1940, CCF, Yankton, Box 4, RG 75, RA; "Certificate of Election," 24 August 1940, CCF, Yankton, Box 14, RG 75, NA.

101. Hoover, *Yankton Sioux*, 61. There were three other communal colonies on the Yankton Reservation.

102. *Statistical Supplement to the Annual Report of the Commissioner of Indian Affairs* (Washington, D.C.: GPO, 1939), 80; Yankton Census, Rosebud, Microfilm Series 595, Roll 445, RG 75, NA. Five of the fifty-six who died were infants.

103. "Suggestions for the Rehabilitation of Yankton Sioux Indians," 10 June 1943; "Yankton Agenda," 1945, Yankton Rehabilitation Committee, CCF, Yankton, Box 3, RG 75, RA; "Yankton Reservation—Basic Data," March 1944, CCF, Rosebud, RG 75, NA, IAIS.

104. Deloria, *Speaking of Indians*, 89–98: Iverson, *"We Are Still Here,"* 105–11.

105. Hoover, *Yankton Sioux*, 64–65.

106. Asa Primeaux, Sr., interview by author, 24 September 1991.

107. Paul Picotte, interview by Joseph Cash, 16 August 1968, AIRP; Jim Blue Bird, interview by Omer C. Stewart, 20 June 1971.

108. Hurt, "The Urbanization of the Yankton Indians"; Hoover, *Yankton Sioux,* 95.

109. Asa Primeaux, Sr., interview by author, 17 September 1991.

110. Hurt, "Urbanization of the Yankton Indians"; Hurt and Brown, "Social Drinking Patterns of the Yankton Sioux."

111. Asa Primeaux, Sr., interview by author, 4 October 1991; Hurt, "Urbanization of the Yankton Indians," 230.

112. Pauline Necklace Kezena, interview by author, 17 September 1991.

113. Asa Primeaux, Sr., interview by author, 24 September 1991; Selma Sully Walker, interview by author, 16 August 1994, AIRP.

114. Loretta Rainbow Primeaux, interview by author, 10 June 1997.

115. Michael L. Lawson, "Historical Analysis of the Impact of Missouri River Pick-Sloan Dam Projects on the Yankton and Santee Sioux Indian Tribes," 32–38, 62–64.

116. Ramona O'Connor, "History of White Swan Community and Inundation," *Sioux Messenger: Ihanktonwan Monthly News* (January 2000): 4.

117. Lawson, "Historical Analysis," 20–42.

118. For full coverage, see *Sioux Messenger: Ihanktonwan Monthly News* (December 1999; January, February, and March 2000); "Court Decision Due for Sioux Burial Site," *USA Today* (11 January 2000): 10D. The January 2000 issue contains a summary of Lawson's "Historical Analysis." "Yankton, Santee to Receive Just Compensation," *Indian Country Today,* 14 March 2001, D3; "Stand Off Begins to Protect Sacred Site," *Indian Country Today,* 14 May 2003, A1, 6; "Unity in Support of Yankton Stand," *Indian Country Today,* 28 May 2003, A1, 6; "National Boycott Has Impact," *Indian Country Today,* 11 June 2003, B1. In December 2002 Congress passed the compensation bill. "Congress Completes Work on Land Compensation Bills," *Lakota Journal,* 27 December–3 January 2003.

119. Selma Sully Walker, interview by author, 16 August 1994, AIRP; Asa Primeaux, Sr., interview by author, 30 January 1992.

120. Parnell Necklace, interview by author, 16 October 1991; Asa Primeaux, Sr., interview by author, 24 September 1991.

121. Joe Packard, interview by author, 16 September 1991, AIRP; Loretta Rainbow Primeaux, interview by author, 10 June 1997.

122. I want to thank Jerome Kills Small for the translation.

123. Names are not used in order to protect the privacy of those involved.

124. Szasz, *Between Indian and White Worlds.*

125. Medicine, "Indian Women and the Renaissance of Traditional Religion," 159.

126. Asa Primeaux, Sr., interview by author, 20 September 1991.

127. Bruce Iron Necklace, interview by author, 30 May 1993. The quotation is Bruce's paraphrasing of his grandmother.

128. Nancy Rockboy, narrator, 15 August 1982. Germaine Sitting Crow, who was also at the naming ceremony, translated the tape for me in 1991.

129. Asa Primeaux, Sr., narrator, 6 January 1983.

CHAPTER SEVEN. THE PEYOTE ROAD AND YANKTON SOCIETY

1. Stewart, "Peyote Religion." Stewart wrote this in 1991 just before he passed away. Swan, *Peyote Religious Art*, 21, gives the second estimate.

2. Clow, "Tribal Populations in Transition," 386–87.

3. Iverson, *"We Are Still Here,"* 121–35.

4. Clow, "Tribal Populations," 388.

5. Hoover, *Yankton Sioux*, 65–66.

6. Hurt, "Urbanization of the Yankton Indians," 229; Wesley R. Hurt, Jr. Papers, IAIS. These papers contain the police and education data and the interviews conducted with the Yanktons.

7. Bessie Red Hawk, interview by Richard Loder, 1968, AIRP.

8. St. Pierre and Long Soldier, *Walking in the Sacred Manner*, 87–90.

9. I am using "grandma" and "grandmas" as they are used in today's vernacular.

10. I attended the honoring ceremonies and giveaways for Grandma Eunice's last four birthdays.

11. Wesley Hurt Papers, IAIS.

12. Katherine Sing Necklace, interview by author, 1 October 1992; Parnell Necklace, interview by author, 30 September 1991; Loretta Rainbow Primeaux, interview by author, 10 June 1997; Alice Hope Rabbit, interview by author, 25 June 1999; Germaine Sitting Crow, interview by author, 30 May 1993; Eunice Rainbow Dog Soldier, interview by author, 17 September 1991; Asa Primeaux, Sr., interview by author, 11 May 1992.

13. Parnell Necklace, interview by author, 30 September 1991. Parnell's conversation with his grandma was in Dakota. I asked him to tell me about his grandma's death.

14. Nancy Rockboy, narrator, 15 August 1982. The family made this tape during the naming ceremony.

15. Hoover, *Yankton Sioux*, 77 (Professor Hoover is quoting spiritual leader Charles Kills Enemy); Aberle, *Peyote Religion among the Navaho*, xxxviii.

16. Aberle, *Peyote Religion among the Navaho*, vi, 110–13, 403–405; Stewart, *Peyote Religion*, 296, 301.

17. "Button, Button . . . ," *Time*, 18 June 1951, 82–83.

18. *Time*, 9 July 1951, 6, 8.

19. *Science* 114 (30 November 1951): 582–83. The statement is signed by Weston LaBarre, David McAllester, J. S. Slotkin, Omer Stewart, and Sol Tax; Collier, "The Peyote Cult."

20. *Saturday Review* 37:6 (1954): 14–15; *Time*, 9 August 1954, 49–50; LaBarre, *Peyote Cult*, 206. Copies of the *Quarterly Bulletin of the Native American Church* are

located in the Omer C. Stewart Papers, Boxes 46–47. Each issue describes how to order Peyote and lists prices.

21. The relationship between anthropologists and American Indians has been contentious, as recent literature has shown. The situation with anthropologists who have studied Peyotism is different. They have not been detached observers; from Mooney (not a professionally trained anthropologist, but one of the Smithsonian's most competent ethnologists) to Schultes, LaBarre, Slotkin, McAllester, Stewart, and others, they have been defenders of the faith, as well as scholars, and were welcomed as participants by the Peyote communities. There has not been an appeals case or congressional hearing on Peyote legislation in which anthropologists have not testified in the defense of Peyotism. This includes Professor Hoover of the University of South Dakota, who has been a participant in the Native American Church of Charles Mix County and a supporter of Peyotism. See Bilosi and Zimmerman, eds., *Indians and Anthropologists.*

22. Stewart, *Peyote Religion*, 308–10.

23. Ibid., 310–16; Aberle, *Peyote Religion among the Navaho*, xii, xxxviii. Aberle wrote this in 1991 for a reprint of the 2nd edition.

24. Leonard Bruguier, interview by author, 31 October 1991.

25. *Catholic Indian Herald* 11:4 (1 August 1942).

26. Several of the people I interviewed verified the presence of these artworks on the walls at least since the 1950s. When I first visited the church in 1990 the prints I described (and photographed) were on the walls. By 1998 the prints were gone, as the church was used very infrequently.

27. I want to thank Germaine Sitting Crow for giving me a copy of this photograph.

28. Leonard Bruguier, interview by author, 31 October 1991. The interview with Dr. Bruguier is based on his experiences as a lifelong member of the Native American Church, not as a scholar of American Indian history.

29. Wesley Hurt Papers, IAIS.

30. I met Shane Paterson in 1999. He was invited by the Primeaux family to be the Sun Dance chief for the four-year cycle. The fourth year was completed in 2002. He presently lives in Manitoba, Canada, with his family but returns to the Yankton Reservation in the summer. During these four Sun Dances (1999–2002) I assisted as fireman and cedarman.

31. Daniel Dion was forty-three years old at the time of the interview.

32. Leonard Bruguier, interview by author, 31 October 1991.

33. Bach, "A Study of Speech and Auditory Changes during a Peyote Ceremony of the Native American Church of North America." These are the responses of the twenty Yanktons who were present.

34. William Cape to Dean Walter L. Hard, 18 December 1958; John Artichoker, Director, Indian Education to Kelsey, 30 January 1959, Institute of American Indian Studies Papers, Box 1, RA.

35. Kelsey, "The Pharmacology of Peyote," 233.

36. Cape to Kelsey, 6 February 1959, IAIS Papers, Box 1, RA. The institute reprinted and distributed copies of Wesley Hurt's "Factors in the Persistence of Peyote." Hurt was director of the institute from 1955 to 1958 and 1962 to 1963.

37. "Resolution," 8 April 1959 (a copy of this document is in the files of the Institute of American Indian Studies); Jim Blue Bird to Omer Stewart, 15 December 1960, Omer Stewart Papers, Box 32. Blue Bird lists the fifteen communities.

38. Hall to Kelsey, 8 June 1960, IAIS Papers, Box 2, RA.

39. An account of the convention is included in the institute's *News Report* 13 (15 August 1960). Copies of the *News Report* are located in IAIS Papers, Box 32, RA. The *News Report* was distributed free of charge.

40. Hall to Francis Weston, 8 November 1960, 21 December 1960, 28 March, 21 December 1961, IAIS Papers, Box 2, RA.

41. Hall to Dean Clabaugh, Director, Legislative Research Council, 13 January 1961, IAIS Papers, Box 2, RA.

42. *News Report* 15 (August 1962).

43. Stewart, *Peyote Religion,* 238. The correspondence between the institute and South Dakota's congressional representatives is in IAIS Papers, Box 2, June–July 1964, RA.

44. William O'Connor, interview by Wesley Hurt, 8 July 1959, IAIS Papers, Box 1, RA. This is a typescript of an interview discussing plans for a new constitution. It contains the viewpoints of the competing Yankton factions; William O'Connor, interview by Joseph Cash, 27 August 1968, AIRP.

45. Fay, *Charters, Constitutions and By-laws of the Indian Tribes of North America,* 109–20 (contains a copy of the 1963 constitution and bylaws).

46. Prucha, *Great Father,* 1095–1120.

47. Stewart, "Peyote and the Law," 52; Stewart, *Peyote Religion,* 333–34.

48. Ginsberg, *Howl and Other Poems,* 10.

49. Seymour Krim, ed., *The Beats* (New York: Fawcett Publications, 1960), 94–107.

50. *Sioux Messenger* 3:30 (May 1973).

51. On 8 December 1972 *Radio Oyate,* sponsored by USD, had a panel discussion on AIM. The discussants included Leonard Crow Dog, Asa Primeaux, Neulon Dion, and Adam Sitting Crow. They ended the program with Peyote songs. See Oyate Radio Program, AIRP.

52. Spider, "The Native American Church of Jesus Christ," 197.

53. Ibid., 197, 207.

54. Leonard Bruguier, interview by author, 31 October 1991.

55. Ibid.

56. In 1985 three brothers—Asa Primeaux, Francis Primeaux, and Paul George Godfrey—committed to sponsoring three consecutive Sun Dances, lasting twelve years. Paul George held the first four at his home on the Rosebud Reservation, 1986–89 (I attended the last two years), and Asa followed the next four years, 1990–93. Subsequently Francis and Paul George passed away. In 1995 the third Sun Dance cycle was initiated by Asa and an adopted son, Jim Fallis. In 1999 the

Primeaux family began another four-year Sun Dance. In all, the family had sponsored sixteen Sun Dances by 2002.

57. Crow Dog and Erdoes, *Crow Dog,* 91.

58. *Radio Oyate,* 8 December 1972, Oyate Radio Program, AIRP.

59. Herbert Hoover, interview by author, 23 November 1991.

60. Ibid. See St. Pierre and Long Soldier, *Walking in the Sacred Manner,* for a photo taken by Hoover of Kills Enemy and his wife, Isabel Ten Fingers.

61. Hoover, interview by author, 23 November 1991. Hoover conducted interviews with Joe Rockboy for the oral history collection at USD (tapes 47 and 889, AIRP).

62. Asa Primeaux, Sr., narrator, 6 June 1983; Asa Primeaux, Sr., interview by author, 20 September 1991. Asa described these experiences at two different times. The first was at a family gathering, where he recorded some of his experiences; and the second was in a taped interview with me.

63. Hoover, *Yankton Sioux,* 77, describes Kills Enemy's ecumenical views. Hoover told me the story of the three fingers in our interview.

64. Swan, *Peyote Religious Art,* x.

65. Ibid., figure 2:16 on 39, figure 4:19 on 81.

66. Gerald Primeaux, interview by author, 15 June 2000.

67. Swan, *Peyote Religious Art,* 70–79, figures 4:8, 4:9, 4:10.

68. Douglas and D'Harnoncourt, *Indian Art of the United States,* 210; Wiedman and Greene, "Early Kiowa Peyote Ritual and Symbolism."

69. *Contemporary Southern Plains Indian Art.*

70. Lessard, "Instruments of Prayer," 24. Lessard makes this point about South Dakota; he did not see any Peyote ritual items for sale. This has also been my experience throughout the 1990s. Swan makes the same observation (*Peyote Religious Art,* xi).

71. Lessard, "Instruments of Prayer," 27.

72. For examples of the Rockboys' beadwork, see Hoover, *Yankton Sioux,* 84; Lessard, "Instruments of Prayer," 27.

73. Prucha, *Great Father,* 1186–88.

74. Ibid., 1187.

75. "Church Apologizes to Former Indian Students," *Indian Country Today,* 27 April–4 May 1998.

76. Stewart, "Peyote and the Law," 58–59.

77. Lawson and Morris, "The Native American Church and the New Court"; Long, *Religious Freedom and Indian Rights,* 105–202.

78. Lawson and Morris, "Native American Church." Over one hundred scholarly articles have been published on the *Smith* case. See the bibliographic essay in Long, *Religious Freedom.*

79. Lawson and Morris, "Native American Church," 84.

80. Al Smith to Asa Primeaux, 13 April 1990. I have a copy of this letter.

81. Peregoy et al., "Congress Overturns Supreme Court's Peyote Ruling," 19–20.

82. I have a copy of the information packet.

83. *The Peyote Road: Ancient Religion in Contemporary Crisis* (prod. Reuben A. Snake); John D. Loftin, rev. of *The Peyote Road, American Indian Religions* 1:2 (Spring 1994); 197–200. Unfortunately this review refers to the Peyote faith as a cult.

84. Senator Inouye's speech is reprinted in *Native American Rights Fund Legal Review* 20:1 (Winter/Spring 1995): 3–5.

85. Peregoy et al., "Congress Overturns Supreme Court's Peyote Ruling," 16–17. In 1997 the Supreme Court, in *City of Boerne* v. *Flores*, ruled the Religious Freedom Restoration Act (1993) unconstitutional in that it violated the principles of federalism and the separation of powers. The *Boerne* decision, however, has not affected the 1994 American Indian Religious Freedom Act Amendment. Long, *Religious Freedom*, 248–50, 273.

86. Barnett quoted in "Will Yankton Sioux Reservation Cease to Exist?" *Indian Country Today,* 5–11 June 2000, 1, 3. Virtually every recent issue of the *Sioux Messenger* has an update on this case. For a history of the diminishment of the Yankton Reservation, see Ritter, "Dispossession to Diminishment."

87. "Yankton Sioux Tribe Officials under Fire," *Indian Country Today,* 22–29 March 1999, B1; "First Yankton Sioux Chairwoman Seated," ibid., 1.

88. "The Women's Lodge: A Safe Place," *Sioux Messenger,* November 1999, 22.

89. "Brave Heart Society Coming Back," *Indian Country Today,* 21–28 July 1997, C3; "Bravehearts Travel to Sexual Abuse Conference," *Sioux Messenger,* June 1999, 10; "Coming of Age Ceremony," *Sioux Messenger,* July 1999, 13; "Traditional Lessons Swell Brave Hearts," *Indian Country Today,* 23 February 2000, "Healing Journey" insert, 12–13. For more information on the coming of age ceremony, see Medicine, "Indian Women and Traditional Medicine," 168–69; Brown, *Sacred Pipe,* 116–26; St. Pierre and Long Soldier, *Walking in the Sacred Manner,* 67–75.

90. Neihardt, *Black Elk Speaks,* 198.

91. Hoover, *Yankton Sioux,* 76–77. "Chairmen Meet to Protest Operation Eagle," *Lakota Times,* 23 June 1983.

92. Asa Primeaux to Senator Dick Schafrath, n.d. I have a copy of this letter.

93. Doll, *Vision Quest,* 126–27, includes a photograph, brief biography, and interview with Asa Primeaux. Also see two articles on Asa by Cook-Lynn: "Monograph of a Peyote Singer" and "Profile."

94. "Indians Want Court to Say Peyote Is OK," *Columbus (Ohio) Dispatch,* 3 November 1989, B8.

95. Mark Welsh, interview by author, 23 March 2000.

96. A preliminary draft of articles of incorporation was prepared.

97. Gerald Primeaux, interview by author, 15 June 2000; Anderson, "The Peyote Gardens of Southern Texas"; "A Field Full of Buttons," *Economist* 351 (3 April 1999): 27; "For Indian Church, a Critical Shortage," *New York Times,* 20 March 1995, A10.

98. Herbert Hoover, interview by author, 23 November 1991; Asa Primeaux, Sr., interview by author, 20 September 1991.

99. I attended the entire conference, including all the business meetings and all the Peyote services.

100. For biographical information and his earlier views, see Spider, "The Native American Church of Jesus Church," 189–209. Although published in 1987, this interview took place in 1982.

101. Emerson Spider, Sr., interview by author, 25 June 1999. At the convention I saw Reverend Spider sitting in a truck resting. I went over and introduced myself, intending to say hello but not conduct an interview. We ended up talking for almost an hour. I did not have my tape recorder with me; but after ten minutes I asked him if he minded if I took notes. He said he did not mind. He was incredibly gracious, open, and willing to share his thoughts with me.

102. Asa Primeaux, Sr., interview by author, 4 May 1991.

103. Twelve Sun Dances have been held on Asa and Loretta's grounds.

104. Asa Primeaux, Sr., narrator, 6 June 1983.

EPILOGUE

1. Hertzberg, *Search for an American Indian Identity*, 239.

2. James H. Howard, "The Pan-Indian Culture of Oklahoma."

Bibliography

GOVERNMENT DOCUMENTS

Federal Government

Congressional Record. Report of the Yankton Indian Commission, 53rd Congress, 2nd Session, Senate, Ex. Doc. No. 27, 18 January 1894, 1–101.

U.S. Congress. *Peyote.* Hearings on H.R. 2614 before a Subcommittee of the Committee on Indian Affairs, House of Representatives, 65th Congress, 2nd Session, February–March 1918.

———. *Prohibition of Use of Peyote.* Documents and Reports, House of Representatives, Committee on Indian Affairs, 65th Congress, 2nd Session, 13 May 1918.

U.S. Department of the Interior. Bureau of Indian Affairs. *Annual Reports of the Commissioner of Indian Affairs.*

U.S. Office of Indian Affairs. *Peyote.* Bulletin 21, 1923. (Mimeographed.)

South Dakota

State of South Dakota: Biennial Report of the Attorney General, 1923–1924. Pierre, S.Dak.: Hipple Printing Co., 1925.

State of South Dakota: Proceedings of the House of Representatives, Eighteenth Legislative Session. Pierre, S.Dak.: State Publishing Co., 1923.

State of South Dakota: Proceedings of the Senate, Eighteenth Legislative Session. Pierre, S.Dak.: State Publishing Co., 1923.

Yankton Sioux Tribe, Marty, South Dakota

Yankton Sioux Allottee Books, 2 vols. n.d.

Yankton Sioux Base Roll, 1921.

ARCHIVES

National Archives, Washington, D.C.
　　Record Group 75
　　　　Central Classified Files
　　　　　　Law and Order Section
　　　　　　　　Correspondence of Chief Special Officer Relating to Peyote, 1908–11,
　　　　　　　　　　1915–18
　　　　　　　　Liquor Traffic, 1907–39
　　　　　　　　Weekly Narrative Reports of Special Officers and Deputies Liquor
　　　　　　　　　　Traffic, 1907–39
　　　　　　　Rosebud, 1907–39
　　　　　　　Yankton Sioux, 1907–39
　　　　　　Indian Census Rolls, Microfilm Series 595, Rolls 444–45, 680–88, Rosebud
　　　　　　　　Agency, Yankton Agency
　　　　　　Superintendent's Annual Narrative and Statistical Reports: Field Jurisdictions
　　　　　　　　of Bureau of Indian Affairs, 1907–38, Microfilm Series 1011, Rolls 172,
　　　　　　　　173, Yankton Agency
National Archives, Kansas City
　　Record Group 75
　　　　Yankton Agency
　　　　Flandreau School and Agency
Richardson Archives, USD
　　National Archives, Record Group 75, Central Classified Files, Rosebud
　　　　Box 3: Folder: Rosebud 1912–39, Culture
　　　　Box 4: Folder: Rosebud 1907–38, Law and Order
　　National Archives, Record Group 75, Central Classified Files, Yankton
　　　　Box 1: Folder: Yankton: 1909–28, Tribal Rights—Enrollment
　　　　　　　Folder: Yankton: 1925–33, Tribal Rights—Enrollment
　　　　Box 2: Folder: Yankton: 1908–32, Law and Order
　　　　　　　Folder: Yankton: 1933–37, Law and Order
　　　　　　　Folder: Yankton: 1912, Tribal Councils—Organization
　　　　　　　Folder: Yankton: 1913–32, Employment
　　　　Box 3: Folder: Yankton: 1926, Tribal Council Minutes
　　　　　　　Folder: Yankton: 1931–32, Tribal Council: Minutes—Correspondence
　　　　　　　Folder: Yankton: 1935–39, Reorganization Act—General
　　　　　　　Folder: Yankton: 1935–39, Reorganization Act—General
　　　　Box 4: Folder: Yankton: 1939–45, Administrative Reports
　　　　　　　Folder: Yankton: 1923–40, Tribal Relations—Complaints
　　　　　　　Folder: Yankton: 1912–29, Miscellaneous
　　　　　　　Folder: Yankton: 1910–11, Culture—Dancing
　　　　　　　Folder: Yankton: 1927–32, Administrative Reports
　　　　　　　Folder: Yankton: Culture

Sylvester Eisenman Papers
Institute of American Indian Studies Papers: General Correspondence
     Box 1: January–June 1959
     Box 2: July 1959–1965
     Box 3: 1966–1968
University of Colorado at Boulder Archives
   Omer C. Stewart Collection—2nd Acquisition
      IV. Peyote Files: Boxes: 32–92
University of South Dakota
   Institute of American Indian Studies: South Dakota Oral History Center
     American Indian Research Project (AIRP)
     South Dakota Oral History Project

BOOKS

Abel, Annie Heloise, ed. *Tabeau's Narrative of Loisel's Expedition to the Upper Missouri.* Norman: University of Oklahoma Press, 1939.

Aberle, David F. *The Peyote Religion among the Navaho.* Chicago: Aldine Publishing Co., 1966. 2nd ed., Chicago: University of Chicago Press, 1982. Reprint, Norman: University of Oklahoma Press, 1991.

Anderson, Edward F. *Peyote: The Divine Cactus.* Tucson: University of Arizona Press, 1980. 2nd ed., 1996.

Anderson, Guy Clayton. *Kinsmen of Another Kind: Dakota White Relations in the Upper Mississippi Valley, 1650–1862.* Lincoln: University of Nebraska Press, 1984. Reprint, Minneapolis: Minnesota Historical Society, 1997.

Armstrong, Joe C. W. *From Sea unto Sea: Art and Discovery Maps of Canada.* Scarborough, Ontario, Canada: Fleet Publishing, 1982.

Barton, Winifred W. *John P. Williamson: A Brother to the Sioux.* n.p.: Fleming H. Revell Company, 1910. Reprint, Clements, Minn.: Sunnycrest Publishing, 1980.

Beuchel, Eugene. S.J. *A Dictionary of the Teton Dakota Sioux Language.* Vermillion: University of South Dakota Press, 1970.

Bilosi, Thomas, and Larry Zimmerman, eds. *Indians and Anthropologists: Vine Deloria, Jr., and the Critique of Anthropology.* Tucson: University of Arizona Press, 1997.

Brito, Silvester J. *The Way of the Peyote Roadman.* New York: Peter Lang, 1989.

Brown, Joseph Epes, ed. *The Sacred Pipe: Black Elk's Account of the Seven Rites of the Oglala Sioux.* Norman: University of Oklahoma Press, 1953.

Brumble, H. David. *American Indian Autobiography.* Berkeley: University of California Press, 1988.

Carson, Mary E. *Blackrobe for the Yankton Sioux: Fr. Sylvester Eisenman, O.S.B. (1891–1948).* Chamberlain, S.Dak.: Tipi Press, 1989.

Cash, Joseph H., and Herbert T. Hoover, eds. *To Be An Indian: An Oral History.* New York: Holt, Rinehart and Winston, 1971. Reprint, St. Paul: Minnesota Historical Society, 1995.

Catches, Sr. Pete S. *Sacred Fireplace (Oceti Wakan): Life and Teachings of a Lakota Medicine Man.* Santa Fe, N.Mex.: Clear Light Publishers, 1999.

Catlin, George. *Letters and Notes on the Manners, Customs, and Conditions of the North American Indians* [1841]. 2 vols. New York: Dover Publications, 1973.

Champe, John L. and Michael F. Foley. *An Analysis of the Course of Dealings between the United States Government and the Yankton Sioux Tribe, 1858–1900.* Indian Claims Docket 332-C. Washington, D.C.: n.p., 1976.

Clifton, James E., ed. *Being and Becoming Indian: Biographical Studies of North American Frontiers.* Chicago: Waveland Press, 1989.

Contemporary Southern Plains Indian Art. Anadarko: Oklahoma Indian Arts and Crafts Cooperative, 1969.

Cragon, John W. *Petitioner's Proposed Findings of Fact and Brief for Yankton Sioux Tribe of Indians v. United States of America.* Washington, D.C.: Wilkinson, Cragon and Barker, Attorneys, 1968.

Crow Dog, Leonard, and Richard Erdoes. *Crow Dog: Four Generations of Sioux Medicine Men.* New York: Harper Collins, 1995.

Cutright, Paul Leonard. *Lewis and Clark: Pioneering Naturalists.* Lincoln: University of Nebraska Press, 1969.

Davies, Wade. *Healing Ways: Navajo Health Care in the Twentieth Century.* Albuquerque: University of New Mexico Press, 2001.

Deloria, Ella C. *Dakota Grammar.* 1941. Reprint, Vermillion: University of South Dakota Press, 1982.

———. *Dakota Texts.* Publication of the American Ethnological Society, 1932. Vol. 14. Reprint, Vermillion: University of South Dakota Press, 1978.

———. *Speaking of Indians.* New York: Friendship Press, 1944. Reprint, Vermillion: University of South Dakota Press, 1979. Reprint, Lincoln: University of Nebraska Press, 1998.

Deloria, Vine, Jr. *Singing for a Spirit: A Portrait of the Dakota Sioux.* Santa Fe, N.Mex.: Clear Light Publishers, 1999.

Deloria, Vine, Jr., and Clifford M. Lytle. *The Nations Within: The Past and Future of American Indian Sovereignty.* 2nd ed. Austin: University of Texas Press, 1998.

DeMallie, Raymond J., ed. *Plains.* 2 vols. Vol. 13, *Handbook of North American Indians.* Washington, D.C.: Smithsonian Institution, 2001.

———, ed. *The Sixth Grandfather: Black Elk's Teachings Given to John G. Neihardt.* Lincoln: University of Nebraska Press, 1984.

DeMallie, Raymond J., and Douglas R. Parks, eds. *Sioux Indian Religion: Tradition and Innovation.* Norman: University of Oklahoma Press, 1987.

Doll, Don. *Vision Quest: Men, Women, and Sacred Sites of the Sioux Nation.* New York: Crown Publishers, 1994.

Douglas, F. H., and R. D'Harnoncourt. *Indian Art of the United States.* New York: Museum of Modern Art, 1941.

Dudley, Joseph Iron Eye. *Choteau Creek: A Sioux Reminiscence.* New York: Warner Books, 1992.

Duratschek, Mary C., O.S.B. *Crusading along Sioux Trails: A History of the Catholic Missions of South Dakota.* Yankton, S.Dak.: Benedictine Convent, Grail Publications, 1947.

Fay, George. *Charters, Constitutions and By-laws of the Indian Tribes of North America.* Greeley: Colorado State College, 1967.

Foley, Michael F. *Yankton Tribal Lands: An Historical Analysis of the Opening and Development from 1849 to 1869.* New York: Clearwater Publishers, 1976.

Frazier, Patrick. ed. *Many Nations: A Library of Congress Guide for the Study of Indian and Alaskan Native People of the United States.* Washington, D.C.: Library of Congress, 1996.

Furst, Peter T. *People of the Peyote: Huichol Indian History, Religion, and Survival.* Albuquerque: University of New Mexico Press, 1996.

Ginsberg, Allen. *Howl and Other Poems.* San Francisco: City Lights Books, 1956.

Grobsmith, Elizabeth. *Lakota of the Rosebud: A Contemporary Ethnography.* New York: Holt, Rinehart and Winston, 1981.

Hagan, William T. *Quanah Parker: Comanche Chief.* Norman: University of Oklahoma Press, 1993.

Haines, Francis. *The Buffalo.* New York: Thomas Y. Crowell Co., 1970; Apollo edition, 1975.

Hanna, Archibald, ed. *The Lewis and Clark Expedition, by Meriwether Lewis, the 1813 Edition.* Unabridged. Philadelphia: J. B. Lippincott, 1961.

Hassrick, Royal B. *The Sioux: Life and Customs of a Warrior Society.* Norman: University of Oklahoma Press, 1964.

Henige, David. *Oral Historiography.* New York: Longman, 1982.

Hertzberg, Hazel W. *The Search for an American Indian Identity: Modern Pan-Indian Movements.* Syracuse: Syracuse University Press, 1971.

Hodge, Frederick W., ed. *Handbook of American Indians North of Mexico.* 2 vols. Washington, D.C.: GPO, 1907–1910.

Hoover, Herbert T. *The Yankton Sioux.* New York: Chelsea House, 1988.

Hoover, Herbert T., and Karen Zimmerman, eds. *The Sioux and Other Native American Cultures of the Dakotas.* Greenwich, Conn.: Greenwood Publishing, 1994.

Howard, James H. *The Dakota or Sioux Indians.* Vermillion, S.Dak.: Dakota Museum, 1966.

Howe, M. A. DeWolfe. *Life and Labors of Bishop Hare.* New York: Sturgis & Walton, 1912.

Howell, Carol L., comp. and ed. *Cannibalism Is an Acquired Taste, and Other Notes, from Conversations with Anthropologist Omer C. Stewart.* Niwot: University Press of Colorado, 1998.

Hoxie, Frederick. *The Final Promise: The Campaign to Assimilate Indians, 1880–1920.* Lincoln: University of Nebraska Press, 1984.

Hultkrantz, Ake. *The Attraction of Peyote: An Inquiry into the Basic Conditions for the Diffusion of the Peyote Religion in North America.* Stockholm, Sweden: Almqvist & Wiksell, 1997.

————. *Belief and Worship in Native North America.* Syracuse: Syracuse University Press, 1981.

Hurt, Wesley R. *Anthropological Report on Indian Occupancy by the Dakota Sioux Indians and by Rival Tribal Claimants.* New York: Clearwater Press, 1973.

Irwin, Lee. *The Dream Seekers: Native American Visionary Traditions of the Great Plains.* Norman: University of Oklahoma Press, 1994.

Iverson, Peter. *"We Are Still Here": American Indians in the Twentieth Century.* Wheeling, Ill.: Harlan Davidson, 1998.

Kehoe, Alice Beck. *The Ghost Dance: Ethnohistory and Revitalization.* New York: Holt, Rinehart & Winston, 1989.

LaBarre, Weston. *The Peyote Cult.* New Haven: Yale University Press, 1938. 5th ed., Norman: University of Oklahoma Press, 1989.

Lame Deer, John (Fire), and Richard Erdoes. *Lame Deer: Seeker of Visions.* New York: Simon & Schuster, 1972.

Lane, Anne W., and Louise H. Wall. *The Letters of Franklin K. Lane: Personal and Political.* New York: Houghton Mifflin, 1922.

Larkin, Georgia. *Chief Blue Cloud: Biography of the Yankton Sioux Chief.* Marvin, S.Dak.: Blue Cloud Abbey, 1964.

Lewis, Meriwether, and William Clark. *History of the Lewis and Clark Expedition.* Ed. Elliott Coues. 3 vols. New York: Francis P. Harper, 1893. Reprint, New York: Dover Publications, 1965.

Long, Carolyn. *Religious Freedom and Indian Rights: The Case of Oregon v. Smith.* Lawrence: University of Kansas Press, 2000.

Lurie, Nancy O., ed. *Mountain Wolf Woman, Sister of Crashing Thunder: Autobiography of a Winnebago Indian.* Ann Arbor: University of Michigan Press, 1961.

Marriott, Alice, and Carol K. Rachlin. *Peyote.* New York: Thomas Y. Crowell, 1971.

McAllester, David P. *Peyote Music.* New York: Viking Fund, 1949. Reprint, New York: Johnson Reprint Group, 1971.

McCall, Daniel. *Africa in Time-Perspective: A Discussion of Historical Reconstruction from Unwritten Sources.* Boston: Boston University Press, 1964.

McDonnell, Janet. *The Dispossession of the American Indian, 1887–1934.* Bloomington: University of Indiana Press, 1991.

Meriam, Lewis. *The Problem of Indian Administration.* Baltimore, Md.: Johns Hopkins, 1928.

Meritt, Edgar G. *Concerning Peyote.* Washington, D.C.: U.S. Bureau of Indian Affairs, 1919.

Mooney, James. *Ghost Dance Religion and the Sioux Outbreak.* Washington, D.C.: GPO, 1896. Reprint, Lincoln: University of Nebraska Press, 1991.

Moses, L. G. *The Indian Man: A Biography of James Mooney.* Chicago: University of Illinois Press, 1984.

Neihardt, John G. *Black Elk Speaks: Being the Life Story of a Holy Man of the Oglala Sioux.* Lincoln: University of Nebraska Press, 1961.

Newberne, Robert E. L. *Peyote: An Abridged Compilation from the Files of the Bureau of Indian Affairs.* Washington, D.C.: GPO, 1922.

Olden, Sarah Emilia. *The People of Tipi Sapa.* Milwaukee, Wis.: Morehouse Publishing, 1918.

Paulson, T. Emogene. *Sioux Collections.* Vermillion: University of South Dakota Press, 1982.

Petrullo, Vincenzo. *The Diabolic Root: A Study of Peyotism, the New Indian Religion among the Delawares.* Philadelphia: University of Pennsylvania Press, 1934. Reprint, New York: Octagon Books, 1975.

Powell, John Wesley. *Indian Linguistic Families of America North of Mexico.* Washington, D.C.: GPO, 1891. Reprint, Lincoln: University of Nebraska Press, 1966.

Powers, William K. *Oglala Religion.* Lincoln: University of Nebraska Press, 1975.

———. *Yuwipi: Vision and Experience in Oglala Ritual.* Lincoln: University of Nebraska Press, 1982.

Prucha, Francis Paul. *The Great Father: The United States Government and the American Indian.* Abridged ed. Lincoln: University of Nebraska Press, 1986.

———. *The Great Father: The United States Government and the American Indian.* 2 vols. Lincoln: University of Nebraska Press, 1984; unabridged ed., 1 vol., 1995.

Radin, Paul, ed. *Autobiography of a Winnebago Indian: Life Ways, Acculturation, and the Peyote Cult.* Berkeley: University of California, 1920. Reprinted as *Crashing Thunder: Autobiography of a Winnebago Indian.* New York: Appleton, 1926. Reprint, New York: Dover, 1963. Reprint, Lincoln: University of Nebraska Press, 1983.

———. *The Winnebago Tribe.* Washington, D.C.: Bureau of American Ethnology, 1923. Reprint, Lincoln: University of Nebraska Press, 1970.

Rice, Julian. *Black Elk's Story: Distinguishing Its Lakota Purpose.* Albuquerque: University of New Mexico Press, 1991.

Riggs, Stephen R. *A Dakota-English Dictionary.* Washington, D.C.: GPO, 1890. Reprint, St. Paul: Minnesota Historical Society, 1992.

———. *Dakota Grammar, Texts, and Ethnography.* Washington, D.C.: GPO, 1893. Reprint, Minneapolis: Ross & Haines, 1973.

Ronda, James P. *Lewis and Clark among the Indians.* Lincoln: University of Nebraska Press, 1984.

Rouhier, Alexandre. *La plante qui fait les yeux émerveilles—Le Peyotl.* Paris: Doin, 1927.

Sansom-Flood, Renée. *Lessons from Chouteau Creek: Yankton Memories of Dakota Territorial Intrigue.* Sioux Falls, S.Dak.: Center for Western Studies, 1986.

Sansom-Flood, Renée, and Shirley A. Bernie. *Remember Your Relatives: Yankton Sioux Images, 1851–1904.* Vol. 1. Marty, S.Dak.: Marty Indian School, 1985.

Sansom-Flood, Renée, Shirley A. Bernie, and Leonard R. Bruguier. *Remember Your Relatives: Yankton Sioux Images, 1865–1915.* Vol. 2. Marty, S.Dak.: Yankton Sioux Elderly Advisory Board, 1989.

Siskin, Edgar E. *Washo Shamans and Peyotists.* Salt Lake City: University of Utah Press, 1983.

Slotkin, J. S. *The Peyote Religion: A Study in Indian White Relations.* Glencoe, Ill.: Free Press, 1956. Reprint, New York: Octagon Books, 1975.

Smith, Huston, and Reuben Snake, eds. *One Nation under God: The Triumph of the Native American Church.* Santa Fe, N.Mex.: Clear Light Publishers, 1996.

Steinmetz, Paul B. *Pipe, Bible and Peyote among the Oglala Lakota.* Knoxville: University of Tennessee Press, 1990.

Stewart, Omer C. *Peyote Religion: A History.* Norman: University of Oklahoma Press, 1987.

Stewart, Omer C., and David F. Aberle. *Peyotism in the West.* Salt Lake City: University of Utah Press, 1984.

St. Pierre, Mark, and Tilda Long Soldier. *Walking in the Sacred Manner: Healers, Dreamers, and Pipe Carriers—Medicine Women of the Plains Indians.* New York: Simon and Schuster, 1995.

Swan, Daniel C. *Peyote Religious Art: Symbols of Faith and Belief.* Jackson: University of Mississippi Press, 1999.

Szasz, Margaret, ed. *Between Indian and White Worlds: The Cultural Broker.* Norman: University of Oklahoma Press, 1994.

Utley, Robert M. *The Last Days of the Sioux Nation.* New Haven: Yale University Press, 1963.

Utley, Robert M., and Wilcomb E. Washburn. *Indian Wars.* Boston: Houghton Mifflin, 1977.

Vansina, Jan. *Oral Tradition.* Chicago: University of Chicago Press, 1965.

———. *Oral Tradition as History.* Madison: University of Wisconsin Press, 1985.

Vecsey, Christopher. *Handbook of American Indian Religious Freedom.* New York: Crossroad, 1991.

———. *Imagine Ourselves Richly: Mythic Narratives of North American Indians.* New York: Crossroad, 1988. Reprint, New York: HarperCollins, 1991.

Walker, James R. *Lakota Belief and Ritual.* Ed. Raymond J. DeMallie and Elaine A. Johnson. Lincoln: University of Nebraska Press, 1980.

Weeks, Philip. *Farewell, My Nation: The American Indian and the United States, 1820–1890.* Arlington Heights, Ill.: Harlan Davidson, 1990.

Werbner, Richard. *Tears of the Dead: The Social Biography of an African Family.* Washington, D.C.: Smithsonian Institution, 1991.

White, Phillip M. *Peyotism and the Native American Church: An Annotated Bibliography.* Westport, Conn.: Greenwood Press, 2000.

Williamson, John Poage, *An English-Dakota Dictionary.* New York: American Tract Society, 1902. Reprint, St. Paul: Minnesota Historical Society, 1992.

Wood, W. Raymond, and Margot Liberty, eds. *Anthropology on the Great Plains.* Lincoln: University of Nebraska Press, 1980.

Woolworth, Alan R. *Ethnohistorical Report on the Indian Occupancy of Royce Area 410, Yankton Sioux in South Dakota.* Indian Claims Commission Report No. 332-A. New York: Clearwater Publishing Co., 1973.

———. *Sioux Indians III: Ethnohistorical Report on the Yankton Sioux.* With John L. Champe, "Yankton Chronology." New York: Garland Publishing, 1974.

Zitkala-Ša [Red Bird or Gertrude Bonnin]. *American Indian Stories.* Washington, D.C.: Hayworth Publishing House, 1921. Reprint, Lincoln: University of Nebraska Press, 1985.

─────. *Old Indian Legends.* Boston: Ginn, 1901. Reprint, Lincoln: University of Nebraska Press, 1985.

ARTICLES

Adams, David W. "From Bullets to Boarding Schools: The Educational Assault on the American Indian." In *The American Indian Experience,* ed. Philip Weeks, 218–39. Arlington Heights, Ill.: Forum Press, 1988.

Amiotte, Arthur. "The Lakota Sun Dance: Historical and Contemporary Perspectives." In *Sioux Indian Religion: Tradition and Innovation,* ed. Raymond DeMallie and Douglas Parks, 75–89. Norman: University of Oklahoma Press, 1987.

Anderson, Edward F. "The Peyote Gardens of Southern Texas: A Conservation Crisis?" *Cactus and Succulent Journal* 67 (1995): 67–73.

Anderson, Gary C. "Early Dakota Migration and Intertribal Wars: A Revision." *Western Historical Quarterly* 11 (January 1980): 17–36.

Barber, Bernard. "A Socio-cultural Interpretation of the Peyote Cult." *American Anthropologist* 43 (1944): 673–75.

Barber, Carroll. "Peyote and the Definition of Narcotic." *American Anthropologist* 61:4 (August 1959): 641–46.

Boyd, Carolyn E. "Pictographic Evidence of Peyotism in Lower Pecos, Texas Archaic." In *The Archeology of Rock-Art,* ed. Christopher Chippendale and Paul S. C. Tacon, 227–46. Cambridge: Cambridge University Press, 1998.

Brant, Charles S. "Joe Blackbear's Story of the Origin of the Peyote Religion." *Plains Anthropologist* 8 (1963): 180–81.

Bromert, Roger. "The Sioux and the Indian—CCC." *South Dakota History* 8:4 (Fall 1978): 340–56.

─────. "Sioux Rehabilitation Colonies: Experiments in Self-sufficiency, 1936–1942." *South Dakota History* 14:1 (Spring 1984): 31–47.

Campbell, Thomas. "Origin of the Mescal Bean Cult." *American Anthropologist* 60 (1958): 156–60.

"The Case against Peyote." *Outlook* (24 May 1916): 162–63.

Catches, Vincent. "Native American Church: The Half-Moon Way." *Wicazo Sa Review* 7:1 (Spring 1991): 17–24.

Champe, John L. "Yankton Chronology." In *Sioux Indians III: Ethnohistorical Report on the Yankton Sioux* by Alan R. Woolworth. New York: Garland Publishing Inc., 1974.

Clow, Richard L. "Tribal Populations in Transition: Sioux Reservations and Federal Policy, 1934–1965." *South Dakota History* 19:3 (Fall 1989): 362–91.

Collier, John. "The Peyote Cult." *Science* 115 (1952): 503–504.

Cook-Lynn, Elizabeth. "A Monograph of a Peyote Singer: Asa Primeaux, Sr." *Wicazo Sa Review* 7:1 (Spring 1991): 1–15.

─────. "Profile: Asa Primeaux." *Wicazo Sa Review* 1:1, 1:2 (1985).

Corbett, William P. "The Red Pipestone Quarry: The Yanktons Defend a Sacred Tradition, 1859–1929." *South Dakota History* 8 (Winter 1977, Fall 1978): 99–116.

Deloria, Ella C. "Some Notes on the Yankton." *Museum News: University of South Dakota* 28:3–4 (1967): 1–30.

DeMallie, Raymond J. "Sioux until 1850." In *Plains*, ed. Raymond J. DeMallie, 718–60. Vol. 13. *Handbook of North American Indians*. Washington, D.C.: Smithsonian Institute, 2001.

———. "Yankton and Yanktonai." In *Plains*, ed. Raymond J. DeMallie, 777–93. Vol. 13. *Handbook of North American Indians*. Washington, D.C.: Smithsonian Institution, 2001.

"Digest of Reports of the Indian Commissioner 1815 through 1852." *South Dakota Historical Collections and Report* 26 (1952): 456–533.

Dorsey, James O. "Siouan Sociology." In *15th Annual Report of the Bureau of American Ethnology*, 205–44. Washington, D.C.: GPO, 1897.

Echo Hawk, Walter R. "Native American Religious Liberty: Five Hundred Years after Columbus." *American Indian Culture and Research Journal* 17:3 (1993): 33–52.

Ellis, Havelock. "Mescal: A Study of a Divine Plant." *Popular Science Monthly* 41 (1902): 52–71.

Foster, Michael K. "Language and the Culture History of North America." In *Languages*, ed. Ives Goddard, 64–110. Vol. 17. *Handbook of North American Indians*. Washington, D.C.: Smithsonian Institution, 1996.

Goddard, Ives. "The Classification of the Native Languages of North America." In *Languages*, ed. Ives Goddard, 290–324. Vol. 17. *Handbook of North American Indians*. Washington, D.C.: Smithsonian Institution, 1996.

Grinnell, George Bird. "The Last of the Buffalo." *Scribner's Magazine* 12:3 (September 1892): 267–86.

Hafen, P. Jane. "Zitkala Ša: Sentimentality and Sovereignty." *Wicazo Sa Review* 13 (Fall 1997): 31–41.

Hare, DeWitt. "The Yankton Indians." *South Dakota Historical Collections* 6 (1912): 320–28.

Harwood, W. S. "Opening the Yankton Reservation to Settlement." *Harper's Weekly* 20 (20 April 1895): 381.

Hollow, Robert C., and Douglas R. Parks. "Studies in Plains Linguistics: A Review." In *Anthropology on the Great Plains*, ed. W. Raymond Wood and Margot Liberty, 68–97. Lincoln: University of Nebraska Press, 1980.

Hoover, Herbert T. "Arikara, Sioux, and Government Farmers: Three American Indian Agricultural Legacies." *South Dakota History* 13:1–2 (1983): 22–48.

———. "Interview: Noah White." *South Dakota Review* 8:3 (Autumn 1970): 171–77.

———. "Yankton Sioux Experience in the Great Indian Depression, 1900–1930." In *The American West: Essays in Honor of W. Eugene Hollon*, ed. Ronald Lora, 53–71. Toledo, Ohio: University of Toledo Press, 1980.

———. "Yankton Sioux Tribal Claims against the United States, 1917–1975." *Western Historical Quarterly* 7 (April 1976): 125–42.

Howard, James H. "The Dakota or Sioux Tribe." *Museum News: South Dakota Museum* 27:5–6 (May–June 1966): 1–10.

———. "Half Moon Way: The Peyote Ritual of Chief White Bear." *Museum News: South Dakota Museum* 25:1–2 (January–February 1967): 1–39.

———. "The Mescal Bean Cult of the Central and Southern Plains: An Ancestor of the Peyote Cult?" *American Anthropologist* 59 (1957): 75–85.

———. "Notes on the Ethnogeography of the Yankton Dakota." *Plains Anthropologist* 17 (November 1972): 281–307.

———. "The Pan-Indian Culture of Oklahoma." *Scientific Monthly* 18:5 (1955): 215–20.

Hoxie, Frederick. "From Prison to Homeland: The Cheyenne River Indian Reservation before World War I." *South Dakota History* 9:4 (1979): 1–24.

Hurt, Wesley R. "Factors in the Persistence of Peyote in the Northern Plains." *Plains Anthropologist* 5:9 (May 1960): 16–27.

———. "The Urbanization of the Yankton Indians." *Human Organization* 20:4 (Winter 1961–62): 226–31.

———. "The Urbanization of the Yankton Indians." *Museum News: South Dakota Museum* 21:3 (April 1960): 1–6.

Hurt, Wesley R., and Richard M. Brown. "Social Drinking Patterns of the Yankton Sioux." *Human Organization* 24:3 (Fall 1965): 222–30.

Johnson, David L., and Raymond Wilson. "Gertrude Simmons Bonnin, 1876–1938: Americanize the First American." *American Indian Quarterly* 12 (Winter 1988): 28–40.

Kelsey, F. E. "The Pharmacology of Peyote." *South Dakota Journal of Medicine and Pharmacy* 12:6 (1959): 231–33.

Kracht, Benjamin R. "The Kiowa Ghost Dance, 1894–1916: An Unheralded Revitalization Movement." *Ethnohistory* 39:4 (Fall 1992): 452–77.

LaBarre, Weston. "Mescalism and Peyotism." *American Anthropologist* 59 (1957): 708–11.

———. "Statement on Peyote." *Science* 114 (30 November 1951): 582–83.

———. "Twenty Years of Peyote Studies." *Current Anthropology* 1:1 (January 1960): 45–60.

Lawson, Michael L. "Historical Analysis of the Impact of Missouri River Pick–Sloan Dam Projects on the Yankton and Santee Sioux Indian Tribes." Washington, D.C.: Morgan Angel and Associates, 1999 (unpublished policy paper).

Lawson, Paul E., and C. Patrick Morris. "The Native American Church and the New Court: The Smith Case and Indian Religious Freedoms." *American Indian Culture and Research* Journal 15:1 (1991): 79–91.

Leonard, Irving A. "A Decree against Peyote, Mexican Inquisition, 1620." *American Anthropologist* 44 (1942): 324–26.

Lessard, Dennis. "Instruments of Prayer: The Peyote Art of the Sioux." *American Indian Art* 9:2 (Spring 1984): 24–27.

Lewis, David Rich. "Reservation Leadership and the Progressive-Traditional Dichotomy: William Wash and the Northern Utes, 1865–1928." *Ethnohistory* 38:2 (Spring 1991): 124–48.

Looking Horse, Arvol. "The Sacred Pipe In Modern Life." In *Sioux Indian Religion: Tradition and Innovation,* ed. Raymond DeMallie and Douglas Parks, 67–73. Norman: University of Oklahoma Press, 1984.

Maroukis, Thomas C. "Yankton Sioux Tribal Fairs." *Bulletin of the Institute of American Indian Studies, University of South Dakota* 127 (August 1992): 38–42.

McNickle, D'Arcy. "Peyote and the Indian." *Scientific Monthly* 57 (1943): 220–29.

Medicine, Beatrice. "Indian Women and the Renaissance of Traditional Religion." In *Sioux Indian Religion: Tradition and Innovation,* ed. Raymond DeMallie and Douglas R. Parks, 159–71. Norman: University of Oklahoma Press, 1987.

Merriam, Alan, and Warren L. d'Azevedo. "Washo Peyote Songs." *American Anthropologist* 59:4 (August 1957): 615–44.

Mooney, James. "The Mescal Plant and Ceremony." *Therapeutic Gazette,* 3rd series, 12:1 (January 1896): 7–11.

———. "Peyote." In *Handbook of American Indians North of Mexico,* Part 2, 237. Washington, D.C.: GPO, 1906.

Morgan, George. "Recollections of the Peyote Road." In *Psychedelic Reflections,* ed. Lester Grinspoon and James Bakalar, 91–95. New York: Human Sciences, 1983.

Nydahl, Theodore L. "The Pipestone Quarry and the Indians." *Minnesota History* 31 (December 1950): 193–208.

Parks, Douglas R., and Robert L. Rankin. "Siouan Languages." In *Plains,* ed. Raymond J. DeMallie, 94–114. Vol. 13. *Handbook of North American Indians.* Washington, D.C.: Smithsonian Institution, 2001.

Paulson, Howard W. "Federal Indian Policy and the Dakota Indians: 1800–1840." *South Dakota History* 3:3 (Summer 1973): 285–309.

Peregoy, Robert, Walter R. Echo-Hawk, and James Butsford. "Congress Overturns Supreme Court's Peyote Ruling." *Native American Rights Fund Legal Review* 20:1 (Winter/Spring l995): 1, 6–25.

Petrullo, Vincenzo. "Peyotism as an Emergent Indian Culture." *Indians at Work* 8:8 (1940): 51–60.

Radin, Paul. "Personal Reminiscences of a Winnebago Indian [Sam Blowsnake]." *Journal of American Folklore* 26 (1913): 293–318.

———. "The Peyote Cult." In *Thirty-seventh Annual Report of the Bureau of American Ethnology,* 388–426. Washington, D.C.: GPO, 1916.

———. "A Sketch of the Peyote Cult of the Winnebago: A Study in Borrowing." *Journal of Religious Psychology* 7:1 (1914): 1–22.

"A Ritual of Citizenship." *Outlook* (24 May 1916): 161–62.

Robinson, Doane. "A History of the Dakota or Sioux Indians." *South Dakota Historical Collections* 2 (1904): 1–583.

Robinson, William. "Digest of Reports of the Commissioner of Indian Affairs (1853–72)." *South Dakota Historical Collections* 27, 28 (1954, 1956): 160–515, 179–344.

Rood, David S., and Allan R. Taylor. "Sketch of Lakhota, a Siouan Language." In *Languages,* 440–82. Vol. 17. *Handbook of North American Indians.* Washington, D.C.: Smithsonian Institution, 1996.

Sanders, W. E. "Trail of the Ancient Sioux: An Introduction to Their Ethnic History." *South Dakota Historical Collections* 26 (1952): 278–433.

Schilz, Thomas F., and Joyce L. D. Schilz. "Beads, Bangles and Buffalo Robes: The Rise and Fall of the Indian Fur Trade along the Missouri and Des Moines Rivers, 1700–1820." *Annals of Iowa* 49 (1987): 5–22.

Schultes, Richard Evans. "The Appeal of Peyote (Lophophora Williamsii) as a Medicine." *American Anthropologist* 40:4 (1938): 698–715.

———. "Peyote and the American Indian." *Nature Magazine* 30:3 (September 1937): 155–57.

———. "Peyote and Plants Confused with It." *Botanical Museum Leaflets, Harvard University* 5:5 (1937): 61–89.

Seymour, Gertrude. "Peyote Worship: An Indian Cult and a Powerful Drug." *Survey* 34:7 (13 May 1916): 181–84.

Shonle, Ruth. "Peyote, the Giver of Visions." *American Anthropologist* 27 (1925): 53–75.

Slotkin, J. S. "Early Eighteenth Century Documents on Peyotism North of the Rio Grande." *American Anthropologist* 53:1 (1951): 420–27.

———. "Menomini Peyotism: A Study of Individual Variation in a Primary Group with a Homogeneous Culture." *American Philosophical Society* 42:4 (1952): 565–700.

———. "Peyotism, 1521–1891." *American Anthropologist* 57 (1955): 202–30.

Smits, David D. "The Frontier Army and the Destruction of the Buffalo: 1865–1883." *Western Historical Quarterly* 25 (Autumn 1994): 313–38.

Spider, Emerson, Sr. "The Native American Church of Jesus Christ." In *Sioux Indian Religion: Tradition and Innovation,* ed. Raymond DeMallie and Douglas R. Parks, 189–210. Norman: University of Oklahoma Press, 1987.

Stahl, Robert J. "The Peyote Religion and the Sioux to 1945." Unpublished paper, Institute of American Indian Studies, University of South Dakota, n.d.

Steinhard, Edward. "Introduction." *Ethnohistory* 36:1 (Winter 1989): 1–8.

Stewart, Omer C. "American Indian Religion: Past, Present, Future." *Wassaja: The Indian Historian* 13:1 (1980): 15–18.

———. "Anthropological Theory and History of Peyotism." *Ethnohistory* 26:3 (1979): 277–81.

———. "Gertrude Simmons Bonnin." *Bulletin of the Institute of American Indian Studies: University of South Dakota* 87 (May 1981).

———. "The Native American Church." In *Anthropology on the Great Plains,* ed. W. Raymond Wood and Margot Liberty, 188–96. Lincoln: University of Nebraska Press, 1980.

———. "Origin of the Peyote Religion in the United States." *Plains Anthropologist* 19 (1974): 211–23.

———. "Peyote and the Law." In *Handbook of American Indian Religious Freedom,* ed. Christopher Vecsey, 44–62. New York: Crossroad Publishing, 1991.

———. "The Peyote Religion." In *Great Basin,* 673–81. Vol. 11. *Handbook of North American Indians.* Washington, D.C.: Smithsonian Institution, 1986.

————. "Peyote Religion." In *Native America in the Twentieth Century: An Encyclopedia,* ed. Mary B. Davis, 446–49. New York: Garland Publishing, 1996.

————. "The Peyote Religion and the Ghost Dance." *Indian Historian* 3:4 (Winter 1972): 27–30.

Swan, Daniel C. "Early Osage Peyotism." *Plains Anthropologist* 43:163 (1998): 51–71.

————. "Peyote Arts in the Collections of the Gilcrease Museum." *American Indian Art Magazine* 24:2 (1999): 37–45.

Swanton, John R. "Siouan Tribes and the Ohio Valley." *American Anthropologist* 45:1 (1943): 49–66.

Thomas, Sidney J. "A Sioux Medicine Bundle." *American Anthropologist* 43 (1941): 605–609.

Thornton, Russell. "Boundary Dissolution and Revitalization Movements: The Case of the Nineteenth-Century Cherokees." *Ethnohistory* 40:3 (Summer 1993): 359–83.

Voegelin, Charles F. "Internal Relationships of Siouan Languages." *American Anthropologist* 43:2 (1941): 246–49.

Wallace, Anthony. "Revitalization Movements." *American Anthropologist* 58 (1956): 264–81.

Weeks, Philip. "Humanity and Reform: Indian Policy and the Hayes Presidency." In *The American Indian Experience,* 174–88. Arlington Heights, Ill.: Forum Press, 1988.

Welsh, Herbert. "Peyote—An Insidious Evil." *Indian Rights Association,* 2nd series, no. 114 (1915): 1–6.

White, Richard. "The Winning of the West: The Expansion of the Western Sioux in the Eighteenth and Nineteenth Centuries." *Journal of American History* 65 (September 1978): 319–43.

Wiedman, Dennis. "Big and Little Moon Peyotism as Health Care Delivery Systems." *Medical Anthropology* 12:4 (November 1990): 371–87.

Wiedman, Dennis, and Candace Greene. "Early Kiowa Peyote Ritual and Symbolism: The 1891 Drawing Books of Silverhorn." *American Indian Art Magazine* 13:4 (Autumn 1988): 32–41.

Willard, William. "The First Amendment, Anglo-Conformity and American Indian Religious Freedom." *Wicazo Sa Review* 7:1 (Spring 1991): 25–41.

Wolff, Gerald W. "Father Sylvester Eisenman and Marty Mission." *South Dakota History* 5:4 (Fall 1975): 360–89.

Woodruff, K. Brent. "The Episcopal Mission to the Dakotas, 1860–1898." *South Dakota Historical Collections* 17 (1934): 553–603.

Young, Gertrude. "The Journal of a Missionary to the Yankton Sioux: 1875–1902." *South Dakota Historical Collections* 29 (1958): 63–86.

Young, Gloria A. "Intertribal Religious Movements." In *Plains,* ed. Raymond J. DeMallie, 996–1010. Vol. 13. *Handbook of North American Indians.* Washington, D.C.: Smithsonian Institution, 2001.

Zens, M. Serena. "The Educational Work of the Catholic Church among the Indians of South Dakota from the Beginning to 1935." *South Dakota Historical Collections* 20 (1940): 299–356.

Zitkala Ša [Gertrude Simmons Bonnin]. "An Indian Teacher among Indians." *Atlantic Monthly* 89 (March 1900): 381–86.

———. "The School Days of an Indian Girl." *Atlantic Monthly* 89 (February 1900): 45–47, 190–94.

DISSERTATIONS AND THESES

Bach, Lloyd Carl. "A Study of Speech and Auditory Changes during the Peyote Ceremony of the Native American Church of North America." M.A. thesis, University of South Dakota, 1961.

Bruguier, Leonard R. "The Yankton Sioux Tribe: People of the Pipestone, 1634–1888." Ph.D. diss., Oklahoma State University, 1993.

Cwach, Elmer D. "A History of the Yankton Indian Agency during the Nineteenth Century." M.A. thesis, University of South Dakota, 1958.

Morgan, George R. "Man, Plant, and Religion: Peyote Trade on the Mustang Plains of Texas." Ph.D. diss., University of Colorado, 1976.

Ritter, Beth R. "Dispossession to Diminishment: The Yankton Sioux Reservation, 1858–1998." Ph.D. diss., University of Nebraska, 1999.

Suttmiller, Father Francis, O.S.B. "A History of St. Paul's Indian School at Marty, South Dakota." M.A. thesis, University of South Dakota, 1963.

Swan, Daniel C. "West Moon East Moon: An Ethnohistory of the Peyote Religion among the Osage Indians, 1890–1930." Ph.D. diss., University of Oklahoma, 1990.

Welch, Deborah S. "Zitkala-Ša: An American Indian Leader, 1876–1938." Ph.D. diss., University of Wyoming, 1985.

INTERVIEWS

Interviews by Author

Bruguier, Leonard. 31 October 1991. Vermillion, S.Dak. Taped.

Bruguier, Quentin. 6 June 1993. Lake Andes, S.Dak. Field notes.

Dog Soldier, Eunice Rainbow. 17 September 1991. Marty, S.Dak. Taped.

Hoover, Herbert. 23 November 1991. Vermillion, S.Dak. Taped.

Iron Necklace, Bruce. 30 May 1993. Columbus, Ohio. Taped.

Kezena, Pauline Necklace. 17 September 1991. Greenwood, S.Dak. Field notes.

Necklace, Katherine Sing. 1 October 1992. Miamisburg, Ohio. Field notes.

Necklace, Parnell. 30 September 1991. Vermillion, S.Dak. Field notes.

———. 16 October 1991. Vermillion, S.Dak. Taped.

Packard, Joe. 16 September 1991. Marty, S.Dak. Tape 1229, AIRP.

———. 5 October 1991. Marty, S.Dak. Tape 1230, AIRP.

Primeaux, Asa, Jr. 11 May 1991. Marty, S.Dak. Taped.

———. 8 June 1996. Marty, S.Dak. Field notes.

Primeaux, Asa, Sr. 4 May 1991, 16 September 1991, 17 September 1991, 20 September 1991, 24 September 1991, 4 October 1991, Marty, S.Dak.; 30 January 1992, 11 May 1992, Columbus, Ohio. Field notes.

————. 4 June 1991. Marty, S.Dak. Taped.

————. 16 September 1991. Marty, S.Dak. Taped.

————. 20 September 1991. Marty, S.Dak. Taped.

————. 24 September 1991. Marty, S.Dak. Taped.

————. 25 September 1991. Marty, S.Dak. Taped.

————. 17 November 1991. Marty, S.Dak. Taped.

Primeaux, Gerald. 10 June 2002. Marty, S.Dak. Taped.

————. 15 June 2000, 8 June 2002. Marty, S.Dak. Field notes.

Primeaux, Loretta Rainbow. 10 June 1997. Marty, S.Dak. Field notes.

Rabbit, Alice Hope. 25 June 1999. Gregory, S.Dak. Field notes.

Rockboy, Clarence. 25 November 1991. Lake Andes, S.Dak. Field notes.

Sitting Crow, Adam, Jr. 30 October 1991. Vermillion, S.Dak. Taped.

Sitting Crow, Germaine. 28 October 1991. Vermillion, S.Dak. Taped.

————. 29 October 1991. Vermillion, S.Dak. Field notes.

————. 30 May 1993. Vermillion, S.Dak. Field notes.

Spider, Emerson, Sr. 25 June 1999. Marty, S.Dak. Field notes.

Walker, Selma Sully. 16 August 1994. Columbus, Ohio. Tape 1442, AIRP.

Welsh, Mark. 23 March 2000. Columbus, Ohio. Field notes.

Miscellaneous: Taped

Primeaux, Asa, Sr. Narrator. 6 January 1983. Marty, S.Dak.

Primeaux, Asa, Sr., and Nancy Rockboy, Narrators. 15 August 1982. Vermillion, S.Dak.

Oral History Center, Institute of American Indian Studies, University of South Dakota

AMERICAN INDIAN RESEARCH PROJECT

Archambeau, Percy. Interview by Joseph Cash. 19 August 1968. Greenwood, S.Dak. Tape 014.

Cournoyer, Stephen. Interview by Herbert Hoover. 11 March 1974. Marty, S.Dak. Tape 486.

Eastman, Fred. Interview by M. Edward McGaa. Spring 1968. Marty, S.Dak. Tape 693.

Eastman, Mae. Interview by Vince Pratt. 28 July 1971. Marty, S.Dak. Tape 754.

Eller, Cornelia. Interview by Herbert Hoover. Summer 1972. Tape 773.

Foreman, Clarence. Interview by Joseph Cash. 26 August 1968. Armour, S.Dak. Tape 012.

Fredrick, Agnes. Interview by M. Keeler. 1968. Armour, S.Dak. Tape 099.

Good Thunder, Lottie. Interview by Vince Pratt. 11 August 1971. Tape 804.

Kot, Father Casimir. Interview by Joseph Cash. 1968. Marty, S.Dak. Tape 153.

Madlon, Father Daniel. Interview by Patricia Mylott. 9 June 1973. Marty, S.Dak. Tape 901.

Nichols, Eva. Interview by Joseph Cash. 9 August 1968. Pierre, S.Dak. Tape 066.

O'Connor, William. Interview by Joseph Cash. 27 August 1968. Lake Andes, S.Dak. Tape 002.

Oyate Radio Program. 8 December 1972. Vermillion, S.Dak. Tape 1065 (contains discussion with Leonard Crow Dog, Neulan Dion, Asa Primeaux, and Adam Sitting Crow).

Picotte, Grace. Interview by Herbert Hoover. 7 July 1973. Lake Andes, S.Dak. Tape 932.

Picotte, Norbert. Interview by Herbert Hoover. 3 February 1978. Lake Andes, S.Dak. Tape 1050.

Picotte, Paul. Interview by Joseph Cash. 16 August 1968. Lake Andes, S.Dak. Tape 67.

———. Interview by Richard Loder. Summer 1969. Lake Andes, S.Dak. Tape 428.

———. Tape 1169. No interviewer [1969?].

Primeaux, Asa, Sr. Interview by Herbert Hoover. 1 June 1973. Wagner, S.Dak. Tape 897.

———. Moderator Herbert Hoover. 20 October 1987. Tape 1208.

Primeaux, Harry. Interview by Herbert Hoover. 1 June 1973. Marty, S.Dak. Tape 895.

Provost, Cecil. Interview by Joseph Cash. 19 August 1968. Marty, S.Dak. Tape 013.

Red Hawk, Bessie. Interview by Richard Loder. 1968. Wagner, S.Dak. Tape 080.

Rockboy, Joe. Interview by Herbert Hoover. 18 December 1972. Vermillion, S.Dak. Tape 889.

———. Interview by Herbert Hoover. 19 February 1975. Vermillion, S.Dak. Tape 047.

Shubert, George. Interview by Joseph Cash. 13 June 1968. Marty, S.Dak. Tape 020.

Sitting Crow, Adam, Sr. Interview by Herbert Hoover. 5 May 1971. Vermillion, S.Dak. Tape 677.

———. Interview by Herbert Hoover. 26 May 1971. Vermillion, S.Dak. Tape 678.

Snake, Sterling. Interview by Herbert Hoover. 29 July 1970. Winnebago, Neb. Tape 534.

Spider, Emerson. Interview by Jerome Kills Small. 20 May 1999. Pine Ridge Reservation. Tape 1976.

Stinson, Mildred. Interview by M. Edward McGaa. Spring 1968. Tape 009.

Stricker, John. Interview by Joseph Cash. 23 August 1968. Marty, S.Dak. Tape 058.

White, Noah. Interview by Herbert Hoover. 25 June 1970. Prairie Island, Minn. Tape 507.

Yankton Sioux Peyote Music. Miscellaneous tapes, 1266, 1290, 1292–1304.

Yankton Sioux Peyote Songs. Recorded by Herbert Hoover. Joe Rockboy, Clarence Rockboy, Quentin Bruguier, Asa Primeaux. 6 January 1971. Vermillion, S.Dak. Tape 1159.

Yankton Sioux Peyote Songs. Recorded by Leonard Bruguier. May 1985. Greenwood, S.Dak. Tape 1236.

Delahoyde, Father Louis J. Interview by Gerald Wolff. 15 March 1974. Marty, S.Dak. Tape 1029.

Omer C. Stewart Papers, University of Colorado at Boulder Archives, Peyote Files: Boxes 32, 38

Blue Bird, Jim. Interview by Omer C. Stewart. 20–21 June 1971. Allen, S.Dak.
Stricker, Louie. Interview by Omer C. Stewart. 1972. Lake Andes, S.Dak.

YANKTON SIOUX PEYOTE MUSIC: SELECT DISCOGRAPHY

Abdo, Joe, Sr., et al. *Yankton Sioux Peyote Songs.* Indian House, Vols. 1–4, IH 4371C–IH 4374C, 1976–78. Reissued 2003.
Primeaux, Asa, Sr., and Sons. *Yankton Sioux Peyote Harmonizing Songs.* Indian Records, Inc. Vols. 1–6, 1171A–71F, n.d.
Primeaux, Gerald. *Songs of Prayer for Life,* Cool Runnings Music, CRM 050402, 2002.
———. *Yankton Sioux Peyote Songs.* Cool Runnings Music, CRM 081100, 2000.
Primeaux, Gerald, and Neulan Dion, Jr. *Primeaux-Dion: Yankton Sioux Peyote Songs, In Loving Memory.* Cool Runnings Music, CRM 052699, 1999.
Primeaux, Verdell, and Johnny Mike. *Bless The People: Harmonized Peyote Songs.* Canyon Records, CR-6317, 2001.
———. *Primeaux & Mike: Peyote Songs in Sioux & Navajo.* Canyon Records, CR-16301, 1993.
Primeaux, Verdell, Johnny Mike, and Robert Atteson. *Primeaux, Mike & Atteson: Healing & Peyote Songs in Sioux and Navajo.* Canyon Records, CR-16302, 1994.
———. *Primeaux, Mike & Atteson: Peyote Songs in Sioux & Navajo.* Canyon Records, CR-16303, 1994.
Shields, Joe, Sr., et al. *Yankton Sioux Peyote Songs.* Indian House, Vols. 5–8, IH 4375C–IH 4378C, 1980–81.
Shields, Joseph, Sr. *Songs of the Native American Church.* Indian House, IH 4379, 1979.

FILMS

The Peyote Road: Ancient Religion in Contemporary Crisis. San Francisco: Kifaru Productions, 1993.
The Traditional Use of Peyote by Members of the Native American Church of North America. San Francisco: Kifaru Productions, 1993.

Index

DeSmet, Fr. Pierre-Jean, 17, 32, 49
Devil's Lake Reservation. *See* Spirit Lake Reservation
Dion family, *192, 193,* 257–58, 269–72, 280, 308
Disease, 4, 33, 114. *See also* Health/health care
Divorce, 135
Dog Rainbow, Sam, 218
Dog Soldier, Eunice Rainbow. *See* Rainbow family
Dragg family, 214, 254, 258
Dream catchers, 162
Drums, 126, 176–78, *189, 190,* 220. *See also*
Music
Duratschek, Sr. Mary, 49, 208

Eagles, 20, 60–61, 128, 167, 172–74, 294
Eaglethunder, William J., 139
Eastman, Charles, 130
Economic development, 265–66, 289–90
Education: degree of blood in, 84; missionary attitudes, 144; off-reservation, 246; Peyote and, 157–58; reform movement, 59; Sam Necklace, 67–70, 216, 231–32, 239; school attendance, 180; Treaty of 1858, 49; tribal sovereignty, 283. *See also* Boarding schools; Schools
Eisenmann, Fr. Sylvester, 133, 137, 142–43, 197, 205, 208–209
Emmanuel School, 48, 67
Employment: boarding school, 69–70; Depression, 198; economic development, 207, 289–90; off-reservation, 258; on-reservation, 47, 74–75, 144, 158, 180, 197; postwar, 243–44; relocation and termination, 246; Sam Necklace, 78, 82, 123–24, 222–23, 231–33; wartime, 229–32
Enrollment, tribal, 83, 145–46, 148–49; 264
Episcopalian Church, 48–49, 67, 70–71, 74, 133, 142–43

Fairs. *See* Tribal fairs
Family, extended. *See* Tiospaye
Feather in His Ear, Chief, 39, 47–48, 62, 79
Fee patents, 59, 85–89, 122–23
Fire and fireplaces, 126–27, 175–76, 277
First Born Church of Christ, 96–97, 129
Five Civilized Tribes, 109
Flandreau Indian Industrial School, 52, 67, 119, 344n.118
Fool Bull family, 300–301, 308
Forced resettlement. *See* Concentration policy; Reservation system
Ford, Gerald, 265
Foreman, Clarence, 203, 210, 228
Fort Totten Reservation, 111–12
Fox Indians. *See* Sac and Fox Indians
Fraud. *See* Corruption and fraud
Frederick, Nick, 228
French explorers and traders, 7, 10, 17
Full-blood: anti-Peyote efforts, 145; cultural revival, 270; IRA opposition, 199–206; Necklace family as, 120; religious practices, 157–58; Sam Necklace as, 52, 69, 84, 195–96, 212, 223–28; tribal politics and, 84, 146–47

Gambling, 81, 117–19, 124, 243, 281, 289–90
Gandy, Harvey L., 129, 132, 141–42
Gassman, John, 46, 49–50, 50
Ghost Dance movement, 51, 106–107, 172, 179
Ginsberg, Allen, 267–68
"Giveaways", 16, 47, 76, 115–19, 248, 266–67
Godfrey, Paul George. *See* Primeaux family
Goodhouse, Johnson, 94, 111, 139, 182, 214, 239
Goshute Indians, 110
Government. *See* Tribal government; U.S. Government
Grabbingbear, Joseph, 202–203
Grandma White Tallow, 79, 115, 145, 217
Grant, Ulysses S., 50, 57
Great Depression, The, 196–207, 222
Greenwood, Alfred B., 38
Greenwood, SD, 42–43, 66–67, 81
Gros Ventre Indians, 34

Half Moon ceremony: cultural renaissance, 270–71; introduction, 99–100, 110–11; ritual and symbols, 162, 167–68, 176, 221; traditional religion, 140, 297–98
Hampton Institute, 109
Hare, Bishop William Hobart, 48–49, 71
Hare family, 6, 30, 40, 225, 228
Harney, William S. (Gen.), 37, 40
Harvey, Leo, 254
Haskell Institute, 109, 151
Hayden, Carl, 129, 132, 136
Hayes, Rutherford B., 50, 57
Healing ceremonies: buffalo role, 21; Fr. Louis Hennepin, 7; music and drums, 177, 220; Peyote and, 102, 109, 119, 131, 153–57, 154–55; revival, 269; Sam Necklace, 3, 213, 217–19; *tiospaye* in, 156; vision traditions, 172
Health/health care: housing and, 47, 229; peyote and, 91, 154–55; reform movement, 196; reservation, 4, 114, 134, 180; Wagner Indian hospital, 198; women in, 292–93
Hennepin, Fr. Louis, 7
Hensley, Albert, 90, 93–94, 96, 110, 141, 299
Hickman, C. C., 200–202
Hidatsa Indians, 6, 27
Ho-Chunk Indians. *See* Winnebago Indians
Homesteaders, 72, 78. *See also* Squatters
Honoring ceremonies, 179
Hoover, Herbert, 196
Hope Indian School, 67. *See also* Springfield Indian School
Horses, 15–17, 81, 117, 119, 124–25
Housing, 36, 47, 80, 197, 232, 246, 289
Huichol Indians, 101
Huxley, Aldous, 267–68

Ickes, Harold, 197, 226
Ihanktonwan Dakota, 15, 306. *See also* Yankton Sioux
Ihanktonwan Presbyterian Church. *See* Presbyterian Church